Social Dancing in America

SOCIAL DANCING
in America

A History and Reference

VOLUME ONE

Fair Terpsichore to the Ghost Dance, 1607–1900

Ralph G. Giordano

Greenwood Press
Westport, Connecticut • London

Library of Congress Cataloging-in-Publication Data

Giordano, Ralph G.
    Social dancing in America : a history and reference / Ralph G. Giordano
        p. cm.
    Includes bibliographical references and index.
    ISBN 0–313–33756–X (set : alk. paper)—ISBN 0–313–33403–X (vol. 1 : alk. paper)—
    ISBN 0–313–33352–1 (vol. 2 : alk. paper) 1. Ballroom dancing—United States—
    History. I. Title.
GV1623.G56 2007
792.3'3—dc22   2006026183

British Library Cataloguing in Publication Data is available.

Library of Congress Catalog Card Number: 2006026183
ISBN: 0–313–33756–X (set)   ISBN13: 978–0–313–33756–7 (set)
         0–313–33403–X (vol. 1)   978–0–313–33403–0 (vol. 1)
         0–313–33352–1 (vol. 2)   978–0–313–33352–1 (vol. 2)

First published in 2007

Greenwood Press, 88 Post Road West, Westport, CT 06881
An imprint of Greenwood Publishing Group, Inc.
www.greenwood.com

Printed in the United States of America

∞

The paper used in this book complies with the
Permanent Paper Standard issued by the National
Information Standards Organization (Z39.48-1984).

10 9 8 7 6 5 4 3 2 1

To
Thelma Lynn Olsen,
Debby Adams,
Rock-it, Gumball, Brandy,
and
All of those who live to dance

Life, ideally, I think, should be like the Minuet or the Virginia Reel or the Turkey Trot, something easily mastered in a dancing school.
—Kurt Vonnegut, *Slapstick* (1976)

Contents

Acknowledgments

As I was writing this book, I was also rereading the novel *Slapstick* (1976) written by Kurt Vonnegut. I have been an avid fan of Mr. Vonnegut's writing for a long time and appreciate his analysis of American society. What surprised me most about Vonnegut is that quite often he wrote a sentence or two in direct reference to American social dancing. Therefore, as I read his quote, "Life, ideally, I think, should be like the Minuet or the Virginia Reel or the Turkey Trot, something easily mastered in a dancing school," it made much more sense to me (48). Having spent so much time myself researching those same dances, I can certainly appreciate the novel approach (no pun intended) that Vonnegut applied to the sheer innocence and joy of social dancing.

In that same manner, although dancing throughout American history was enjoyed for fun, recreation, exhilaration, and sociability, many facets of American society all too often attacked the dances and dancing itself. The negative forces included the clergy, moralists, and sometimes municipal governments. Therefore, as you read the direct quotes from the anti-dance crusaders, they might sometimes appear to have come directly from a Vonnegut novel—but sadly they have not. Unlike the fictional novel, the anti-dance attacks were all too true.

My connection with Mr. Vonnegut might also stem from the fact that both his father and grandfather were architects. Because I am also an architect, although one who has ventured off into other areas such as this book, I certainly understand Vonnegut's appreciation of an often-overlooked aspect of American culture such as the practice of architecture. For, despite it all, it is architecture that has continually provided me with the organizational tools and research capabilities to work on a project of the nature of this book. In a manner similar to Vonnegut, F. Scott Fitzgerald included social dancing as a backdrop in his brilliant works, especially in *The Great Gatsby* (1925). His novels were also stories of fiction, but Fitzgerald told the truth about contemporary American society and culture.

An individual who also has a strong appreciation and understanding of Fitzgerald is Debby Adams, who is also my editor. With that said, my most heartfelt thanks and appreciation is extended to Debby. This book would not have happened without a contract in place from Greenwood Publishing Group, and for that I am also sincerely grateful. Other members of the Greenwood staff who deserve thanks are Nicole Azze, Leanne Small, and Kaitlin Ciarmiello. In addition, my thanks go to the staff at BeaconPMG, especially Kathy Breit.

But being faced with a project that doubled in size (two volumes) and the prospect of delivering both projects concurrently, I do have to admit that I was very excited about my project on twentieth century social dancing, but not all that enthusiastic about this volume of the earlier periods. In fact, it was my wife, Thelma Lynn Olsen, who made me recognize that each project required individual attention. Therefore, I wrote the twentieth century book first and as a result was able to devote my full efforts to this volume on the earlier periods. Once immersed in evaluating the research, I was utterly amazed at not only the amount of original source material but also the affectionate firsthand accounts in response to social dancing. Upon reading that material, I slowly came to the realization that American social dancing was an integral part throughout all of American history. That history began from the point when Christopher Columbus first set foot in the North American region. In fact, many accounts indicate that he was greeted in dance by the indigenous tribes; therefore, the history of American social dancing was already in place. A significant amount of that original material was available from the Library of Congress, including the American Memory Collection, the Prints and Photographs Division, and especially the Music Division and their on-line compilation *An American Ballroom Companion Dance Instruction Manuals Ca. 1490–1920.* The Web site contains an invaluable catalog of rare books, illustrations, and videos that otherwise might have been virtually unattainable.

A special thank you goes to one of my College of Staten Island students, Sierra Kessler. Apparently she overheard me discussing my research for this book. As a result, one day she dropped a note in my mailbox informing me of a ten-week course in English Country-dancing sponsored by the Staten Island Historical Society at Richmondtown. I was certainly interested, and my wife, Thelma Lynn, and I did, in fact, participate in a ten-week course taught by Tom Amesse and his wife, Susan. The session culminated in a Dance Assembly, in which we also dressed in period costumes lent to us by avid English Country-dancers and reenactors Donna and Tom Briggs. Once again, I cannot express my appreciation for each of those individuals. The experience of social participation in authentic English Country-dancing provided me with a better understanding of the written works such as the likes of John Playford who first described the patterns and step figures over 350 years ago. Dance historian Lloyd Shaw probably said it best when he wrote:

> It isn't enough to read such books, you get only part of their impact. But if you put on a phonograph record, and dance, you get a moving, kinetic, living idea of what it's all about (34).

Shaw wrote that statement in 1948, but it certainly applies to social dancing throughout all facets of American history. In that same manner, there are so many aspects about social dancing that simply cannot be expressed in mere words or even photographs. Attached to it all is human emotion. How can one person describe the fun, the relaxation, the sociability, the friendships, and the exhilaration?

Throughout the years, I have danced in many places all over America. What I have learned best about the social dance world is that an individual is judged on only one aspect—his or her individual willingness to participate. Regardless of what happens in the outside world, we do not judge on political persuasion, economic status, or even sexual preference. The bottom line is "Do they dance?" Also, it matters little what his/her last name is or what his/her function is within American society, for the common attraction to the dancing is the music and an available dance floor. For almost all, the dancing and music serve as an escape from the outside world and in turn allow us all to cope with the toils and tribulations of life itself.

Needless to say, I have also been very fortunate to have an individual in my life who has certainly helped me "to cope with the toils and tribulations" of daily life. That person is not only my wife, Thelma Lynn, but she is also my best friend and partner-in-life-in-dancing. Little did I know that as she was growing up she always had a secret desire to "dance big" at a family wedding to Bobby Darin's hit song "Mack the Knife." Well, a short time after we met she fulfilled that dream with me as her dance partner. For it

The author and his wife, Thelma Lynn, swing dancing at a vacation resort in Jamaica. Author's archives.

was through dancing that Thelma Lynn and I also first met. Since the mid-1990s we have danced together, and hardly a week has gone by without us dancing for a few hours. Granted, we continually dance in our hearts each day, and if given a choice we certainly would rather always be dancing. Together we danced in over 20 states across America and in literally hundreds of dance venues, including Country, Shag, Swing, Ballroom, Social, Disco, Historical, and, of course, at family weddings and celebrations. At no time do we compete, for that would take all the fun out of the spontaneity of just getting up and dancing. However, I will admit that at one time at a vacation resort in Jamaica we were awarded a "first prize" of a bottle of rum—which we still have not opened.

Researching a book is not without the assistance of some very talented and dedicated people. First and foremost, my most heartfelt thanks and gratitude go to Angie DeMartinis who services the interlibrary loan section at the College of

Acknowledgments

Staten Island Library. Her promptness and professionalism made the acquisition of some very difficult documents and publications an easy process. Individual thanks also go to Carol Butler of Brown Brothers, Terri Torretto of Dover Publications, the Library of the United States Military Academy at West Point, The Granger Collection, Corbis-Bettmann, the New York Public Library, Jeannine Pedersen, Curator of Collections at the Catalina Island Museum, and Howard Mandelbaum, Ed Maguire, and Ron Mandelbaum at Photofest.

I also thank my family of Giordanos, Dattilos, Leavers, Kargos, Clarkes, Quattrochis, Garcias, Demolas, and all the rest. It was mainly from my family that I first experienced the joy of social dancing. All of our family weddings were certainly an amazing joyful experience of American social dancing. All week long they could all toil through the tribulations of life—both good and bad—deal with family arguments, yet they never took those problems to the dance floor. And I must, of course, mention my own parents, Phyllis and Thomas Giordano—oh, how they loved to dance. That experience was passed on to not only myself, but also my brother Thomas Giordano, Jr., who is a Battalion Chief in the Fire Department of the City of New York. Both he and his wife, Helene, never miss an opportunity to enjoy a whirl on the dance floor. Many of us were extremely relieved after all those awful months following September 2001 when Tommy and Helene finally got back on the dance floor. In fact, they also attended many social dance functions sponsored by the Fire Department. On many an occasion, Tommy has told me that the organizers always remembered to include a "Lindy set for the Chief and his wife."

But mostly, I do wish to thank anyone who has had the simple desire to just experience the fun of social dancing and who has also continued to read to this point of the acknowledgements. I sincerely hope you find somewhere within this book the common element that social dancing can provide within all our lives. And I hope you enjoy this book, for dancing has certainly been a vital part in shaping the American way of life throughout all of our shared history.

Introduction

Social dancing was not new to the development of America. Social dance traditions can be traced to ancient Greece and Rome, as well as to Biblical locales and just about every civilization throughout the world. In America, social dancing was an integral part of its history beginning from the point when Christopher Columbus first set foot in the North American region. In fact, many accounts indicate that he was greeted in dance by the indigenous tribes; therefore, in reality the history of American social dancing was already in place. But, as the first Europeans settled into areas, such as the Spanish in the Southwest, the French in the Louisiana territories, and the British in New England and Virginia, they pushed aside the native American Indian tribal customs and instilled their own social customs, including dancing.

Throughout the seventeenth, eighteenth, and nineteenth centuries, American communities, cities, and western territories regularly sponsored social activities that included dancing. Americans danced, young and old, male and female, mostly at communal events such as weddings. In America, the emerging republic of the Founding Fathers, for example, held steadfast in the tradition of social dancing. George Washington was an avid social dancer from his days prior to the American Revolution and continuing through his presidency. He incorporated the etiquette and manners of dances such as the Minuet as a means of diplomacy to secure European allies, such as France, during the War of Independence. During his presidency he toured the country and was honored at each occurrence with a dance in his honor. After his death, Americans continued to celebrate his birthday with a grand ball that included dancing.

At the time, social dancing was one of the important talents of Virginia gentlemen, including Washington. While in Paris, in 1785, another Virginian, Thomas Jefferson, wrote to Abigail Adams of a life "where we have singing, dancing, laughter and merriment." Both Jefferson and Washington were typical of many Colonial Americans who intertwined a culture of music and dancing within their lives; however, that culture was distinctly European. In almost all instances the social dance trends were copied directly from Europe, mainly London and Paris. During the early years, those dances were mainly English Country-dances and Quadrilles.

As European immigrants continued to enter America, they also brought traditional folk dances from their native countries, such as the Jig, Clogging, the Schottische, and the Polka. During the development of America as a nation, social dancing in itself offered a parallel of the social, economic, and cultural traditions of each particular time period. For example, slavery, segregation, and the "Jim Crow" mentality was cemented in place all over the United States. In that same manner, prejudice against the indigenous Native American Indian tribes was rampant. As a result, the dominant European culture sought to obliterate the minority social customs that included dancing. In the case of African Americans, the social dance traditions survived and morphed with other ethnic European traditions. However, that was not the case as it applied to the American Indians.

During the latter half of the nineteenth century, the social elite attended dance functions at elaborate ballrooms and resorts, where it was considered proper etiquette for a socialite to have a *dance card*. The dance card listed a set list of songs that would be played during the evening and a space where the names of gentlemen dance partners would be written in advance of the event. The predetermined dances were usually smooth flowing, dignified, sedate dances. In order not to extend too much excitement, the typical dance format usually included a rest period after each dance. However, with the development of Ragtime music in the late 1890s, the music and the dances were faster and more energetic, and the rest periods were reduced (and eventually eliminated), which appealed mostly to the younger people.

Throughout the development of social dancing from the colonial period through the end of the nineteenth century, many Americans relied on dance instruction books. As opposed to *why* Americans danced, many of the social dance instruction books simply provided descriptions and step-by-step instructions on "how to dance" and added strict etiquette guidelines for mannerisms within the ballroom. Most, if not all, of the new dance trends started in Europe and were copied in the American ballrooms. Some dances, such as the Minuet, simply faded out and others, such as the Waltz and Polka, became American standards. Therefore, in order to understand the development of "American" social dancing, a discussion of the "European" social dances is essential. As a result, the first chapter provides a comprehensive discussion including ancient times beginning with the Greek Goddess Terpsichore and continuing through European Medieval and Renaissance dances.

This work also traces a consistent theme that contemporary American social dances were more often than not initially perceived as "scandalous" and usually attacked by purists and religious groups as immoral. However, with time, each preceding dance moved from scandalous to public acceptability and respectability. In that same manner, although dancing throughout American history was enjoyed only for fun, recreation, exhilaration, and sociability, many facets of American society all too often continued attacking the newer dances and social dancing itself. The negative forces included the clergy, moralists, and sometimes municipal governments. Therefore, in that same sense, the anti-dance sections have taken up a significant portion of the book.

Although this work encompasses a broad historical period and provides step descriptions for many specific dances, the intent is *not* to teach people "How to Dance." There are thousands of publications available that can do just that, many of which are listed in the bibliography. This book not only places social dancing in a historical, social, cultural, and political context, it also traces the integral part that social dancing played in the lives of individuals in America from the first settlements in 1607, through the birth of the nation in 1776, and through the nineteenth century. This volume also encompasses the global nature of the ethnic contributions to the formation of many unique American social dances. Those influences during the seventeenth, eighteenth, and nineteenth centuries were mainly European but also included the Native American Indian, Spanish, Caribbean, African, and other ethnic cultures. Therefore, each chapter within this volume contains a brief introduction of the social, political, and cultural climate. Some questions discussed throughout the book are as follows:

- How did the historical, political, and cultural events influence dance styles?
- What was the history of the most popular dances and where did they begin?
- What attracted men and women to social dancing in these periods?
- What was their ethnic and economic background?
- How was their dancing and choice of dance style viewed by contemporary society?
- What specific dances crossed over from "scandalous" to public acceptance?
- Which dances survived the test of time and why?
- What dances and dance venues were hindered by municipal regulations?
- What dances and dance venues were hindered by moral or religious objections?

Some points that should be noted are that some of the dance instruction manuals and historical texts list the names of the dances in lowercase spelling. On the other hand, a significant number of dance manuals also capitalized the spelling of the names of specific dances. In the case that the dance was referenced as a noun, most of the contemporary writings capitalized the word. In that same sense the name of the dance was often in lowercase since it was also referenced as a verb because dancing represents an action. In some instances, the spellings of some of the dances also vary such as Schottische (sometimes Schottisch) and Cotillion (sometimes Cotillon, which is the French spelling). Therefore, since this book is about the dances and dancing in itself, I decided to capitalize the spelling of names of the individual dances throughout the text, for example, the Waltz, Polka, Quadrille, and English Country-dancing. The only instances where I did not are within a direct quote. With that said, I encourage you to read this book and hope that this history of American social dancing transcends your current understanding of why Americans freely decided upon the choice to dance.

Chronology of Dance

Chapter 1: The Minuet, Puritans, and Anti-Dance Reformation: 1607–1740

PRE-RENAISSANCE

- Black Hat Dance, Ancient Civilization through 1500 (Tibet)
- Choral Dancing, earliest civilization through 1500
- Ring Around the Rosy, mid-14th century through 20th century (Europe)
- St. Vitus, Middle Ages (Europe)
- Tarantella, mid-14th century through 20th century (Italy)
- Basses Dansés 14th century to early 16th century (Europe)
    - Carole
    - Estampie
    - Farandole
- Branle, 1400 to 1550 (Europe)

RENAISSANCE

- Allemande, 16th and 17th century (France)
- Ballo, 1450 to mid-1500s (Italy)
- Courante, mid-1500s through 18th century (Italy and France)
- Fandango, 17th century through 19th century (Spain)
- Galliard, late 16th century to early 17th century (Italian and French)
- Gavotte, 1580 to mid-1700s (France)
- Pavane, 1500 to 1600 (Italy or Spain)
- Sarabande, late 16th century (Spain)
- Volta, mid-1500s (Italy)

17TH CENTURY TO EARLY 18TH CENTURY

- Contredanse, 1680 through 19th century (France)
- English Country-Dance, 1650 through 19th century (England)
- Pueblo Circle Dance, 10,000 B.C. through 17th century (North America)
- Maypole, early 1600s through 19th century (England and Ancient Times)
- Minuet, early 1600s through 18th century (France)

Chapter 2 : The Virginia Reel, George Washington, and the Waltz: 1740–1820

- American Colonial Minuet, 1770 to 1820 (France)
- Big Circle Dances, 1800 through 19th century (England)
- Breakdown, mid-1700s to early-1800s (African)
- Clog Dancing, early 1700s to 1800s (Scotland, Wales, England, Ireland, and French Canada)
- Contra Dancing, 1770 through 18th century (France and England)
- Cotillion, 1760 through 19th century (France)
- English Country-Dance, 1650 through 19th century (England)
- Hornpipe, 1700 to 19th century (England, Wales, Scotland, and Ireland)
- Jig, 16th century through 19th century (Ireland and Scotland)
- Quadrille, 1800 through 19th century (England)
- Rigaudon, 1700 to 19th century (France or Italy)
- Square Order Shuffle, 1770s (England)
- Viennese Waltz, 1776 through 19th century (Vienna, Austria)
- Virginia Reel, early 18th century through 19th century (England)

Chapter 3: The Buffalo Dance, Cotillions, and the Polka: 1820–1865

- Buffalo Dance, 1800s (Mandan and Sioux)
- Dancing the Slaves, 1607 to 1820
- The Galop Dance, 1800 through 19th century (Europe)
- Polka, 1844 through 19th century (Czech Republic and Slovakia)
  - Mazurka
  - Polka Mazurka
  - Redowa
  - Polka Redowa

- Ring Shout (African tribal)
- Schottische, 1844 to 1900 (Bavaria sometimes "Schottisch")
- Waltz, 1834 through 19th century (German)
  - Boston Waltz
  - Spanish Waltz (Europe and Mexican Folk)
  - Waltz *à* Deux Temps
  - Waltz *à* Trois Temps

Chapter 4: The Ghost Dance, the Cakewalk, and the Two-Step: 1865–1900

- Cakewalk, 1890 to 1905 (African American)
- Cancan, 1890 to 1910 (France)
- The German, 1870 to 1910 (France)
- Ghost Dance, 1870 to 1893 (Native American Indian)
- Square Dance Calling, 1870 through 20th century (American vernacular)
- Two-Step, 1890 to 1910 (American vernacular)

1

The Minuet, Puritans, and Anti-Dance Reformation: 1607–1740

All the disasters of mankind, all the fatal misfortunes that histories are so full of, the blunders of politicians, the miscarriages of great commanders, all this comes from want of skill in dancing.

—Moliere, 1670

The Political, Social, and Cultural Climate

The first British colonists who settled in Jamestown, Virginia, in 1607 and Plymouth, Massachusetts, in 1620 did not "dance" off the boat into a world of established social society. Many Puritans left Anglican England for the wilderness of New England in search of a land to practice their religion, and many settlers in Virginia left England to seek economic reward. Both the settlements of the New England and Virginia colonies, although for different reasons, were a direct result of English history. In the case of the Puritans, they were directly linked to the Reformation and Restoration in England.

During the sixteenth century, a religious movement in Europe against the Catholic Church termed the "Reformation" (sometimes the "Protestant Reformation") established the new Protestant religion throughout northern Europe. The beginning of the Reformation was attributed to 1517 and the German theologian Martin Luther who proclaimed a "faith based on the guidance contained in the Bible." In England, the Puritans represented a radical arm of Protestantism that sought to rid England of all traces of Catholicism. As a result, the safe haven of the Puritans rested in the personality of the English monarch ("Reformation," n.d.).

King Henry VIII, for example, who ruled from 1509 to 1547, favored the Protestant Reformation in England. Upon Henry's death his ten-year-old son, Edward VI, was crowned King and ruled Protestant England from 1547 to 1553. Edward was succeeded by Queen Mary I who sought to restore the Catholic Church and in doing so also persecuted Protestants. In 1558, Mary died and was followed by Elizabeth I (from 1558 to 1603) who attempted to maintain a balance between the Protestants and the Catholic Church. The kings following Elizabeth, James I (from 1603 to 1625) and his son Charles I (from 1625 to 1640), also had a disdain for Puritans. It was within that unsettling climate that the Puritans welcomed a refuge in New England ("England," n.d.).

In 1628, the Massachusetts Bay Company, by charter of King Charles I of England, secured settlement rights to expand to the ports of Salem (1629) and Boston (1630). The settlements were to spread the idea of a "religious utopia." In the case of Boston, Massachusetts, those Puritans who arrived on the sailing ship the *Arebella* made a covenant with God. Led by the onboard sermon of John Winthrop, the covenant decreed:

> If we shall neglect the observation of these articles which are the ends we have propounded, and dissembling with our God, shall fail to embrace this world and prosecute our carnal intentions, seeking great things for ourselves and our posterity, the Lord will surely break out in wrath against us, be revenged of such perjured people, and make us know the price of the breach of such a covenant (quoted in Marks 1975, 3–4).

Winthrop termed the land of Boston their "city upon the hill."

As a result of the need for food, materials, and land, the colonists continued to extend settlements along the coastal areas. The New England settlers expanded into the Massachusetts Bay Area and into Connecticut. The Virginia settlers probed into the Carolinas, Maryland, and the West Indies. However, as the settlements continued to grow, the indigenous Native American Indian tribes were displaced.

As the settlers continued moving along the bay area, many of the coastal Indians died from diseases transmitted by Europeans (estimates range as high as 90 percent). In other cases, such as the Pequot Indian tribe near Mystic, Connecticut, they were attacked and killed by Puritan soldiers. The survivors were forced to move westward, where they were enslaved by rival Indian tribes. Historian Joseph E. Marks in *America Learns to Dance* noted,

> The Puritans came to the new world in order to set up a society based on a Calvinistic interpretation of the Bible. They believed they were a chosen people and that by coming to a new land and making their own laws and regulations they could keep their "Bible religion" pure (1957, 13).

Therefore, the first government of the Puritan colony in Massachusetts was a theocracy under the auspices of Puritan ministers. By 1640, the Massachusetts Bay Company enacted laws forbidding the Native American Indian tribes from practicing their own religion and cultural heritage. Some New England colonists, such as Roger Williams and Anne Hutchinson, spoke out against the Puritan rule and were banished from the Massachusetts colony. At that time, the total number of British colonists in New England and Virginia numbered a little over 26,000 (Goldfield, Abbott, et al., 2001, A-29).

At about the same time, from 1640 to 1642, England was engaged in a civil war fought between the armies of King Charles I and Parliament led by Oliver Cromwell, a "devout Calvinist." (Charles I believed in the divine monarchial right of kings and did not feel accountable to Parliament). Cromwell's armies defeated King Charles (who was beheaded in 1649) and began a Puritan rule in England. Cromwell declared himself "Lord Protector" of England. One result was the closing of all theaters in London and banishing actors and theater participants to the other side of the Thames River.

In 1658, Cromwell died and was succeeded by his eldest son, Richard. However, in 1660, Richard Cromwell was deposed, and a monarchical government was reestablished in England with the crowning of King Charles II (son of Charles I, and King of Ireland during Cromwell's rule). It was termed the "Restoration." Under the reign of Charles II (1660 to 1685), Protestant dissenters who did not conform to the Church of England were either prosecuted or banished. In addition, Catholics were removed from Parliament. Then again, during his reign, Charles II promoted the study of natural science by granting a charter in 1662 to the Royal Society. As a result, England established empirical publications such as Isaac Newton's *Principia* (1687), which integrated "the laws of motion with the idea of universal gravitation," and John Locke's *Two Treatises of Government* (1690) and *Essay Concerning Human Understanding* (1690). At the time, debates arose over religion versus science and rational thought. Newton's scientific reasoning and Locke's essays in particular intrigued eighteenth century American statesmen such as Benjamin Franklin, Thomas Paine, John Adams, and Thomas Jefferson as the fledging American colonies sought to separate from England (see Chapter 2). Another aspect in Europe and American society was sorcery and witchcraft ("Restoration," n.d.).

In late 1691, some young girls in the village of Salem, Massachusetts, supposedly began to act strange. They told tales of a local African American woman who told fortunes and talked of sorcery. The magistrates and ministers of Salem prompted the young girls to name the slave women as well as two other Salem women as "witches." The paranoia mounted and continued as over 340 local residents were accused as witches. Many were imprisoned and some executed. In late 1692, when the wife of Salem Governor William Phips was accused, he grew concerned. He implemented a system of pardons for all those who were currently in prison and suspended executions for a few others. By mid-1693, the Salem witch hunts were over (Boyer, Clark, et al., 2000, 59).

One area that was not initially colonized by the British was New York. In 1609, Henry Hudson first explored the harbor of New York and sailed up the river to Albany. Beginning in 1614, the area along the river (named the Hudson River after the explorer) was settled by the Dutch and developed for agricultural resources and fur trading with the Iroquois Indian tribes. At Albany was Fort Orange, and the area of New York City was named New Amsterdam. The entire Dutch region was known as the New Netherlands. In 1640, New York claimed only about 450 settlers. However, the area was profitable and tolerant of many different religious and ethnic settlers. By 1664, when it was taken over by the British, the cosmopolitan city had over 6,000 people ("United States History," n.d.).

The southern colonies of Virginia differed from the towns of New England and the growing city of the New Netherlands (New York). In 1607, Jamestown in Virginia was the first British colony in America. The area on the east coast of modern-day south Virginia was located near the James River. Both the colony and the river were named for England's King James I, who granted a Royal Charter to the speculative London Company for the settlement. During the first few years, the settlers faced extreme hardship, and many of the original settlers died from disease or were killed by resentful Indians. The colonists soon discovered the profitability of tobacco, and within a few years the area was producing a steady flow of profitable tobacco. By 1619, slave labor was imported into the region for the tobacco crops. During the same year, the first representative assembly was held. A college was attempted as early as 1619, but local Indians killed the intruding settlers. By 1676, a combination of rebellious colonists and Indian attacks caused the abandonment of Jamestown. Many of the residents moved, along with the main governing body, to Williamsburg. In 1693, the College of William and Mary was established in Williamsburg, so named for the popular and likeable King and Queen of England who ruled England at that time ("Jamestown (Virginia)," n.d.).

Because of the profitability of tobacco, the Chesapeake region attracted many new settlers and colonies expanded to other areas of Virginia, into Maryland, and eventually into the Carolinas. Life on plantations followed the educational, political, and cultural patterns of England and not necessarily the church as in New England. In Virginia the wealthy plantation owners built "Great Houses" modeled from the architectural pattern books of Europe. Furnishings and decorations, including windows and other architectural details, were usually imported from Europe. The gentlemen and ladies patterned their manners and fashions after those in the Royal Courts of England and France. However, most of the colonists lived in one-story homes with either one or two rooms, where all the cooking, cleaning, housework, and sleeping was done.

The French, on the other hand, maintained trading outposts and religious missions in Newfoundland along the St. Lawrence River, which had an abundance of fishing areas. Some French settlers lived in Quebec (1608) and Montreal (1642), mainly trading furs with the Huron Indians. The French also had settlements in central Canada, along most of the Mississippi River, and at the port of New Orleans. French control was based mainly on trading outposts and peaceful dealings directly with Indian tribes. By 1700, the total French population was about 15,000. Spanish settlements in the southwest and Florida numbered only about 5,000. The French and Spanish control, however, marked about two-thirds of the contemporary continental United States. In contrast, the British settlements numbered over 250,000 along the eastern coast of America (Boyer, Clark, et al., 2000, 77–79).

During the seventeenth century British settlement colonies on mainland America included Virginia (1607), Massachusetts (1620), New Hampshire (1630), Maryland (1634), Rhode Island (1636), Connecticut (1636), the Carolinas (1663), New York (captured from the Dutch in 1664), New Jersey (1664), and

Pennsylvania (1681). The British also had territorial possessions in the West Indies, mainly for sugar crops, including St. Christopher (1624), Barbados (1627), Nevis (1628), Antigua (1632), Monserrat (1632), and Jamaica (captured from Spain in 1655), collectively known as the "Sugar Islands." In order to ensure a profitable return on the sugar crop in the West Indies, the British instituted a large scale system of slave labor. The British rule on the Sugar Islands was quite harsh, and slaves, imported from Africa, and Indians, from mainland America, supplied the labor.

Although accurate records were kept of the slave trade from Africa, no accurate records were kept of American Indian enslavement. What is known is that the need for slaves was so great that plantation owners in the Carolinas raided the Spanish possession of Florida and enslaved American Indians. Many of those Indians were shipped to the West Indies. They did not acclimate to the conditions or develop immunity against European diseases such as smallpox, tuberculosis, malaria, and diphtheria. As a result, almost all of the Native American Indians enslaved in the West Indies died there (Goldfield, Abbott, et al., 2001, 55).

The very first settlements in Massachusetts and Virginia also involved a significant number of indentured servants and a few African slaves. Indentured servants were poorer Europeans who, in exchange for passage to America, consented to a predetermined length of service (usually three years). After the time period was up, the indentured servant was granted both his release and a parcel of land. However, because of the profitability of rice in South Carolina and tobacco in Virginia and Maryland, the demand for labor was so great (a typical rice farm required 60–65 slaves for 130 acres of farmland) that the only way to meet the demand was to increase the amount of slave labor. As a result, large numbers of African slaves were being marketed to mainland America. In 1661, concern over the growing slave population prompted Maryland to define slavery as a "lifelong, inheritable racial status." In 1670, Virginia did the same, and the other southern colonies followed. By 1690, the African slave market to America increased dramatically, and by 1700, the number of slaves in most of the southern British colonies outnumbered the white European settlers (Goldfield, Abbott, et al., 2001, 49–56).

With the importation of Africans into America also came their tribal dance and music, which many of the slaves employed as a distraction from the forced incarceration of a life in slavery. However, in 1739, after a series of slave rebellions, many of the southern colonies passed laws prohibiting African Americans from using drums. It was thought that the drums incited the African slaves "to insurrection" (DeMille 1980, xi).

The colonial cities of Boston, New York, Philadelphia, and Charleston, South Carolina, might be considered provincial by contemporary standards. In 1685, Boston was the most populous at about 7,000 inhabitants. However, many of the later arriving immigrants did not seek the same covenant as the first Puritan settlers. Many of the new settlers sought the cities with their seaports with the idea of economic prosperity. Throughout the settlements of the English colonies along the eastern coast of America, many other religious groups settled in, such as Dutch Protestants in New York, Quakers and Moravians in Pennsylvania, Moravians and Huguenots in North Carolina, Anglicans in Virginia and the Carolinas, and French and Spanish Catholics in Louisiana.

Nevertheless, the irony, as it applied to the social establishments of the European courts, was that the same colonists who fled England and Europe in search of freedom from religious oppression soon used their own religious beliefs in an attempt to oppress the indigenous American Indian tribes, the African slaves, and even the European settlers themselves. In many instances, the cultural oppression involved the pursuit of dancing.

The main thought of the Puritans and most of the religious groups at the time was that dancing was completely unacceptable as part of a religious function. Noted dance choreographer Agnes DeMille noted that during the seventeenth century "in America even the social value of dancing was barely accepted and then only in certain restricted classes and areas of communal life" (DeMille 1980, 3). Conversely, historian William B. Weeden's description of the American colonies noted, "Social life was bare and spiritless beyond the possibility of description. Opportunities for pleasure would hardly satisfy the common laborer of two centuries later" (quoted in Csida and Csida 1978, 19). However, that would soon change.

After 1700, a greater number of English and northern European immigrants, including people from Scotland, Ireland, and Germany, immigrated to the British colonies. By 1740, the population in the British colonies exceeded 900,000. The white population was about 630,000 and the African slaves 270,000 (Goldfield, Abbott, et al., 2001, A-29). The sheer numbers of immigrants from different regions of Europe weakened the Puritan notion of religious utopia. In New England, the focus of immigration shifted from religious autonomy to economic speculation. And with that also came the need for recreation and enjoyment—the most favored was dancing.

In all areas of the colonies and settlements, the Europeans brought their homeland culture including the European dance traditions. In New York, for example, the Dutch brought with them the dance traditions of their native Holland. They continued a tradition of dancing on the holidays of Christmas, Pinkster, and Kermis. According to historian Joseph Marks, in 1641, in America, Governor Willem Kieft of the New Netherlands "established fairs to encourage the agricultural pursuits of the people" that included outdoor dancing. The Dutch also practiced social entertainment within their homes, and the men gathered at local taverns or members of social clubs. Soon, both the taverns and the clubs also established traditions of social dancing (Marks 1957, 22).

It is no wonder that in 1670, Molière, a French dramatist, in *Le Bourgeois Gentilhomme*, I, 2 (translated as *The Would-Be Gentleman*) wrote of the necessity of dancing. He claimed that, "There is nothing so necessary for men as dancing.... Without dancing a man can do nothing." Molière also satirically added:

> All the disasters of mankind, all the fatal misfortunes that histories are so full of, the blunders of politicians, the miscarriages of great commanders, all this comes from want of skill in dancing.

Noted dance historian Curt Sachs, who translated the French writings, agreed with Molière's statement. Sachs added, "This is not at all exaggerated" (1963, 400).

The Dances

Who so danceth not, knoweth not what cometh to pass. . . . Thou that dancest, perceive what I do.

—Jesus, 33 A.D.

But, without a knowledge of dancing, I could not please the damsels, upon whom, it seems to me, the entire reputation of an eligible young man depends.

—Capriol, 1589

If she were to meet with some hindrance while moving backwards, she might fall, a mishap for which you would receive the blame and suffer a rapid decline in her good graces.

—Thoinot Arbeau, 1589

I have seen a Minuet begun at the Bottom of the Room, and ended at the Upper End; which could not possibly have happened, had they observed the preceding Rules.

—Kellom Tomlinson, 1735

THE EARLIEST DANCES

Terpsichore: "The Fair Goddess of Dancing" and Choral Dance

The history of dancing has proliferated throughout history and has been recorded in factual, ancient, mythical, legendary, and even Biblical tales and stories. The earliest recorded history of the dance might be from rock paintings created around 10,000 B.C. to 20,000 B.C. by primitive man in the region of the south of France. In addition, Biblical tales such as David "dancing and leaping before the Lord" also traced dancing to earlier times. Throughout recorded history there have been all sorts of ceremonial dances including marriage dances, fertility dances, funeral dances, war dances, initiation dances, harvest dances, scalp dances, exorcism dances, dances honoring the gods, and even dances honoring one God, to name but a very few.

Almost all of the dances were performed in a circle or round dance known as Choral dance—which is the oldest and the most basic form of dancing. The round dances were associated with the community itself in that they lived in circular huts, and sometimes the ceremonial dance was performed around a fire or in the center of the village. In some cultures that built rectangular huts instead of circular huts the Choral dance was usually done in a straight line. Choral dancing was practiced by just about every human civilization (both cultured and primal) throughout the world. The unifying theme was to include the immediate community of the tribe or town (Sachs 1963, 144–145).

In Tibet, for example, as part of the Tibetan New Year's ceremonies, chanting monks in most monasteries performed the Black Hat Dance. The dramatic dance supposedly predated Buddhism and combined history, legend, and comedy to perform "a solemn rite of exorcism...to expel the evils of the past year and to symbolically defeat the enemies of Buddhism." The monks wore costumes of "animals, demons, and other mythical beings" and were accompanied by the music of trumpets, cymbals, drums, and bells (Museum text, The American Museum of Natural History, New York).

In fact, dancing in itself, whether for social enjoyment, religious ritual, or ceremony, can be traced to just about every civilization including the ancient Greeks and Romans. Homer's epic poem *The Iliad*, for example, provided a description of the ancient dancing of the Greeks at marriage ceremonies or even "together with the maidens" of the gods and goddesses. One description of the dance of Hellenes was described as follows:

> Also did the glorious lame god devise a dancing-place like unto that which once in wide Knossos Daidalos...There were youths dancing, and maidens of costly wooing, their hands upon one another's wrists....Fair wreaths had the maidens, and the youth daggers of gold hanging from silver baldrics....they would run in lines to meet each other. And a great company stood round the lovely dance in joy (*Iliad*, XVIII, 509–606; Sachs 1963, 237).

Choral dancing was, as were all forms of art, architecture, music, and poetry, an important component to Greek society. Throughout ancient Greece and Macedonia society, Greek mythology believed that individual gods and goddesses were responsible for individual components of life. It was the nine "Muses," born as daughters to the great Greek god Zeus and Mnemosyne who provided the artistic merits. The Muses along with Apollo, the god of music, sat beside the throne of Zeus and collectively sang of all the heroic efforts and great deeds of the gods and mythical heroes. In Roman society of the third to fifth centuries, the Muses were specifically thought to be associated with one facet of the arts. For example, Calliope was the muse of epic poetry, Clio for historical accounts, Erato for the poetry of love, Euterpe for lyrical poetry, Polyhymnia for sacred poetry, Melpomene for drama and tragedy, Thalia for comedy, Urania for the science of astronomy, and Terpsichore as the goddess of choral songs and dancing ("Muses," n.d.).

Italian Dance Master Carlo Blasis, in an important dance treatise of his time titled *The Code of Terpsichore* (1830), wrote lovingly of the goddess Terpsichore. He offered a description of her graceful motions as an example for the student of social dancing. He wrote:

> Terpsichore, the Goddess of Dancing, finding herself alone, betakes herself to the pleasures of graceful movements: first, she retires, then advances, displaying, as she lightly trips along, a beauteous knee. Her attention is fixed, on the harmonious sounds, while she arranges her steps in prelude....On her small foot she pauses skillfully, and gives to every limb some graceful attitude. . . . By such well-studied motion, and so light, the Goddess scarcely deigns to touch the earth. She wantons gaily, and springs aloft with such velocity, that her winged feet deceive the sight, and seldom can we

detect which foot it is that prints the soil. Shooting along in airy bounds, she traces circles with her limber feet; then, with step exact, retraces them...so are the motions of her twinkling feet, whether on earth, or quivering in the air; whether she lightly trips, or firmly treads the ground....Harmonious symmetry prevails throughout her person....The linked, and entwined figures of her dance are varied to the change of melody; marking each note, and minding every pause, promptly she obeys each phrase of music, which she respects as mistress of every motion (Blasis 1831, 47).

During ancient times through the Middle Ages, into the Renaissance, and beyond, the Choral dance and circle dances were sometimes viewed "as an earthly counterpart of the heavenly dance of the angels." One source actually claimed that Jesus and his Apostles joined in a Choral dance (Sachs 1963, 57).

According to a second century account, attributed to the Apostle John, Jesus and the Apostles joined in a Choral dance. At the Last Supper (the feast of Passover) before Jesus left his Apostles to meet his destiny at the Crucifixion, he asked his Apostles to join hands and dance around him in a circle. Within the circle Jesus sang a hymn, and the Apostles responded and repeated his words. According to dance historian Curt Sachs, the dance as commanded by Jesus to his Apostles was a Choral dance that "takes over the form of mystic circling, in which power jumps across from those on the outside to the one on the inside or vice versa" (Sachs 1963, 57).

The story of Jesus dancing with the Apostles is from a second century writing (possibly A.D. 130) that is contained in the Gnostic Society Library titled, "*The Hymn of Jesus* and *The Mystery of the Cross* from *The Acts of John.*" According to the Apostle John, Jesus said:

Who so danceth not, knoweth not what cometh to pass....Now answer thou unto my dancing. Behold thyself in me who speak, and seeing what I do, keep silence about my mysteries. Thou that dancest, perceive what I do, for thine is this passion of the manhood, which I am about to suffer.

"Terpsichore" from William De Garmo, *The Dance of Society* in Library of Congress. Library of Congress, Music Division, http://memory.loc.gov/musdi/.

Upon completion of the dance, John added, "Thus, my beloved, having danced with us the Lord went forth" (*The Hymn of Jesus*, n.d.).

It might be legend, or it might be fact. In either case, an important item of note is that during the thirteenth century, dancing as part of religious ritual was removed from the teachings of the Catholic Church. Therefore, if, in fact, the tale of the Apostle John existed at that time, it is quite possible that it too was removed from any printed editions of the Bible (DeMille 1980, 3).

However, unlike the Choral dance that had precedent throughout the world, the development of European dance had a distinction upon itself. The European dances developed the tradition of a man and woman dancing as a couple, first side-by-side and eventually face-to-face. The specific manner of partners dancing and moving together as a single couple in harmonious unison is strictly a European creation.

Christopher Columbus and his three ships land at Hispaniola on December 6, 1492. "Indians" can be observed dancing in the background. Library of Congress, Prints and Photographs Division, LC-USZ62-59702.

EUROPEAN DANCES OF THE MIDDLE AGES

St. Vitus' Dance, "Ring Around the Rosy," and the Tarantella

It is said that, during the journeys of Christopher Columbus and the discovery of the New World, he had his crew dance both for the joy of finding the new world and for the enjoyment of the natives. Some reports also indicated that Columbus, upon landing on Hispaniola, observed dancing among the native indigenous tribes. He termed those natives "Indians." Columbus's voyages (which actually placed him as discoverer of the Caribbean and West Indies islands of present day Bahamas, Dominican Republic, Haiti, Jamaica, and Cuba among others) were under the auspices of Spain and opened up exploration into the North American continent. As Columbus and other voyagers explored the New World that was soon called America, the courts of Europe, specifically France and England (and to a lesser extent Germany, Austria, Italy, and Spain), held a long-standing tradition of social dancing for courtship and enjoyment leading back from the Middle Ages (fifth to fifteenth centuries).

Accounts from as early as 1284 indicate that group round dancing usually followed the completion of medieval tournaments. The dancing was informal and usually involved the entire community. The group round dances did not necessarily have specific set steps. Sometimes a hop was included, or the circle would break into couples and they might whirl around "wildly" or stamp their feet. And they would return to the group circle for more frivolity (Dannett and Rachel 1954, 16–17). In the early fourteenth century, for example, during Kumis ceremonies the Yakut tribespeople of central Asia employed a pattern of moving rhythmically in circles. The ceremonial dancing encompassed thousands of villagers (Museum text, The American Museum of Natural History, New York).

At the time, most, if not all of the dancing, occurred outdoors. It was not until the late Middle Ages that an architectural development enabled dancing indoors. In an age before technological innovation in heating and cooling, rooms had a fireplace in the center of the room for heating and cooking with the smoke filtered through a simple hole in the ceiling. The development of the "chimney"

"Albrecht Dürer Dancing Peasant Couple."—Engraving c. 1514. Bradley Collection. Library of Congress, Prints and Photographs Division, LC- USZ62-127107.

allowed the fireplace to be built on the far walls of an interior space, thereby freeing up the interior space and eliminating smoke-filled rooms. Prior to that, any interior dancing was usually limited to circular dances that were literally around the fire (Clarke and Crisp 1981, 93).

About the mid-fourteenth century, during the devastating Bubonic Plague (also known as the "Black Plague" or "Black Death"), there were numerous reports of "uncontrollable dance madness" throughout Europe. The condition was actually involuntary neurological movements, coupled with severe twitches and facial grimacing and sometimes associated with rheumatic fever, but in all likelihood caused as a result of the plague. The applied medical term of *Sydenham's chorea* (sometimes "*chorea major*") was actually derived from Greek and Latin words that mean "dancing"—it was commonly known as the St. Vitus' Dance.

It appears that during the Middle Ages, as the Bubonic Plague devastated Europe, townspeople were desperate for any known cure. Some thought that they could put flower petals in their pockets and ward off death with the fresh scent. Others, mainly in Germany, traveled to the shrine of St. Vitus, which was considered a place of healing. (St. Vitus was actually a fourth century Sicilian martyr who was canonized for his healing powers and is also considered the patron saint of actors and dancers.) Many of those who made the pilgrimage had the neurological disorder associated with the plague. Therefore, as they traveled to the shrine they were observed to be twitching nervously—a sign that was most likely misinterpreted as dancing.

In later years, St. Vitus' feast day of June 15 was celebrated in many areas of Europe with a community dance. During the late twentieth and early twenty-first centuries, many swing dance aficionados picked up on the legend and sponsored a "St. Vitus Day Dance" typically on June 15 ("Saint Vitus," n.d.).

Many historians agree that the dancing was a method to ward off the plague. In many instances, townspeople, both young and old, gathered in a circle as they danced and sang along. One of the first known instances broke out in the Rhine Valley of Germany. The song that they sang as they danced seemed to mock the plague:

> Amidst our people here it come,
> The madness of the dance.
> In every town there now are some
> Who fall upon a trance.
> It drives them ever night and day,
> They scarcely stop for breath,
> Till some have dropped along the way
> And some are met by death. (Sachs 1963, 253)

In some cases, the singing and dancing continued for hours or until the townspeople literally collapsed either from sheer exhaustion or from the plague. Legend has it that the child's game "Ring Around the Rosy" was actually devised by peasants during the Bubonic Plague. Ring Around the Rosy is a circle dance that has the participants sing along. One verse containing the words "Pockets full of posy" was a reference to the fragrance of the flower petals to ward off the plague. The dance ends with all the hand-holding participants falling down in mocked death. The supposed "evil" of the dancing continued for many months as the plague ravaged Europe (Sachs 1963, 253–254).

In southern Europe, another form of dance mania known as "Tarantism," was reported in the Italian town of Tarentum. Some attributed that the madness was caused by the poisonous bite of a spider. Legend claims that the cure for the poison was obtained by performing the superstitious ritual dance known as the Tarantella. The dance was a group circle dance where the dancers held their arms high above their shoulders while they alternately lifted each foot and crossed it over the body, stepping to the ground mimicking stepping on a spider. Music was kept in time by the beats on a tambourine and the shaking of bells and even castanets. Some confusion existed that at the time the Tarantella might have been only "for girls" (Sachs 1963, 253–254). However, the Tarantella was performed as a circle dance by both men and women (although sometimes gender specific) among the entire southern portion of Italy. The Tarantella continued as a "high-spirited" Italian folk dance well into the nineteenth century. Immigrants during the late nineteenth and twentieth centuries brought it to America, and it was a popular social dance at weddings and other festive occasions into the twenty-first century.

EUROPEAN DANCES OF THE LATE MIDDLE AGES

Basses Dansés and Branles (1400–1550)

Some of the earliest known forms of social dancing that did have detailed written information included the *Basses Dansé* and the Branles. In all likelihood, the earliest known book of dance description for the Basse Dansé (sometimes "Basses Danses" or either "bassadanza" or "Bassa Danza" in Italian) is *Les Basses danses de Marguerite d'Autriche*, published in 1490. The book contained music and descriptions for over 50 contemporary Basses Dansés and also might be the earliest known book of dance instruction in general. The original manuscript is in the Brussels Bibliothèque Royale, and a digital facsimile is viewable online at the Library of Congress *An American Ballroom Companion: Dance Instruction Manuals Ca. 1490–1920* (see bibliography).

The Basse Dansé was common from the fourteenth century through the early part of the sixteenth century. It was a group processional dance usually performed to a "grave and solemn" Psalm tune. According to the Music Division of the Library of Congress, the instrumental music was performed with

> Soft, mellow musical instruments such as the vielle, (a bowed string instrument), or recorders were used for small, indoor occasions. The most popular musical accompaniment, however, consisted of an ensemble of three loud, shrill instruments: two were double-reed woodwind instruments called shawms (the forerunner of the oboe) and one was the sackbut, a brass instrument that later was developed into the trombone ("Burgundian Dance in the Late Middle Ages," n.d.).

The steps that accompanied the music were slow simple gliding movements. In the latter part of the fifteenth century, the dance consisted of only five simple steps that combined single and double progressive walking steps that were either forward or backward. The steps were accentuated on the gliding movement with a slight rise on the toes and a graceful lowering of the body. When performed in the courts of the nobility, the couples touched hands at a respectable arm's length, and they lined up with one couple behind the other. They promenaded throughout the room led by the couple of the highest-ranking social order (Clarke and Crisp 1981, 94).

Although the classes did *not* intermingle, both the nobility and peasants danced as a form of courtship. On the other hand, the peasants danced mainly to celebrate festive occasions and to escape the routine of daily life. The nobility danced to exhibit "social grace" and to show off their aristocratic social standing. The Basses Dansés that were done by both the peasants and nobility included the same simple dances such as the Carole, Estampie, Farandole, and Branle.

The Carole (sometimes "Carol") was a "chain dance" with as many participants who wanted to dance linked together in a line. The Carole was usually accompanied by the dancers singing along. In the south of France, the Estampie was another slow and dignified dance that had a man and a woman holding hands and standing side-by-side. The Farandole was also done with couples in single file with the dancers linking hands. When it was danced as a circular round dance, it was called the Branles (Clarke and Crisp 1981, 93).

According to the Music Division of the Library of Congress, Thoinot Arbeau's publication *Orchésographie* (1589) is the only contemporary Renaissance source for the Branles. Arbeau cited that the dance of peasant origin included over 20 different variations including "Branle Simple," "Branle Double," "Mixed Branles," "Haut Barrois Branle," "Maltese Branle," "Pease Branle," and "Washerwomen's Branle." The Branles were all circle dances for as many couples who wished to join in, and all began with a sideways step to the left. The basic Branles (or the "Branle Simple") was a sequence of single or double steps. The Mixed Branles included the single and double steps from the "Branle Simple" and also included a series of jumps. A third type added facial expressions and "mime gestures." Video clips of a demonstration of the basic Branle step as well as double and mixed steps are viewable from the Music Division of the Library of Congress online source *An American Ballroom Companion: Dance Instruction Manuals Ca. 1490–1920* (see bibliography).

By the sixteenth century, the Basses Dansés were out of fashion. In 1589, Arbeau's dance instruction manual, *Orchésographie*, provided similar information on the description of the dances. Arbeau did note that at the time the Basses Dansés had "been out of date some forty or fifty years, but I foresee that wise and dignified matrons will restore it to fashion as being a type of dance full of virtue and decorum" (51).

The Pavane, Etiquette, and How to Avoid Dancing Into a Wall

The Basses Dansés fell out of favor and the Pavane (sometimes "*Pauanes*" in French, "Pavan," in English, and "Pavana" in Italian) replaced it as a courtly processional dance. The Pavane was important in that it was usually the dance that opened all the formal balls and courtly affairs of that time. The Pavane most likely originated in Italy or possibly Spain around 1500. It was similar to the Basses Dansés as it was also a "gliding dance" done to solemn music. In 1508, the first written description of the Pavane was in *Intabolatura de Lauto* by Petrucci (Sachs 1963, 356). In 1581, Dance Master Fabritio Caroso provided a description of the "Pavana" in *Pavana Matthei*. Caroso also described the Pavane as a solemn ceremonial ballroom dance for a solo couple. The music for the Pavane was played with woodwind-type instruments and was also danced at weddings and festive ceremonial feasts. In 1589, Thoinot Arbeau described the Pavane as a solo couple's dance "walking with decorum and measured gravity" ("Renaissance Dance," n.d.).

The Pavane was performed in a predetermined sequence of steps (known as "choreography"). The basic dance contained two simple single walking steps and one double step moving either forward or backward. A simple Pavane choreography included "two *simples* and one *double* forward and two *simples* and one *double* backward." Prior to beginning the steps, the couple performed a "*révérence*," which was a bow by the man and a curtsy by the woman towards the guests, usually at the front (or "top") of the ballroom. (A *révérence* was usually done before every dance of the time period.) The Pavane begins with the feet in the First Position (heels together and both feet turned outward at a 45 degree angle) and proceeds with two "Simple Steps" as follows:

Step 1: (Two Counts) Step forward with the left foot and hold.
Step 2: (Two counts) Bring the right foot forward and next to the left and hold. Do not put weight on the right foot (The first "simple step.")
Step 3: (Two counts) Step forward with the right foot and hold.
Step 4: (Two counts) Bring the left foot forward and next to the right and hold. Do not put weight on the left foot. (The second "simple step.")

The left foot is free to repeat the simple step. A variation was to add a double step to the simple step. The double step is added to the end of the first two simple steps to make one continuous motion as follows:

Step 1–2: The first "simple step."
Step 3–4: The second "simple step."
Step 5: Step forward with the left foot.
Step 6: Step forward with the right foot and pass the left as in walking.
Step 7: Step forward with the left foot; and pass the right as in walking.
Step 8: Step forward with the right and bring the right foot beside the left with the heels together in the First Position.

(Note: Arbeau's notation and the Music Division of the Library of Congress describe the dance with counts assigned to the first bar, second bar, third bar, and fourth bar of music. Each simple step was performed in four bars of music necessitating the hold, and the double step was also performed in four bars of music, hence the continuous walking movement) ("How to Read a Dance Manual," n.d.).

The basic Pavane could also be done backwards using the same sequence of simple or double steps. The option of moving in either direction allowed the dancing couple to make conversation with the "multitude of guests" within the ballroom. (At the time, the written descriptions began to describe the dances as a "ball" and the room to hold the dance and guests as a "ballroom.") The idea of the Pavane was, according to Arbeau, to "circle the hall two or three times." Therefore, a continuous combination of forward and backward sequences would not take the couple very far.

Apparently, the straight-line forward and backward motion of the dance did not necessarily include the ability to avoid a ballroom hindrance such as a wall. According to Arbeau, "That is so, and if one does not wish to move backwards one may continue to advance all the time." As an alternative, he offered the following suggestion:

> Sometimes the hall is so thronged with a multitude of guests that the space for dancing is limited and therefore when you near the end of the room you are faced with two alternatives, either you, and the damsel with whom you are dancing, must move backwards or you must make a *conversion.*

In Arbeau's description of the Pavane, he elaborated upon the importance of the "conversion." He added,

> It means that upon approaching the end of the hall you continue to guide the damsel forward while you yourself move backwards as she advances, until you are facing in the opposite direction from which you started (58).

The conversion suggested that, rather than moving backwards, the dancers could turn around while doing the double steps. The gentleman basically stayed in place doing small steps backward and turning while he led the lady gracefully around him. The idea to turn around, rather than move backward was so that the lady could see where she was going. Once again, regardless of the time period, simple etiquette in any ballroom warned that it was entirely impolite to collide with another couple while dancing. In avoiding collision, Arbeau placed the sole responsibility with the gentleman. He warned:

> In my opinion it is better to make a conversion, in order that the damsel may always see where she is going. Because if she were to meet with some hindrance while moving backwards, she might fall, a mishap for which you would receive the blame and suffer a rapid decline in her good graces (58).

The Pavane not only presented (and also "showed off") each of the couples in a dignified and stately manner, it also allowed each couple to see all of the other guests and what they were wearing.

Regardless of the time period, going to a dance or a ball usually involved wearing the best clothes that one owned. Arbeau's brief description of the clothing included:

> A cavalier may dance the pavan wearing his cloak and sword, and others...dressed in ...long gowns, walking with decorum and measured gravity. And the damsels with demure mien, their eyes lowered save to cast an occasional glance of virginal modesty at the onlookers (59).

The Pavane was also a favorite of the Royal Court of Louis XIV (see later in this chapter), and after 1540 it was also common in the English courts. British dance historian Thomas Reginald St. Johnston in *A History of Dancing* (1906) noted that it was one of England's earliest "courtly dances." In regards to the origin of the Pavane, St. Johnston speculated the following:

The name of this dance is probably derived from the Latin pavo, a peacock, because of the stateliness of its movements, but some say it takes its name from Padua in Italy.... Concerning the stateliness of the dance, Sir John Hawkins has written in his "History of Music," It is a grave and majestic dance; the method of dancing it anciently, was by gentlemen dressed with caps and swords, by those of the long robe in their gowns, by the peers in their mantles, and by the ladies in gowns with long trains, the motion whereof in dancing resembled that of a peacock (134).

St. Johnston, however, believed that the Pavane might have originated in Spain around 1500. He "refuted by the fact" of the Italian origin and claimed that the dance "was almost undoubtedly of Spanish origin." St. Johnston based his belief on a contemporary Spanish proverb that proclaimed "Every Pavane must have its Galliard" (134).

After 1600, the Pavane faded from popularity of the Royal Courts and the ballrooms. It was replaced as the opening dance by the Minuet (see later in this chapter) and in some cases by the Grand March or Polonaise (see Chapter 4). The Pavane, although not performed as a social dance in America, did influence a basic step that many a school-age American individual or an attendant at a wedding was inadvertently aware in almost all formal settings from the nineteenth through the twentieth centuries. The basic step-close with alternating feet of the Pavane was so ardently taught as schoolchildren struggled during their graduation processional, usually to the tune of "Pomp and Circumstance." In addition, bridesmaids, ushers, and the bride employed the similar step well into the twenty-first century during a wedding ceremony ("How to Read a Dance Manual," n.d.).

EUROPEAN DANCES OF THE RENAISSANCE

The Galliard, Volta, Courante, Gavotte, and the Allemande

At the time, the Galliard was a dance that was usually danced at the end of the Pavane. In contrast to the slow Pavane, the Galliard (sometimes "Galliarde" in French and "Gagliarda" in Italian) was a spirited couple's dance also popular in the Italian and French courts during the late 1500s. The basic Galliard pattern was five steps within six beats of music. The male portion of the dance was energetic and considered "a showcase dance for male dancers." The idea was that the man would display his athletic ability to his female dancing partner. The first four steps of the Galliard, corresponding with single beats of music, were short springing steps followed by a jump or a leap with a foot change on the fifth beat with a change in the feet in the air for the landing on the sixth beat. There were many variations of the basic Five-step Galliard. Some variations included linking two series of six beats of music for an 11-step variation. The female's pattern was "demure" and admiring of her male counterpart without any leaps or jumps. Contemporary descriptions of the Galliard included two books by Fabritio Caroso *Il ballarino* (1581) and *Nobiltà de dame* (1600), as well as Cesare Negri's *Nuvone inventioni di balli* (1604) ("Renaissance Dance," n.d.).

Another dance that was usually danced within the Renaissance courts was the Volta. The Volta (sometimes "Volte") was an Italian Renaissance dance that was also in favor in the French and English courts during the 1500s. It was a "turning dance" that might have been the predecessor to the Waltz (see Chapter 2). The Volta was danced as a couple, and portions of the dance were in the face-to-face position, which also had the couple turning together. During the dance the man lifted the lady high in the air and turned her about halfway around and gently placed her on the dance floor. The Volta was considered quite scandalous since the man not only lifted the lady from the floor but also exposed the underside of her corset; both of which broke with the strict decorum of the time (*500 Years of Social Dance*, Dancetime Publications DVD, n.d.).

In addition to the Volta, another Renaissance dance was "Les Bouffons," a sword dance. A sword dance was done solely by men (usually in a group) and combined the valued masculine traits of the time, which was dancing and swordsmanship. Famed twentieth century dance choreographer Agnes DeMille noted in her book on dance history, *America Dances*, that, "The ability to dance well was as indispensable to an ambitious gentleman as the ability to fence well" (3). Arbeau also provided some of the earliest descriptions for other popular contemporary court dances including the Courante, the Gavotte, and the Allemande.

The Courante originated during the 1500s and remained a popular court dance through the eighteenth century. It was a couple's dance with short bouncing steps and gliding steps with music in 3/2 time. In the Italian courts it was danced a bit faster than in the French courts. The Courante had two distinct steps, which were a *pas coupé* and a *temps de courante*. A description of the Courante was found in two French Dance manuals: Francois de Lauze's *Apologie de la Dansé*, published in France in 1623, and in Pierre Rameau's *Le Maître à Danser*, published in Paris in 1725 and translated into English by John Essex as *The Dancing-Master: or, The Art of Dancing Explained*, published in London in 1728 ("Renaissance Dance," n.d.).

The Gavotte (known as *Gavots* by the peasants) was a French dance from around 1580 to the mid-1700s. It was a group dance that linked together the Branles with some movements from the Galliard. One couple would dance in the middle of either a circle or two opposite lines. During the dance it was the custom for the lead couple to end the set with a "kiss" towards each other. At the completion of the dance the gentleman would then kiss all the ladies and the lady would kiss all the gentlemen. Another couple would then take the place in the center and repeat the custom (Sachs 1963, 388). A contemporary account by Thoinot Arbeau described it as follows:

> When those taking part have danced a little while, one couple detaches itself from the rest and executes a few passages in the centre of the room within view of all the others. Then, this first dancer proceeds to kiss all the damsels in the room and his partner kisses all the young men, after which they return to their rightful places. This accomplished, the second couple do likewise and so on throughout the company (175).

The Allemande (sometimes "Allamande") was another French court dance of the sixteenth and seventeenth centuries that was also common in England and danced throughout Europe during the 1600s. The dance, most likely of German origin, was developed from the French Basses Dansés and incorporated similar balance and gliding steps. It was danced either as a couple or as a group in a chain with basic chassé steps, turns, and changing partners. The term "allemande" (sometimes "allamand") was later used to describe a set pattern in English Country-dances and American Square dancing ("Allemande," n.d.).

Video clips of a demonstration of the Pavane (including the conversion and *révérence*), the Galliard, the Volta, and also the Courante, the Gavotte, and the Allemande are viewable from the Music Division of the Library of Congress online source *An American Ballroom Companion: Dance Instruction Manuals Ca.1490-1920*, as well as Dancetime Publications *500 Years of Social Dance: Volume I: The 15th to 19th Centuries* (see bibliography).

Catherine de Medici, Italian Dance Masters, and Thoinot Arbeau

In 1533, Catherine de Medici of Italy married Henry II of France, and together they ruled as King and Queen of France from 1547 to 1559. During her reign, Catherine introduced dances such as the Pavane, the Galliard, and the Volta by importing Italian Dance Masters who in turn taught the dances to members of the aristocracy at the French Royal Court. The musical accompaniment to the dances was by such contemporary composers as Bach, Handel, Haydn, and Corelli. As a result of Catherine de Medici's influence, Paris was the model of social dance styles and etiquette and remained as such until the dawn of the twentieth century (Dannett and Rachel 1954, 20–21).

At the time, Catherine de Medici reflected the standard practice of the European nobility as the cultural leaders of the Renaissance. The Renaissance, which is placed historically from the late fourteenth century through the seventeenth century, spread throughout most of Europe. Much of the influence was derived from the ancient Greek and Roman civilizations. The main emphasis produced improvements in art, architecture, literature, philosophy, illustration, printing, humanism, and secular scientific thought.

It was during the Renaissance that the idea of a Dance Master as a profession came to be known. A Dance Master, described in contemporary terms, was in essence a professional dance instructor. The Dance Master was employed first in the Italian Courts to teach the proper steps necessary and required of the Aristocracy not only to display proper decorum and etiquette but also to be *au courant*. (In later years, the style or term would continue as it was known as being "up to date," "stylish," "modern," "in vogue," "hip," "cool," "trendy," or one of many other fad terms.) (Dannett and Rachel 1954, 18–19).

Around 1450, Italian Dance Masters first devised a choreographed dance known as the Ballo (sometimes "Balli" or "baletti"). The dance changed rhythms with various changes in the music and placed emphasis on pantomime movements. The Ballo was considered as the precursor to the modern "Ballet." It was the Dance Masters who also developed specific instructions on how to properly place the feet in one of five basic positions during a particular dance. In all five positions both feet are turned outward at a 45 degree angle with the heels toward the center of the body and the toes pointing away and to the front. In all five positions, the left

19

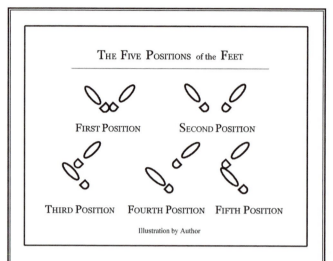

THE FIVE POSITIONS of the FEET

FIRST POSITION   SECOND POSITION

THIRD POSITION   FOURTH POSITION   FIFTH POSITION

Illustration by Author

The Five Positions are described as follows: The First Position, the feet are heels together. The Second Position, the feet are about shoulders width apart. The Third Position, the right heel is placed against the instep of the left foot. The Fourth Position, the right foot is placed about one foot in front aligned with the center of the left foot. The Fifth Position, the right heel is placed against the front side of the left foot.

From these five positions was the combination of all the variations of steps—backward, forward, and sideways—while still maintaining balance, and most importantly defining that no large dance step should be taken—they instead remained no more than one foot apart. Although the five positions were taught by the Dance Masters, they were not fully standardized until Charles Beauchamp (b. 1636, d. 1705) defined them while he was the Royal Dance Master for King Louis XIV of France. Thereafter, the Five Positions of the Feet became standard among classical dancers and for ballet dancers, as well as essential for the aristocracy in the Royal Courts (Sachs 1963, 395).

foot remains in the natural position forming a straight line with the left shoulder and left hip.

With the introduction of Dance Masters into the Royal Courts, dancing styles among the peasant and gentry class separated from that of the nobility. The simple dances, including the Branles and Pavane, that were done in a circle, line, or couple among the peasants at merry occasions usually did not require either the Five Positions of the Feet, much practice, or even a Dance Master. In addition, the dances of the townspeople included any number of participants. However, when the Branles and Pavane were danced as processional dances, or mainly reserved for the royal courts—and later dances such as the Galliard, the Volta, the Courante, the Gavotte, and the Allemande—they required specific steps, set figures, patterns, and posture that could be taught only by a Dance Master. In many cases the nobility danced as few as one couple in order that the dance could "be viewed" by the other aristocrats in attendance ("Renaissance Dance," n.d.). The result, according to dance historian Curt Sachs, was that:

> The dance, which hitherto had been the child of passion and irresistible impulse, is now the product at once artistic and artificial of the masters. It is a work of art, the correct figures, positions, and steps of which must be learned according to rule (1963, 302).

In an age before the twentieth century technological developments of reproducible photographs, film, videos, and DVDs, the way to learn a dance was either from a Dance Master, a dance instruction manual, or, preferably, both. Many of the Dance Masters also published their own books (some with music, rudimentary dance notation, or illustrations), which they sold to their patrons and also took with them as they traveled from town to town ("How to Read a Dance Manual," n.d.).

In the case of Italian Dance Master Fabritio Caroso (b. 1535, d. 1605), his dance manual, *Il ballarino*, (1581) not only described the most popular dances of the contemporary royal courts but also provided specific choreography for 80 dances. He preceded each dance with an illustration showing the proper starting position. He also provided detailed written information for the "appropriate music" and etiquette, including the proper use of "swords" within the ballroom. In 1600, Caroso also published another dance manual titled *Nobiltà di dame*. A second edition was released in 1605 and reissued in 1630. In 1630, Caroso's *Nobiltà di dame* was also translated into Spanish. However, Thoinot Arbeau's *Orchésographie* (1589) is probably the most important of the sixteenth century dance manuals ("From Renaissance Dance To Baroque Dance," n.d.).

Born Jehan Tabourot (b. 1520, d. 1595), Thoinot Arbeau wrote his dance treatise under an anagram of his own name. However, his biographer, Mary Stewart Evans, claimed that Arbeau "was no ordinary dancing master." At the time of publication, he was a 69-year-old French Catholic monk and was part of a small group of religious leaders who reintroduced dancing as part of Church ceremony in France. Evans added, "He continually [stressed] the valuable function of dancing in the life of the community....He belongs to that honourable line of scholarly churchmen in the Roman tradition who combine spiritual with worldly wisdom to the advantage of both." It should be noted that Arbeau wrote his dance manual and praised the value of dancing at a time when a "series of edicts" dating back to the Middle Ages still prohibited "dances in churches, churchyards, and public procession" (5). However, during the Renaissance, which was an age devoted to humanistic studies, there was a fair amount of latitude for individual Catholic monks, such as Arbeau, to determine for themselves the value of dancing for both the community and as part of Catholic religious ceremonies (Sutton "explanatory notes," in Evans translation, *Orchesography* 1967, 208).

Consequently, Arbeau's *Orchésographie* provides a valuable detailed account of the contemporary French dancing and social customs from 1550 through the 1580s. The entire manual, subtitled a *Dialogue Upon the Dance and the Manner of Dancing*, was written as a conversation between himself and a young student named Capriol. Hence, Capriol had left his hometown of Langres and had been absent for "six or seven years," during which time he had studied law in Paris, but by his own admission had "neglected to learn fine manners." Upon his return to the city of Langres, Capriol understood that law was "necessary in the conduct of [everyday] affairs"; however, he discovered that simply being able to work at a job was not enough. Capriol regretted that during his hours of study in Paris he did not make the time "to have acquired skill in dancing." He added, "I have found myself in society, where to put it briefly, I was tongue-tied and awkward, and regarded as little more than a block of wood." Capriol explained his reason to want to learn dancing. He said:

> I much enjoyed fencing and tennis and this placed me upon friendly terms with the young men. But, without a knowledge of dancing, I could not please the damsels, upon whom, it seems to me, the entire reputation of an eligible young man depends (11).

Arbeau consoled the young lad stating, "You took consolation in the fact that the learned professors excused this shortcoming in recognition of the learning you had acquired." Arbeau offered the simple solution that learning how to dance "will be an easy thing by reading French books"—especially *Orchésographie* (11).

Within the course of conversation with Capriol, Arbeau provided a detailed treatise including the history of dance, as well as the etiquette and révérences of the ballroom. Arbeau offered his definition of dance and dancing as follows:

> The noun dance comes from the verb to dance, which in Latin is called *saltare*. To dance is to jump, to hop, to skip, to sway, to stamp, to tiptoe, and to employ the feet, hands, and body in certain rhythmic movements (14).

The illustrations in *Orchésographie* also provided a good indication that the dance steps were restricted by the fashion decorum. The clothing was bulky, as all parts of the body except the hands and face were covered. (In some cases, such as masquerade balls, the faces were, in fact, covered.) Women were restricted by tight-laced corsets for the upper body. Men also wore similar tight-laced upper body coats and usually wore their swords. The head was somewhat restricted by the fashionable ruffs worn around the neck by both genders.

Specific dances discussed included the Branle, the Pavane, the Galliard, the Volta, the Courante, the Gavotte, and the Allemande. To represent the descriptions of the specific dance steps, Arbeau introduced a tabulation chart corresponding each dance step with the appropriate musical note. Arbeau's original illustrations were simple vertical charts of five musical lines read top to bottom along the left side of the page. The appropriate step was written out horizontally on the right side of the vertical scale. Unfortunately, subsequent editions and translations of *Orchésographie* in 1878, 1888, and 1925 did not provide a faithful reproduction of the original tablature. In 1967, Mary Stewart Evans's translation titled *Orchesography* reproduced an accurate facsimile of Arbeau's original illustrations. Evans called Arbeau's tablature "an ingenious device to enable the pupil

In 1589, Thoinot Arbeau's *Orchésographie* provided a detailed account of the contemporary French dancing from the 1550s through the 1580s. The version depicted here is a translated version by Mary Stewart Evans titled *Orchesography*, released by Dover Publications in 1967. The illustration is a round dance indicative of sixteenth century fashion.   Courtesy of Dover Publications. Cover design by Ted Menten.

to see at a glance which notes and steps corresponded by placing them opposite to one another on the page." Evans added that Arbeau continually emphasized "the importance of musicality in a dancer and the dependence of the dance upon the music" (6).

After 1600, some changes in dance style were noted that included a "turnout from the hip," and most importantly the leaps and jumps of the earlier dances were replaced by specific dance steps that were close to the ground. A contemporary account was provided by Francois de Lauze's *Apologie de la danse* (1623) and Juan de Esquivel Navarro's *Discvrsos sobre el arte del dançado* (1640). Each dance manual noted the "turnout from the hip," as well as the Five Positions of the Feet ("From Renaissance Dance To Baroque Dance," n.d.).

Other dances that were favored at the time included the Brando (a form of Branle), the Moresco, the Passépied (which included three steps and a leap), the Nizzarda, the French Buffins (which pantomimed a mock swordfight from France), the So Ben Mi Chi Ha Bon Tempo (written in 1602 by Italian Dance Master Cesare Negri), and the Canari, among others. The Canari (sometimes Canary), from the Canary Islands, was a courtship type of dance that involved enticing gestures by the man towards the woman (*500 Years of Social Dance: Volume I*, n.d.).

NATIVE AMERICAN DANCING

The Sarabande, the Fandango, the Spanish in Southwest America, and the Pueblo Indians

In the late sixteenth century the Sarabande was another favored court dance. It is thought to have originated in Spain and may have developed from Spanish folk dances of the peasants such as the Chacona. The Sarabande combined twists and turns, as well as some backwards motion. It was danced to both slow and fast tempos. But by the mid-seventeenth century in Spain, it was danced only in slow tempo. At that time, the Sarabande was also a choreographed dance on the theater stage ("Baroque Dance," n.d.).

Around 1583, some parts of Spain banned the dance and punished those found dancing the Sarabande. Dance historian Curt Sachs cited an account by a contemporary Jesuit historian named Juan de Mariana (b. 1536, d. 1623) who wrote, "In these years appeared a dance and song, so indecent in its text, so repulsive in its movements, that even the most respectable people were influenced by it." Other contemporary accounts described the Sarabande "with absurd twists of the body, hands, and feet" and "unimpaired primitivism" (367).

However, it is quite possible that the dance was banned since it might have actually originated with the "unimpaired primitivism" of native indigenous Indian tribes from either Central or North America. Sachs claimed that the Sarabande dance was also sometimes spelled "Zarabanda" and that a Guatemalan musical instrument similar to a flute was called the *zarabanda*. Therefore, Sachs asserted, "Never has an instrument been named for a dance, but dances, on the other hand, have frequently been called after instruments." As a result, the Sarabande might have been the first dance "of the mixed races of Central America" to influence Europe (Sachs 1963, 367–372).

Another similar type of Spanish dance was the Fandango, danced in a mixture of 3/8 and 3/4 time. The Fandango was a favored courtship dance in Spain. In 1767, the writer Casanova saw the dance in Spain. He described it as "always danced by only two persons, who never touch each other even with the hand...never move more than three steps as they click their castanets with the music of the orchestra. They take a thousand attitudes, make a thousand gestures so lascivious that nothing can compare with them." Some claim that the Fandango was indigenous to Spain and the castanets were traced back 2,000 years to the Phoenicians. However, dance historian Curt Sachs also speculated that the "courtship dance of Spain" might have actually originated with the *Reinos de las Indias*—the American Indians (quoted in Sachs 1963, 98–99).

From as early as 10,000 B.C., evidence of Paleo-Indian tribes existed in North America. Agriculture and shelter by descendants of those Indians were found dating before the birth of Christ. Intricate pueblos (multiple housing units made of adobe) dated from at least 1290. Shortly after the discovery of the New World, beginning in 1519 to 1521 with the conquest of the Aztecs by Hernán Cortés, Spain began extensive exploration, conquest, and colonization of many areas of the Caribbean, Mexico, and Peru—mainly in search of gold and silver. In 1513, Ponce de León first explored Florida. In 1528 and 1539, Spain followed with expeditions of the southeast portion of America. The expedition in 1539, led by Hernán deSoto, explored to the Mississippi River. In 1540 to 1542, Francisco Vásquez Coronado led Spanish explorations into the area of New Mexico, Arizona, and Colorado. As a result, by 1550, Spain effectively controlled Mexico and Central America, and in 1565, a permanent outpost and settlement was established in St. Augustine, Florida (Goldfield, Abbott, et al., 2001, 3–15).

As early as 1598, the Spanish conquest of Mexico (known as New Spain) spread into the southwest territory of America into the region of the southwest known as "New Mexico." The Spanish built a series of forts known as "missions," to convert the Indians to Catholicism. The implementation of Catholicism upon the indigenous Native North American Indians included a suppression of their native culture including centuries old dancing. Dance historian Curt Sachs described an ancient courtship dance ritual of the Pueblo Indians similar to the circle dances of Europe. In comparison to Europe where the man danced around the woman, with the Pueblo Indians "the encircled woman spins like a top." He also surmised that, "Since Mexico lies on the outer border of the territory in which this motif is to be found, we must suppose that we have in that country [America] the oldest form [of dance]" (Sachs 1963, 95).

However, the Spanish colonial rule upon the Pueblo Indian tribes was harsh and ruthless. The Spanish raided the Pueblo underground Kivas, which was their equivalent of a church, and also destroyed the Indian ritual artifacts. Choreographer and dance historian Agnes DeMille in *America Dances* pointed out that, "The Europeans took kindly to the Indians' tobacco, maize, potatoes, leatherwork, and furs, but not to any of their art forms." In regards to the Indian art form and dancing, DeMille added, "The early settlers saw plenty of Indian dances wherever they went, but they feared and scorned them, considering them goings-on of heathens and savages...They did not observe Indian dances with the slightest aesthetic or anthropological curiosity." Unfortunately, this statement not only applied to the Spanish, but also to all the European settlers who entered America from the earliest days until well into the twentieth century (DeMille 1980, 4).

In 1680, Native American Indian tribes in the Southwest, including Taos, Tewa, Apache, and Comanche, rebelled against the Spanish conquerors. Known in American history as the Pueblo Revolt of 1680, the Indians were successful in forcing the Spanish soldiers out of the region. Unfortunately, the successful rebellion lasted only about 20 years. The Spanish returned and by 1700 reestablished the missions. The most famous of those was the Alamo established in 1718 in San Antonio, Texas (see Chapter 3). Although the total number of Spanish was only about 1,800, they were able to control the Native American Indians with the use of guns and horses. In fact, it was the Spanish who introduced both the horse and the gun to the North American continent. In contrast to the life of the Native American Indian, although with a history of both peaceful tribes and warring tribes, once again, Agnes DeMille so aptly points out, "A gun had never been fired on the North American continent before the Spaniards and Englishmen came" (3). Spanish colonies were also firmly reestablished throughout the American Southwest as well as Florida. In the process, the Spanish also displaced Russian outposts in California to maintain and protect shipping trade to the Philippine Islands. In doing so, they established a series of forts along the coast of California from San Diego to San Francisco (Goldfield, Abbott, et al., 2001, 117).

After the reconquest, the Pueblos devised methods to maintain their native culture under Spanish rule. Historian Jill Sweet in *Keeping the Rituals Alive* noted that the Tewas, Pueblos, and other Native American Indian tribes maintained their dance tradition by "compartmentalization." Compartmentalization is an anthropological term that was defined as "adopting but deliberately practicing separately (that is, keeping in separate 'compartments') certain aspects of Spanish culture, the Pueblos managed to keep the borrowed traits as additions to, rather than replacements for, their native customs." In the case of their native dance rituals the Tewas, for example, incorporated dance as part of the Catholic mass celebration (Sweet 1985, 41).

EUROPEAN DANCE TRADITIONS AND THE AMERICAN COLONIES

King Louis XIV, Feuillet's Dance Notation, Pierre Rameau, and the Minuet

For the most part, the dances prior to the seventeenth century were performed by any number of couples at the same time, and the orientation of the dance within the ballroom was not of major importance. However, by the mid-seventeenth century the court dances were usually precisely regulated to the form of a singular couple dance known as a *danses à deux*. The dances were performed one couple at a time and designed to be orientated towards the guests at the front or top of the dance hall. This area usually had seating reserved for the most prominent or highest-ranking couple such as the King and Queen. (Most ballrooms of the time had seating on three sides of the room.) This standard format was devised during the reign of King Louis XIV (1643–1715) of France ("Baroque Dance," n.d.).

In 1643, when Louis XIV became King, France was a dominant political and military power. As King, he established the French Royal Court and established France as an influential cultural authority—especially for social dancing. In 1661, Louis commissioned the Royal Academy of Dance under the direction of Charles Beauchamp, who was also the official Dance Master to the King. At the Royal Academy, training was available for all styles of dance including dancing for the theater and for the Royal Court, as well as social dancing for the public ballrooms. The standard dances, under the supervision of Beauchamp included the Branle, Courante, Gavotte, Allemande, and Minuet, among many others. At the Royal Academy of Dance, the King mandated a standardized teaching method of dance including the Five Positions of the Feet, body position, and gestures, as well as the protocol, decorum, manners, and révérence for the court dances.

During the end of the seventeenth century, in association with the Royal Academy of Dance, King Louis XIV commissioned Dance Master Raoul-Auger Feuillet to create a uniform visual dance notation for the court dances. As a result, Feuillet developed (or "notated") a precise uniform system for the five positions of the feet, orientation of the body, and gestures and movements for the legs, arms, torso, and head. Prior to Feuillet, dance instruction manuals placed little emphasis on describing the arm movements and gestures of the upper body and head. (They were, however, taught by personal instruction from a Dance Master.) Feuillet's notation system provided an illustration of a couple in dance position, and at the bottom of the page he placed a drawing "that traced the pattern of the dance." He placed symbols on the sides of the tract for the dance steps. Along the top of the page, he illustrated the "bar lines" of the appropriate music for the dance. In 1700, the "Feuillet Notation" system was published in his dance manual titled *Chorégraphie*. By 1713, it was reissued three times, and Feuillet had recorded over 300 dances of the Royal Court ("Baroque," n.d.).

The Feuillet Notation system, as well as the multitude of dance step descriptions and ballroom etiquette was widely copied and spread throughout Europe. *Chorégraphie* was translated into other

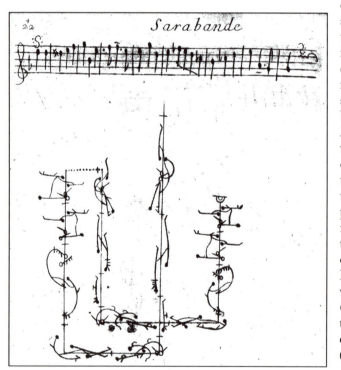

An illustration of the Sarabande dance in "Feuillet Notation" from Raoul-Auger Feuillet as published in his dance manual titled *Chorégraphie*, c. 1700. Library of Congress, Music Division, http://memory.loc.gov/musdi/073/0024.gif.

languages including English in 1706 by John Weaver (*Orchesography*, reissued in 1715) and into German in 1717 by Gottfried Taubert (*Rechtschaffener Tanz-Meister*). Other dance manuals, such as the Italian Giovanni Battista Dufort's *Trattato del Ballo Nobile* (1728), Spain's Pablo Minguet é Irol's *Arte de Danzar a la Francesa* (1758), and the Portuguese Natal Jacome Bonem's *Tratado dos Principaes Fundamentos* (1767) borrowed much of Feuillet's publication and notation system. Feuillet's notation system was the universally accepted standard until it was replaced by the system of Labanotation in the early twentieth century ("Baroque Dance," n.d.).

In 1928, Rudolf von Laban of Hungary devised and published a standardized system for recording any human body movement. Shortly thereafter, in America, Ann Hutchinson adjusted the system that became universally accepted as a "non-verbal symbology, posing no language barriers for research." Hutchinson explained that, "Labanotation serves the art of dance much as music notation serves the art of music." Labanotation uses a vertical staff similar to a column and is read from the bottom to the top of the page. Therefore, by placing the column in the vertical direction, what is written on the left side of the vertical chart pertains to the left side of the body and similar for the right side. Every change of the center of weight, including body gestures, arm movements, and leg movements, are recorded within the vertical column lines. The system also allows for charting movement paths as well as floor plans for location and movement of dancers, which are written into the column at the far right of the chart. Throughout the twentieth century and into the twenty-first century, Labanotation was used to archive all forms of dances including theatrical, ballet, and social dancing (Griesbeck 1996).

In 1682, Louis XIV established the official Royal Court of Versailles for "official dances," which lasted until Louis's death in 1724. Throughout his reign, dances and balls were frequent. (Although the palace of Versailles itself did not necessarily have a formal ballroom, there were numerous ballrooms in the homes and palaces of the aristocracy.) The pattern of dancing at the French balls "set the standard for social dancing throughout Europe" (Harris-Warwick, "Ballroom Dancing at the Court of Louis XIV," 1986, 41).

The opening of each ball usually included, as the first four dances, the Branle, Courante, Gavotte, and Allemande. The protocol was strictly maintained that the attendees at the ball formed a column in couples in descending rank of social order. The King selected a partner and danced the first dance. The King and his partner then proceeded to the end of the line. Each couple performed the same dance until the King was back at the front of the line. He then selected another dance, and the other couples followed his lead. After this procedure was completed for the four dances, the King usually took a seat on his throne, which was at the top of the ballroom, and continued to watch the others dance (Sachs 1963, 396).

In 1725, Pierre Rameau, in *Le Maître à Danser*, provided a contemporary account of the "social behavior" of a dance at the Royal Court, as well as the order of dances to open a formal ball of that time. Rameau had attended dances at the Royal Court of the King and wrote his account the year after the death of Louis XIV. He described it as follows:

The king takes his place at the part of the room where the dancing is to start, which is near the orchestra. In the time of [Louis XIV], it was the queen whom His Majesty took as his partner, or in her absence, the first princess of the blood. . .

They place themselves at the head of the group, and the others take their places behind them in a line, according to rank, with the gentlemen on the left side and the ladies on the right. In this same order they make a *reverence* to each other, and then the king and his partner lead the Branle, which was the dance with which court balls were opened. All the gentlemen and ladies follow Their Majesties, each on his own side, and at the end of the *couplet*, the king and queen go to the end of the line, and the next couple leads the Branle. This continues until Their Majesties are at the head of the line again. . . .

Then comes the *danses à deux*. In the past the Courante was danced after the Branles, and Louis XIV of happy memory danced it better than anyone else at his court, but now the Minuet is danced after the Branles (quoted in Harris-Warwick, "Ballroom Dancing at the Court of Louis XIV," 1986, 41–42).

King Louis XIV at a court ball for a *danses à deux*. The dances were performed one couple at a time and were designed to be orientated towards the guests at the front or top of the dance hall. This area usually had seating reserved for the most prominent or highest-ranking couple such as the King and Queen. Copper engraving, c. 1682. The Granger Collection, New York, ID: 0027055.

After the death of Louis XIV, the French Court diminished as "the official arbiter of the acceptable social dances" in Europe. The Minuet, however, maintained an unprecedented popularity for well over 150 years and would become a favorite dance in America, especially by George Washington (see Chapter 2) ("Baroque Dance" n.p.).

The Minuet (also *Menuet*) was a folk dance that originated among the countryside and townspeople in Poitou, France. Some sources said the dance was also known as the "Poitou," and often described it as "ugly," "insignificant," and "lowly" (Sachs 1963, 396). In all likelihood, the description was in keeping with the social decorum of the day. The Aristocracy viewed themselves as the social arbiters of culture and therefore did not speak highly of anything from the peasants from the lower social order. Among the townspeople the Minuet (Poitou) was considered "carefree and lively"; however, by the time it appeared before King Louis XIV, it was "a slow and stately" elegant dance. Following the social decorum set down in the rules of the Five Positions of the Feet, the steps in the Minuet were also short or "small." It is possible that the name of the Minuet was derived from the small steps taken in the dance. The steps were defined either as *menu* (which is the French word for "small") or *menuet* (which is French for "tiny") ("Baroque Dance," n.d.).

In 1650, when the Minuet was officially "presented" at the French Court of King Louis XIV, it was elegant and befitting of the Royal Court. The dance was led by the highest-ranking members of the social order. In the case of Louis XIV, it was the King and Queen (or someone that he personally selected) who led the dance and was followed by the descending aristocracy rank. The Minuet danced by Louis XIV remained basically the same from 1660 to 1820. Some of the most famous classical composers who scored music for the Minuet included Jean-Baptiste Lully, George Frideric Handel, Johann Sebastian Bach, Franz Joseph Haydn, and Wolfgang Amadeus Mozart, among others (Richardson 1960, 18).

The Minuet might be the first dance that is very much a reflection of the fashion of the times. The clothing was also a key ingredient, and the stately minuet reflected the grace to maintain both the charm and the balance of the contemporary attire. In regards to the Minuet specifically, the fashion at the time of the Royal Court required men to wear buckled shoes, white knee-length stockings, knee britches as pants, and a heavy knee-length bright colored coat. Under the coat was a puffy shirt with a high collar and sleeves with lace cuffs that extruded beyond the jacket and hung down below the palm of the hand. The gentleman's attire was completed with a powdered wig. The lady of the court wore a full-length hooped dress of many layers of fabric. Her sleeves were three-quarter length, and the collar was low-cut accentuating the bosom. The woman also wore a powdered wig, although it was much more elaborate than the gentleman and could be almost one-foot high. The lady completed her attire with a display of jewelry and restrictive high-heeled shoes (Shaw 1949, 50–51).

Therefore, because of the bulkiness, formality, and weight of the clothes, the style of dance was restricted to a slow, stately, graceful dance such as the Minuet. Needless to say, with the weight of the clothes and especially the lady's headdress and the gentleman's powdered wig, balance and daintiness were essential, for any sudden quick movements or leaps might cause the headdress to come undone. And certainly the restrictive heavy bulky clothing was not conducive to an athletic movement such as a leap or a jump. As dance historian Lloyd Shaw so aptly advised: "This relationship of costume and dance must always be kept in mind. Study the costume, if you wish to understand the dance" (50–51).

However, the Minuet that was danced at the Royal Court was certainly not one that could be learned by "watching" or for that matter danced with any joy or frivolity. The Minuet danced before the eyes of the King required precise steps, gestures, movements, turnouts of the knees and legs, and close coordination with the music that could be attained only from the dour tutelage of a Dance Master from the Royal Academy (Marks 1957, 27).

Minuet music was in 3/4 time and danced accordingly in a set of six steps, or two measures of music. It was danced one couple at a time, in the aforementioned social rank. The Minuet started with an introduction of a révérence or an acknowledgment to the partner. The couple joined hands, and the dance started with a series of elegant precise small steps and balance with a rise and bend of the knee and feet.

One step forward was in the side-by-side (gentleman on the left side of the lady) and two steps facing each other as the couple traced a predescribed floor pattern. (At first the floor pattern was outlined as a figure 8; later it varied as an S, a 2, or a Z. After 1770, it was standardized as a Z.) The face-to-face position had two hands joined together placed diagonally on the top inner corner of the Z floor pattern. The couple separated their hands and performed two steps down the horizontal line of the Z and two steps back up. It was followed by two more steps back down the diagonal line. A turn put them on the bottom inner corner of the Z. They danced two steps forward and two steps back along the bottom horizontal of the Z. The pattern was counterrepeated along the floor pattern of the Z to return the couple to the original start position. The S or Z figure could be repeated as often as the gentleman decided. The small steps were accompanied by equally dignified slow and precise arm and hand movements that included "the giving of right hands," "the giving of left hands," and "the giving of both hands." In addition, there were frequent presentations of courtly gestures, bows, and curtsies. [Video clips of a demonstration of some of the basic Minuet movements are viewable from the Music Division of the Library of Congress online source *An American Ballroom Companion: Dance Instruction Manuals Ca. 1490–1920* (see bibliography) (Sachs 1963, 407; Dannett and Rachel 1954, 24; Keller and Hendrickson 1998, 123; "Baroque Dance," n.d.).]

The Minuet was also carefully described in many eighteenth-century dance manuals. During the course of providing written instructions for the dance, the instruction manuals spent many words describing the proper bows, curtsies, and etiquette. In the simple manner of the opening "bow," for example, one dance instructor wrote two full chapters, another over 60 pages, and yet another almost an entire book. Some of the most complete descriptions for all phases of the Minuet were included in contemporary accounts in two manuals by Pierre Rameau in *Le Maître à Danser* (1725) and *Abbrégé de la nouvelle méthode* (1725), and one by Kellom Tomlinson's *The Art of Dancing...first design'd in the year 1724* (1735) (Sachs 1963, 398).

In 1725, Pierre Rameau's *Le Maître à Danser* attempted to cover all forms of dancing for the social dancer, the gentry, and the nobility, as well as for the theater stage. Rameau even included a complete description of all the pageantry and ceremony of the King's Grand Ball. He declared that the Grand Ball should be "the model for any similar event held anywhere else." In 1728, Rameau's work was translated into English by John Essex (b. 1680, d. 1744) as *The Dancing-Master: or, The Art of Dancing*. By that time, the Minuet was the most favored and revered dance throughout Europe. During the course of over 150 years, almost every noted court or state ball in Europe and America opened the dancing with the Minuet ("Ballroom Dancing at the Court of Louis XIV," 41).

Kellom Tomlinson and "The Art of Dancing"

In 1735, English Dance Master Kellom Tomlinson (b. 1690, d. 1753) in *The Art of Dancing* devoted an entire publication to the method of French dancing, which was for distribution in England. In addition, the number of pages (well over 100) dedicated to the Minuet provides support of the widespread influence and immense popularity of the dance. He described the Minuet as follows:

> The Minuet Step is composed of four plain straight Steps or Walks, and may be performed forwards, backward, sideways, [and] four different Ways, to which there are the like Number of Names annexed, to distinguish them from one another, arising, not improperly speaking, from the Placing of the Marks upon them: For Example, a Movement or Sink and Rise, being added to the first Step of the three belonging to the Minuet Step, produces a Bourrée; and the like to the fourth and last a Half Coupee, which together compose what is commonly called the English Minuet Step (1735, 103–104).

Tomlinson described in-depth variations, or other "Methods" for the basic Minuet Step, as well as a complete description for the proper distribution for the "Weight of the Body" and the specific postures and movements required to complete the Minuet. He was careful to point out, "It is to be noted, that it always begins with the right and ends with the left foot; and it is performed faster or slower, according to the Tune that is played, which the Dancer is obliged to follow" (1735, 106).

Tomlinson actually finished writing *The Art of Dancing* in 1724, and in order to properly describe the Minuet and the other dances, he supplemented the text with 35 full pages of illustrations in Feuillet Notation. However, because of the high cost of printing the illustrations, it took Tomlinson over ten years to raise the money for publication. (At the time, many authors, especially the Dance Masters, paid the cost of printing and distributed the books themselves.) When *The Art of Dancing* was finally published in 1735, Tomlinson's complete title explained it all. The full title read:

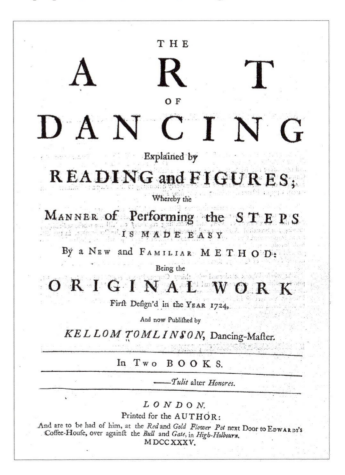

The art of dancing explained by reading and figures; whereby the manner of performing the steps is made easy by a new and familiar method: being the original work, first design'd in the year 1724, and now published by Kellom Tomlinson, dancing-master.

The cover from Kellom Tomlinson's *The Art of Dancing* with an example of a long descriptive title, c. 1735. Library of Congress, Music Division, http://memory.loc.gov/musdi/158/0003.gif.

An illustration in Feuillet Notation for the "révérence" to begin the Minuet, from Kellom Tomlinson's *The Art of Dancing*, c. 1735. Library of Congress, Music Division, http://memory.loc.gov/musdi/158/0208.gif.

The wait might have been long but the end result was worth it, according to the Library of Congress: "Tomlinson's treatise is today considered an important tool in the understanding of eighteenth-century dance because of his combination of text and graphically depicted dance steps in the plates." Therefore, it also serves as a valuable reference for twenty-first century readers to "get a feel" for the writing of dance instruction during the time ("How to Read a Dance Manual," n.d.).

Similar to Tomlinson's long title, during the eighteenth century, you could "judge a book by its cover." Unlike late twentieth century and early twenty-first century publications, which provided a synopsis of the content on the back of the book, eighteenth century publications did not print any information at all on the back cover. Hence, many of the publications of the day provided long in-depth titles as part of the cover page, which in essence gave a thorough description of what was inside the book. Tomlinson's dance manual also found its way to America and provided a basis for the formulation of dancing in the American colonies.

Tomlinson provided an in-depth description of the Minuet including the "Posture of the Body" as well as the "Motion or Stepping of the Feet upon the aforesaid Tract or Line." The weight is on the left foot in "the first Position" and the motion began sideways to the right. The step began with the right foot "by making a Sink and Step, open off from the left Foot." He noted that the rise and the fall of the body were kept in time to the music "ending in the same Position upon the right Foot, with the left disengaged to perform the Bourrée or second Part of the said Step sideways." The right foot follows with

a plain open Step sideways to the same [side]…leaving the left upon the Point, in the very Place the Body rested before, in Readiness to make the second Step,…upon which the third and last Step of the Bourrée and Minuet Step is made to the third Note of the second Measure of the Tune, by drawing the left Foot, pointed as it is firm to the Floor into the fifth Position behind the right (106–107).

Tomlinson's description also incorporated the Five Positions of the Feet, and for the eighteenth century uninitiated dancer he described it as follows:

> The Positions, from which Dancing dates its Original, consist of five Principles: As, first, when the Toes turning outwards, the two Heels are equally placed together. Secondly, when both Heels are considerably separated or open. Thirdly, when the Poise rests upon one Foot, the other being inclosed [sic] or placed before the Ankle of that Foot by which the Weight is supported. Fourthly, when the inclosed [sic] Foot is advanced upon a right Line, about the Length of a Step in Walking. And, Fifthly, when the Heel of the advanced Foot is crossed and placed before the Toe of that Foot on which the Body rests, as that the Turning may be made, and yet one Foot not, in the least, interrupt the other (5).

Tomlinson also described the proper révérence for an individual whether in simple conversation, standing, walking, or "leaving a Room," but most importantly "to begin the Minuet." In regards to the multitude of uses for the révérence, he did offer the following explanation:

An illustration in Feuillet Notation for the Minuet, from Kellom Tomlinson's *The Art of Dancing*, c. 1735.   Library of Congress, Music Division, http://memory.loc.gov/musdi/158/0214.gif.

> Bows or Courtesies are the outward Marks of Respect we pay to others, which, in one Sex, are shewed [sic] by bowing the Body, but, in the other, by bending the Knees; and, if made in a regular Manner, they are, indeed, very grand, noble, and highly ornamental (7).

The length and stride of the Minuet steps, however, would need adjustment "which may be either more or less, according to the Largeness or Smallness of the Room in which the Dance is performed" (110).

The formality of the dances, especially the Minuet required a specific predescribed floor tract. Therefore, in order to properly execute the dance, it was necessary to fit the predescribed "S" or "Z" floor pattern to fit the particular shape of the ballroom. Tomlinson felt that even before he provided any descriptions of the Minuet "it will be necessary to describe the Room in which the Dancing or Steps are to be performed." Therefore, he devoted an entire chapter describing the

"Dancing-Room." He offered up the "Service," of describing the various rooms in order to remove any "Causes of Disorder and Confusion." In keeping with the order of the day, Tomlinson provided extensive discussion. Some excerpts as follows:

> First then, you are to observe, that the Shape and Figure of Rooms differ exceedingly; for some are of a direct Square, others not square but oblong or longish, namely, when the two Sides are somewhat longer than the Top or Bottom, and various others that, in Reality, are of no Form at all; which renders Dancing extremely difficult and confused to those, who have not a just and true Idea of the Room, in its different Situations; because, if this be wanting, altho' [sic] they may perform very handsomely, at their own Houses, or in School with a Master, yet, in Assemblies or Rooms Abroad, they are as much disordered and at a Stand, as if in an Uninhabited Island....I have of rendering them Service, by endeavouring [sic] to remove the above mentioned Causes of Disorder and Confusion (18).

Tomlinson continued:

> I proceed to inform the Gentlemen and Ladies, that, when they are about to dance in a Room of the first Sort, viz. a direct Square, the dance may be begun, at any of the four Sides or Parts of the Square or Room; but then they are to note, that the Side or Part, on which the Dance begins, is always called the Bottom or Lower End; the Side or Part which they face, the Prefence or Upper End; and the two remaining Parts or Sides of the Room receive their Names, according to the Hand they are on (18–19).

In regards to a room of a different shape, he said:

> As to the longish or second Sort of Rooms, they differ from the square, in the Sides being longer than the Ends; and it of Course follows, that the Dance must begin, at one of the said Ends, which is likewise decided by the Company; or, if the Door be hung near the End of one of the Sides, as usually it is . . . the Dance commonly begins, at the End next the Door (19-20).

In order to provide a clearer understanding of the room description, Tomlinson provided rudimentary floor plans and marked the plans by letters and numbers to indicate the lower end, upper end, the sides, and doorway among others. In an attempt to be as complete and informative as possible, he also offered up that when the dance begins the "right side" of the room is that which is on "the right Shoulder" of the dancer and the other side is obviously the left. Therefore, "the Back is to the Lower End of the Room, and the Face to the Upper." Tomlinson sought to be as clear as possible that the Minuet *must* be performed in a predescribed "correctness" regardless of who, where, or when it was danced. Therefore, it must have been quite shocking that Tomlinson offered up the startling revelation that at one time:

> I have seen a Minuet begun at the Bottom of the Room, and ended at the Upper End; which could not possibly have happened, had they observed the preceding Rules (20).

Queen Elizabeth I, English Country-Dancing, John Playford, and Contredanse

At about the same time that the Minuet was introduced in the French Court, John Playford published in England a dance instruction manual titled *The English Dancing-Master: or Plaine and easie Rules for the Dancing of Country Dances, with the tune to each Dance*. However, by 1651, when Playford published a listing of 105 country-dances and the accompanying music, they reflected an English tradition that was many years old and that was established among the countryside and townspeople. As with almost all of the traditional dances among the peasants, they were simple fun dances learned and performed in the villages, towns, and countryside, and passed along the generations mainly by watching and participation. Since none of those dances were written down (a large portion of the peasants were illiterate), some of the dances in Playford's publication might have been obtained by observation and in all likelihood also included a number of the traditional country-dances that were performed at the court of Queen Elizabeth I.

Written accounts of English Country-dancing were first noted in the mid-sixteenth century during the reign of Queen Elizabeth I (1558–1603). Elizabeth, the daughter of Henry VIII and his second wife, Anne Boleyn, was considered one of England's greatest royal leaders. Her reign, which became known as the Elizabethan Age, was considered a time of great prosperity. Under her rule in 1588, the English navy defeated the Spanish Armada, thereby averting an invasion of England. The naval victory also established Great Britain as a major naval power and soon led to colonization throughout the world, including America. Her Royal Court also established an atmosphere conducive to the arts including scholarly works, poetry, literature, music, and dancing. Although it is known that Queen Elizabeth both encouraged and enjoyed watching the English Country-dances, it is not certain if she actually danced them. But, there are accounts that she did enjoy vigorous dancing and that she did partake in the Volta with the Earl of Leicester (McDonagh 1986, 60; "Elizabeth I," n.d.).

Country-dancing did continue sporadically in the courts of King James I and King Charles I. It is not certain, however, to what extent Cromwell embraced the country-dances, but it is known that he allowed dancing at the wedding of his daughter. In either case, after 1660, the English Country-dances were fully restored in the Royal court during the Restoration under King Charles II. Within these transitional periods, the peasants in the countryside simply continued the tradition of the country-dances.

In contrast to the French dances and the "correctness" of the Minuet, each of the English Country-dances relied on geometric patterns rather than intricate footwork. Unlike the European court dances such as the Courante, Allemande, Galliard, and Volta, which required specific precise steps, the steps within the English Country-dances were unimportant. What was important was the movement of the couple in a common geometric pattern. The formations included circle dances, square formations, single lines, and longways.

During the course of any of the longways dances the first couple at the head of the line (who sometimes were allowed to request a specific dance) performed a set figure either between themselves or in or around some of the other dancers.

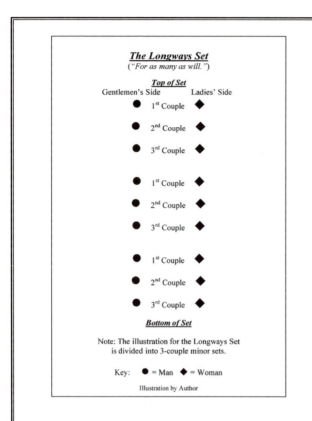

The Longways Set
("For as many as will.")

Top of Set
Gentlemen's Side   Ladies' Side

● 1st Couple ◆

● 2nd Couple ◆

● 3rd Couple ◆

● 1st Couple ◆

● 2nd Couple ◆

● 3rd Couple ◆

● 1st Couple ◆

● 2nd Couple ◆

● 3rd Couple ◆

Bottom of Set

Note: The illustration for the Longways Set
is divided into 3-couple minor sets.

Key: ● = Man   ◆ = Woman

Illustration by Author

A "longways" formation was simply two opposing (or "contra") lines with the gentlemen on one side shoulder-to-shoulder about one full-body width between each other. They faced the ladies who were about four to six feet opposite their male partners in a similar shoulder-to-shoulder formation. (Many of the dances allowed "for as many as will" in any of the dance formations.) In the longways formation, the dancers moved in unison as a couple rather than actually embracing, and performed a series of set patterns moving up or down the line, across the line, or weaving (known as "haying") in and out of the other couples. Throughout the series of sets, the dancers met, came together (usually in the center of the longways line or circle), and then parted, taking their places back in line. Sometimes their set pattern involved going under an arch or traveling in a set circle (known as a "star pattern"), among others. Upon completion of a set figure, the second couple would perform the same figure and then the third couple and so on down the line for the fourth, fifth, sixth, or as many couples who wanted to join in the dance.

Upon completion of their set they actually changed places in line with the 2nd couple. Therefore the 2nd couple became the "head" or 1st couple. And the 3rd couple became the 2nd and in turn after the former 2nd couple completed the set, the former 3rd couple took the place as the head couple. As a result of the constant progression of the couples up the longways line where eventually every couple got a turn as the head or 1st couple, English Country-dancing was usually described as "a democratic dance." In turn, the "democratic" nature of the dance relies on the cooperative interaction between couples as a group and often included changing partners as well. In addition, as a new dance tune was played, an entirely new couple took its turn starting as the lead couple (Keller and Shimer 2002, 61–62).

Since the description of the dance allowed for the number of dancers to be "as many as will," eventually many of the dances were divided into "minor sets" of two or three couples. For example, if there were 60 people, they could be in ten "minor sets" with each set having a 1st, 2nd, and 3rd couple. Therefore, with the beginning of the music the ten couples began dancing, thereby eliminating a lot of waiting and standing in line. Throughout it all, none of the steps for any of the country-dances were written down until Playford's publication.

In 1651, Playford's publication of *The English Dancing-Master* listed 105 country-dances including 38 longways, 41 "for a limited amount of couples," 14 circle dances, and the remainder for square formations and single lines. John Playford (b. 1623, d. 1684) was not necessarily a "Dancing Master" per se; rather he was a musician and also operated a bookshop, which he opened in 1647. In addition, *The English Dancing-Master* was not necessarily a technical manual in the manner of a Pierre Rameau or a Kellom Tomlinson publication. In contrast, Playford's was a pocket-size manual that included only the basic outlines of each dance in a very simple unrefined dance notation. Because he was a musician, he did provide an appropriate dance tune for each of the listed dances. Under the name of the dance and the music, he provided a short list and a simple word description for the set of dance figures for the particular dance. He described them in short catchall phrases such as "Back all, meet again" and "Sides all, set and turn." As a result, the "pretentious tone" of the dancing style of the Royal Courts was diminished (Sachs 1963, 400).

Playford's publication met with such a good response that in 1652 he quickly published a second edition under the new title *The dancing-master; or, Directions for dancing country-dances, with the tunes to each dance, for the treble-violin. Vol. the 2d.* He followed with a third edition in 1665 and a fourth in 1670. Within Playford's lifetime, the manual went through six editions. The fourth edition, for example, was expanded with over 360 dances and "tunes" that were used at both the courts and "other publick places." Playford noted in his foreword that, "The whole work [was] revised…and much more correct than any former editions." In 1684, his son Henry Playford released a seventh edition, which also added more dances and continued publication under the simple name *The Dancing Master*. The Preface for the tenth edition in 1698, for example, retained the original first half written by

The illustrated cover from the 7th edition of John Playford's *The Dancing-Master*, c. 1698.   Library of Congress, Music Division, http://memory.loc.gov/musdi/004/0001.gif.

John Playford in 1651 and the last two sentences added by his son Henry Playford.

In 1706 (after the death of Henry Playford), John Young continued its publication and expanded it to a multivolume set. In 1728, the seventeenth and final edition of *The Dancing-Master* contained descriptions and tunes for over 918 dances (of which 904 were for longways formations). The name of John Playford became so "synonymous" with English Country-dancing that the social dancing of his time is described as "Playford dances" and any type of assembly or ball pertaining to English Country-dancing is usually known as a "Playford Ball" (Keller and Shimer 2002, 62–63).

Sometime in the 1680s, French Dance Master André Lorin traveled to England and brought some of the English Country-dances to the court of King Louis XIV. In France the English Country-dances were known as *anglaise danses* or *angloise danses,* which simply meant "English dances." Shortly thereafter, the French termed them "Contredanse" (sometimes "Contredance"; some sources claim it was a derivative of "contra dance," and others thought it a slang for "country dance"). Lorin published many of them in 1697–1698 under the title *Livre de contredance présenté au Roy.* Within his publication, Lorin provided illustrated diagrams to describe the geometric patterns of the Contredances. During the late seventeenth century, the Contredance, in the style of the English Country-dance, shared equal time in the French Royal Court with the Minuet, Galliard, Courante, Allemande, and Volta. However, after 1700, the earlier court dances soon gave way to the rising popularity of the Contredances, and soon only the Minuet and the Contredances were danced ("From Renaissance Dance To Baroque Dance," n.d.).

Although John Playford was not concerned about the specific steps, similar to the Minuet, the French pattern of Contredance advocated steps in the Feuillet Notation. In 1706, in France Raoul-Auger Feuillet published a book on the French "contredance" version of the English Country-dancing titled

Recüeil de contredances mises en chorégraphie, d'une maniére si aisée, que toutes personnes peuvent facilement les apprendre, sans le secours d'aucun maitre et même sans avoir en aucune connoissance de la Chorégraphie Par Mr. Feuillet. Paris: L'auteur, 1706.

When translated into English in 1710 by Dance Master John Essex, the long-title read

For the Furthur Improvement of Dancing: A treatise of chorography, or, Ye art of dancing country dances after a new charact: in which the figures, steps & manner of performing are describ'd & ye rules demonstrated in an easie method adapted to the meanest capacity / translated from the French of Monsr. Feuillet, and improv'd with many additions, all fairly engrav'd on copperplates, and a new collection of country dances describ'd in ye same character by John Essex, dancing master; London: Sold by I. Walsh & P. Randall & by ye author, 1710.

The English Country-dances under the French form of Contredance spread throughout Europe. In 1714, it was danced in Spain, and around the same time in Italy and Germany. A contemporary French account from 1717 noted that the Contredances and the Minuet were also danced by the gentry and the peasants "everywhere we look now, whether in the distinguished courts, or in the towns at weddings, parties, and banquets, absolutely nothing is danced but the minuet and some English dances" (quoted in Sachs 1963, 397).

However, shortly thereafter, although the same dances were being done, the dancing styles separated between the "country style" and the "courtly style." The country style was the uninhibited easy-to-learn Contredances that peasants and townspeople performed, and the courtly style was the manner used to perform the Contredances throughout the Royal Courts of Europe.

In England, the English Country-dances were in no way specific only to John Playford. Between 1700 and 1830, over 25,000 different English Country-dances were published in similar books in England and also became popular in America. At the same time, in the American colonies, the number of English Country-dances in published dance manuals numbered a little over 2,700. By 1670, English Country-dancing was a primary source of recreation and community activity in all the British colonies in America (Keller 1996, "The Eighteenth-Century Ballroom," 23).

In books such as Playford's, and for those dances that preceded him and for the most part all the dances of the early periods, it is difficult to determine the exact dance step or sequence of steps. Dance historian Lloyd Shaw noted, "I would have had so much more fun dancing them than merely reading about them. But of course it is impossible for anyone to be sure about these older dances. Any interpretation is in part a guess, unless you can have the ghost of the old dancing master beside you" (Shaw 1949, 34).

The dance that has survived as probably the most well-known of the longways dances is the "Roger of Coverly" (sometimes "Roger de Coverly"), a longways dance "for as many as will." The entire description, as printed by Playford, is as follows:

The 1st. Man go below the 2nd. Wo[men]. then round her, and go below the 2nd. Man into his own place then 1st Wo[men]. Go below the 2nd. Man, then round him, and go below the 2nd. Wo[men]. Into her own place. The 1st. [couple] cross over below the 2nd. [couple] and take hands and turn round twice, then lead up thro' and cast off into the 2nd. [couples] place (Playford, 7th edition, 167).

In the American colonies the Roger of Coverly dance would become known as "The Virginia Reel" (see Chapter 2).

A sample of the dance description for the "Roger of Coverly" from the seventh edition of John Playford's *The Dancing-Master*, c. 1698.   Library of Congress, Prints and Photographs Division LC-USZ62-64031.

The Places to Dance

The unchaste Touches and Gesticulations used by Dancers, have a palpable tendency to that which is evil.

—Increase Mather, 1684

For everyone who has belittled dancing, scores of others have praised and esteemed it.
—Thoinot Arbeau, 1589

Dance is a Work of Satan, one of his Pomps and Vanities, which all Baptised Persons are under Vows to Renounce.

—Cotton Mather, 1700

BEAU NASH IN BATH AND THE PUBLIC ASSEMBLY ROOMS

In the early years, the comparisons of Paris and London with the provincial cities of the American colonies could not be further apart. The handful of American cities with populations of only 4,000 to 5,000 people (Boston was the most populous at about 7,000) could not compare with the massive urban centers of London and Paris with populations in the hundreds of thousands. Therefore, dancing in the American colonies, for the most part followed the established traditions of Europe. For those in the British colonies of Virginia and New England, they looked to England and France—both in the Royal Courts, the countryside, and the public assembly room. After 1700, the most influential in the proper manners of dancing and etiquette was just outside of London in the resort city of Bath. The city, known for its natural hot water mineral springs regularly attracted royalty, the aristocracy, and even commoners. But the main attraction was the elaborate social activity and dancing provided by Richard "Beau" Nash.

In *A History of Dancing* (1906) Thomas Reginald St. Johnston called Beau Nash "one of the most interesting figures of the eighteenth century" (140). He described Nash as

> One of the acknowledged leaders of the day, and his horses, clothes, and dinners, had begun to set their mark on the "beau monde." Living, as he did, upon no apparent income whatever,...In whatever way his income was derived, he certainly stands out as one of the greatest "chevaliers d'industrie" in an age when this was almost one of the fashionable professions (140).

In 1705, Beau Nash arrived in Bath and served as an aide to then Master of Ceremonies Captain Webster. At the time, the title "Master of Ceremonies" was given to the person who arranged "society's social life" including formal balls and dancing. Nash, of Welsh background, had earlier resigned his own commission in the army claiming that "he did not care to be trammeled by the narrowness of a military life." Shortly thereafter, Webster was killed in a duel, and Nash assumed the duties as Master of Ceremonies. In a short time, Nash, the self-proclaimed "King of Bath," created a legacy that changed the social habits of public dancing. It was in the city of Bath that Nash first conceived the idea of an assembly room that allowed public access upon payment of an entry fee. In 1708, Nash opened the newly built Bath Assembly House and within a few years it was "the most desirable location" in all England and even attracted visitors from the European continent ("Beau Nash," n.d.).

According to dance historian Philip J.S. Richardson in *The Social Dances of the Nineteenth Century in England*, at Bath Beau Nash "drew up that extraordinary set of rules which regulated not only the conduct of frequenters of the Assemblies but the general behaviour of the visitor to the City" (22). For example, it had always been customary for men to wear calf-length boots, but Nash thought them vulgar and clumsy so he advocated the adornment of shoes and stockings for men, which were very quickly adopted and found to be far more agreeable to the dance floor. Nash also felt that the public ballroom required a new degree of "respectability." Therefore, he prohibited any swearing, spitting, and unruly behavior. Most importantly, within the Bath Assembly House Nash introduced a new code of social conduct that cut across the social divides that allowed the aristocrats and commoners access to the same dance floor. According to the official history of England recorded by the BBC,

> [Nash] was so successful in leveling society that people could be found creating friendships across the classes that would not have been dreamt of in London. Bath had become the platform for social change ("Beau Nash," n.d.).

In addition, as an advocate for social change, Nash introduced a style of clothing that was unlike any other of the time. Unlike the customary powdered white wigs in fashionable society, for example, Nash sought to be different and wore a black wig "with a bejeweled cream, beaver-trimmed hat worn at a raffish angle." His formal attire was described as an "exaggerated elegance" characterized by a "braided and laced coat...worn open to show off his waistcoat and ruffled shirt" ("Beau Nash," n.d.).

As part of the fashionable life of the resort spa at Bath, dancing took place in the evenings several times during the week (usually on Tuesdays and Wednesdays), and Nash adhered to a very strict schedule. At Bath, for example, the dance programs were strictly followed, starting with a Minuet that most of the time was begun by Nash himself. The first Minuet began precisely at 6:00 P.M. and was followed by about two hours of Minuets followed by English Country-dancing as preselected by Nash. At exactly 9:00 P.M. he called for an intermission for tea. Shortly thereafter, he signaled the musicians, and the dancing began again with English Country-dancing. At precisely 11:00 P.M. he raised his finger signaling the music to stop and the dancing to end. A short time was allowed for final refreshments and farewells as the public left the assembly room. Most historians agree that Nash "ruled the assemblies with an iron hand." His well-known "Code of Etiquette at Bath" was actually posted on signs in the public assembly room, and anyone who did not abide by the rules was quickly dismissed (St. Johnston 1906, 141; Clarke and Crisp 1981, 99; "Beau Nash," n.d.).

On February 3, 1761, Nash died at the age of 87. Although he died almost penniless, the city of Bath provided him with a "lavish funeral." As with his lifetime, however, Beau Nash left a lasting legacy. For the most part, the newly established social decorum and manners of the ballroom did not stay confined to Bath. The enjoyment was such that, upon their return home, the visitors to Bath not only spread the glorious tales of dancing in the assembly room but also extolled the same etiquette and format of the dancing within their own social circles ("Beau Nash," n.d.).

As a result of the enthusiastic response of the patrons at the public assembly room at Bath, during the early part of the 1700s many other fashionable assembly rooms opened in and around London. Some of the first were at other English resort spas including Tunbridge Wells, Epsom, and Hampstead. The dancing within these fashionable resorts was also fictionalized and romanticized by the noted writer Jane Austen (Clarke and Crisp 1981, 101). The notoriety of Nash, however, was so widespread that it quickly spread to the European continent and the American colonies. The pattern set in the public assembly room at Bath was slavishly followed in American cities including New York, Philadelphia, Hartford, as well as Newport, Rhode Island, and Williamsburg, Virginia.

THE PURITANS, THE MAYPOLE, AND DANCING SCHOOLS IN BOSTON

In sixteenth and seventeenth century England, some of the noted writers of the time valued dance for education and recreation. In 1571, Roger Ascham, for example, wrote of the positive benefits of dancing in his educational treatise *The Scholemaster*. In 1644, Puritan poet John Milton (author of *Paradise Lost*) wrote of the delights and physical education benefits of dance in *Tracate on Education*. In 1690, philosopher John Locke wrote in *Some Thoughts Concerning Education* the value of teaching children as early as possible dance: "Dancing being that which gives *graceful Motions* all the Life, and above all things Manliness, and a becoming confidence to young Children, I think cannot be learned too early" (Marks 1957, 17; Locke, 174).

At the time, the rule of Cromwell (1640–1660) in England coincided with the Puritanical ideas of the New England colonists. Cromwell enforced the stricter moral code established during the Commonwealth and in 1642 even closed the theaters throughout London. Within the churches, the Puritans removed musical instruments including organs, eliminated choir-singing ornaments, and eliminated elaborate ornamentation. Within England the Puritans maintained a continuous presence until the restoration of King Charles II in 1660. Curiously, Cromwell was noted as an aficionado of music, and in November 1657, he even allowed mixed dancing at the wedding of his daughter. It is agreed by most historians that the dances were most likely country-dances from John Playford's *The English Dancing-Master*, which was actually a Puritan publication (Nevell 1977, 29). Dance historian Joseph Marks explained,

> Because dance taught manners and manners were considered a part of morals, the Puritans could justify its use. Playford's dances also were democratic in that they were circle or round dances and, therefore, there was not a head couple, a position which in the dances of the court was reserved for the elite (Marks 1957, 18).

Ironically in England, with the overthrow of Cromwell and the Restoration of King Charles II, there arose a new popularity of social dancing. The social dancing, however, was not patterned after the Royal Courts, but rather after the country-dances. In 1706, Dance Master John Weaver indicated that "the polite activity of dancing, once associated entirely with the court, was now spreading throughout the gentry." The overall influence of the French and English Royal Courts in respect to dancing and the arts in general was declining (Clarke and Crisp 1981, 100).

In America, the Puritans in the Massachusetts colonies were consistent with the rule of the Commonwealth in England under Oliver Cromwell. In fact, the Puritans in New England were not totally against dancing. Actually, they did approve of dancing in certain situations, but only if it did *not* involve "mixt dancing" between men and women. Although very little documentation exists, in all likelihood the dances were also English Country-dances similar to those in Playford's publication.

Dancing in the New England colonies was usually associated with a festive occasion such as a "husking" or a wedding. The revelry also included games and music, but throughout the 1600s, although the weddings included dancing, overall they were usually solemn affairs. The Puritans, however, did scorn dancing that was associated with most secular feasts and public festivities such as dancing around a Maypole (Daniels 1995, 119). In 1628, for example, a festival of Maypole dancing in Merry Mount, Massachusetts, was deemed "too close to the pagan feast." In response, magistrate John Indecott (sometimes Endecott) ordered the Maypole cut down and admonished the participants "for their profanes" (quoted in Marks 1975, 9–10).

The Maypole has its origins in Ancient Greece and Rome. It was also danced in ancient England. At the time of the first settling of the Colonies in America, the Maypole was danced in rural areas of England in celebration of May Day, May 1, which celebrated the coming of spring. After 1400, Maypole dances in England were usually celebrated in June. Some associated it with the "Feast of Flora," who was the ancient goddess of flowers, when participants decorated both the Maypole and themselves with flowers. For many, the celebration signified the beginning of spring and the forthcoming of harvest.

The Maypole was a vertical pole (usually cut from a nearby tree) usually 12 to 20 feet in height (but could also be as high as 60 feet). Numerous multicolored ribbons were draped from the top of the pole to the ground. Two concentric circles were formed with villagers each holding one of the ribbons. Most villages celebrated with young girls who were entering into "womanhood" dancing around the Maypole. The older girls were usually on the outside circle and the younger girls on the inside circle. Each circle would go in opposite directions and weave in and out of the outer and inner circles forming a braid around the Maypole. The local legends said that if the ribbons did not break the village would be bestowed with good fortune, which usually meant a good harvest ("Maypole," n.d.).

By the end of the nineteenth century the Maypole was included as part of a Cotillion, which was a series of party games. In 1878, *Dick's Quadrille Call-Book and Ball-Room Prompter*, for example, described the Maypole:

> A pole, about ten feet in height, is inserted in a box filled with earth to give the foundation, weight, and stability. To the top of the pole six (or eight) ribbons of different colors are fastened, each being about four yards long, with a loop at the lower end. Three couples (or, if eight ribbons, four couples) form a circle a round the pole, each gentleman having his partner on his right hand. Each takes a ribbon, holding the loop, the gentleman in his right hand, and the lady in her left, all face partners. At a signal they all form the *Grand Chain* without touching hands, the ladies going to the left, and the gentlemen to the right, each gentleman first passing inside his partner, then outside the next lady, and so on, until the ribbons are braided upon the pole. At a signal, when each gentleman faces his original partner, all turn half-round, changing the ribbons to the outer hand, and reverse the movement, unwinding the ribbons. Afterwards all waltz (*Dick's Quadrille Call-Book* 1878, 199).

In the mid to latter part of the twentieth century, the Maypole was mainly a children's dance that was performed during part of the school year, usually during spring.

The cutting down of the Maypole in 1628 in Merry Mount, Massachusetts, was not an isolated incident. In 1687, a similar incident was also documented. In Charlestown, Massachusetts, Judge Samuel Sewall noted that the Maypole had also been ordered cut down, but the people of the town put up a new one. Sewall noted in his diary, "Now a bigger is set up and a garland upon it" (quoted in Marks 1975, 9–10).

Municipal interference in social dancing was not necessarily limited to the cutting down of Maypoles. In regards to his study of early colonial dance in America, dance historian Joseph Marks presented interesting evidence stating, "That there was dancing in seventeenth-century New England is shown by the fact that many of the court cases mention dancing in connection with other offenses" (1957, 16). Dance historian Richard Kraus concurred; he added that in New England, "the court records during the 17th century…frequently mention severe punishment for mixed dancing, dancing in taverns, and similar offenses" (Kraus and Chapman 1981, 90).

Throughout the colonies the taverns offered an opportunity "to dance and make merry well through the night." In New England, this type of dancing appeared at least as early as 1651. At that time, Nathaniel B. Shurtleff, editor of the *Records of the Governor and Company of Massachusetts Bay in New England*, noted that the General Court of Massachusetts issued an edict to end the practice by declaring "upon the paine [sic] of five shillings for every person that shall so daunce [dance] in ordinarys [taverns]" (quoted in Cole, "The Puritan and Fair Terpsichore," 1942, 17).

The cutting down of the Maypole by order of Massachusetts Governor John Endicott, c. 1628. The Granger Collection, New York, ID: 0036016.

The town of Cambridge, Massachusetts, for example, specifically prohibited dancing in any of the local taverns or inns. If found guilty, the offenders were levied a fine of "five shillings." However, dancing was allowed if done in the proper place and at the proper time, although the "proper place" and "proper time" were not fully defined. In 1638, for example, Lawrence Waters with his wife and friend were charged with dancing in Cambridge. The court records simply listed that all three "were admonished to avoyed [sic] dancing." In 1651, the *Records of the Colony of New Plymouth in New England from [1620–1692]* recorded that a Mr. Samuel Eaton and Goodwife Halle in the town of Duxburrow were charged by the court with "mixt dancing." Although no sentence was imposed, they too were "released with admonition." In that same year the court records "observed that there were many abuses & disorders by dauncing [sic] in ordinarys [taverns], whether mixt or unmixt, upon marriage of some person." In 1662, another court record listed an indentured servant named John Clark, who had attempted on numerous occasions to run away from "his master." The records indicate that Clark appealed to the court that his running away was to search for his own liberty and also to "live merrily and sing & daunce [sic]" (Marks 1957, 16).

On the other hand, dancing schools and Dance Masters that were an established tradition in Europe did not fare any better when transplanted to Boston. In 1672, Dance Master Henry Sherlot attempted to set up a dancing school in Boston. Apparently the Boston ministers did not take kindly to the immigrant Frenchman and ordered him to leave. They claimed he was a "person very Insolent & of ill fame that Raues & scoffes at religion, of a Turbulent spirit no way fitt [sic] to be tolerated to live in this place." As a result, Sherlot was not only ordered to leave Boston, but was actually banished from the entire New England colony by the ministers (quoted in Marks 1957, 19).

In the years 1676, 1681, and 1685 other dancing schools were also noted as being opened in Boston. However, local authorities quickly shut each down. In 1685, for example, Francis Stepney's attempt at opening a dancing school for "mixt dancing" in Boston was met with swift retribution. Unbeknownst to Stepney, he picked as his first scheduled day of dance classes the same day as church worship in Boston. It also appeared that Stepney, in an attempt to publicize his newfound venture, was a bit arrogant. He claimed that dancing could serve the inhabitants of Boston better than any religious teachings. Stepney might very well have totally crossed the line and infuriated the Puritan ministers when he claimed that dancing would better serve the community "than attending church on Sunday."

As a result, Stepney was reviled for "questionable activities" and charged by the ministers of Boston with "Blasphemous Words; and Reviling the Government." According to the court proceedings as recorded by Judge Samuel Sewall in his diary for November 12, 1685, he wrote:

> After the Ministers of this Town Came to the Court and complained against a Dancing Master who seek to set up here and hath mixt Dances, and his time of Meeting is Lecture-Day; and 'tis reported he should say that by one Play he could teach more Divinity than Mr. Willard or the Old Testament. Mr. Moody said 'Twas not time for [New England] to dance. Mr. [Increase] Mather struck at the Root, speaking against mixt Dances (quoted in Marks 1957, 19).

Stepney was tried by a jury in court and found guilty. He was ordered by the court to close the dancing school and was fined an astonishing sum of "100 pounds." The debt was quite steep, and therefore, rather than risk incarceration in "debtors' prison," Stepney fled the colony to avoid payment (Marks 1975, 12–14).

In 1687, Francis Stepney, fresh from fleeing his debt in Boston, was also forbidden to teach dance in the Dutch territories. During that time, Stepney tried to open a dancing school in New York but was turned down by the ruling governor's council. It is quite possible that the Dutch had heard of his confrontation in Boston and his nonpayment of debt. The Governor's Council of the New Netherlands also gave warning that he would be ordered out of the province "unless he could show that he would not become a public charge" (Marks 1957, 22).

INCREASE MATHER AND AN ARROW AGAINST "GYNECANDRICAL DANCING"

At the time of the Stepney incident, the Ministers of Boston issued the infamous pamphlet titled *An Arrow Against Profane and Promiscuous Dancing Drawn Out of the Quiver of Scriptures*. The 30-page discourse, which became the benchmark for a continuous series of anti-dance literature against American social dancing, was first published in Boston by Samuel Green in 1684, and the cover credited authorship to "the Ministers of Christ at Boston in New-England." Although the treatise was credited to the "Ministers," it is a widely held belief that it was written solely by Increase Mather (Marks 1957, 13–19).

Increase Mather was born in 1639 in the town of Dorchester, Massachusetts. His father was a notable godly Puritan named Richard Mather, as was his father-in-law, John Cotton. Increase was educated at Harvard and during the reign of Cromwell went to Ireland and England for divinity school and eventual pastorate. However, with the Restoration of King Charles II, Mather found he could not live within the Anglican climate of England. As a result, he returned to his father's church in New England. In 1681, the Second Church in Boston elected him minister, and he was a leading voice of the Boston Ministers, which at the time controlled the political process of the colony (Marks 1975, 1–2).

Prior to Increase Mather, the leading voice of Puritanism in the colony was John Cotton (father-in-law to Increase Mather). John Cotton was not necessarily against dancing but was adamantly against, "Lascivious dancing to wanton ditties, and amorous gestures and wanton dalliances." According to anti-dance historian Ann Wagner, "lascivious dancing" was defined by the Puritan ministers as "any dancing that allowed men and women to touch or hold each other, was forbidden, as was any association between alcohol and dancing." As a result, Wagner asserted that "virtually no organized dances or mixed-sex dancing took place in the first generation of New England's settlement." Any dancing that was done was of the spontaneous nature either in the home or outdoors during a celebration (Wagner 1997, 110).

On the other hand, in *An Arrow Against Profane and Promiscuous Dancing Drawn Out of the Quiver of Scriptures*, Increase Mather presented a clear and explicated condemnation of just about any sort of dancing that involved interaction between a man and a woman. Mather offered that the "Design of Dancing is only to teach Children good Behavior and decent Carriage...provided it be done without provocation to Uncleanness, and be not a Nurse of Pride and Vanity" (1684, 24). In the first paragraph, Mather explained,

> The Question is not, whether all *Dancing* be in itself sinful...Nor is the question, whether a sober and grave *Dancing* of Men with Men, or of Women with Women, be not allowable; we make no doubt of that, where it may be done without offence, in due season, and with moderation....But our question is concerning *Gynecandrical Dancing*, or that which is commonly called *Mixt* [sic] or *Promiscuous Dancing*, viz. of

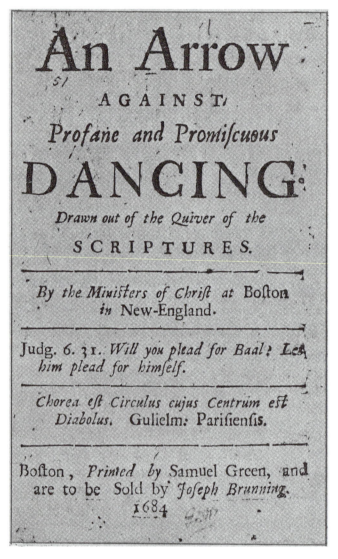

An Arrow

AGAINST

Profane and Promiscuous

DANCING

Drawn out of the Quiver of the

SCRIPTURES.

By the Ministers of Christ at Boston
in New-England.

Judg. 6. 31. Will you plead for Baal? Let
him plead for himself.

Chorea est Circulus cujus Centrum est
Diabolus. Gulielm: Parisiensis.

Boston, Printed by Samuel Green, and
are to be Sold by Joseph Brunning.
1684

The cover from Increase Mather's *An Arrow Against Profane and Promiscuous Dancing*, c. 1684. (A brief explanatory note: In reading the title cover of *An Arrow Against Profane and Promiscuous Dancing* the word "Promiscuous" appears as "Promifcuous." In similar fashion so do "himfelf" and "Bofton." During colonial times American writings usually wrote an "f,'" whereas in later years it was written with the correct "s." As a point of reference, the same instances appear in the original Declaration of Independence written in 1776 by Thomas Jefferson).

Men and Woman (be they elder or younger persons) together: Now this we affirm to be utterly unlawful, and it cannot be tollerated [sic] in such a place as *New-England*, without great Sin (1684, 1–2).

Increase Mather asserted that the interaction of the men and women by means of *dancing* was in violation of the Seventh Commandment ("Thou shalt not commit adultery" *Exodus 20:14*). Mather also cited other "Scriptures" with tales of the Israelites, the Daughters of Sion in Isaiah 3:16, the Apostle Paul in Romans 13:13 and Peter 4:3, among others. With this combination of brief cryptic sentences from within the Bible, he concluded "the Scripture does expressly, and by name condemn *Dancing* as a vicious practice" (Mather 1684, 6).

From that point on Mather expanded his condemnation. He decried, "The unchaste Touches and Gesticulations used by *Dancers*, have a palpable tendency to that which is evil." He added, "that the Devil was the first inventor of the impleaded *Dances*, and the Gentiles, who worshipped him, the first Practitioners in this Art" (Mather 1684, 3, 8). In support of his adverse claim of "dancing with the Devil," Mather cited a supposed historical source of a religious group known as the Waldenses. A fifteenth century French historian named Jean Paul Perrin claimed that they were a religious group that "professed the truth of the Gospel and sealed it with their blood" (Marks 1975, 41). Supposedly, the Waldenses were in existence 100 years before Martin Luther and the Protestant Reformation. Mather cited a text titled *History of the Doctrine and Discipline of the Waldenses* written by Perrin. He chose an excerpt from page 63 that claimed the following:

A Dance is the Devils Procession. He that enters into a dance, enters into his Possession. The Devil is the Guide, the middle and the end of the Dance. A man sinneth in dancing…for all his steps are numbered…We will prove first from Scripture, and then by other Reasons, how wicked a thing it is to Dance. He that Danceth maintaineth the Devil's Pomp…In a Dance, a man breaks the Ten Commandments of God. The very motion of the Body, which is used in dancing, giveth Testimony enough of evil. Austin saith, The miserable Dancer knoweth not, that as many Paces as he makes in dancing, so many steps he makes to Hell (Mather 1684, 13–14).

Mather continued to pile on the historical and Biblical precedents against dancing in general. Mather even refuted and posited a twist on the celebrated Ecclesiastes.

In regards to dancing, joyous celebrations, and life in general, many dance historians throughout American history offered up the Biblical verse provided by Ecclesiastes, which read in part:

To every *thing there* is a season, and a time to every purpose under the heaven.…A time to weep, and a time to laugh; a time to mourn, and a time to dance (Ecclesiastes 3:1,4).

Mather refuted the New Testament and somehow claimed that Ecclesiastes "does not speak a syllable for the Justification of such *Dancing* as we are writing against, nor indeed for any other *Dancing*, since the meaning of the place is not that there is a *lawful time*, but only a *limited time* to Dance" (1684, 20). Although there are other scriptures in the Bible in support of dancing, often interpreted as "positive" acceptance of dancing, Mather incredulously refuted them as just the opposite. They included:

- And David danced before the Lord with all his might (2 Samuel 6:14).
- Then shall the virgin rejoice in the dance (Jeremiah 31:13).
- Let them praise his name in the dance: let them sing praises unto him with the timbrel and harp (Psalms 149 1:3).

In *Adversaries of Dance: From Puritans to the Present* (1997), Ann Wagner argued, "since the Bible nowhere expressly prohibits dancing, [Increase] Mather [had] to rely on passages that stipulate a generalized behavior forbidden to the Christian." Mather claimed his basis on early Christian theologians Junius, Rivet, and Ravenel who according to Wagner "interpret that Scripture (Isaiah 3:16) to prohibit the artificial postures learned in dancing schools." Mather also cited 1 Peter 4:30, which referred to "rioting and reveling." Mather, as others before him such as Calvin, Daneau, and Cicero, interpreted "reveling" to mean dancing. Wagner presented the question posed by Mather "But who can seriously pray to the Holy God to be with him when he is going to a Promiscuous dance?" Wagner ably answered that Mather's rhetorical question "contains no possible answer, but an implied negative response is meant to make the respondent feel guilty" (Wagner, 50–51).

In all likelihood, Increase Mather's anti-dance treatise was based on the writings of European predecessors such as John Northbrooke, Sir Thomas Elyot, and John Calvin. In 1566, Northbrooke, a Protestant minister in England under Elizabeth I, wrote that "dauncing is the vilest vice of all." At about the same time Elyot in *Gentlemen Boke* wrote on the value of dance only, but only as it applied in the education of manners in children. However, the highly influential Protestant leader John Calvin also attributed dancing with the "work of the devil." Calvin declared "in seeking to hoppe [sic] and daunce [sic] like stray beasts, and to do such other like things: let us understand that it is not of late beginning, but that the Divell [sic] hath raigned at all times" (Wagner, 19–27).

In searching for anti-dance literature among religious leaders, it appears that Mather conveniently avoided the writings of the French Catholic monk Thoinot Arbeau (see earlier in this chapter). In 1589, Arbeau's dance treatise titled *Orchésographie* not only supported dance for religious ceremony and community involvement, he also had disdain for the anti-dance reformers in France and England. He wrote:

> But it has chagrined me to find that many have condemned dancing, have even judged it shameless and an effeminate pastime, unworthy of the dignity of a man. For everyone who has belittled dancing, scores of others have praised and esteemed it (Arbeau, 12).

In all likelihood, Arbeau was well aware of two contemporary sixteenth century French publications: *Le Blason des danses* (1566) by G. Paradin, and *Traité des danses* (1580) by the Reverend Lambert Daneau. Each publication discussed the bad effects of dancing and Daneau in particular rejected dancing as "too much enjoyment" (Sutton *explanatory notes* in Evans 1967, 208). Arbeau, as a Catholic monk, was obviously also aware of the scriptures. In defense of dancing he said, "You can moreover quote Our Lord (St. Matthew [11:17] and St. Luke Chap. III) when he reproached the Pharisees for their obstinacy and ill will. 'We have piped unto you, and ye have not danced'" (13).

However, it appears that Arbeau did not have patience for the absurd writings of his contemporaries. Therefore, rather than spend too much time writing a long rebuttal, he simply offered the following explanation and solution:

> We take part in such rejoicing to celebrate wedding days and in the rites of our religious festivals, in spite of the abhorrence of reformers, which latter deserve to be fed upon goat's meat cooked in a pie without bacon (13).

In 1967, according to notes added to the Dover publication translated version, Julia Sutton concurred, adding that both Paradin and Daneau "obviously deserve the dreadful recipe Arbeau describes" (Evans, 208).

It might also be prudent to wonder if Increase Mather and his predecessors read the second century *Hymn of Jesus* that attributed the words of Jesus to say, "Who so danceth not, knoweth not what cometh to pass.... Thou that dancest, perceive what I do." But the reason that Mather did not quote from Arbeau or the *Hymn of Jesus* can be attributed to the fact that the basic principle of Puritanism was to reject any teachings of the Catholic Church. But Mather did not stop with the inhabitants of Boston; he also condemned the Native American dances.

In regards to the neighboring Native America Indian tribes, such as the Pequots, the association was not a tranquil one. Since the Indian tribal cultures were different from their own, the Puritans viewed them with suspicion and disposed the Indian worship as "pagan ritual." Mather wrote:

> It is known from their own Confessions that amongst the *Indians* in this *America*, oftentimes at their *Dances* the Devil appears in bodily shape, and takes away one of them alive. In some places of this Wilderness there are great heaps of Stones, which the *Indians* have laid together, as an horrid Remembrance of so hideous a fruit of their *Satanical Dances* (23).

Unfortunately, Mather's writings were not confined to either Boston or even the seventeenth century. Mather's anti-dance tract "Arrow Against Profane and Promiscuous Dancing Drawn Out of the Quiver of Scriptures" laid the firm foundation for numerous religious leaders and municipal authorities to continue a long lineage of anti-dance reformation well into the twenty-first century—especially if it involved "mixt dancing." The rhetoric applied in anti-dance reformation often harkened back to the same arguments as presented by Increase Mather in 1684. Unfortunately, most who read the tract or who heard it applied from the pulpit in the form of a religious sermon were not aware that the argument was a recycled version of Increase Mather's tract. Luckily, most Americans valued the pursuit of happiness of dancing so much that they persevered and just continued to dance.

COUNTRY-DANCING IN NEW ENGLAND AND ORDINATION BALLS

In 1689, the Glorious Revolution in England was a bloodless transfer of power that gave sovereign power to William and Mary as King and Queen of England. In doing so, William and Mary restored the monarchy and reestablished the Church of England, thereby nullifying any future accession of either a Catholic or a Puritan monarch. Shortly thereafter, the repercussions were felt in the English colonies in America, especially New England, where a new governor was appointed by the King and Queen of England. In 1714, at King's Chapel in Boston, for example, the new governor not only allowed the use of an organ (which was considered by Puritans as a "dangerous innovation"), but also allowed the organ master the ability to supplement his income by teaching music and dancing.

After 1700, the English immigrants in America soon embraced dancing as a social custom. For the most part, however, of those social dance customs that were accepted by ministers and towns, the style of dancing most favored was English Country-dancing in the Playford style, rather than mixed dancing. The acceptance of the dancing involving sets and formations was usually justified on the basis that they taught "good manners" and social interaction, but many strictly avoided any of the one-on-one intergender European dances. In essence, the New England dances were in direct opposition to the Court dances of Europe, such as the Minuet. Historian Joy Van Cleef, in an article titled "Rural Felicity: Social Dance in 18th Century Connecticut," explained:

> The country dances were not dances of self-presentation like those ordinarily performed by one couple at a time while the rest of the company watched, dancers taking

the floor in the order of their rank and position. They were not "show-off" dances. Nor were they extravagant or spectacular like the Galliard, nor bold and indecorous like the Volta, which required the man to lift…his partner into the air while executing rapid turns…The country-dance was a democratic affair in which a number of people danced together. Its interest lay in the figures, or patterns—sometimes extremely intricate (requiring) a team effort on the part of the whole group, or set, in order to succeed (7–8).

By that time, dancing had become an integral part of New England social life. It soon became fashionable that the main method for a person of wealth to show off his or her prominence was to sponsor a ball with dancing as the featured activity. In addition, the dancing schools also became a valuable source to teach not only children, but also adults "Decency of Behaviour" and how to "carry themselves handsomely" (Marks 1957, 21–22).

In addition, from about 1700 through the 1730s, it was also common that a newly ordained minister was honored with an Ordination Ball. The main feature at an Ordination Ball was music and dancing—usually the English Country-dances. It is almost certain that none of the Late Middle Ages or Renaissance dances that involved singular couples were danced. Therefore the "lascivious dancing" that the Puritan ministers frowned upon was usually avoided, but it is important to note that the strict Puritanical hold over social dancing was, in fact, severed.

In 1721, for example, Ebenezer Parkman, a recent Harvard graduate (which at the time still trained many of its graduates for the ministry), was scheduled to be ordained as a minister in Westborough, Massachusetts. In a research article titled "Early American Social Dance," Kate Van Winkle Keller discovered that Parkman "played the fiddle and kept a pocket-size notebook in which he wrote psalm tunes, songs of love, and tunes from [Playford's] *The Dancing-Master*" (Keller, "Early American Social Dance," 2001). Another local minister, Timothy Edwards, was also honored with an Ordination Ball. Edwards was the father of the famed Jonathan Edwards, who was instrumental in the religious revival termed the Great Awakening in the 1730s and 1740s in British Colonial America (see Chapter 2).

COTTON MATHER IN "A CLOUD" AND THE NARROW "GATE OF HEAVEN"

By the end of the 1600s, the climate of a strictly Puritan New England was fading. However, in Boston Cotton Mather continued the Puritan crusade set down by his father Increase Mather. But, unlike his father, Cotton Mather was not totally against "mixt dancing." He did concede that it was acceptable if it was in conjunction "with God's people in the Old Testament." (But Cotton did not fully define what was acceptable in the Old Testament.) At the time, many "People of Quality" in and around Boston "began to give balls." Therefore, Cotton Mather's argument shifted to the case at hand, which was mainly against the ball itself. As a result, in 1700, he wrote a tract titled: *A Cloud of Witness Against Balls and Dances* (1700). The publication published in Boston was subtitled *Darting out Light upon a Case, too Unseasonably made Seasonable to be Discoursed On* (Marks 1957, 15).

Within his introductory passage of *A Cloud of Witness Against Balls and Dances*, Mather explained:

The Case before us is not whether people of quality may not employ a dancing master with due circumstances of modesty...[but] whether the dancing humour [sic] as it now prevails and especially in balls or in circumstances that lead young people of both sexes unto great liberties (Mather 1700, 2–4).

Cotton claimed that the "lascivious dancing [led] to wanton ditties, and amorous gestures and wanton dalliances, especially after feasts" and therefore was forbidden by Christianity. Consequently, Cotton threatened that any "that go to Dances shall be Reproved; and if...they persist therein, they are to be excluded from communion." He reminded his congregation that, "Dance is a Work of Satan, one of his Pomps and Vanities, which all Baptised Persons are under Vows to Renounce" (reprinted in Marks 1975, 65–69).

According to anti-dance historian Bruce C. Daniels in *Puritans at Play* (1995), he claimed that Cotton Mather's response against dances and balls in general was a reaction against Anglicanism. It appears that at the time Puritan youth were attending dances within the community sponsored by members of the Anglican faith. Therefore, Daniels concluded,

[Cotton Mather] placed his opposition to extravagant balls and dancing parties in the larger context of Puritan fears of Anglicanism. Puritan young men and women attended Anglican parties because of the opportunity to dance they offered; late hours, immodest dress, vanity, lewdness, and, of course, eventual spiritual loss (112).

However, Cotton Mather was not the only Puritan minister who was concerned about the "accompanying vices" of involvement in a community dance.

Another contemporary Puritan writer named William Prynne also wrote a strong condemnation against dancing. Prynne wrote with all fire and brimstone that dancing occurred only on the "beaten pleasant road that leads to Hell." He warned:

Dancing for the most part is attended with many amorous smiles, wanton compliments, unchaste kisses, scurrilous songs and sonnets, effeminate music, lust provoking attire, ridiculous love pranks, all of which savor only of sensuality, of raging fleshly lusts! Therefore, it is wholly to be abandoned of all good Christians. Dancing serves no necessary use!... The way to heaven is too steep, too narrow for men to dance and keep revel rout....The Gate of Heaven is too narrow for whole rounds, whole troops of dancers to march in together (quoted in Nevell 1977, 29).

Prynne's response was most likely in obvious reference to the community style English Country-dances, which were becoming more common throughout the New England area.

"FRENCH DANCES" IN WILLIAMSBURG, VIRGINIA—AND THE STAGGS

During the first decades of colonial settlement in Virginia, the living conditions were similar to those in New England. The conditions were harsh, and the main focus was on working the land. The Virginia Legislative Assembly of 1618 to

1619, for example, decreed that every person should work and pronounced "we resolve to suffer no Idle persons in Virginia." In addition, the legislative assembly decreed strict observance of the Sabbath within the colony. Therefore, they enacted laws against dancing on the Sabbath as well as a prohibition on fiddle-playing, throwing dice, card-playing, hunting, and even fishing (Marks 1957, 24).

However, in contrast to New England, as the cash crops of the region brought a significant amount of wealth to the large plantation owners, a three-tier hierarchal social class system developed that was based closer to their ties with England. The social system included the wealthy class of plantation owners, the middle group of small landowners with mainly the immediate family to provide labor, and the lowest social class of the indentured servants and African American slaves.

In general, as the conditions of life within the colony improved, the enforcement of the laws of the first legislative assembly diminished. And as the wealthy Virginia plantation landowners became accustomed to the labor provided by slaves and indentured servants, they had more leisure time. In turn, as noted by leisure historian Max Kaplan, "Virginians were more generally permitted to make the most of whatever opportunities for recreation their expanding life presented" (151). Therefore, as a result of the higher level of wealth, they patterned their social amusements after the aristocracy of England and France. In many cases, that involved social dancing both within the home and as part of elite functions.

Between 1711 and 1741, for example, Virginian aristocrat William Byrd noted numerous occasions of parties within his home that involved dancing among his invited guests. On other occasions he noted that both he and his wife attended formal balls at the Governor's mansion in Williamsburg. An entry in Byrd's diary on February 6, 1711, noted that at Williamsburg the ball was officially opened "with a French dance" (most likely the Minuet). In keeping with the custom of the French Royal Court, Governor Alexander Spotswood selected Mrs. Byrd to dance the first dance. William Byrd led the second dance as he selected the Governor's wife. The ball continued with "several more French dances" among the other invited guests. After the conclusion of the French dances, Byrd noted, "we danced country dances for an hour" (Keller and Fogg 2000, 8).

But social dancing among the Virginia aristocrats involved more than just dancing. Dance historian Joseph Marks noted that in eighteenth century Virginia, "Dance served an even more important role than that of social amusement. It was believed to be one of the accomplishments proper for a gentleman, and not having knowledge of dance showed a lack of the proper education" (1957, 25).

Typically, a Virginia plantation owner had a small library that contained a few books dealing with the education and manners of a "gentleman." The most noted of the time was Richard Brathwaite's *The English Gentleman* (1630). The book outlined a complete "gentleman's education" and gave the "most commendation" to dancing and fencing. He suggested that dancing "with a reserved grace to come off bravely and sprightly, rather than with affected curiosity." In Brathwaite's opinion, the mark of a true gentleman was, "To lead a dance gracefully" (204). As for the lady, Brathwaite, in *The English Gentlewoman* (1631), suggested that she learn to "dance gracefully." However, he cautioned that she not put dancing before her "religious tasks" (76–77). In 1633, a second edition of *The English Gentleman* was published, and in 1641, a single combined volume was released titled *The English Gentleman; and the English Gentlewoman.*

Many plantation owners also had books on dancing. Plantation owner Robert Beverly, for example, had in his personal library a translated version of Pierre Rameau's *Le maître à danser* (1725). It was most likely a copy of John Essex's translated version of 1728 titled *The Dancing-Master: or, The Art of Dancing Explained.* As much as the writers on aristocratic education expected that a gentleman and lady learn to dance well, they did not expect them to become so proficient that they rivaled the dancing master (Marks 1957, 26, 49).

Similar to that of Europe, in Virginia and the other southern colonies, the mark of true social status was to employ a Dance Master. Unlike Europe, however, the Dance Masters in the southern colonies often traveled with African slaves as assistants. During the early 1670s, for example, Charles Cheat was a dancing master traveling the Virginia area with his servant named Clason Wheeler who played fiddle accompaniment. In fact, it was common for traveling Dance Masters to have an African American slave who played an instrument for musical accompaniment. In some cases, the African American slaves also taught dancing.

On August 13, 1739, in the *Virginia Gazette*, Jones Irvine, for example, advertised that he would open dancing schools in both Hampton and Yorktown in Virginia. The Dance Master was listed as one Stephen Tenoe, who was an African American slave. As was the social custom of the day, slaves were property of the owner. Therefore, Irvine noted that "all Sum and Sums of Mony due for teaching [by Tenoe] to dance, is due payable to me [Jones Irvine] by the subscriber." On August 17, 1739, the same newspaper listed an ad for a runaway slave named Thomas Macoum who "professes Dancing." The same notice also indicated that another runaway slave named Robin went with Macoum. Apparently Robin was a fiddle player, and together they most likely sought to escape to freedom in the North and employ themselves with their skills (Marks 1957, 41).

In 1716, in Williamsburg, Virginia, Charles Stagg and his wife, Mary Stagg, announced plans to perform stage plays in a theater and also teach dancing. The Staggs entered into partnership with a tavern owner by the name of William Levingston to build a theater adjacent to the Palace Green in Williamsburg. During construction, Levingston arranged for permission from the College of William and Mary to provide temporary quarters for the Staggs' dancing school. At the time, it was apparent the College of William and Mary not only agreed with but also placed a value on dance and education. The Staggs' agreement with the college read in part to teach "the scholars and others to dance until his own dancing school in Williamsburg be finished."

The Staggs eventually opened a permanent theater and dancing school in Williamsburg. To develop their expertise Mary and Charles Stagg had in their personal library translated versions of Raoul Ager Feuillet's *Chorégraphie* and Pierre Rameau's *Le maître à danser* (*The Dancing-Master*). Feuillet's publication contained a standard system of dance notation (see earlier this chapter) that was valuable to anyone interested in teaching dance. For the most part, Feuillet's publication was purchased by other Dance Masters, who in turn taught the European dances to those who planned to accept an invitation to dance at a formal ball (Marks 1957, 48).

In particular, Rameau's *The Dancing-Master* served as a valuable resource for the Staggs to teach the protocol and etiquette for the Virginia gentleman and lady. Rameau held it essential to meticulously teach the five positions of the feet and the proper posture for dancing. In a translated version by C.W. Beaumont, Rameau suggested:

> The head must be held erect without any suggestion of stiffness, the shoulders pressed well back, for this expands the chest and affords more grace to the body. The arms should hang at the side, the hands be neither quite open nor quite closed, the waist steady, the legs straight and the feet turned outwards (Beaumont 1931, vii–viii).

As eighteenth century dance historian Joseph Marks explained, "As one studies Rameau's *The Dancing Master*, it becomes evident what strict discipline was taught and was considered so necessary for the young lady and gentlemen [of Virginia]" (1957, 49–50).

Mary and Charles Stagg taught dance in the same manner as prescribed by the likes of Feuillet and Rameau. At the time, although dancing in itself was considered a form of recreation or amusement, the main purpose was for the student to develop a graceful dance style in order to display his or her social status. The Staggs maintained a successful dancing school teaching the proper manners of the Virginia gentleman and lady. They continued teaching dance together until Charles Stagg's death in 1736. Mary Stagg continued teaching dances and sponsoring assembly balls until 1745 (Wright 1957, 180).

PROVINCIAL DANCING, THE NEWPORT ASSEMBLY, AND MR. PELHAM'S DANCING SCHOOL

By 1700, similar to the southern colonies in Virginia, the conditions of life for the American colonists in New England also improved. Towns and cities, although provincial by European standards, slowly developed a social structure involving recreation and amusement. Manuscripts in the Rhode Island Historical Society, for example, indicated that Newport, Rhode Island, offered a series of assembly balls. The assembly was a large dance usually by invitation only or as a guest of the invited. The dances were sometimes sponsored by a fraternal group or a dignitary of society, such as a wealthy socialite or the governor of the colony.

In similar fashion to the public assembly ballrooms of London and Europe, most of the American assembly balls followed the same rules of etiquette as prescribed by Beau Nash. The Newport assembly, for example, always began promptly at 6:00 P.M. and ended precisely at midnight. The ball was opened with a series of Minuets and followed by a set of country-dances. In similar fashion, the invitation listed a set of rules and etiquette for the ballroom. An excerpt follows:

> Every member at the time of subscribing will be presented with a list of such Ladies as are to have a general invitation, to each of whom will be give a ticket for their constant admittance. With respect to dancing of minuets, the gentlemen shall dance with such Ladies as the Master of Ceremonies shall appoint...with this privilege to the Master

of Ceremonies, that he shall always chuse [sic] his own Partner and open the Ball (quoted in Van Cleef, "Rural Felicity," 1976, 12).

Records of the time also indicated that other New England cities introduced a social structure similar to Newport. In Connecticut, they included Hartford, Norwich, New Haven, and Durham, as well as Portsmouth, New Hampshire, and Providence, Rhode Island. In Massachusetts, a regular series of assembly balls were staged in Newburyport, Greenfield, Brookfield, and Boston.

By the early eighteenth century, Dance Masters "like preachers, doctors, lawyers, peddlers, and many other trades and professions...traveled from town to town, often advertising ahead that they planned to open a dancing school." George Brownell was one example of a Dance Master of the time who traveled from town to town. In 1712, for example, Brownell taught in Boston where he offered "Writing, ciphering, Dancing, treble Violin, Flute, Spinet, &c." In 1727 and 1730, he taught in Philadelphia; in 1731, he was in New York, and was back in Boston in 1734 and Philadelphia in 1735. As late as 1744, he even traveled into Charleston, South Carolina. During that time many cities also had Dance Masters as permanent residents (Marks 1957, 38–40).

In contrast to the 1600s, when the magistrates and ministers of Boston closed down numerous dancing schools, after 1700, Boston joined Newport, Rhode Island, as the major dance centers within New England. By 1720, Boston boasted four "competing dance schools." At the same time, a dancing school was open across the Charles River in Charlestown. The nearby town of Salem (notorious for their "witch hunts" of 1691 to 1692) opened a dancing school in 1727, and a second one opened in 1739. By 1730, the population of Boston was around 12,000 people and the most populous city in the American colonies. In addition, contemporary accounts in Boston listed at least eight dancing schools under the auspices of a Dance Master. However, some Bostonians still had their doubts about dancing as evidenced by an incident involving a dancing school opened in 1732 by Peter Pelham (Cole, "The Puritan and Fair Terpsichore," 1942, 15–16).

On November 20, 1732, the *Boston Gazette* printed an editorial that complained about "Mr. Pelham's Dancing School." The editorial noted that a letter to the editor from a "pious" religious elder claimed that Pelham's dancing school was a "Licentious and Expensive diversion" among the youth of Boston. The letter writer claimed that he was given a flyer outside of Mr. Pelham's Dancing School advertising an upcoming evening of "Entertainment of Music and Dancing." He scolded the idea of both dancing schools such as Mr. Pelham's and dancing in general, He claimed that dancing was "hastening the ruin of our country, and are evils which call loudly for a Remedy." However, despite the plea by the Boston elder, Peter Pelham stayed in business. It appears that by that time the social climate of Boston was changing and was not under the political control of the religious elders. In 1738, for example, advertisements from January 16–23 appeared in the *Boston Gazette* for Pelham's dancing school that offered dancing lessons for "Young Gentlemen and Ladies" (Marks 1957, 32; Cole, "The Puritan and Fair Terpsichore," 1942, 15–16).

During the early 1700s, Boston was not the only city that had religious leaders object to dancing. In 1706, in Philadelphia, the Quaker Society of Friends presented a written decree to city authorities that proclaimed, "Friends are generally grieved that a dancing & fencing school, are tolerated in this place, which [we] fear will tend to the corruption of [our] children." The Quaker Society of Friends continued meeting on a monthly basis. And from 1706 to 1739, they adopted a platform at their Yearly Meeting to continually "condemn dancing and fencing." In addition, each year they petitioned the Governor and city authorities to not only condemn dancing but also close the dancing schools. But despite the condemnations, dancing schools flourished in the City of Brotherly Love (Marks 1957, 32–33).

Throughout Philadelphia, as with the rest of the American colonies, great pains were taken to offer the same stylish etiquette and manners that were offered in England and Europe. In 1738, in Philadelphia, for example, Theobald Hacket, advertised in the August 24–31 issue of the *Pennsylvania Gazette* that he taught "all sorts of fashionable English and French Dances, after the newest and politest manner practiced in London Dublin, and Paris" (quoted in Keller, "The Eighteenth Century Ballroom," 1996, 19).

NEW YORK, JAMES ALEXANDER, THE BLACK HORSE TAVERN, AND MR. ISAAC

At that time in New York, dancing could be had at a formal ball, assembly, local tavern, an "informal house party," or even within the home for practice or instruction. In 1729, *The New York-York Gazette* noted a sale of a building within New York City that formerly housed "the Dancing school." In 1731, the same newspaper carried an advertisement that traveling Dance Master George Brownell announced that he would teach dancing and also offered private lessons as well in the home. By that time there was already an established tradition of dancing in New York as evidenced by the diary of James Alexander.

James Alexander (b. 1691, d. 1756) was born in Scotland and studied law in London. In 1715 he emigrated to New York and by 1730 was an accomplished lawyer. By that time he had also previously served as the Surveyor General of both New Jersey and New York, and as Attorney General of New York. As did most colonial gentlemen of the day, Alexander kept a pocket dairy. His "Commonplace Book" contained "professional notes on surveys and legal matters, [and] a remedy for rattlesnake bite." Within his notes of May and November of 1730, he wrote down information for 27 country-dances. At the time he was 39 years old, was married, and had children; therefore, in all likelihood, he had copied the country-dances for his children to learn. It was speculated that he copied from another source, quite possibly from a friend or maybe even an edition of John Playford's *The Dancing-Master*. All of the dances that he wrote down were newer dances, in longways formation, introduced between 1710 and 1730. Some of the choices were also those that were popular in London at the time he left in 1715. Alexander and his wife quite possibly also danced the English country-dances. With their social status, in all likelihood they attended formal balls at the Black Horse Tavern in New York City (Keller and Fogg 2000, 6–8).

Throughout most of the eighteenth century, the Black Horse Tavern "was the scene of many political conferences and dances." In 1736, one such occasion was a celebration of both the birthday and recent marriage of the Prince of Wales. (Since the colonists were British citizens, the marriage of the future King and Queen of the British empire was a significant event.) The dance program at the Black Horse Tavern followed the same tradition as in Bath, England. The first half was reserved for the formalities as prescribed by the Minuet and possibly followed by a Courante, Gavotte, and Allemande. The second half of the dance program included the English Country-dances. (Keller and Fogg 2000, 8).

The event held in honor of the Prince of Wales on January 19, 1736, was described in *The New-York Weekly Journal* as follows:

> The 19th instant being his Royal Highness the Prince of Wales's birth day. It was celebrated at the Black Horse in a most elegant and genteel manner. There was a most magnificent appearance of gentlemen and ladies. The ball began with French dances. And then the company proceeded to country dances, upon which Mrs. Norris led up two new country dances made upon the occasion; the first of which was called, The Prince of Wales, and the second, The Princess of saxe-Gotha, in honour of the day. There was a most sumptuous entertainment afterward...The whole was conducted with utmost decency, mirth, and cheerfulness (*The New-York Weekly Journal*, January 26, 1736).

The two new dances "made upon the occasion" were a common practice of the day —one that had been established a few years earlier by Mr. Isaac.

At the time Mr. Isaac (b. 1640, d. 1720) was a noted choreographer and Dance Master to the Royal English Court. He wrote quite a few of the contemporary English Country-dances that were also danced in the American colonies. In 1711, the "Rigadoon Royal," for example, was a new dance choreographed by Mr. Isaac for the Queen's birthday. It was designed for one couple as an "eight couplet dance in duple meter." Mr. Isaac presented a tract drawing of the pattern of the dance and illustrated in Feuillet Notation (see earlier this chapter).

In 1706, John Weaver published a collection of dances by Mr. Isaac in *A collection of ball-dances perform'd at court*. In 1703, some of Mr. Isaac's dances also appeared in the latest edition of John Playford's *The Dancing-Master*. He also had some dances published in Edmund Pemberton's *An essay for the further improvement of dancing* (1711). Pemberton was the Dancing Master at a girls' boarding school in England. His publication was part of the school's curriculum to teach students a series of minuets and country-dances. After 1706, many of Mr. Isaac's dances were published and available in small singular pamphlets. Some of the most popular included special dances in honor of the Queen's birthday such as The Princess (1707), The Royal Portuguese (1709), The Royal Gailliarde (1710), The Royal Ann (1712), The Pastorall (1713), and The Godolphin (1714). Other dances included The Royall (1712), The Northumberland (1713), and The Friendship in honor of the New Year of 1715 ("An American Ballroom Companion" 2000).

By the early 1700s, dancing as a social activity was firmly entrenched in the American colonial society. What is most interesting is that, despite the threat of punishment and condemnation by the ministers throughout the American colonies, the colonists in communities both large and small followed the lead of the mother country of England and continued to dance. For the most part, the social dancing was first established in the provincial American cities and in turn influenced the smaller towns and villages. Shortly thereafter, a distinct geographic pattern of social dancing was firmly established. In many areas of New England, for example, they favored English Country-dancing. The southern colonies in Virginia, Maryland, and the Chesapeake Bay area adopted both English Country-dancing as well as other dances from the Royal Courts of France. The French in New Orleans and other provinces chose Contredanse and in the Spanish territories the Fandango and Bolero (Kraus and Chapman 1981, 90; Needham 2002, 2).

2

The Virginia Reel, George Washington, and the Waltz: 1740–1820

Virginians are of genuine Blood—they will dance or die!

—Philip Fithian, 1774

The Political, Social, and Cultural Climate

The time, from 1740 to 1820, represented a revolutionary change in America. During that time, the American colonies fostered a growing desire for independence and separation from the British Empire. In the ensuing years, an emergent revolutionary climate permeated through the colonies, culminating in a rebellion and long drawn out war of separation from England. The result of the American Revolution was the formation of the United States of America. Prior to the American Revolution, however, the American colonies were strictly subjugated by England—for in reality all the colonists were British subjects. Although the American colonies were separated by almost 3,000 miles of the Atlantic Ocean, the governing body was with Parliament in England. In essence, they were politically, economically, socially, and culturally dependent upon Great Britain.

In 1740, the total population in the 13 American colonies was a little over 900,000. The settlements, ranging from the Sea Islands of Georgia to Newfoundland, were concentrated near the coastline. At the most, some small settlements extended only 150 miles inland. The colony of Virginia was the most populated with over 350,000 people almost evenly divided between colonists and slaves. The Carolinas contained about 25,000 colonists, 40,000 slaves, and approximately 60,000 Indians. (The total inclusion of Native American Indians into the U.S. Census was not official until after 1930 in the twentieth century.) A few thousand non-

British Europeans were sparsely scattered throughout the Spanish and French territories (Zinn 2003, 49–54).

Over 70 percent of the population lived in rural areas and on small farms. They were as self-sufficient as the land and their capabilities allowed. They planted and harvested their own food, with labor mainly provided by immediate family members. In addition, they baked, spun cloth, and sewed their own clothing, and many built their own homes, furnishings, and wagons. Slave labor was mainly concentrated on the large plantations and some moderate sized farms throughout the southern colonies. In all the colonies, including the cities, slaves were also engaged for domestic labor, dockhands, and many other types of labor (Risjord 2002, 6–7).

The major seaboard cities with a population over 10,000 included Boston, New York, Philadelphia, Baltimore, and Charleston. In fact, only about 5 percent of the entire population of the colonies lived in a town or city with more than 2,500 people. The city of Newport, Rhode Island, with a population of about 7,500 residents, was a thriving seaport at the entrance to Narragansett Bay. At the time, Newport was considered a "modern" American city with many of the commercial buildings two and three stories in height. Almost all of the streets were paved with cobblestone and lit at night by whale-oil streetlights. In addition, the residents of Newport maintained an enviable social life that included sociable conversation circles, first-rate food, and dancing at assembly balls. During the summer months, the city served as a retreat for wealthy plantation owners from Georgia and the Carolinas.

Travel between cities was by horseback and an occasional wagon, but was difficult due to unreliable roads. The travel speed was no faster than by walking or by horseback, a travel speed that had not changed in the previous hundreds, if not thousands of years. Improvements in roads made the travel a bit more bearable, as did rudimentary ferries and flatboats along highways to traverse streams and rivers. Wherever possible, travel by waterway was the most reliable, that is, depending upon favorable wind for the sails. Most of the products and goods were also shipped by water. In 1760, for example, travel to the colonies from England was exclusively by sailing ship, and a one-way trip took about 30 days. Within the colonies, the 160-mile travel between Albany and New York City by sailing ship on the Hudson River took four days (Risjord 2002, 1–8).

The Hudson River was a valuable waterway that was traversable up to the interior of North America into Newfoundland and the Midwest. At the southern entry to the river was New York City, with possibly "the finest natural harbor on the seaboard." In 1740, New York City was the second most populous city (behind Philadelphia) with a population of 12,000 of which 2,000 were African slaves. At the time, the area of the city extended only about one mile on the Hudson River side and about two miles up on the East River side. Dutch influence was still evident and many of the narrow streets contained brick buildings four and five stories high. By 1800, however, the immigration into cities increased dramatically. Philadelphia was the most populous city with 73,000 residents followed by New York with 63,000, and Boston by comparison claimed 38,000 inhabitants. Similar to Newport, Rhode Island, New York along with the other seaport cities of Boston, Philadelphia, Baltimore, and Charleston developed a cosmopolitan social life patterned on the likes of England (Risjord, 9; Glaab 1963, 78).

With well over 100 years since the first British settlements in Virginia and New England and the continued influx of immigrants from England, Scotland, Ireland, France, Germany, Scandinavia, and Africa, the result was that Americans still did not have a distinct cultural identity. However, that was slowly changing. As early as 1743, American statesman Benjamin Franklin, a Philadelphia resident, had observed the social changes in the American colonies. He wrote:

> The first Drudgery of Settling new Colonies, which confines the Attention of the People to mere Necessaries is now pretty well over; and there are many in every Province in Circumstances that set them at Ease, and afford leisure to cultivate the finer Arts (quoted in Csida and Csida 1978, 19).

Franklin had earned a living as a printer until about the age of 42. In his later years, he invented the lightning rod, bifocal glasses, the Franklin stove, and the glass harmonica. He was also instrumental in developing a state university in Philadelphia and the first American public library. Franklin was part of a growing number of American statesmen whose ideas were shaped by the Age of Enlightenment.

The Enlightenment developed in Europe as an outgrowth of the Renaissance by such leading contemporary "thinkers" as John Locke, Isaac Newton, Voltaire, Thomas Hobbes, and Jean Jacques Rousseau. Sometimes known collectively as *Philosophes*, they based their ideas and beliefs in the rational exploration of the laws of science and nature and applied those ideas as a means towards social progress. Unlike the contemporary Christian leaders who believed all answers for the universe could be derived from the Bible, the Philosophes put emphasis on the fact that God did not control the events of life or human nature. Instead, they claimed that God gave the power to acquire knowledge, and therefore human beings, through reasoning and rational thought, could improve the social conditions of humans and their environment. According to historians in *The American Journey: A History of the United States*, the Enlightenment thinkers "emphasized the need to reform Christian society and believed that this reform could be accomplished through education that was based on the great writings of ancient Greece and Rome." Voltaire, for example, believed that "the Renaissance was a crucial stage in liberating the mind from the superstition and error that he believed characterized Christian society during the Middle Ages" (Goldfield, Abbott, et al., 2001, 104).

In 1762, Rousseau introduced the idea of individual civil liberty, as opposed to monarchial or Church rule, in his treatise *The Social Contract*. The political philosophy was an extension of John Locke's *Two Treatises of Government* (1690). The Enlightenment idea that government entered into a "social contract" with the people it governed was the human reasoning that Thomas Jefferson applied in writing *The Declaration of Independence* as justification for the American Revolution.

In fact, the American Revolution, as important as it was to the development of the country, was not a cultural revolution but a social revolution of political discourse. During the time of 1763 through 1775, a series of events created political unrest that led to the eventual separation of the American colonies from the British Empire. It was not until 1774 that some American colonists (known as Whigs) wanted complete separation from England. On the other hand, a significant number of British loyalists (known as Tories) did not agree and wished to stay loyal to the British Crown. But after a long period of civil unrest, culminating in 1775 in the first battles at Lexington, Concord, and Bunker Hill, Parliament declared the Massachusetts colony in a state of rebellion and sent a large military force. By 1776, the American colonies were engaged in a full-fledged war with Great Britain.

In 1776, two important documents set the course for no turning back in America's war for independence. In January 1776, Thomas Paine's 47-page pamphlet *Common Sense* provided in plain language that the everyday common man could understand the reason for the war. In July of that same year, the Continental Congress met in Philadelphia and commissioned Thomas Jefferson to write a petition to the King of England stating the reason for independence. Jefferson's document, The Declaration of Independence, ratified on July 4, 1776, claimed that King George set out to destroy the natural rights of the American colonists. On July 9, 1776, when the Declaration of Independence was read in Bowling Green, New York, near a statue of England's King George III, the assemblage of city residents and Washington's troops were incited to tear down the statue.

During the war years of 1775 to 1781, General George Washington engaged in a series of battles with British troops. The battles began in the north and traveled into the southern colonies. The year 1781 marked a significant turning point in the war. In October of that year, Washington's forces on land coupled with the allied French Navy Blockade of sea trapped the main British army at the Yorktown peninsula in Virginia. Within days the British General surrendered, signifying an end to the warfare. In 1783, in the Treaty of Paris, Great Britain recognized American independence as the British evacuated their remaining forces from New York. The significance of the American Revolution loomed larger than life on the world stage. The victory meant that the ideas and theories of the enlightenment were possible with a workable system of government based on the individual and the idea of liberty.

In 1787, the American Congress drafted a new Constitution to develop a workable form of government to replace the Articles of Confederation. (In 1777, the fledging United States Congress adopted the Articles of Confederation creating a loose confederation of autonomous states.) In 1789, the Constitution of the United Sates of America was "officially" adopted by the 13 original colonies. In that same year in Europe, the French Revolution, also based on the ideas of the Enlightenment, brought with it a "spirit of individualism." In effect, both the American and French revolutions put an official end to the old form of monarchial government as expressed by the King and the Royal Courts.

As a consequence of the Peace Treaty with England, former British lands and Tory loyalist lands were confiscated and became property of the Revolutionary forces. Some land was sold in small parcels at low prices and some was given as parcels and land grants of the American soldiers of the revolution. The result was a change in the makeup of America to a nation of small landowners, mostly for farming. In addition, American settlers began a westbound expansion into the Louisiana territories. By 1800, according to *The Monthly Magazine and American Review* in January 1800,

The grand division of the United States is into two parts. The first is that which lies on the Atlantic Ocean and among those streams that flow into it. The second is the region adjacent to the lakes and Mississippi...Eastern or Atlantic portion [and] the western portion (quoted in Marks 1957, 29–30).

The Mississippi River was of prime importance for those Americans west of the Appalachian Mountains for shipment of goods to European markets.

The city of New Orleans was of particular importance due to its strategic location at the mouth of the Mississippi River. On the other hand, the uncharted territories of Louisiana and beyond might have been deemed "unknown" to the fledgling United States, but it was occupied by indigenous Native American Indian tribes for many centuries and had been traversed by French fur traders for many years. However, in the fall of 1802, the Spanish closed the port of New Orleans to American trade, and talk of an American war with Spain heated up.

At about the same time in Europe, the French under Napoleon Bonaparte defeated Spain in a war and gained control of the area. But, Napoleon also suffered a devastating defeat of one of his armies in the West Indies. He realized that the area was well beyond his reach of power and therefore offered not only New Orleans but also the entire Louisiana territory for sale to the United States. The sale, known in American history as the "Louisiana Purchase," represented the single largest peaceful transition of land ownership in the history of the United States. As a result, the land size of the United States literally doubled, satisfying the quest for America's westward expansion. In May 1804, in order to chart the territory, Jefferson sponsored an expedition under the joint command of Meriwether Lewis and William Clark (Risjord 2002, 349–351).

In 1805, shortly after the Louisiana Purchase, England soundly defeated the French navy and gained control of the Atlantic trade routes. The British attempted to dictate overseas trade policy of the fledgling United States and prohibited any dealings with the French. English ships also routinely raided American cargo vessels, seizing the goods as well as forcing the sailors into service of the British empire. The practice continued until 1812, when the United States declared war on England. The United States could not effectively fight the British on the seas; therefore, the British were able to attack various American coastal cities including Baltimore, Washington, D.C., and New Orleans. In the process, they destroyed much of the nation's capitol city, including burning the recently built White House and Capitol building. In Baltimore, however, they were turned back at Fort McHenry, the event that inspired Francis Scott Key to write "The Star Spangled Banner." The British attack on New Orleans was of utmost strategic importance as American forces led by Andrew Jackson soundly defeated the British. Although the Battle of New Orleans, fought on January 8, 1815, was actually about a month after a peace treaty was signed (neither side knew that the war had ended), the victory firmly established America as an independent nation ("United States (History)," n.p.).

During the course of events that changed America from a series of British colonies into the United States of America, dancing was a well-established tradition. Dancing, for example, was a social necessity of the Virginia gentlemen. Historian Stephen Ambrose in his book *Undaunted Courage*, chronicling the adventures of

Meriwether Lewis and William Clark, stated that social dancing was one of the important talents of Virginia gentlemen. In 1774, Philip Fithian, a Presbyterian tutor, toured the southern colonies and kept a journal of his observations. During his journeys, he partook in many of the social amusements and attended some dances. In Virginia he was particularly impressed and exclaimed: "Virginians are of genuine Blood—they will dance or die!" By that time, however, the air of revolution might have tinged that statement. Nevertheless, the dancing climate in America was certainly breaking away from the provincial beginnings of the first settlers at Jamestown, Virginia, and New England (Williams 1934, 235).

The Dances

Dancing is incontestably an elegant and amiable accomplishment; it confers grace and dignity of carriage . . . Nature gives us limbs, and art teaches us to use them.

—Amelia, 1796

But, alas, our dancing days are over. We wish, however, all those who relish so innocent and agreeable an amusement all the pleasure the season will afford them.

—George Washington, 1799

CONTRA DANCING, THE COTILLION, THE QUADRILLE, AND THE BIG CIRCLE DANCES

During the 1700s, the English Country-dances were commonly danced among the city folk and townspeople, as well as in the countryside. By the 1770s, the Minuet and the French cotillion were introduced in the American colonies to the cities and larger towns. At that time the cities favored the European model of opening a formal ball with a Minuet, followed by a long set of other French dances such as the Cotillion. The French dances concluded the first part as an intermission was taken, usually for refreshments and sometimes supper. The second half was usually devoted entirely to English Country-dances. All in all, Americans still followed the European lead for new dance styles—especially the French.

In the French Royal Court, many of the English Country-dances or *anglaise danses* (see Chapter 1) were reworked and danced with some of the longways formations in opposite lines with alternating couples. Therefore, the French term of *Contredanse* (or sometimes in France as the *contredanse francaise*) was commonly used to denote those dances that differed from the Longways set "for as many as will." In 1706, for example, French Dance Master Raoul-Auger Feuillet's *Recueil de Contredanses* published over 30 dances in the Contra longways formation. In 1710, Dance Master John Essex translated Feuillet's book of Contredanses into English titled *For the Furthur Improvement of Dancing*. However, Feuillet's system of dance notation (see Chapter 1) was a bit cumbersome for dances that contained multiple couples. The French *contredanse* was composed of a specific "sequence of figures" arranged in combinations of "two- or four-bar step combinations." Interspersed with the set figures of the dance was a series of 12 changes that alternated with the figures ("Late Eighteenth-Century Social Dance" n.d.).

During the years 1760 to 1785, two French publishers, Landrin and La Cuisse published numerous collections of dance instruction manuals and also issued an "annual collections of dances." They included all sorts of *Contredanses* and Cotillions, including a series of 12 figured *Contredanses* and English Country-dances. Most of the publications by La Cuisse were four-page pamphlets for a single dance that included step descriptions, an illustration, and suggested music. In 1762, La Cuisse in *Le répertoire des bals* improved on Feuillet's dance notation system as applied for the French Contredanse and Cotillion. The dance instruction manual contained over 85 *Contredanses* and variations. When the popular French Contredanse was danced back in England, it was translated into English as "Contra Dancing" ("Late Eighteenth-Century Social Dance" n.d.).

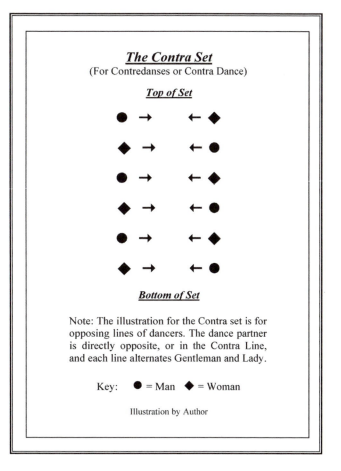

The Contra Set
(For Contredanses or Contra Dance)

Top of Set

Bottom of Set

Note: The illustration for the Contra set is for opposing lines of dancers. The dance partner is directly opposite, or in the Contra Line, and each line alternates Gentleman and Lady.

Key: ● = Man ◆ = Woman

Illustration by Author

Similar to English Country-dancing, Contra dancing employed many of the same techniques and figures, such as smooth interweaving figures and the camaraderie of the couples. The French also adapted the English round dances such as described in Playford's editions of *The Dancing-Master*. However, many of the French dances were limited to a "round for eight," which was a circle dance with a maximum of four couples. Both the reworked Contra formation and circle dances were grouped under the general title of *cotillon* (Cotillion in English). The French word *cotillon* was loosely translated as simply "petticoat," which was a bulky undergarment worn under a lady's skirt (Sachs 1963, 421–422).

The Cotillion was first popular in France around 1723. After 1740, it was picked up in Germany. In 1755, the German Dance Master Hänsel noted that the "Cotillons are very popular at large weddings, parties, and balls, and for a variety are the most common, the gayest and the best next to the English [country] dances." Around 1760, in England, the refined French Cotillon was welcomed in the British ballrooms, where it was also enhanced with a greater number of figures and geometric patterns. At about the same time it was also danced in the American colonies. By the late part of the nineteenth century, "Cotillion" was the word used to

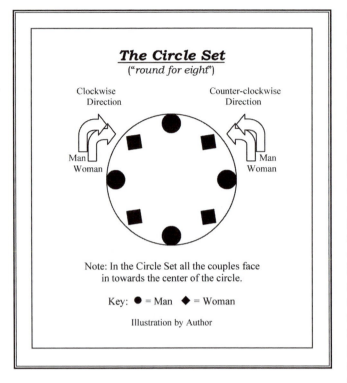

The Circle Set
("round for eight")

Clockwise
Direction

Counter-clockwise
Direction

Man
Woman

Man
Woman

Note: In the Circle Set all the couples face
in towards the center of the circle.

Key: ● = Man   ◆ = Woman

Illustration by Author

describe either the final dance or set of dances that ended a formal ball or assembly. During the twentieth century, the term replaced "assembly" and was usually applied to denote "fancy-dress ball" (Sachs 1963, 421–422; Clarke and Crisp 1981, 97; Page 1977, 29–31).

The Cotillion was originally a dance of four couples, sometimes starting in a circle formation of a "round for eight" or sometimes in a square formation. Any number of formations of eight couples could fill the floor as the size of the room allowed. The groups of eight all danced at the same time, and, depending upon the particular figure, they might all dance together hand-in-hand, or sometimes as separate couples. At the end of a particular figure they would resume the original circle or square. In patterns such as the *grande chaîne*, for example, the couples all joined hands and moved in a circle either clockwise or counterclockwise depending upon the called figure. A similar description of the *chaîne* actually appeared in numerous editions of John Playford's *The Dancing-Master* under the description of a "hey" and "heying" (Sachs 1963, 422–423).

During the eighteenth century, most of the Cotillion patterns were simple and contained two basic parts. The first part was "the changes or verses," which was the standard opening of all the cotillion dances. In similar fashion to the révérence in the minuet (see Chapter 1), the Cotillion began with an "honors," which was "a salute" to the partner, and then a similar acknowledgment to the other couples in the set. The second part was a series of set figures (known as the "chorus") that was distinctive to the particular dance. According to dance historians Kate Van Winkle Keller and Charles Cyril Hendrickson, "The opening phrase is played once through for the dancers to honor their partners and their corners, then played twice again for the first change" (1998, 109).

From 1760 and 1820, the Cotillion was particularly popular in the American colonies. In 1788, American John Griffith's *A Collection of the Newest and Most Fashionable Country Dances and Cotillions* listed 13 different Cotillions. One Cotillion, named "The Forty-Second," was described by Griffith as follows:

All round, Halfway—back again—the first and second couple meet together—set and chassee Halfway—then stand still—the third and fourth couple do the same—first and second couple chassee back—set and turn Partners quite round with Hand—set —third and fourth couples do the same (quoted in Page 1977, 29).

In 1798, another American, John Trumbull of Norwich, Connecticut, published a 24-page pamphlet on dance instruction titled *The Gentlemen & Lady's Companion; Containing, The Newest Cotillions and Country Dances; To Which Is Added, Instances Of Ill Manners to be carefully avoided by Youth of both sexes.* One of the Cotillions described by Trumbull, named "The York Fusiliers," began as a Circle set broken into a Longways set and back to the Circle set. He described the pattern as follows:

> All round, first and opposite couples, balance in the middle, set, and turn, contrary partners, and retreat to your places, the other two couples do the same, chasse all eight and turn the lady to your right quite round, chasse back to your places and turn the lady to your left, then form two lines long way four each side, balance, cross hands tour, each corners, balance again, and cross hands back, and come to your former places (4).

In addition to the descriptions of 12 dances, Trumbull added two pages of ballroom etiquette to complete the title portion of "Instances Of Ill Manners to be carefully avoided by Youth of both sexes." Some of the "instances of ill manners" that Trumbull listed in regards to the dance floor included:

> OMITTING to pay proper respect to company, on entering or leaving a room; or paying it only to one person, when more are present. Entering a room with the hat on, and leaving it [on] in the same manner.... Passing between the fire and persons sitting at it....Whispering, or pointing in company... Contradicting your parents or strangers who are any way engaged in conversation. Laughing loudly, when in company, and drumming with feet or hands. Swinging the arms, and all other awkward gestures [and] ...All actions that have the most remote tendency to indelicacy....Contempt in looks, words, or actions, for a partner in dancing, or other persons (22–23).

Trumbull also included some other basic rules of etiquette that included rising from one's seat upon "the entrance of your instructor, strangers, or parents." In addition, all sorts of rude behavior were not acceptable, including "ridicule of every kind," "surliness of all kinds," "lolling on a chair when speaking or when spoken to," "throwing things instead of handing them," and basically any instance that might be misinterpreted by any other individual within the ballroom as inappropriate. As a final note, Trumbull advised a "constant smile" during the entire course of dancing (24).

By about 1800, the "round for eight" had been smoothed out to a square of four couples. In addition, the British, both in England and in the American colonies, adapted the contra lines of sometimes only two couples and eventually a set of four couples in a square and termed it a Quadrille (Clarke and Crisp 1981, 97).

The *Le Pantalon* figure, for example, was composed of an English chaîne for eight bars of music, a Balancé (which was a set to the partners) for four bars, turning with your partner for four bars, a chaîne just of the Ladies for eight bars, a half promenade for four bars, and half of the English chaîne for four bars. Video clips of a demonstration of the *Le Pantalon* figure are viewable from the Music Division of the Library of Congress online source *An American Ballroom Companion: Dance Instruction Manuals Ca. 1490–1920* (see bibliography) ("Nineteenth Century Social Dance," n.d.).

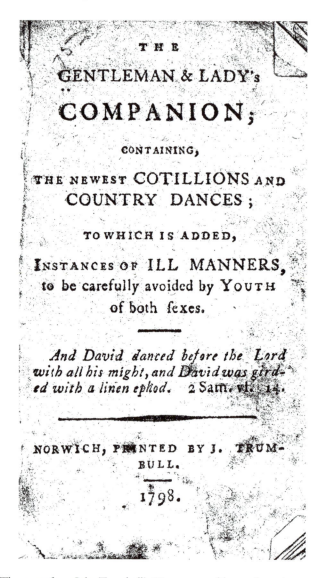

THE

GENTLEMAN & LADY's

COMPANION;

CONTAINING,

THE NEWEST COTILLIONS AND
COUNTRY DANCES;

TO WHICH IS ADDED,

INSTANCES OF ILL MANNERS,
to be carefully avoided by YOUTH
of both fexes.

*And David danced before the Lord
with all his might, and David was gird-
ed with a linen ephod.* 2 Sam. vi. 14.

NORWICH, PRINTED BY J. TRUM-
BULL.

1798.

The cover from John Trumbull's 24-page pamphlet on dance instruction titled *The Gentlemen & Lady's Companion; Containing, The Newest Cotillions and Country Dances; To Which Is Added, Instances Of Ill Manners to be carefully avoided by Youth of both sexes,* c. 1798. Library of Congress, Music Division, http://memory.loc.gov/musdi/114/0001.gif.

In regards to the origin of the Quadrille, British dance historian Thomas Reginald St. Johnston in *A History of Dancing* (1906) noted that the Quadrille "was originally a card game for four people." He speculated that since the cardplayers faced each other in a square, or at a square table, that might have been the reason the name was applied to the dance. Others thought the name might have derived from the Italian *Quadriglia,* which was a "military square of tournament horsemen." In either case, in France the full name of the dance was "Quadrille de Contre Danse," indicating that the "dance itself was probably a direct descendant" from the French Contredanse and that the name was first "given to a dance introduced into the French ballets about 1745." St. Johnston added that, although the Quadrille was introduced in England around 1808, it did not become "fashionable" until it was "danced...in Almack's rooms in 1815" (see later in this chapter). He described it as follows:

> The French Quadrille was for two, four, or any number of couples, but four pairs seem to have been the ideal number in England. The dance itself was divided into figures, usually five, being Le Pantalon, L'Eté, La Poule, La Tremise [Frenis], and Le Final, and with each figure there were appropriate movements and phases of almost a pantomimic nature...but later on these adjuncts were left out, though the figures remained, as names only, for a very long time afterwards.

At first, the French Quadrille was quite formal and each couple remained with each other and did not interchange with the other couples (St. Johnston 1906, 143–144).

The first part of the Quadrille began with a bow and was followed by a set series of promenades, circles, and turns. The second part had different sets of figures. One of the better descriptions is found in a contemporary Thomas Wilson's *The Quadrille and Cotillion Panorama* (1818). Wilson described it as

This fashionable species of Dancing is entirely of French origin, and only differs from the well known dance, the Cotillon, by leaving out the changes …being much shorter, and frequently composed of Figures that require but four persons to their performance; as may be seen from the first set of French Quadrilles that were publicly danced in [England]…

A set of Quadrilles generally consist of four, which are danced in succession…these are usually danced before the company sit down or separate; to which is generally added one more, or is what is generally termed a Finale.

Wilson was one of the leading English Dance Masters of his time, and his dance instruction manual was published in both London and New York under various titles including the *Quadrille panorama* and *Treatise on quadrille dancing*. The complete title of his publication was

> *The quadrille and cotillion panorama, or, Treatise on quadrille dancing, in two parts: with an explanation, in French and English, of all the quadrille & cotillion figures generally adopted, as described by diagrams on the plate, by Thomas Wilson.*

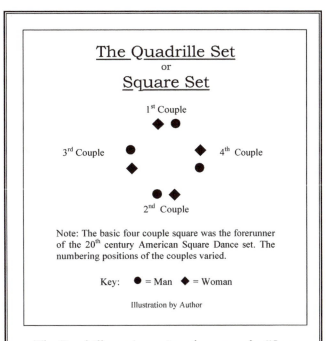

The Quadrille Set
or
Square Set

1st Couple

3rd Couple   4th Couple

2nd Couple

Note: The basic four couple square was the forerunner of the 20th century American Square Dance set. The numbering positions of the couples varied.

Key: ● = Man   ◆ = Woman

Illustration by Author

The Quadrille set (sometimes known as the "Square set") consisted of four couples in a square formation, with each couple facing inward on each side of a square. As it developed in France, the dance was arranged with a very specific predescribed sequence of five different figures. The first four figures called *Le Pantalon*, *L'Eté*, *La Poule*, and *La Frenis* were derived from the popular Contredanses, and the fifth was from the French Cotillion known as *Le Final* (Harris et al., 2000, 125–126).

In 1822, a second edition was published that contained a "three-color-fold-out and nine [illustrated] plates." That version was also reissued in 1839. Within *The Quadrille and Cotillion Panorama*, Wilson provided a detailed analysis of the particular figures and intricacies of the Quadrille. His book was divided into two sections, one part for the step descriptions and another part for the suggested music. Typically the names of the Quadrille dances were given the same name as the accompanying musical tune. Other contemporary dance manuals that included step descriptions for the Quadrille were Barclay Dun's *A Translation of Nine of the Most Fashionable Quadrilles* (1818), J.H. Gourdoux-Daux's *Elements and Principles of the Art of Dancing* (1817), and Alexander Strathy's *Elements of the Art of Dancing* (1822) ("Nineteenth Century Social Dance," n.d.).

By 1800, in America, dances in the Square Set were replacing Longways set English Country-dances. A contributing factor was the rising tensions and dislike of all things British that began with the American Revolution and culminated in the War of 1812. From about 1800 through 1815, anti-British sentiment was at an all-time high, especially among the cities that almost universally rejected the English style dances. Therefore, the adaptation of the French Cotillions and Quadrilles was particularly suited to the Americans preference. According to dance historian Richard Nevell, "While this square formation was certainly not an invention of the French, it was their enthusiastic importation of the dance to America that sowed the seeds for great changes in dancing throughout the nineteenth century." As a result, the budding new American country adapted the dances of their European ancestors, and the Quadrille was the forerunner of the Lancers (see Chapter 3) and the twentieth century American Square Dance (Nevell 1977, 35–39).

In the American colonies, the quadrille was also known as a "Running Set" or "Square Dance." In the Running set the dance moved around the outside of the square, rather than through or across it, and sometimes in a big circle. Unlike the "round for eight" or set square for eight people, it could also include as many couples who wished to join in the dance. The Running set was usually danced during a social occasion such as a wedding or a harvest, and any of a series of figures was called that involved all the dancers. Some of the calls included the entire group holding hands either in a "circle left" or a "circle right," a promenade, or even a swing your partner. In the Running set a "caller" called out the figures from inside the formation. Other forms of big circle dances eventually developed including the "Mountain Square Dance," the "Appalachian Big Circle," the "Great Circle," and the "Big Circle Square." Each of them remained popular in the mountain regions until well into the twentieth century. The Running set remained virtually unchanged, and very little was written about it until 1917. At that time, Englishman Cecil Sharp (see Chapter 4) traveled through the Appalachian Mountains of Kentucky and named the four-couple square formation the "Kentucky Running Set" (Nevell 1977, 41; Harris, Pittman, et al., 2000, 84–85, 127).

GEORGE WASHINGTON AND THE AMERICAN COLONIAL MINUET

Throughout the history of America, George Washington is considered, almost universally, as the most famous American individual. Many historians would be hard-pressed to disavow his importance and stature as it applied to America, not only within his own lifetime, but also for all succeeding generations both politically and publicly. But, unbeknownst to most students of American history, Washington was greatly admired and revered for his dancing and leadership in establishing American social decorum within the ballroom. In that same spirit, Washington was most likely the most famous dancer within his own lifetime.

Throughout Washington's military career in the American Revolution and subsequent presidency of the United States, there are numerous accounts of his dancing. His dance of choice to start the evening was the Minuet, followed by Country-dances. Although accounts of Washington dancing after 1770 are numerous, very little is known about his own dance education. It is most plausible that since he was a Virginia gentleman of wealth, it was a necessity that he be well versed in fencing and dancing (Ambrose 1996, 30)

Washington's prowess in the Minuet could only mean that he spent many hours learning the dance from a Dance Master. However, it is not known where or how Washington learned the graceful skill of the Minuet. It is known that in 1747, the 14-year-old Washington obtained a copy of William Winstanley's *Rules of Civility and Decent Behaviour* (1722, reprinted 1733). From one of the editions, he copied a list of rules and manners. The first rule, for example, was "1st Every Action done in Company, ought to be with Some Sign of Respect, to those that are Present." Washington both as president and on the ballroom dance floor artfully applied this basic rule. The rule also applied to the stately grace that was required to properly dance the Minuet (Keller, *Early American Social Dance*, n.d.).

Some documentation existed that he did hire a Dance Master to instruct his children and nieces. On September 12, 1770, for example, Washington noted in his diary that a "Mr. Christian and his scholars came here to Dancing." The "here" was his home at Mount Vernon in Virginia, and the dancing was to instruct his nieces Patsy Custis and Milly Possey (Marks 1957, 41). By that time, it was considered an outward sign of social prestige that a family could afford the services of dancing instruction for both themselves and their children. For that matter, whether it was in New York, Philadelphia, Boston, Newport, Charleston, South Carolina, or even Virginia, the employment of a dancing master within one's own home was held in the highest social esteem. It was also quite common that the parents had their children "show off" their learned dancing talents for assembled guests. Typically the children danced a Minuet or a similar intricate French dance learned from the Dance Master.

At the time, both the Minuet and the Gavotte (see Chapter 1) were danced in the America colonies in the same style and flavor of the French Royal Courts of King Louis XVI and Marie Antoinette. Both of the dances required specific skillful steps, and in the American colonies, as in Europe, persons of wealth or esteemed social standing favored the dances. In the colonies the Minuet was danced in the same stately and graceful manner, but also a bit slower than in France. In addition, after the first Minuet, in many instances, more than one couple danced subsequent Minuets at the same time. However, the colonists also followed the same protocol of opening a formal dance with a Minuet led by the highest-ranking social member. During the American Revolution and the ensuing years, that honor was reserved for George Washington.

In 1976, in honor of America's Bicentennial, dance historian Leon Dorfman chose to present a "bicentennial," of American social dancing from the "Minuet of 1776" to the "Hustle of 1976." In *The Cavalcade of American Ballroom Dancing*, Dorfman described the American Colonial Minuet as

> Characterized by deep bows and curtseys, the gentleman held the lady's hand high and led her through elaborate patterns. With pointed toe leading, the steps were carefully and gracefully executed to music in 3/4 time (1).

Dorfman recounted that a Minuet danced at the Philadelphia Assembly of 1776 might have consisted of a routine including a Strut Walk, Balance and Change Places, Side Cross and Walk Around, Reverse Turns, and finished with a Side Cross and Balance Steps (Dorfman 1976, 2–3).

In the American colonies the employment of a dancing master within one's own home was held in the highest social esteem. It was also quite common that the parents had their children "show off" their learned dancing talents for assembled guests. Typically the children danced a Minuet or a similar intricate French dance learned from the Dance Master. This undated illustration is from about 1760 to 1780.   Library of Congress, Prints and Photographs LC-USZ62-85568.

Kate Van Winkle Keller and Charles Cyril Hendrickson in *George Washington: A Biography in Social Dance* (1998) added that the American Colonial Minuet was also danced in the predescribed Z floor pattern (see Chapter 1). They described it as follows:

> All movement appears to float without effort; the dancer's sinking into a demi-plié is a push down through the heel into the floor, and the rise to the demi-coupé is a release upward. Movement is direct, the body does not sway or waver, and the paths are straight or in clear curves.... The man leads the dance and signals his partner with his arm movements and the management of his hat.... As each Z track is performed, the dancers may either pass each other without touching, or take hands in the center and turn by the right, the left, and finally both hands. The number of steps they use and the number of times they perform each figure is optional and may or may not conform to the phrases of the music. The dance is completed with honors to the company and partner (123).

Washington's adoption of the Minuet might have had bigger reasons politically.

Prior to the war of independence from Britain, the American colonies still followed the European lead as it applied to culture and dancing. In looking to separate from any provincial association as uncultured colonists, individuals such as Washington attached to an accepted cultural pattern, as was the case in England, France, and the rest of Europe. During the revolution, Washington's army and the Continental Congress needed European allies—especially France. In fact, Washington and his armies were dependent upon the aid of both the French army and the French navy as well as the German general Baron Friedrich Wilhelm von Steuben. Therefore, an acceptance of the French and European cultural customs, especially as it applied to dancing, provided the necessary diplomacy in dealing with the French both militarily and politically.

And finally after the revolution, the infant United States of America needed to establish its position as a "civilized" society among the political, economical, and social world that was still controlled mainly by England and France. For those reasons, according to dance historian Curt Sachs, in choosing a dance such as the Minuet, regardless of the situation, Washington was allowed "without self-consciousness, to address a person of rank with decorum" (Sachs 1963, 400).

However, the year 1777 did not fare well for Washington and his army. In August 1777, faced with an overwhelming British force, Washington and his army barely escaped, and retreated across Brooklyn, into Manhattan, and finally New Jersey. On the other hand, in October 1777, an American army commanded by General Horatio Gates won a major battle at Saratoga, New York. The victorious battle proved to the French that the Americans could indeed meet and defeat the British on an open battlefield. As a result, France joined as an ally of the American Revolutionary forces in the war against Great Britain. But the one victory did not necessarily guarantee success for Washington.

In fact, the American army that Washington brought into winter encampment at Valley Forge, New Jersey, during 1777–1778, was an undisciplined ragtag assemblage of untrained militia. Washington, therefore, enlisted the aid of German General Baron von Steuben. It was because of the precise military training and discipline instilled by von Steuben that Washington's army turned into an organized disciplined fighting force. (In fact, in later years it was von Steuben who suggested that the United States form an established military academy that eventually transpired to become West Point—see Chapter 3.) As part of the training, von Steuben recommended dancing.

During the winter at Valley Forge, the hospital staff hired the services of John Trotter and opened a dancing school. The lessons held every afternoon in Country-dancing were twofold. The first was to provide some recreation as an alternative to the military training, and the second was obviously an attempt to keep the soldiers' circulation moving in the freezing temperatures. Subsequent winter encampments at Middlebrook in 1777–1778, Pluckmein in 1778–1779, and Morristown 1779–1780 also offered the same instruction in Country-dancing (Van Cleef, "Rural Felicity," 1976, 22).

During the winter encampments, the American officers also danced; however, they followed the formal European pattern of Minuets, French dances, and Country-dances. During the winter of 1778–1779, for example, American artillery commander General Henry Knox and his wife sponsored a series of balls. In a letter to his brother dated February 28, 1779, Knox noted that, on one particular occasion, over 400 people attended. The high attendance was attributed to the attendance of a special honored guest—General George Washington. The honor of the first dance obviously went to Washington. Knox added, "We had above seventy ladies...We danced all night [in] an elegant room" (Keller and Hendrickson 1998, 6–7).

While Washington and the American revolutionary army were in winter encampment, the British nestled in the coastal cities including New York and Newport, Rhode Island, also made the best of the winter season by dancing. In New York, for example, General William Howe attended a lavish ball given in his honor by his officers prior to his return to England (Wharton 1893, 2). From 1775 to 1783, throughout the duration of the war, the British controlled most of the coastal cities. In 1780, however, when news arrived that the French fleet was sailing for Newport, the British evacuated the city. In the process of evacuation they set fires and destroyed as much as they could. Despite the destruction, upon arrival of the French navy, the town residents scraped together what they could and held a dance in their honor. One eyewitness account noted that the French "are fond of dancing which they do most unpretentiously" (Page 1977, 27).

Shortly thereafter in Newport, French commander Comte de Jean Baptiste Rochambeau arranged a dance in honor of a special guest—General George Washington. The dance held at Mrs. Cowley's Assembly Rooms located on Church Street symbolically represented the "official" joining of two nations as allies. The honor of opening the dance was given to Washington, and Rochambeau played among the musicians. Washington selected a local debutante named Peggy Champlin "known for her grace and sweetness" and led her in a dance. One eyewitness account wrote,

> The noble dames, "though robbed of their wealth by war," appeared in superb brocades with embroidered petticoats and were pleased to "foot it" with such noblemen ...The soft light from silver candelabra was reflected in beautiful mirrors loaned from old mansions, as Washington opened the ball with beautiful Miss Champlin under festoons of bunting looped with rosettes of swords and pistols; Rochambeau...tooke [sic] the instruments and played the dance selected by the partner of General Washington, "A Successful Campaign," followed by "Pea Straw," and "I'll be Married in my Old Clothes," and "Boston's Delight," in honor of the guest from that city (quoted in Page 1977, 27).

At the time, all the dances listed in the eyewitness account, "A Successful Campaign," "Pea Straw," "I'll be Married in my Old Clothes," and "Boston's Delight" were all quite common and listed in numerous contemporary dance instruction manuals. However, they were all Country-dances (Page 1977, 27–28).

This account is certainly accurate; however, in all likelihood, this sequence of dancing most likely happened as the opening to a second set of dancing after a break for either refreshments or dinner. Washington was well versed in the decorum of the European dances opening with a Minuet, and he most likely did, in fact, open the dance with the Minuet. Especially since the honors for the dance were to acknowledge the alliance with France, it would be highly unlikely, given

Washington's impeccable record for decorum in all phases of public appearances, that he would have insulted his French guests (and valuable allies for the success of the revolution) by opening with any dance other than the Minuet.

During the course of the remaining years of the military campaign, both the Americans and the British held numerous Assembly balls. In 1782, for example, Captain Erasmus Wolcott noted that during winter encampment in Hudson, Connecticut, the militia regularly attended to dancing. Wolcott wrote in his journal, "We have built ourselves a large ballroom in which we are instructing ourselves in the polite arts of Dancing and fencing" (Van Cleef, "Rural Felicity," 1976, 23). In 1783, the conclusion of the American Revolutionary War (and also at the conclusion of the second war with England during the War of 1812) was celebrated by a "Peace Ball" in most of the major cities (Cole, "The Puritan and Fair Terpsichore," 1942, 19).

After the revolution, the United States needed to establish itself as an independent country and also sought to shed the provincial colonial status in the eyes of the world. Washington, therefore, continued the European refined cultural etiquette and manners, especially as applied in the ballroom. On May 7, 1789, the

This image titled "First in Peace" depicts George Washington leading a lady in the Minuet. During Washington's presidency he traveled throughout the entire 13 colonies, and in all instances he was greeted warmly and honored by a formal dance in his honor.   Picture Collection, The Branch Libraries, The New York Public Library, Astor, Lenox, and Tilden Foundations. Picture Collection ID: 815078.

New York Assembly, located on Broadway near Wall Street, held the first Inaugural Ball in honor of the presidency of George Washington. The formal dance followed the traditional pattern of opening with a Minuet, followed by other French dances, and finally Country-dances. Washington, of course, was given the honor of the first dance. The Official History of the White House maintained, "Washington enjoyed the theater and liked to dance, especially the minuet, which he danced with great pleasure at his inaugural ball." On May 27, 1789, about one month after the inauguration, Washington's wife, Martha, arrived in New York. On November 25 of that same year, he wrote in his journal that both he and Martha attended the New York Assembly ball ("White House History," n.d.; Wharton 1893, 80–88).

In the following years, from 1789 to 1791, both George and Martha Washington traveled throughout the entire 13 colonies. In all instances, they were greeted warmly and honored by a dance in his honor. And in all instances he was given the honor of selecting a noted society lady to open the first dance, which in all cases was the Minuet. However, no records exist of Martha Washington ever dancing in public, with or without her husband.

In the fall of 1789, Washington attended assembly balls in both Salem and Boston, Massachusetts. In early November 1789, he attended another Assembly ball in Portsmouth, New Hampshire, sponsored by Colonel John Langdon. In his journal, Washington described his Portsmouth visit as follows:

> About 2 O'clock I recd. [received] an Address from the Executive of the State of New Hampshire; and in half an hour after dined with them and a large Company at their Assembly room which is one of the best I have seen any where in the United States. At half after Seven [p.m.], I went to the Assembly where there were about 75 well dressed, and many of them very handsome Ladies—among whom (as was also the case at the Salem & Boston Assemblies) were a greater proportion with much blacker hair than are usually seen in the Southern States. About 9 [p.m.] I returned to my Quarters (Jackson and Twohig, Vol. 5, 1979, 490).

In 1790, Washington visited the city of Hartford, Connecticut, and attended the first in a series of Assembly balls that were held every two weeks for a ten-week winter season. (The Hartford Assembly continued annually until stopped by another war with England in 1813.) In December 1790, both he and Martha attended the Philadelphia Dance Assembly (see later in this chapter). In April and May of 1791, they traveled to the southern colonies, stopping to attend dances in his honor at Charleston, South Carolina; New Bern, North Carolina; and Savannah, Georgia, to name a few. Although Washington danced on each occasion, Martha did not (Keller and Hendrickson 1998, 91–93).

In Savannah, Georgia, for example, the evening dance was held in the Long Room of the Filature, a public assembly hall in Reynolds Square. A newspaper account wrote that Washington arrived at 8:30 P.M. The account of the arrival noted the following:

> [Washington] was personally introduced to 96 ladies, who were elegantly dressed, some of whom displayed infinite taste in the emblems and devices on their sashes and head dresses, out of respect to the happy occasion. The room, which had been lately

handsomely fitted up, and was well lighted, afforded the President an excellent opportunity of viewing the fair sex of our city and vicinity, and the ladies the gratification of paying their respects to our Federal Chief. After a few minuets were moved, and one country-dance led down, the President and his suite retired about 11 o'clock. At 12 o'clock the supper room was opened, and the ladies partook of a repast, after which dances continued until 3 [a.m.] o'clock (*Dunlap's American Daily Adv.* [Philadelphia], 31 May 1791, in Jackson and Twohig, Vol. 6, 1979, 138).

Washington continued his travels, attending more Assembly balls along the way.

In 1796, Washington retired from the presidency after serving two consecutive four-year terms. (His voluntary resignation after two terms set a tradition among future two-term presidents until Franklin D. Roosevelt broke with the tradition in 1940. Shortly thereafter, a Constitutional amendment was added to make Washington's "tradition" of a two-term presidency maximum.) However, Washington's dancing days were not over.

In 1798, Nelly Custis (grandchild to Martha and George Washington) wrote of a ball that she had attended with her grandparents in Alexandria, Virginia, in celebration of Washington's birthday. Custis told her friend, "The room was

A PRESIDENTIAL RECEPTION IN 1789.
BY GENERAL AND MRS. WASHINGTON.

After his inauguration as first president of the United States of America on May 7, 1789, both George and Martha Washington traveled throughout the entire 13 colonies. In all instances, they were greeted warmly and honored by a dance in his honor. However, no records exist of Martha Washington ever dancing in public, with or without her husband. This illustration titled "A presidential reception in 1789" was issued by Currier & Ives, c. 1876. Library of Congress, Prints and Photographs LC-USZ62-2262.

MOUNT VERNON, Va., November 12, 1799.
GENTLEMEN : Mrs. Washington and myself have been honored by your polite invitation to the assemblies in Alexandria this winter and thank you for this mark of attention. But, alas, our dancing days are over. We wish, however, all those who relish so innocent and agreeable an amusement all the pleasure the season will afford them.
I am, gentlemen, your most obedient and obliged Humble servant, GEORGE WASHINGTON

As it appeared on April 11, 1857, in the *New York Ledger*, p. 1

crowded, there were twenty five or thirty couples in the first two setts." The following day she attended another "charming dance" arranged by a Mrs. Potts. Nelly claimed that she "danced twenty four dances, setts, cotillions, reels, [and] sung twelve songs" (Keller and Hendrickson 1998, 16).

In 1799, one of the last correspondences from Washington was in regards to declining an invitation to an Assembly ball in Alexandria, Virginia. At the time, although Washington and his wife Martha were close by in Mount Vernon, his declining health precluded their attendance. The letter appeared in his journals and was republished in April 11, 1857, in the *New York Ledger* newspaper, which offered its readers "the views of the Father of his Country on dancing." Washington died about a month later.

Shortly after Washington's death, on December 30, 1799, the *Connecticut Courant* noted a special request at the upcoming Hartford Assembly Ball in Hartford, Connecticut. In honor of Washington, they asked that the "ladies dress in white trimmed in black, and the Gentlemen wear a crape on the arm for the evening." Also a long-standing tradition in the United States was a national holiday in celebration of Washington's birthday. Long after Washington's death throughout the nineteenth century, his birthday marked a grand celebration and was usually honored with a dance (Marks 1957, 62).

AMERICAN COUNTRY-DANCES, THE VIRGINIA REEL, AND "AN ANALYSIS OF COUNTRY DANCING"

The death of George Washington also signified the end of the American Colonial Minuet. By that same time in Europe, the Minuet was already out of favor. In Europe by about 1770, the Minuet was slowly replaced by dances such as the Waltz (see later in this chapter). In 1789, the Minuet ended abruptly with the French Revolution. The overthrow of the French monarchy by the "bourgeois" or middle class eliminated all that was associated with the Royal Court. The dances were replaced by Contredanses and later also the Waltz.

The Minuet was also viewed as a thing of the past and not progressive. Voltaire, one of the leading philosophers of the Enlightenment, for example, compared the Minuet to the metaphysical philosophers ("the philosophical study of the ultimate causes and underlining nature of things" dictionary definition). He claimed that similar to the Minuet dancers, the metaphysical philosophers "who most elegantly adorned, bow a few times, mince daintily across the room exhibiting all their charms, move without progressing a single step, and end up on the very spot whence they started" (quoted in Sachs 1963, 407).

Although the Colonists succeeded in their separation from England, their Revolution, it should be noted, was one of political discourse and not a cultural revolution. At the time, the dances were still those that were danced in Europe, and Americans continued to follow European cultural traditions. During the time of American independence, the dances in the English Colonies were mostly based on the English Country-dance tradition (see Chapter 1). After 1800, the urban areas started to distinguish themselves as progressing from the provincial towns into burgeoning cities. The dancing in the cities was also refined in the English and French traditions with ballroom rules of behavior and etiquette. Within the countryside and rural towns the "true country dance" remained virtually unchanged, although, in general, it was sometimes simply known as a "junket" or a "barn dance" and included the English Country-dances such as the Virginia Reel and Arkansas Traveler (Nevell 1977, 39).

In August of 1774, the *New Hampshire Gazette* published a front-page editorial on the practice of English Country-dancing in the colonies. The editors obviously approved, as they wrote the following:

> Country Dances are very simple and agreeable and possess the Mind of Youth with pleasing and sprightly Ideas. The advantage of Dancing adds to every Motion of the Body a certain attractive Grace which never can be sufficiently admired, gives a free and open Air on the Gait; a happy Address in Company and adds the finishing Embellishments in the sexes, to every species of polite education (Page 1977, 29).

Shortly thereafter, during the Revolution some of the dances acquired names such as "Jefferson and Liberty," "The Green Mountain Volunteers," "The Washington Quickstep," and "A Successful Campaign," among many others.

In 1793, what is probably the earliest description of "A Successful Campaign" was published in *Asa Willcox's Book of Figures*. Willcox provided a simple description as follows:

> Cast down two Couple, lead up two Couple, cast Down one. 2nd couple do the Same, turn contrary partners half round, four hands round. Cross over one Couple, right and left at top (4).

Willcox also listed 39 different Country-dances with names such as "Poor Soldier," "Young Widow," "Soldiers Joy," and "Hay Maker." Some of the other popular Country-dances in the American colonies included, "Pea Straw," "Boston's Delight," "Stony Point," and "I'll be Married in my Old Clothes." At the time many of the American Country-dances were written down in journals, diaries, and commonplace books. Some, such as *Asa Willcox's Book of Figures*, were published by the author and received a fair amount of distribution (Page 1977, 28).

The most common of all the American Country-dances was the Virginia Reel. In its basic form, it was danced in the American colonies from the very early part of the eighteenth century through the nineteenth century. It was also kept alive in the Appalachian mountain regions of the United States and danced through the twentieth century. As late as 1878, *Dick's Quadrille Call-Book and Ball-Room Prompter*, for example, reminded its readers that "The Virginia Reel is the same lively dance that is known in England by the name of 'Sir Roger de Coverly'" (104). The Roger de Coverly was an English Country-dance that was popular in England and listed in early seventeenth century publications of John Playford's *The Dancing-Master* (see Chapter 1).

The Virginia Reel was danced to just about any music in 2/4 time and was arranged in a Longways set of three or four couples. *Dick's Quadrille Call-Book and Ball-Room Prompter*, for example, described the set as

> The couples form in two lines down the middle of the room, all the gentlemen on one side, and all the ladies on the other, partners facing each other...each couple in turn becomes top couple and bottom couple at least once during the progress of the dance (104).

The publication, which was reissued numerous times between 1878 and 1895, reminded the dancers that the steps of the Virginia Reel began "commencing with the music" (104). One or two instruments such as a fiddle and banjo provided most of the musical accompaniment. The dancers in the Virginia Reel benefited when a "caller" reminded them what steps to perform at what time to accompany the music.

An example of the basic "Directions for Calling" the Virginia Reel was in addition to the quick reference guide, and the called steps were explained as follows:

> The "*Forward and Back*" involved both the first gentleman and the last lady taking four steps towards each other and four steps back to their original position to eight beats of music.

THE VIRGINIA REEL.

DIRECTIONS FOR CALLING.

First Gentleman:	And Last Lady, Forward and back .	4 bars.
First Lady:	And Last Gentleman, the same . .	4
First Gentleman:	And Last Lady, Swing Right Hands.	4
First Lady:	And Last Gentleman, the same .	4
First Gentleman:	And Last Lady, Swing Left Hands .	4
First Lady:	And Last Gentleman, the same .	4
First Gentleman:	And Last Lady, Swing Both Hands .	4
First Lady:	And Last Gentleman, the same. .	4
First Gentleman:	And Last lady Dos-à-Dos. . .	4
First Lady:	And Last Gentleman, the same. .	4
First Couple:	Turn Right Hands. . . .	2
	Separate and Turn Second couple, Left Hands . . .	2
	Turn Right Hands . . .	2
	Separate and Turn Third Couple, Left Hands . . .	2
	And so on to bottom.	
	Join Hands and back to Places at Top.	
All:	Gentlemen to Left, Ladies to Right, March Down Outside, and Up the Middle.	
Head Couple:	Down the Middle to Bottom.	

Excerpt from: *Dick's Quadrille Call-Book and Ball-Room Prompter*. New York: Behrens Publishing Company, 1878-95, pp. 104-105.

The "*Swing Right Hands*" was performed by a gentleman and a lady meeting face-to-face joining right hands and swinging half round and back to their original position to eight beats of music.

The "*Swing Left Hands*" and the "*Swing Both Hands*" was performed in the same manner as the "*Swing Right Hands*" only with the respective joining of left hands or holding both hands as the call required.

The "*Dos-à-Dos*" had a gentleman and a lady move to the middle and pass each other on their right side. They each side-stepped to the right back-to-back and passed backwards on each others left side without turning and back to their original position to eight beats of music.

The "*Turn Right Hands*" was performed by the gentleman and his partner as they joined right hands made a complete turn and back to their original position to four beats of music.

The "*Separate and Turn Second couple Left Hands*" The first gentleman joined left hands with the second lady and "swings her half round." The lady then joined left hands with the second gentleman who then "swings her half round" and back to their original position to four beats of music.

As the "head couple" (or first couple) reached the bottom they "Join Hands and back to Places at Top," whereas they join hands in a face-to-face position and chassés sideways up through the middle of the set back to their original start position at the top of the set. At that point, a processional march of the entire set began. At the same time, the Gentlemen to the left and the Ladies to the right, marched in line down to the outside of the set and moved up the middle of the set. The first couple marched down the middle of the set and took their places at the bottom of the set. The former second couple assumed the new first couple position, and the entire sequence of forward and back, swings, turns, and dos-à-dos was repeated and followed by a march to change positions. The sequence was continually repeated until all the couples in the set had their turn as the first couple. In some cases, instead of the march the first couple substituted joining their hands in raised arms forming an arch for the other couples in the set to pass under during their march. This in turn left them at the bottom of the set and ready for the sequence to begin again.

In 1868, *Hillgrove's Ballroom Guide* provided another alternative to the processional march as it was danced during the American Civil War. Thomas Hillgrove suggested the following:

> Then the head couple join right hands and turn once and a half round; the head lady then turns with the left hand every gentleman down the line, alternately turning her partner with the right hand; while the gentleman turns every lady with his left hand, alternately turning his partner with the right; when they arrive at the bottom they turn partners and pass up inside to the head again, and then separate, the lady turning to the right and passing down on the outside of the ladies' line, and the gentleman turning to the left and passing down on the outside of the gentlemen, and all follow, meeting their partners at the foot, and return up on the inside to places; the first couple then join hands, chassez followed by the bottom lady and top gentleman...down the middle, and take their position below the last couple. Then the figure commences with a new couple at the head.

Hillgrove reminded the dancers that the musicians played continuously "until each couple has gone entirely through the dance, and the first couple has arrived back to their own places at the head." Upon completion of each of the couples having its turn to dance the Virginia Reel, Hillgrove suggested an added special touch of ballroom etiquette. He suggested that the musicians continue playing as all the couples in unison "all chassez, all forward and back, bow and courtesy, and see their ladies back to their seats" (Hillgrove 1868, 225–226).

Americans, however, danced more than just the Virginia Reel. In fact, they continued dancing all sorts of Country-dances, many of them derived from England. In 1825, Thomas Wilson, in *Analysis of the London Ballroom*, for example, described them as follows:

> Country-Dances are the most popular, the oldest, and as capable of almost unlimited variety the best style of Dancing that the English Ball-Room presents.... The general characteristic of this style of Dancing is simplicity, ease, freedom, and liveliness, rather inclining to the mirthful than the graceful, and to cheerfulness than elegance (Wilson 1825, 67–68).

Thomas Wilson was a London Dance Master whose books, although published in England, were common in America. From the early 1800s to about 1850, his dance instruction manuals encouraged the dancer to learn how to dance "without the aid of a master." Wilson's catalog of at least 15 dance instruction books included *An Analysis of Country Dancing* (1808), *Treasures of Terpsichore* (1809), *The Complete System of English Country Dancing* (1815), *A Description of the Correct Method of Waltzing* (1816), *A Companion to the Ball Room* (1816), *The Quadrille and Cotillion Panorama* (1818), *Quadrille Fan* (1820), and *Analysis of the London Ballroom* (1825).

Wilson's publication *An Analysis of Country Dancing* (1808), in particular, was quite successful and was reissued in 1811, 1815, and 1822. Each successive issue was expanded to include additional information such as descriptive text and helpful illustrations as it applied to English Country-dancing. Typical of the day, the titles were long and descriptive. The complete descriptive title of *An Analysis of Country Dancing* (1808), for example, read as follows:

> *An Analysis of Country Dancing: wherein are displayed All The Figures ever used in Country Dances, In a Way so Easy and Familiar, that Persons of the meanest Capacity may in a short Time acquire (without the aid of a master) A complete Knowledge of that Rational and Polite Amusement. To which are added, Instructions for Dancing some entire New Reels; together with the rules, regulations, and Complete Etiquette of the Ball Room.*

Wilson did not necessarily restrict himself to just an analysis of Country-dancing. In fact, his long list of publications attest to his diverse expertise of dance style. As a prelude to the first edition, Wilson expressed his own admiration for dancing in general. He wrote,

> Dancing is the most enchanting of all human amusements, it is the parent of joy, and the soul and support of cheerfulness; it banishes grief, cheers the evening hours of those who have studied or laboured [sic] in the day, and brings with it a mixture of delightful sensations which enrapture the sense (1808, vi–x).

For the most part, his dance instruction manuals were specific to a particular dance style; however, he maintained a consistency for the overall etiquette as it applied to dance in general.

Some of the "rules, regulations, and complete etiquette of the ballroom" noted by Wilson were actually quite similar to the rules set by Beau Nash at Bath (see Chapter 1). In addition, it was quite apparent that the standard formal organization of dances of opening with a Minuet and concluding with a series of English Country-dances was still the same. For example, Wilson maintained:

Every lady upon entering the ball room must be presented by the Master of the Ceremonies with a ticket...

Any Lady or Gentleman wishing to dance a Minuet must, as soon as they enter the room, make known their intentions to the Master of the Ceremonies...

No Gentlemen must enter the ball room with whole or half boots on, or with canes or sticks in their hands; nor are pantaloons [trousers] considered a proper dress for the assembly room (1808, 134–135).

For the series of English Country-dancing, he reminded the participants of the standard etiquette. Some of the basic suggestions included the following:

When Country Dancing has commenced, and the top couple have gone down three couple[s], the next couple must go off...

When every couple have gone down the dance, and the couple who called it have regained the top and gone down three couple[s], the dance is finished; for the next dance they stand at the bottom...

It is a great breach of good manners for any couple to leave a dance before it is finished...

As soon as a dance is finished the Master of the Ceremonies should make a signal to the leader of the band, to prevent any clapping of hands or unnecessary noise...

No Ladies or Gentlemen must during a Country-dance, attempt to dance Reels or other figures in any part of the room (Wilson 1808, 135–138).

Wilson's "rules, regulations, and complete etiquette of the ballroom" would be applied almost word-for-word in the ballrooms not only throughout London, but also among almost all of the formal Assembly balls in the American colonies (see later in this chapter).

In 1811, Wilson's *An Analysis of Country Dancing* (1808) was revised and reissued under the descriptive title of

An Analysis of Country Dancing, wherein all the figures used in that polite amusement are rendered familiar by engraved lines. Containing also, directions for composing almost any number of figures to one tune, with some entire new reels; together with the complete etiquette of the ball-room. By T. Wilson...Illustrated with engravings on wood by J. Berryman.

This particular edition provided additional descriptive text as well as charts and "color-coded diagrams" to explain the geometrical figures for the various English Country-dances.

In 1815, *An Analysis of Country Dancing* was revised and released under the title:

The Complete System of English Country Dancing, containing All The Figures Ever Used in English Country Dancing, with a variety of New Figures, and New Reels, composed expressly by the author, and elucidated by means of Diagrams. Also Scientific Instructions for the Composing of Country Dances, An Etiquette of the Ball Room. A description of the Various Times, Measures and Styles Of Country Dance Music; together with A Dissertation, comparing the ancient and original wit the present state and style of English Country Dancing, Professors of Dancing, Dancing Masters, and Dancing Rooms. By Thomas Wilson, Teacher of Dancing.

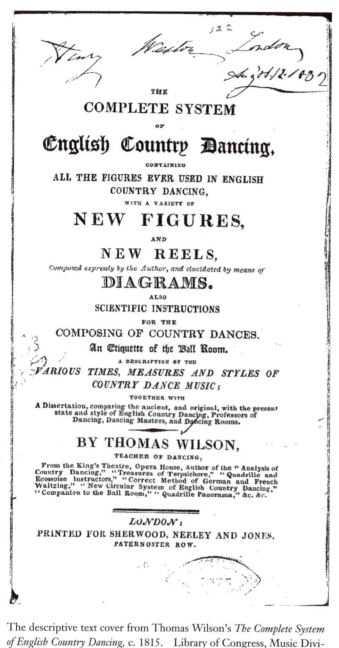

The descriptive text cover from Thomas Wilson's *The Complete System of English Country Dancing*, c. 1815. Library of Congress, Music Division, http://memory.loc.gov/musdi/168/0002.gif.

In 1822, the manual was reissued basically unchanged from the 1811 edition. Wilson's successive editions provided specific in-depth analysis as it applied to English Country-dancing, which he termed "the national Dance of the English." Some of the descriptive text, for example, included the numerous combinations of steps, figures, and positions, as well as how to set up a Longways set.

But Wilson cautioned that Country-dancing was not "a simple, trifling art." He explained that at first glance the figures might "appear paradoxical," they could be "very easily attained" by a person new to English Country-dancing upon learning some of the basic principles. He claimed that the precision figures based on "mathematical and other scientific principles" were merely "self-evident truths" that could easily be demonstrated and explained either by an experienced dancer or by reading the illustrated instructions in any of his dance manuals (3). However, he cautioned that since there were so many different dances and figures, complete knowledge of the system was not easily attainable. In fact, some of the numerous variations that could confuse the beginner included:

- An English Country Dance may be composed either of three couples or one hundred, and have its parts equally complete in both.
- A Dance may be set with either two, or twenty Figures.
- A Dance may be selected so as to afford Dancing only to the leading couples to the same music.
- A Dance may be set so as to actively employ [everyone].
- A Dance may be rendered either very easy or very difficult, though performed to the same music.

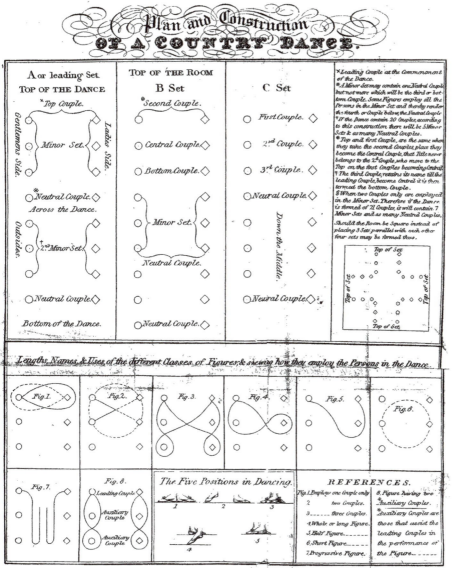

An illustrated chart for the "Plan and Construction of a Country Dance" showing some of the many sets and geometric patterns, from Thomas Wilson's *The Complete System of English Country Dancing*, c. 1822. Library of Congress, Music Division, http://memory.loc.gov/musdi/168/0001.gif.

- A Dance may be selected, that requires a variety of different Steps; and One may be chosen, that may be danced with the greatest propriety with only one Step, and require no more.
- A Dance may be formed, that will require an hour for its performance; and one may be formed to the same music, that may be completed in five minutes.

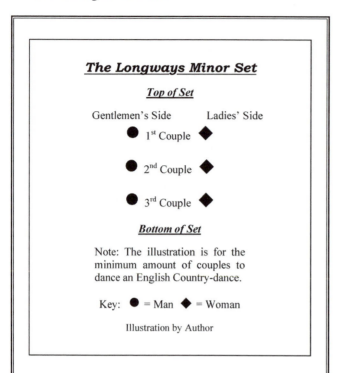

The Longways Minor Set

Top of Set

Gentlemen's Side   Ladies' Side

● 1ˢᵗ Couple ◆

● 2ⁿᵈ Couple ◆

● 3ʳᵈ Couple ◆

Bottom of Set

Note: The illustration is for the minimum amount of couples to dance an English Country-dance.

Key: ● = Man ◆ = Woman

Illustration by Author

Wilson described that the Longways set can be "formed of an indefinite number of Ladies and Gentlemen." However, a minor set of only "six persons [is] sufficient to perform any of the Figures in the System of English Country Dancing." He described the Longways Minor set as follows:

> The Ladies and Gentlemen are placed in two rows or lines parallel with each other; the one consisting of Ladies, which is called the Ladies' side; and the other of Gentlemen, which is called the Gentlemen's side: every Lady is opposite a Gentleman, who are called partners. The couples being so placed, form what is termed "a Set," and are denominated by different technical appellations, according to their situations, or the manner in which they are employed in the Dance (2).

The "System" of English Country-dancing and the Longways set, as described by Wilson, was basically the same as outlined in the numerous editions of John Playford's *The Dancing Master* published between 1651 and 1728 (see Chapter 1).

- A Dance may be set so very easy, that its Figures may be performed by a person never having before attempted; or Set so difficult and complex, as to require all, the skill of a good Dancer.
- A Dance may be wholly composed of circular movement, or of straight lines.

Wilson indicated that many more examples existed "but the foregoing is deemed quite sufficient to shew [sic], that a knowledge of Country Dancing is not so easily attainable." The basic outline was presented even before the description of the steps, which Wilson suggested required a sufficient amount of practice (Wilson 1815, 3–8).

Wilson did offer many examples of the basic steps within the particular figures that were simply explained and were informative. The individual figures were diagrammed mainly for three couples in a Longways Minor set with a "circle" denoting the Gentleman and a "diamond" representing the Lady. The first couple were marked as the "Lady at A, and the Gentleman at B" with various other letters of the alphabet corresponding with his descriptive text. For example, he described the figure for a "Cast Off Two Couple" as follows:

> The Lady at A, and Gentleman at B, move at the same time, the Lady from A to C, and the Gentleman from B to D; they then return to their situations, as shewn [sic] (1808, 8).

Another basic figure, the "Turn Corners," was described in similar fashion as follows:

> The Lady at A, and Gentleman at B, pass each other at C, the Lady moves to D, and the Gentleman to E (1808, 28).

Although reference letters are given as well as directional lines, he also provided some explanatory notes and helpful references. For example, Wilson offered an easy explanation of the difference between the call of "Turn your partner," as opposed to "Swing round your partner." He explained, "The only difference between swinging and turning is that swinging is always performed with one [hand], and turning with both hands…it is a general rule in all turning in Country Dancing, to turn to the left…in returning, you of course turn to the right" (1815, 9–10).

One of the basic figures was a "Lead down the middle," in that the first couple, "Lady and Gentleman," joined hands at the middle and moved down the set in the same direction, taking the place of the bottom third couple. The bottom couple each "Cast Off" on the outside of the set and take the place as the first couple. However, with that basic figure Wilson cautioned,

An illustration of three American couples performing a Country-dance in the Longways Minor set, c. 1820.   The Granger Collection, New York, ID: 0048338.

It is a common practice with bad Dancers, and those unacquainted with the true system of English Country Dancing to gallop, or run down a dozen couple, instead of dancing and keeping this Figure within the compass of three couples, and thereby make it a long Figure instead of a short one, and take for its performance eight bars of music instead of four (1815, 29–30).

After the American Revolution the colonies were still about equally divided in their opinions of the British; however, both during and after the War of 1812, anti-British feelings were rampant throughout America. In many cases, especially in the cities, Americans refused to dance the English Country-dances. Most danced the French Cotillions and Quadrilles. In New England, the anti-British sentiment, as it applied to dancing, was not as evident as many of the people continued with the English Country-dances. Although the anti-British sentiment was based mainly on political oppression, the dance instruction manuals praised English dancing. By about 1825, the English Country-dances fell out of favor in the urban areas and were replaced by the Waltz and Polka. In the rural areas and the countryside, they continued through the American Civil War (see Chapter 3) and eventually developed into Square Dances and Ninepin Reels (see Chapter 4).

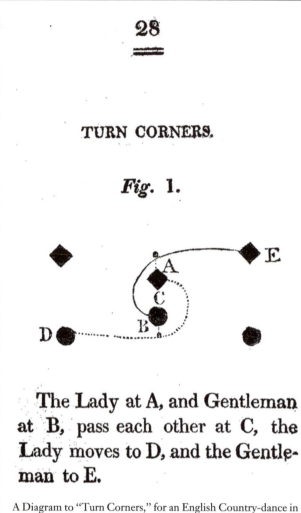

28

TURN CORNERS.

Fig. 1.

The Lady at A, and Gentleman at B, pass each other at C, the Lady moves to D, and the Gentleman to E.

A Diagram to "Turn Corners," for an English Country-dance in the Longways Minor set. The illustration is from Thomas Wilson's *An Analysis of Country Dancing*, c. 1808. Library of Congress, Music Division, http://memory.loc.gov/musdi/170/0072.gif.

THE "IRISH-SCOTCH" JIG, THE RIGAUDON, THE HORNPIPE, THE BREAKDOWN, AND CLOGGING

At the time that the English Country-dances were adapted in the American style, they were also adapted in some solo variations that developed into the Jig, the Breakdown, and the Hornpipe. To the average individual, however, the Hornpipe, the Breakdown, and the Jig were almost indistinguishable. Therefore, in many contemporary accounts they were often confused, and sometimes the word "Jig" was used universally to describe any solo dance.

All-in-all, the Jig was often described as a "lively folk dance" most often attributed to Ireland from as early as the sixteenth or seventeenth century and, therefore, was sometimes known as the "Irish Jig." However, it also maintained a strong folk tradition in Scotland and the English countryside. Some contemporary accounts attributed the name as a "Scotch Jig." In fact, William Shakespeare in his play *Much Ado About Nothing* described one element as "hot and hasty, like a Scotch jig, and full as fantastical" (Act II, Scene I).

Some accounts placed the origin of the Jig with the Royal Court of Queen Elizabeth I in England (see Chapter 1). Although the Jig was also accepted at the Royal Court of King Louis XIV, it is most likely that it was danced among the peasants in the countryside and was

refined for the Royal Courts. In the case of the Jig in France, it was known as "the gigue" and was a subdued dance for couples. ("*Gigue*" was an Old French word that meant "to dance"). In 1700, an account in Raoul-Auger Feuillet's *Chorégraphie* (Feuillet was a Dance Master for Louis XIV—see Chapter 1) recorded a dance called the *gigue á deux*. Dance historian Curt Sachs surmised that, although the addition of the word *á deux* indicated that it was a couple dance, it might have also inferred that it was different from the commonly known *gigue* as a solo dance. Therefore, Feuillet's description might have differentiated the "gigue" as a couple's dance preferred in the Royal Court and a solo dance everywhere else (Sachs 1963, 410).

There were also some other "Jig" references that were earlier than Feuillet's. Dance manuals titled *Irish Hayes, Jiggs and Roundelays*, in 1589, and *Country Measures, Rounds, and Jiggs*, in 1603, both indicated "jig type" dances in the English Country-dance style in a round dance formation. Although the manuals noted that the dances were performed to "jig" music, they might not necessarily be related to the solo Irish Jig since it was common practice of the day to call many of the Country-dances a "jigg." However, a couple dance in Italy known as the *giga* that continued through the twentieth century was definitely "very different" from the Irish Jig and did not necessarily have any influence upon American social dance (Sachs 1963, 410–411).

A concise explanation offered by dance historian Curt Sachs, therefore, can be offered as the most plausible definition. Sachs explained:

> As a matter of fact the true *jig* of the Scots and Irish is not bound to any definite form. Danced by one or more persons, it is quick and fiery...The Scot does not dance with the "insipid formal movements" of the French and English...the *jig* calls for a lively stamping of the heels and rapid foot work with a quiet torso—in which it resembles the other Scottish dances (Sachs 1963, 411).

During the mid to late eighteenth century, a new wave of Scottish and Irish immigrants settled in America. Unlike the first American colonial settlers, the new settlers did not necessarily emigrate to search for religious freedom or to join a particular community such as the Puritans, Shakers, or Quakers. Most of the new settlers were not from European cities, but rather the countryside. In turn, those Scottish and Irish immigrants who came from similar rural and highland areas settled in similar regions of America ranging from the northeast highland areas of New Hampshire and Vermont, down through the Appalachian Mountain regions to the south such as Kentucky, West Virginia, Virginia, North Carolina, and Tennessee. They also brought with them to America the same rural traditions of folklore and traditional dancing styles, such as the Country-dances and the Jig (Nevell 1977, 40).

The rural areas that were far from the urban cities did not necessarily benefit from either a traveling Dance Master or from a local dancing school. In cases where either might have been available, formal dance instruction was certainly beyond the affordable means of the poorer white settlers, mountain folk, and African American slaves. Therefore, many of the dances were learned by observation and passed on by one dancer to the other. In most cases, the dances were learned within a community by family members or neighbors (Nevell 1977, 33–34).

Most of the American colonists in the rural areas learned the dances from watching their parents and growing up watching them at barn dances. Many of the dances were actually held in the barn, which in many cases was recently built with the help of neighbors and the community—which many have speculated was the actual definition of a "barn dance." Sometimes dances were held indoors in the kitchen where all furniture was removed, and they were known as "kitchen rackets" (Nevell 1977, 38).

In 1829, a contemporary account by a visitor in rural Tyler County, Virginia, expressed his amazement at witnessing "five generations of the same family dancing." He wrote, "the father, the grandfather, and the great grandfather; the daughter, mother, and grandmother; the son, and great grandson, all in a dance on the same floor at the same time" (quoted in Needham 2002, 56).

In the case of the Jig, however, usually very little dance instruction was required. Therefore, many variations and improvisations were applied. Historian Bruce C. Daniels in *Puritans at Play: Leisure and Recreation in Colonial New England* (1995), for example, noted the prevalence of Jig dancing in the New England area. He described the Jig as follows:

> Usually done solo, jigs were aggressive dances associated with drunken sailors trying to outdo each other in boastful competition. Always regarded as unsavory by New Englanders, at their least jigs engendered vanity and excessive pride; at their worst they provoked fights and brawls. When men started dancing dueling jigs it was usually a sign that a wedding reception, dance, or waterfront party had gotten out of control (115).

In almost all cases, since the solo Jigs were also commonly danced among the poorer classes, and not at the formal Assembly balls, they were usually deemed as "unsavory" by society. The instruments that accompanied the solo dances were usually a fiddle, a flute, or even a banjo. In some cases, the dancer made his own musical accompaniment by the sound of his own feet.

Another "one of the liveliest dances" that was similar to the Jig was the Rigaudon (sometimes "Rigadoon"). Like many folk-type dances, the historical origin of the Rigaudon is hard to trace. Some sources claimed that the dance was of French origin and named after an inventor named Rigaud. The word might also be derived from the Italian word *rigodone* or *rigolone*. In 1728, one of the earliest descriptions was by Italian Dance Master Giovanni Battista Dufort in his dance treatise *Trattato del Ballo Nobile*. Dufort described the Rigaudon simply as "a changing step plus a leap." Dance historian Curt Sachs seemed to agree with the Italian origin. He suggested that the dance was named as a derivative of the Italian word *rigoletto* which means "circle dance." However, Sachs described the Rigaudon as a solo dance as follows:

> A light dance in duple time and is executed in one spot. Staring with the first position [of the feet] the dancer bends the knee, leaps up, and in so doing thrusts first the right and then the left leg out from the hip. Then comes another *plié*, a leap, and return to the first position.

Other variations were noted in the nineteenth century, and also during the late twentieth century in some isolated regions of France, such as Dauphiné, the Cévennes, and Massif Central, the Rigaudon was actually danced as a turning couples dance. Sachs speculated that the "contradiction is probably explained by the fact that the term *Rigaudon* is not exclusive…[it] is a collective name for the folk dances of southeastern France." In the American colonies, the Rigaudon was learned in similar fashion as the Jig; therefore, many variations also existed. Therefore, very few written accounts of the step descriptions were available. In many cases the Rigaudon, the Jig, and the Hornpipe were danced as part of a theatrical stage show (Sachs 1963, 411–413).

The Hornpipe was another solo type with origins in England, Wales, Scotland, and Ireland. The dance itself was actually named after a medieval musical instrument the *hornpipe*. It was a reed wind-type instrument similar to a flute or sometimes it was two parallel reeds. Sometimes a cow bell or an inflated bag was attached. In some cases specific musical arrangements and Country-dances were also called "hornpipes" ("Hornpipe," n.d.).

The Hornpipe dance contained intricate footwork (with very little written instruction) and was danced to a variety of musical rhythms in 3/2, 6/8, and 2/4 time. In America, it was made famous by John Durang, who has the distinction of being America's first professional stage dancer. As a result, just as Durang's stage dancing, it was modified to the individual skill of the dancer and the steps were adjusted accordingly to fit the various rhythms. Durang, in his memoirs, offered a very brief description of the Hornpipe. He simply stated, "I learned the correct stile of dancing a hornpipe in the French stile, an allemande, and [added] steps for a country dance" (Durang 2002, 140; Needham 2002, 2).

After 1788, one of the better known "Hornpipes" in America was actually a Country-dance devised by John Griffith (sometimes Griffiths) named "Fisher's Hornpipe." Griffith was a Dance Master (see later in this chapter) in New England that published possibly the earliest American collection of dances. Fisher's Hornpipe was most likely done in a Longways Minor set for four couples. Griffith's original text for the dance was as follows:

> Cast off back-up again-lead down the Middle-up again and cast off one Co.-Hands cross at Bottom-Halfway-back again-right and left at Top.

Other variations done at the time of the Hornpipe were the Pigeon Wing and Buck Dancing, and sometimes they were combined and known as the "Buck and Wing."

John Durang's memoir from about 1800 provided an early contemporary description of the Pigeon Wing. He stated that it was "executed in part by jumping up and striking the legs together." As a dance, Durang thought the Pigeon Wing was quite difficult to master and also not easy for another person to explain. He wrote that it "was the only difficulty I had to encounter...nor I never met a dancer since that could show it to me." However, Durang claimed that he uncovered "the mystery" of the Pigeon Wing one night "in bed." He said, "I dream'd [sic] that I was a ball and did the pigeon wing to admiration to the whole company" (Durang 2002, 140).

Durang also performed another solo-type dance named Buck Dancing. A description of Buck Dancing in *Dance a While: Handbook for Folk, Square, Contra, and Social Dance* (2000) noted that "the feet remain very close to the floor. With the exception of the legs, little body movement is used." As with the other dances of its time, simple musical accompaniment was usually just a fiddle or sometimes just the sound of the feet stomping during the dance. All of the solo dances might have also incorporated steps from the Native America Indians and African American slaves (Harris et al., 2000, 88).

In the case of the solo dances in America it appears that the dances done by rural whites also influenced the African American slaves and Free Blacks. African American slaves learned the Irish Jig from watching white dancers, and in all likelihood white Jig dancers also borrowed elements from the African American dance known as the Breakdown. Historians Edwin G. Burrows and Mike Wallace provided a description of the Breakdown in their exhaustive research work *Gotham: A History of New York City to 1898* (1999). They described the dance as "performed on a springy board, with percussive accompaniment made by beating hands on sides of legs, followed by the taking up of a collection from bystanders" (403).

Between 1740 and 1804, many accounts in New York City cited interracial mingling and dancing among poor whites and blacks. The interaction of the races usually occurred in "bawdy" taverns that were also known as "Negro dancing cellars." The places often included alcohol, dancing, and in many cases prostitution. Most of the Negro dancing cellars were located in the lower east side of Manhattan in the notorious area known as the Five Points. Some of the places had names such as Mrs. Cunningham's or Dicken's Dance House and some did not. One unnamed Negro dancing cellar was located on Bancker Street. In 1804, a white sailor named Horace Lane described it as a

> small room, well filled with human beings of both sexes...[with] a big darkie in one corner sweating, and sawing away on a violin....To increase vigour, and elate the spirit of fun, there stood by his side a tall swarthy female who was rattling and flourishing a tambourine with uncommon skill and dexterity.

Lane noted that in response to the music he also observed people dancing. He described their dancing as "Jumping about, twisting and screwing their joints and ankles as if to scour the floor with their feet" (quoted in Burrows and Wallace 1998, 403).

During the late 1700s and early 1800s, both slaves and freed blacks also danced in celebration of holidays—most often in public areas. In contrast to the formal balls and public dance halls for whites, urban African Americans and poor whites often gathered for dancing in informal and nonjudgmental settings such as an outdoor market squares. One contemporary account in New York City noted, "In the afternoon the grown up apprentices and servant girls used to dance on the green in Bayard's farm." (Bayard's farm was an outdoor market west of Broadway.) It was common in the market places of the ports of New York City or in the Brooklyn Village, for visitors to observe upwards of 200 African Americans dancing Jigs or the Breakdown. In many cases they also danced as exhibition for the white observers or in dance competitions, of which they would share in a portion of the winning bets (Burrows and Wallace 1998, 403).

The descriptive accounts of dancing in the market squares of New York City compare with a contemporary account by American architect Benjamin Latrobe during a visit to Congo Square in New Orleans (also see later in this chapter). In February 1819, Latrobe witnessed similar African American dancing in Congo Square that he estimated at about 550 to 600 people. Latrobe, who was out for a leisurely walk, was attracted to the square by a sound that he thought was "horses trampling on a wooden floor." The sound was actually made by solo dances tapping out rhythms with their feet on wood boards. In all likelihood, the dance was either the Jig or the Clog, but most likely it was the Breakdown (Latrobe 2002, 72–73).

Other types of dancing were also going on, but Latrobe noted that he did not see any Quadrilles, Contredanses, English Country-dances, or Waltzes. He did see some other dances of small groups that formed into individual circles around musicians who played within the center. He described it as follows:

> They were formed into circular groups, in the midst of four which that I examined (but there were more of them) was a ring, the largest not ten feet in diameter. In the first were two women dancing. They held each a coarse handkerchief, extended by the corners, in their hands, and set to each other in a miserably dull and slow figure, hardly moving their feet or bodies (Latrobe 2002, 73).

The dance Latrobe described might have been the Haitian Chica dance that was seen by Moreau de Saint-Méry in 1796 (Needham 2002, 58).

Latrobe, however, thought the music and dancing was "too African." He expressed his dislike and left to continue his walk. The "African" music that Latrobe "disliked" was supplied by "two drums and a stringed instrument." One drum was cylindrical and the other was an "open staved" drum that was held between the knees. He described the stringed instrument as a "curious instrument ...which no doubt was imported from Africa." In all likelihood, the stringed instrument was an African "banja," which was the forerunner of the American banjo. In the latter part of the nineteenth century, Congo Square also holds in part the legend as being the birthplace of American Jazz music (74).

Unlike cities such as New York and New Orleans, which had a combination of free blacks and African American slaves, the plantations in the south were almost exclusively slaveholders. On the plantations dancing was a major form of recreation and entertainment. One ex-slave named Isaac Stier remembered:

> Us danced plenty, too. Some o' de [of the] men clogged and pigeoned, but when us had the dances dey was [they were] real cotillions, lak de [like the] white folks had...Long after the [Civil] war was over de white folks would [hire] me to come 'round wid de [with the] band an' call de figgers [the figures] at all de big dances. Dey always paid me well (quoted in Nevell 1977, 46).

In many cases the plantation owners would select the best dancer or "jigger" from among their slaves and used them for profit. The idea was to stage a dance competition against other slaveholders with the intent of wagering large sums of money. Sometimes the dance competitions were staged in nearby towns to involve wagering by the local townspeople.

In 1873, a very descriptive short 12-page pamphlet *Jig, Clog, and Breakdown Dancing Made Easy, with sketches of noted jig dancers*, published by Ed James, provided excellent descriptive information. James asserted,

> Jig Dancing is peculiarly an American institution and had its origin among the slaves of the southern plantations. No white man taught the original darkies [ethnic slur] the arts

An illustration of an African American dancing The Breakdown. The stringed instrument was an African "banja" which was the forerunner of the American banjo. The illustration was originally printed in *Harper's Weekly*, April 13, 1861, 232–233.   Library of Congress, Prints and Photographs Division LC-USZ62-35932.

of Jig or Clog Dancing, and it is equally as indisputable that they did not pick either one of them up from reading books on the subject (1873, 1).

James credited the "first person of any account in the north" who was noted as an accomplished Jig dancer as an African American named William Henry Lane, known as "Master Juba." Around 1835, accounts noted that Juba danced at Dicken's Dance House, a notorious establishment in the poor Five Points section of the lower east side of Manhattan. At Dicken's, he was "discovered" and danced professionally throughout the United States and toured England where he died in 1842 at the age of 26. James contended that Master Juba's "success" encouraged other African Americans to perform the dance professionally (James 1873, 1).

Around 1840, 17-year-old Johnny Diamond was another noted "darkey" dancer who danced the Jig and the Breakdown at "the old Fly Market" in New York City. Diamond was first brought into public notice by the enterprising American show-man P.T. Barnum. That same year Barnum hired Diamond to dance the Jig and Breakdown at London's Vauxhall Garden (see later in this chapter). From about 1841 to 1857, Barnum toured America with Diamond "dancing [competition] matches with whoever came on" (James 1873, 2).

Although dancers such as Master Juba and Johnny Diamond were considered "gifted" in their dancing abilities, James felt that anyone could properly learn the Jig or the Breakdown. He wrote,

> It is not everybody who is gifted with musical ability or elocutionary powers, and these arts are not in general acquired, but almost anybody can become a dancer who has the slightest ear for music or time. As in everything else, it requires patience and practice to become perfect (1).

He suggested that the best musical accompaniment was the banjo. However, if a banjo was not available, the dance could commence with either simple "whistling" or "the old fashioned patting on the thighs." In either case, it was important that the timing was counted out in segments of eight "to get the proper time" (James 1873, 5).

James also described the posture, basic five steps, and a series of step combinations for a Jig dancer. He described the basic Jig posture as follows:

> Hold the head well up, standing erect; do not look at the feet at all, as that has a tendency to stooping, which is a very bad and ugly habit. Let the arms, the hands being open, dangle perpendicular and without straining at the sides. It is necessary to observe an easy balance, with all parts of the body free to act as may be required in dancing the various steps (1873, 3).

The five basic steps were the Strike, Tap, Hit, Hop, and Spring. James described each of the five basic steps as:

> The Strike is made by striking the floor firm and sharp, with either toe or heel, and letting the foot rest at the spot the necessary length of time. The Tap consists of hitting the floor with the ball of the foot and lifting it immediately after the Tap. The Hit is the same as the Tap except that in the Hit the end of the heel or toe is brought into play instead of the ball of the foot. The Hop resembles the Tap except that it is made by hopping on one foot with the other off the floor. The Spring is performed by springing from both feet at once, bringing the feet down separately (1873, 3–5).

Jig dancing, therefore was a variety of combinations of the basic five steps. James, for example, offered a typical combination of a the basic "Hop step" and a "Tap step" as follows:

> Standing in the natural position, hop with the left, giving one tap with the left foot; swing the right foot forward, making a heel and toe tap, and then, with the right foot, give four taps—so, heel, toe, heel, toe. Reverse—Throw the weight from the left to the right, and execute the same movements with the other foot…by springing up with both feet, counting four and giving a tap with each heel, one after the other, commencing with the left, and then give two back taps with the balls of the feet, commencing with the right. Stand natural, give a forward and back tap with the left foot, bringing it back to the original position; throw the weight to the left; give a forward and back tap with the right foot, bringing the back tap in front and across the toe of the left

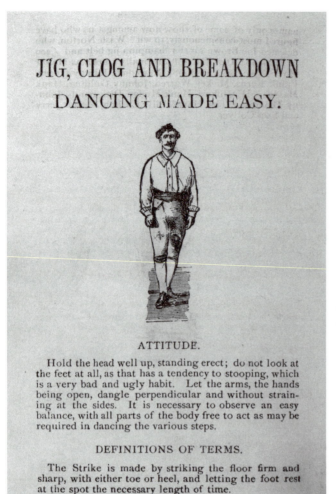

JIG, CLOG AND BREAKDOWN

DANCING MADE EASY.

ATTITUDE.

Hold the head well up, standing erect; do not look at the feet at all, as that has a tendency to stooping, which is a very bad and ugly habit. Let the arms, the hands being open, dangle perpendicular and without straining at the sides. It is necessary to observe an easy balance, with all parts of the body free to act as may be required in dancing the various steps.

DEFINITIONS OF TERMS.

The Strike is made by striking the floor firm and sharp, with either toe or heel, and letting the foot rest at the spot the necessary length of time.

A sample page from *Jig, Clog, and Breakdown Dancing Made Easy*, by Ed James, page 3, c. 1873. Library of Congress Music Division, http://memory.loc.gov/musdi/117/0006.gif.

foot; give a forward and back tap with the left foot, bringing it back, as before (James 1873, 8).

Many of the steps in Jig dancing were also quite similar in appearance to Clog dancing.

Clog dancing (or "Clogging") was another solo dance that was most often described as "a dance of sound." The dance was a combination of many different steps and rhythms from many of the solo dances of the immigrants from Scotland, Wales, England, Ireland, French Canada, as well as American solo dance rhythms such as the Breakdown. The origin can be traced to a small region of the United States in the Appalachian area and Blue Ridge Mountains south of the Pennsylvania border during the 1700s and 1800s. Because of the geographic region, the dance was sometimes called Appalachian Mountain dancing. However, Clog dancing was done in almost all the rural areas of New England as well as French Canada and Nova Scotia (Nevell 1977, 49; "Clog Dance," n.d.).

In fact, in *Jig, Clog, and Breakdown Dancing Made Easy* (1873) Ed James noted that any of the "Jig Dancing steps are equally appropriate for Clog Dancing" with the simple addition of "introducing the 'Clog Break' to finish the eight bars of music." He described the Clog Break as follows:

Stand in the natural position, throwing your weight to the right, giving a strike on the ball of the left foot, stopping it at the heel of the right foot; give the weight to the left; make a forward and back tap with the right; make a strike with the ball of the right foot, stopping it at the heel of the left; give a forward and back tap with the left, make a strike with the ball of the left; throw the weight to the left, and give a forward and back tap with the right; hop from the floor on the ball of the left foot, making one strike, and at the same time swing right (James 1873, 10–11).

In 1874, a similar publication, *Clog Dancing Made Easy* by Henry Tucker, was a 12-page pamphlet that also contained some very good descriptions for executing

Clog dancing steps. Tucker provided sections for "General Advice," the "Use of Clogs," and an "Explanation of Terms used in Describing Steps and Figures," and he also provided sheet music (but no step descriptions) for "Oh, Nicodemus," "Durang's Hornpipe," and "The Original Sailor's Hornpipe." He offered that the Clog dance steps were "comparatively easy" and the references within his pamphlet were sufficient to learn the dance without the aid of a "professional teacher."

Similar to Ed James's publication of *Jig, Clog, and Breakdown Dancing Made Easy*, Tucker indicated that the Clog was composed of five basic steps. The first three, which were the Tap, Hop, and Spring, were executed exactly the same as described by James. In contrast, the Strike step and Hit step of the Jig were replaced by the Shuffle step and the Cross step in the Clog. Tucker described the Shuffle step as follows:

> First draw two diagrams (with chalk or other material), on the floor...Leaving the ends about three inches apart ...Place the heels on the angles of the [chalk] diagram and then with both feet "tap," first No. 1, then No. 2; making the sounds nearly at the same time.

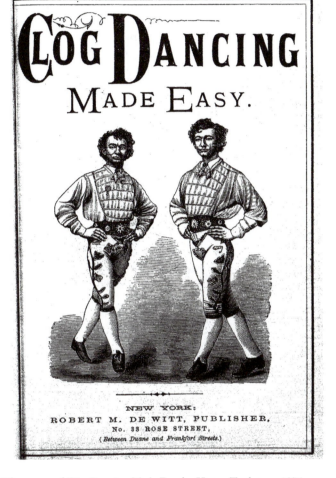

The cover of *Clog Dancing Made Easy* by Henry Tucker, c. 1874. Library of Congress Music Division, http://memory.loc.gov/musdi/ 159/0001.gif.

The Cross step, which was the fifth basic step, contained "eight motions." He described the eight motions in the following sequence:

> 1st. Tap with the left foot. 2d. Tap with the right foot, lift it up in front, and 3d. Hop on left foot. 4th. Tap the right foot, crossing the left foot in front. 5th. Touch the right heel with the toe of the left foot, then 6th. Hop on the right foot. 7th. Tap with the left foot, and, finally, 8th. Bring it down firmly beside the right.

Tucker also included 12 intensive step descriptions as examples of the various combinations of the Clog steps. The "First Step. Example" was described as follows:

1st. Tap with the left foot; 2d. Shuffle with the right; 3d. Tap with the right (extending the foot forward); 4th. Tap with the left foot; 5th. Stamp with the right (forward); Now reverse the above, that is, 1st. Tap with the right foot; 2d. Shuffle with the left; 3d. Tap with the left (extending the foot forward); 4th. Tap with the right foot; 5th. Stamp with the left foot (forward) (2–3).

An example of the "Break" step (also a step characteristic in the African American Breakdown) was described in the following manner:

1st. Tap the left foot; 2d. Shuffle the right; 3d. Tap the right foot; 4th. Shuffle the left; 5th. Tap the left; 6th. Shuffle the right; 7th. Tap the right; 8th. Tap the left; 9th. Shuffle the right; 10th. Hop on the left, crossing the right foot over in front of the left, and resting the tip of the toe on the floor (3).

Tucker suggested that before moving on to learning the other 11 step combinations, he strongly advised continuous practice of the "First Step" and the "Break Step."

At the point that the dancer was "so familiar with it as to be able to perform it perfect, and without hesitation," only then should the dancer move on to the other 11 steps, and in each step, "always perfecting one before attempting the next." Tucker did offer the advice that after becoming so proficient in each of the predescribed steps, "Of course the dancer, having learned these 'primary steps,' is not compelled to follow the exact routine." Therefore, any amount of improvisation or recombination of the steps was acceptable (2–3, 9). Regardless of the step combinations, Tucker reminded the potential Clog dancer that each of the sequence of steps also made a corresponding sound with the feet. Therefore, he advised that it was essential to "Use clogs for all practice, as the learner will experience great difficulty in adapting his steps to clogs after having practised [sic] in shoes; the clogs having unyielding wooden soles" (2–3).

In order to either Jig or Clog, it became necessary to wear clothing, such as knee breeches, hose stockings, and the proper shoes, that would not impede the steps. A basic necessity for clogging was a shoe that could make "noise." Early clogging shoes were made entirely of wood so that the sound of the steps made by the dancer could be heard. In later years, with the advent of industrialization, specialty shoes and clothing for Clogging were available for purchase. In 1873, for example, New York dance instructor Ed James advertised a pair of specialty "Dancing Clogs" at a cost of $4.50. The ad offered, "A large assortment of all sizes of red Leather Clogs, [of the] best make, imported, always on hand." In addition, were the requisite knee breeches available in either velvet or worsted wool in "various colors" (James 1873, 14).

In regards to all of the dances such as the Jig, Breakdown, Clogging, Country-dances, Cotillions, Contras, Quadrilles, and even the courtly dances such as the Minuet, they all had in common "the pronounced lack of physical intimacy." The only physical contact between a man and a woman was an occasional touch of the hands, and that could be only in a manner prescribed by the manners and etiquette of the day. According to dance innovator and choreographer Agnes DeMille, "on the dance floor or in the parlor, there was emphatically no embracing. Casual handling was simply considered too risky" (10). However, all that would change with the introduction of the Waltz.

THE WALTZ, THE SLOW WALTZ, AND THE VIENNESE WALTZ

The exact origin of the Waltz is unclear and difficult to pinpoint. Although the name "Waltz" is derived from the German word *walzen*, which simply means "to revolve," some trace it back to the fifteenth century Renaissance Italian court dance, the Volta, which meant "to turn" (see Chapter 1). Similar to the Waltz, the Volta was also a turning dance in a similar closed dance position and was considered quite scandalous. But, unlike the Waltz, the Volta included lifts and athletic moves that separated the partners. Others say the Waltz evolved from an Austrian couple's dance, the Ländler, which was also danced in 3/4 rhythm and with a similar closed dance position. Most agree, however, that the Waltz that swept through the European ballrooms of the late eighteenth century traced its roots to the traditional turning folk dances of German peasants. The German version, which was danced in the late 1700s, most closely resembled the Waltz that remained throughout the twentieth century in America (Richardson 1960, 18; Panati 1991, 38).

In a description of social dancing in the *St. James Encyclopedia of Popular*

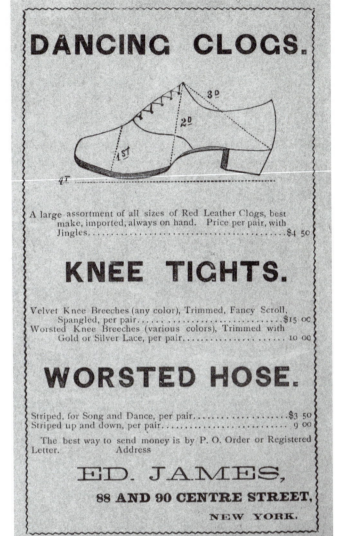

An advertisement for "Dancing Clogs" in *Jig, Clog, and Breakdown Dancing Made Easy*, by Ed James, page 12, c. 1873. Library of Congress Music Division, http://memory.loc.gov/musdi/117/0015.gif.

Culture, dance historian Jeffery Escoffier claimed the Waltz was "the first dance of urban life." He added, "Social dance moved out of the ballroom of the aristocratic court into public dance halls and 'assembly rooms'" (2000, 450). The fact that the Waltz was embraced as a product of "urban life" is attributed to the French Revolution.

Prior to the French Revolution in 1789, the Royal Courts still held sway and dictated the social decorum. In the case of France, the Royal Court of Louis XVI and

Marie Antoinette preferred the glamour and ritual of dances such as the Minuet. The French Revolution abolished the Royal Court and brought with it the rise of the middle class and also a revolution in the arts. After the French revolution, social dancing was no longer regulated by the dictum of dance approval by the Royal Courts. In the example of the Waltz, the dance was first popular among the peasants and was later introduced to the social elite by way of the public dance halls. Therefore, a major significance of the Waltz is that despite the fact that it was not sanctioned by the Royal Courts it became popular among all classes of people. In fact, in its native Germany it was prohibited in the German Imperial house (the German version of the Royal Court). According to dance historian Curt Sachs, "for the first time in centuries a dance conquers the world without the sanction of the powers that be, of courts, of dancing masters, or of France" (1963, 431).

In 1782, poet and writer Johann Wolfgang von Goethe, who had taken dancing lessons in the stately Minuet during his youth at the bequest of his father, admitted that he was smitten by the Waltz. As an adult he frequently danced in public dance halls, and he described the elation of dancing the Waltz. Goethe wrote:

> [Never] have I moved so lightly. I was no longer a human being. To hold the most adorable creature in one's arms and fly around with her like the wind, so that everything around us fades away (quoted in Sachs 1963, 430).

At the time that Goethe described the dance, the first known dance instruction for the Waltz titled *Etwas über das Waltzen* was published in Germany by C. von Zangen (1782).

The Waltz was so popular in Germany that contemporary composers, such as Wolfgang Amadeus Mozart, were writing music in 3/4 time and adapting it for the dance. On January 15, 1787, for example, Mozart visited a public dance hall in Prague named the *Breiten* with an acquaintance named Count Canal. In his diary, he noted the following:

> At six o'clock I went with Count Canal to the so-called *Breiten*, a rustic ball, at which the flower of Prague beauties are in the habit of assembling I saw with wholehearted pleasure how these people jumped around with such sincere enjoyment to the music of my *Figaro* which had been turned into all kinds of *contres* and *Teutsche* [*waltzes*] (quoted in Sachs 1963, 428).

At the time, many early sources simply referred to the Waltz dance as *Deutsche* or *Teutsche*, which in translation simply meant "German."

By 1797, the Waltz was highly favored as the dance of choice throughout Germany. At the same time, however, it was also attacked as indecent. Salomo Jakob Wolf, for example, published *Discussion of the most important causes of the weakness of our generation in regard to the waltz* (1797). His discourse "urgently recommended to the sons and daughters" of Germany of the ill-health and unscrupulous behavior in regards to the effects of the dance upon German society. In 1799, a revised second edition was published under the "new" condemnation title of *Proof that the waltz is a main source of the weakness of body and mind of our generation* (Sachs 1963, 429).

Nevertheless, the dance was soon to sweep all of Europe. After 1800, for example, with Napoleon's invasion of Germany "part of the loot" brought back to Paris was the German Waltz. It is said that his soldiers introduced the Waltz in the Parisian public dance halls. No small feat considering that by time, in Paris alone, there were over 680 public dance halls. Shortly thereafter, the Waltz was so much in demand across the European continent that many dance halls played almost exclusively Waltzes (Sachs 1963, 430–432).

According to dance historians Sylvia Dannett and Frank Rachel, "As compared to the Minuet, the Waltz seemed shameless and abandoned...In the peasant form of the Waltz, the partners, their hands on each other's backs, held each other so closely that their faces touched" (1954, 30). In fact, the Waltz introduced a revolutionary new dance position, the "closed" dance position between a couple. The close embrace was unlike any other type of publicly displayed physical interaction and body contact between a man and a woman. In the "Waltz position" the man and woman started in a face-to-face position; he would literally grasp his right arm around the lady's waist, and she would place her left arm on his right shoulder. He placed his left arm and hand out to the side, and she placed her right hand in his left hand completing the embrace. From the closed dance position they began their joyful turning as they progressed around the perimeter of the dance floor. In fact, without the close contact and embrace between the couple, the Waltz could not be properly danced. The particular hold actually made it possible for a couple to move freely about the floor. The "Waltz Position" was so dominant that it became almost universally known as the basic closed couple dance position and was applied to many different dances through the nineteenth, through the twentieth, and into the twenty-first century (Shaw 1949, 49).

The basic Waltz was danced in a three-four rhythm, known as 3/4 time. The steps corresponded with the first two measures of the music. A strong accent or emphasis was placed on the first beat as the couple began a long first step (man with the left foot and woman with the right foot). The next two beats were de-emphasized as the couple took one step to each beat. The second measure with the same emphasis began with the right foot for the man and the left foot for the woman.

In his dance instruction manual *A Description of the Correct Method of Waltzing* (1816), Wilson provided a description for what he termed "The Slow Waltz":

> The *Slow Waltz Movements*...are commenced by the Gentleman's left foot being brought from the fourth position behind into the second position with a turn of the body...A slow pirouette...immediately follows; and is performed, by bringing the right foot...into the fifth position behind the left; both feet raised on the toes, the knees perfectly straight, and turning round on the points of the toes of both feet together, preserving in the turning an easy Equilibrium of the Body; and, in turning on the toes, passing the heels perfectly close and as much raised as may be. The right Foot...placed in front of the left...finishes the pirouette, and leaves the right foot prepared for the performance of Three Movements forward in the fourth position, technically named, *Pas de Bourée*, which next follows.

Wilson described that the movements, although "performed alike," were not done at the same time by the Lady and Gentleman. He described the *Pas de Bourée* as follows:

> The right foot is passed forward into the fourth position on the toe pointed, and the knee as straight as possible; the left foot being left in the fourth position behind and on the toe pointed, is brought forward into the fourth position in front of the right foot; the right foot being again in the fourth position behind, is again brought forward into the fourth position in front of the left.

He noted that in order to properly execute the *Pas de Bourée*, it must be performed "on the toes, with the knees perfectly straight." However, Wilson suggested that, unlike the rise and fall of the twentieth century Waltz, "a rising and sinking motion of the body be totally avoided." He added that dancing the Waltz "on the toes" was in keeping with the French style of Waltzing.

Wilson's step description was "equally adapted for the instruction of the Lady." He advised, "as the Gentleman passes his left foot into the second position, the Lady commences with her right foot." As the Gentleman performed the *Pas de Bourée* the Lady at the same time performed a slow pirouette. The Lady then performed the *Pas de Bourée* and the Gentleman performed a slow pirouette; thus the couple simultaneously created continuous "Waltzing Movements" (Wilson 1816, 125–128).

The majesty and allure of the turning Waltz was romanticized in many Hollywood films of the twentieth century. One example was *The Great Waltz* (1938), a grand MGM Studio musical, among countless other films. A video clip based on a reconstruction of Thomas Wilson's 1816 Waltz, as well as video clips of a comparison of the early, mid, and late nineteenth century versions of the Waltz are viewable from the Music Division of the Library of Congress online source *An American Ballroom Companion: Dance Instruction Manuals Ca. 1490–1920* (see bibliography).

One contemporary variation was the Viennese Waltz. Sometimes known as the "classic style" and sometimes called "Langaus," the Viennese Waltz began around 1776, in Vienna, Austria. Unlike, the French version, which was danced "on the toes," the Viennese Waltz was danced with a bit more speed and "on the flat foot." The speed was attributed partly to the shoes and smooth wood floors in the ballrooms.

By the time of the Waltz, public ballrooms were quite common in Europe and were beginning to gain acceptance in America. The ballrooms were decorated in elaborate fashion and were complemented by highly polished wood floors. To ensure protection of the wood surfaces, lighter less cumbersome footwear was suggested. Therefore, the awkward "hobnailed" shoes with rough bottoms and smoother flat surfaced shoes replaced narrowed high heels. At the same time that the couples moved around the dance floor, the ladies carefully held up their dresses so that they would not accidentally step on them while dancing. In turn, this led to lighter fabrics and less cumbersome formal dresses. As a result, the combination of the polished wood floor, lighter dresses, and lighter footwear permitted gliding dance steps and in turn allowed for better agility than the smooth flowing grace that the turning in the Waltz required (Sachs 1963, 429–433; Buckman 1978, 114).

The Viennese Waltz was a series of constant turns by the individual couple as they traveled around the perimeter of the dance floor in a counterclockwise rotation. In doing so, the dancers moved at much greater speed than had ever been seen on a dance floor. (The eighteenth and early nineteenth century Waltz was danced much faster than the twentieth century versions.) In order to sustain the speed and equilibrium as a couple, the dancers concentrated on maintaining the closed dance position and not so much on the exact foot positions of the Pas de Bourée and the slow pirouette. According to dance historian Curt Sachs, the dancers "forgot about the characteristic arrangement of the feet one behind the other in the third position on the fifth and six counts of the two measure phrase" (1963, 429).

But, in fact, the fast-paced dance was not as "exhausting" as many made it out to be. According to dance instructor Beale Fletcher:

> When Waltz music is played very fast, it will not tire you nearly so much if you turn. In fact, it is very difficult to dance a fast waltz without turning. Why is this so? Because the Waltz Basic Time Step has a side step which follows a forward step in every measure of the music. Therefore, when the dancers travel without turning there is a constant change of direction from one side to the other. One is actually fighting his own momentum with every step. However, when the dancers are turning, the side step follows the same line of direction as the forward step. In fact, all the steps in the fast Turning waltz follow along one line of direction. Thus, in turning, one does not fight the momentum of his own body weight, but instead he gives in to the momentum and rides it around the room (Fletcher 1956, 35).

As the Waltz was danced in Vienna, Austria, composers such as Johann Strauss wrote accompanying music such as *The Blue Danube* (1867), *Tales From the Vienna Wood* (1868), and *Vienna Life* (1873). The 3/4-time music for the Viennese Waltz overemphasized a strong first beat and underemphasized the second and third beats. The graceful Waltz dance, accompanying music, and the musical composers dominated as the popular music selections and dance of the nineteenth century. Throughout the nineteenth century, the Waltz, in various adaptations, was the predominant ballroom dance. Later variations included the Waltz a Deux Temps, the Waltz a Trois Temps, and the Boston Waltz (see Chapter 3) (Sachs 1963, 433; Panati 1991, 38).

On the other hand, the gracefulness and beauty of the waltz was not shared equally by all. In 1906, dance historian Thomas Reginald St. Johnston wrote:

> Sweeping all precedent on one side, and overturning all the old thoughts and ideas on dancing, the Waltz came and conquered, but not without the severest opposition that a dance has ever had. Such a distinct departure from all established forms was bound to be regarded with disfavour [sic] by those of conservative ideas, for it must be remembered that this was practically the first time in the history of dancing that two people had ever danced [solely] with each other and together; and, to crown all, it was considered by many to be positively immodest! (St. Johnston 1906, 144–145).

The continuous turning was said to have an "intoxicating effect" upon the female —therefore many critics deemed the dance "vulgar." Regardless, of its continued popularity throughout the nineteenth century, one noted eighteenth century French satirist, Vigée, wryly stated, "I can understand that the mothers like the *waltz*, but I cannot understand that they allow their daughters to dance it" (Sachs 1963, 432).

Many of the Dance Masters were also outraged, mainly because the dance gave way to fun and did not require much instruction. In addition, most of the teachers taught grace, balance, feet positions, and slow courtly moves. The fast-turning Waltz did not require much instruction and also seemed to throw all the dance etiquette "to the wind." In contrast to the stately presentation of the European court dances, the Waltz did not place itself in a position to "show off" a dance for others in attendance. The dance was quite different from any previous dance and broke from all dance tradition, even the social decorum of the day. As the couples whirled around the dance floor, they paid attention only to each other. In addition, the dance was not preceded by a bow, and during a night of Waltzing, many of the dancing couples did not necessarily change partners—especially in the public ballrooms. As a result, many critics called the dance antisocial and immoral ("Instrumental Dance Music 1780s–1920s," n.d.).

Some of the dismay and shock was attributed to the fact that as the woman held up her dress (to avoid stepping on it while dancing) she revealed a slight glimpse of the petticoat. In 1804, writer Ernst Moritz Arndt witnessed the Waltz and was shocked. His written account was scornful and insinuated lascivious behavior. Arndt wrote:

> The turning went on in the most indecent positions; the hand holding the dress lay hard against the breasts pressing lasciviously at every movement; the girls, meanwhile, looked half mad and ready to swoon. As they waltzed around on the darker side of the room, the clasp and kisses became still bolder...but I can now quite understand why they have forbidden the *waltz* in certain parts of [Europe] (Sachs 1963, 430).

Dance historian Maureen Needham provided an explanation. She noted:

> The waltz involved such unseemly physical intimacy that, from the moment of its inception, it was labeled indecent immoral, and even worse. By the end of the nineteenth century, the struggle to halt the waltz continued without abating. Moralists, growing even more shrill, contended that "the degrading, lust-creating influence of the waltz" and its "voluptuous, sensual embrace" would automatically lead to a shameful career in prostitution for many a waltzing woman (99).

As a result, according to dance historians Sylvia Dannett and Frank Rachel, "Storms of protest arose from outraged critics. Public ordnances [were] issued insisting that 'both men and women must be decently dressed for the Waltz [and] women and girls must not be thrown about'" (1954, 30). In 1812, for example, poet Lord Byron also expressed his dismay against the Waltz. His objections stemmed from the "low class" origins and also to the "lewd grasp and lawless contact" exhibited by the close embrace between the man and the woman. Byron's outrage led him to insinuate that the dance led to sexual promiscuity. Byron exclaimed that during the Waltz, the "thin clad daughters...[did not] leave much mystery for the nuptial night" (quoted in Buckman 1978, 125). It was also quite apparent that Byron was not alone in his objections.

In July 1816, the Waltz was danced at an eloquent ball in London. A scathing review in the *London Times* was not as accepting of the dance as the general public. It stated:

> We remarked with pain that the indecent foreign dance called the Waltz was introduced...at the English court on Friday last. This is a circumstance which ought not be passed over in silence. National morals depend on national habits; and it is quite sufficient to cast one's eyes on the voluptuous intertwining of the limbs and close compressure on the bodies in their dance, to see that it is indeed far removed from the modest reserve which has hitherto been considered distinctive of English females. So long as this obscene display was confined to prostitutes and adulteresses, we did not think it deserving of notice; but now that it is attempted to be forced on the respectable classes of society by the civil examples of their superiors, we feel it a duty to warn every parent against exposing his daughter to so fatal a contagion....We know not how it has happened (probably by the recommendation of some worthless and ignorant French dancing master) that so indecent a dance has now for the first time been exhibited at the English Court; but the novelty is one deserving of severe reprobation, and we trust it will never again be tolerated in any moral English society (Buckman 1978, 125).

In that same year, London Dance Master Thomas Wilson defended the Waltz, claiming that it was "a promoter of vigorous health and productive of an hilarity of spirits...*not* an enemy to true morals and endangering true virtue" (Wilson 1816, 124).

As late as 1885, comments on the Waltz persisted. American Dance Master Allen Dodworth in *Dancing and Its Relation to Education and Social Life* remarked that the Waltz had survived for over 50 years and "resisted every kind of attack and is today the most popular known" (127). About 50 years earlier in 1834, the Waltz was officially introduced in America by Boston Dance Master Lorenzo Papanti. By the 1880s, America developed a version of the Boston Waltz, a slower gliding dance, and in the 1910s, the Hesitation Waltz eventually developed into the twentieth century version of the Waltz.

The Places to Dance

Assemblies of the gayer sort are frequent here...I was present at two or three such and saw as fine a ring of ladys, as good dancing, and heard musick as I had been witness to anywhere...I saw not one prude while I was here.
—Dr. Alexander Hamilton, 1744

I have already said elsewhere that dancing for the inhabitants of the United States is less a matter of self-display than it is true enjoyment.
—Moreau de Saint-Mery, 1798

FASHIONABLE ASSEMBLY ROOMS, ALMACK'S IN LONDON, LADY JERSEY, AND DANCING ROOMS

During the late eighteenth century, the ballroom manners of dancing that were set at Bath, England, by Beau Nash (see Chapter 1) carried over into the city of London at open-air dance assemblies such as the Pleasure Gardens at Vauxhall and the Ranelagh in Chelsea. Other fully enclosed Assembly rooms were maintained at the Carlisle House in Soho Square (opened in 1763) and the Pantheon on Oxford Street (opened in 1772). In all, about 70 such Assembly rooms and open-air rooms for dancing existed in London. The "traditional dances" included the Minuet, Cotillion, Allemande, and Contredanse, and, after 1815, the Quadrille and the Waltz. Each of these London dance halls maintained a policy of "open to the public." Therefore, those who could afford to pay the admission price—and, of course, abided by the rules—could enter the public dance hall for a varied choice of listening to the music, having tea, enjoying supper, or dancing (Richardson, 23–27).

The Assembly Rooms exhibited an air of elegance and were decorated in the latest European fashion. Particular attention was paid to the interior decoration that usually included ornate pilaster columns, interior balconies adorned with decorations, and walls finished with lively "French" wallpaper. The Ranelagh, for example, was renovated at an astounding cost of over "fifty thousand pounds." Although the interior space was still unfinished on opening night, one contemporary visitor, Horace Walpole, was quite impressed. He described the Assembly rooms at the Ranelagh as follows:

It amazed me myself....The pillars are of artificial giallo antico [yellow antique]. The ceilings...are of the most beautiful stuccos...The ceilings of the ballrooms and the panels are painted like Raphael's [famous Renaissance Italian artist] loggias in the Vatican; a dome like the [ancient Roman] Pantheon glazed (quoted in Richardson 1960, 26).

The interior decoration was complemented by highly polished wood dance floors. Each of the fashionable London Assembly rooms also retained a Master of Ceremonies (see Chapter 1). In addition to welcoming the guests, the Master of Ceremonies arranged a variety of entertainment, including public concerts, masquerade balls, subscription dances, regular dancing evenings, and employed a resident Dance Master.

The most fashionably prominent of all the London Assembly rooms, for both its exclusivity and its Master of Ceremonies, was Almack's. Located at 1765 King Street in the St. James district of London, Almack's subscription price of ten guinea's (about $60) for a once-a-week 12 week season was quite expensive for eighteenth century standards. Simply by virtue of its high subscription price, many Londoners were precluded from entry. Beginning on its very first opening night on February 14, 1765, for example, the Duke of Cumberland attended and wrote that it maintained an air of "Exclusiveness."

Similar to Beau Nash at Bath, Almack's also had a discerning Master of Ceremonies named Lady Jersey. At Almack's, Lady Jersey was also very selective about who was allowed entry. Even if an individual could afford Almack's subscription, she strictly limited the subscription tickets to only a few hundred. In the process, she excluded a large number of London nobility and maintained an air of exclusivity that was similar to the late twentieth century exclusive door policies that were legendary in Disco dance clubs such as New York's famed Studio 54. On two occasions, for example, the Duke of Wellington was even turned away at the door. On one occasion the Duke of Wellington arrived too late, and on another occasion he was inappropriately dressed. Although he was wearing "fashionable" trousers, the rules stated that gentlemen were required to wear "Knee-breeches" (Richardson, 25–26).

Typical of many of the Assembly rooms, Almack's advertised its upcoming subscription dances in the London newspapers. However, it was specifically stated that a ticket was required for entry. In addition, if an unknown individual arrived at the door with a ticket, it had to be known what subscriber had originally purchased the ticket. In 1769, for example, an advertisement in the *London Daily Press* newspaper read in part:

On Friday next, the 10th Instant, at ALMACK'S Assembly Room in King Street St. James, will be the First of the two Nights Subscription for Minuets and Cotillons, or French Country Dances. The Doors will be open at eight. No Person admitted without the Name wrote on the Back of the Ticket (quoted in Richardson, 25).

In 1772, an advertisement in the same newspaper for Almack's Winter season beginning on December 17, 1772, read in part:

There are to be in the twelve Balls four Mask'd Balls, which the Subscribers have for the same Subscription…positively no Person whatever can be admitted without a Ticket, nor any Tickets delivered out upon Ball-Day (Richardson, 25).

In 1815, however, contemporary Dance Master Thomas Wilson noted a severe dislike of the London Assembly rooms. He claimed:

> Public Balls have, it seems, lost their original intention and character, by having become, generally, sources of imaginary profit…in fact, the greatest number of Balls advertised are given by persons little acquainted with Dancing (1815, 325).

According to Wilson, the reason that the proprietors might not have focused solely on dancing was simply because of profits. In fact, he was quite critical of the idea of not only the "subscription fee" but also the additional costs once inside the ballroom. He wrote:

> These Dancing Rooms are supported by persons who visit them, many of whom go out of curiosity…But before the visitors obtain admission into the Room, they are requested to deposit a piece of money, of not less value than sixpence, for the care of their hats, bonnets, [and other outer garments] which must be left with the attendant …Each visitor is also expected to partake of the refreshments which the proprietors provide, as another source of profit; and should the visitors be inclined to depart early, or dislike the company, he has no alternative by way of escape, as the person with whom the hats…were deposited, is not to be seen [until] Coffee has been served up, with a view of inducing persons to spend their money.

Wilson, felt that "one visit is sufficient to convince the visitor" that the motive was not to regulate proper dancing but to simply make money. He claimed that the proprietors "are frequently totally ignorant of the correct manner of performing either Figures or steps" and interested only in "giving invitations for the next 'Dancing night.'" (Wilson 1815, 328–329).

THE GREAT AWAKENING, BLACK SABBATH, AND THE SQUARE ORDER SHUFFLE

From about 1720 through the 1740s a series of religious revivals, termed the "Great Awakening," swept through the American colonies. By 1726, the revival was embraced throughout the Dutch and German communities of the Middle colonies. In New Jersey, for example, the Reverend Theodore J. Frelinghuysen preached of "old-time" religion in the Dutch reform churches. In 1734, in New England the religious enthusiasm was echoed through the preaching of Jonathan Edwards (son of the Reverend Timothy Edwards—see Chapter 1). The preachings of both Edwards and Frelinghuysen converted many people from within their respective communities. The religious conversion soon swept through the American colonies; however, the zenith of the religious fervor came full tilt with the arrival of George Whitfield.

In 1739, Evangelist minister George Whitfield emigrated from Great Britain to Philadelphia. Described as a "fiery evangelist," he wanted to bring the American colonies back to the religious ideals of the early Puritan settlers. Whitfield traveled throughout the colonies, venturing both north and south. In the process, he converted thousands of American colonists with the pretext to forego the "sins" of amusements and idle hours—and in some instances they were successful in eliminating dancing (Goldfield, Abbott, et al., 2001, 102).

From about 1700 to 1739, throughout New England, for example, Ordination Balls for newly ordained ministers were quite common (see Chapter 1). After the Great Awakening, however, they were stopped and most were never revived. From 1706 to 1739, in Philadelphia, The Quaker Society of Friends was unsuccessful in their annual appeal to Philadelphia's municipal authorities to condemn the practice of dancing and dance schools that taught "dancing and fencing" (see Chapter 1). However, in 1742, Whitfield added his voice (and his multitude of followers) to the Quaker Society of Friends in a condemnation of dancing. With the added pressure applied by Whitfield, the Philadelphia Assembly dancing ball was disbanded.

Around the end of the 1740s, the frantic conversion pace of the Great Awakening slowed, mainly as a result of a population increase of newly arrived immigrants of different cultural and religious backgrounds. In addition, the itinerant revivalist's unwavering demand "for sinners to be converted" was usually in a settled community with established religious practices. Therefore, as the evangelist traveled through the towns and communities, they caused an upheaval among the ministers and congregations that caused tension and bickering among the previous harmonious communities ("Great Awakening," n.d.). As a result, in Philadelphia in 1748, for example, the Philadelphia Assembly was resumed. But, although the religious fervor slowed, throughout the 1700s and into the nineteenth century, a growing number of ministers, municipalities, and newspapers continued to denounce dancing (Marks 1957, 31–32).

The appeal for dancing as a social amusement was such a common occurrence among the American colonies that many cities and towns sought to include it as part of their community. In order to attract a qualified Dance Master, many cities would place an advertisement in their local newspapers. At the time, newspapers were usually printed weekly and served as the main source of information within the community.

In records contained in the Connecticut Historical Society for the *Providence Gazette and Country Journal*, between January 15 and February 19, 1763, for example, the town of Providence, Rhode Island, listed an advertisement that a Dance Master was "welcomed to open a school for violin, fencing, and dancing." Unbeknownst to the editors, the simple request spurred a debate among local residents. Shortly after the advertisement, one local resident complained to the newspaper editor against the "importation of a Dance Master," asserting that a dancing school was the equivalent of a "public Stew or Brothel." The letter continued with a declaration that a "Dancing-School" or any public ball would be a "Scene of Lewdness" and "inconsistent with Modesty."

The following week, another local resident disagreed with accusations made to the editors. The response stated in part:

In Regard to Dancing, it is an Amusement neither faulty in itself, nor unlawful; and I dare say, the Gentleman that speaks so bitterly against it, knows very little of the matter …otherwise he could not look upon Dancing as inconsistent with Modesty, or blame an Art, that can change a Romp into a polite Lady, that can give a genteel, free air, to the most awkward creature imaginable, in short, an Art that is capable of working Wonders…That a Dancing-School or Ball should be a Scene of Lewdness, is to me the greatest absurdity in Nature! What effect Dancing may have on the Vulgar, I can't say, but modesty and Exactness are the peculiar Characteristics of a regular School or Assembly.

The debate continued, but eventually dancing and Assembly balls were a regular occurrence in Providence (Marks 1957, 42–43).

In 1796, a similar debate over dancing appeared in the weekly *Philadelphia Minerva*. An editorial was written in opposition to the combination of local dancing schools and assemblies. The editors claimed that,

> Dancing was calculated to eradicate solid thought…In fact, versatility of mind, hatred for study, or sober reflection, are the inseparable companions of dancing schools, and the miseries resulting from them are virtually incalculable (Vol. II, No. 97, December 10, 1796).

A rebuttal the following week by a woman known only as Amelia disagreed. She argued that "dancing is incontestably an elegant and amiable accomplishment; it confers grace and dignity of carriage upon the female sex…Nature gives us limbs, and art teaches us to use them" (Vol. II, No. 98, December 17, 1796).

At the time the general acceptance of dancing in America created a similar debate that occurred among religious leaders and their congregations. Some congregations in New England, for example, continued strict observance of the "Black Sabbath." The Black Sabbath was a full 24-hour religious observance from Saturday evening until Sunday evening. Therefore, those same congregations were totally opposed to any dancing within that period, especially Saturday night dancing. In 1778, a similar such congregation from New England was successful in persuading the Continental Congress in Philadelphia to provide language to disavow any "exhibition of shews [sic], plays, and other expensive diversions and entertainments." Although the word dancing was not specifically mentioned—the idea was to ban dancing during the ongoing war for independence. In light of the potential for interference by the other colonies, the fledgling Continental Congress was careful not to specifically pass a general "law of the land" prohibiting dancing. However, in direct response to the decree, the Wilmington Committee of safety in North Carolina quickly declared, "that all persons concerned in any dance for the future should be properly stigmatized." In contrast, on the same evening that the law was passed, a dance ball was given by the governor of Philadelphia in honor of a visiting French dignitary (Marks 1957, 35–37).

Some religious congregations encouraged dancing as part of their religious rituals. During the 1770s, the Shakers, a strict religious denomination that emigrated from England, brought with them an established pattern of dancing among their congregation. They had an open practice of dancing as part of their religious observance "to rid themselves of their sins." During both the religious observance and the dancing, they maintained a strict separation between the men and women. During the dancing, the men would circle on the outside of a circle of woman and at other times the genders danced on opposite ends of the room. As a result of their dancing, some contemporary observers nicknamed them the "Shaking Quakers" (McDonagh 1979, 4–5).

Shaker religious leaders encouraged dancing, and in some cases they even introduced new dances. In 1788, for example, Father Joseph introduced a formalized Shaker dance known as the "Square Order Shuffle." Rather than giving up to uninspired and uninhibited motions of moving in a circle, Father Joseph organized the men and women in groups facing each other. In an article titled "The Dance in Shaker Ritual," contained in Paul Magriel's *Chronicles of the American Dance* (1948), author E. D. Andrews described the Square Order Shuffle as follows:

> A forward and backward movement of ranks, the brethren and sisters in separate groups shuffling towards and away from each other, three paces each way, with a double step or "tip-tap" at the turn (3–5).

However, just because the strictly religious Shakers accepted dancing did not mean that all religious leaders did the same.

SHAKERS near LEBANON state of N YORK. their mode of worship.

A Shaker congregation in Lebanon, New York, performs the Square Order Shuffle. A dance described as, "A forward and backward movement of ranks, the brethren and sisters in separate groups shuffling towards and away from each other, three paces each way, with a double step or 'tip-tap' at the turn." Library of Congress, Prints and Photographs Division LC-USZ62-13659.

In 1794, the Reverend Devereux Jarratt in Dinwiddie, Virginia, called dancing "wicked." He confessed that as a child he was forced to take dancing lessons and developed a strong dislike for the amusement. He recalled that at the time dancing was "the favorite sport and diversion of the wicked and ungodly were then much in vogue." As a result, some religious leaders decreed a ban on dancing within their own congregations. The following year, for example, in Kentucky, Elizabeth Smith had some invited guests in her home for a party that included dancing. Upon word reaching the local Baptist minister, Smith was prohibited from attending church services. In the French colonies, on the other hand, the religious leaders usually encouraged dancing among both young and old. According to a contemporary account, one French Catholic priest named Henry Howe "lent a sanction and a blessing upon the innocent amusements and useful recreations [including dancing]" (Marks 1957, 34).

Within the boundaries of the newly formed United States of America, some ministers sought objection to dancing by distributing anti-dance pamphlets and booklets. They included John Phillips's 39-page discourse *Familiar Dialogues on Dancing, Between a Minister and a Dancer, Taken From Matter of Fact With an Appendix Containing Some Extracts From the Writings of Pious and Eminent Men Against the Entertainments of the Stage, and Other Vain Amusements*, published in 1798 in New York; a 99-page 1802 Boston publication *A Treatise on Dancing* written under the pseudonym "Saltator"; and in 1807, *An Address to the Congregational Church in Sangerfield: Stating Grievances of a Number of the Members of Said Church*, written and published "By One of the Aggrieved Brethren," near Utica, New York.

In many cases, however, the preaching of one minister could be very powerful. At the time, a local minister did not provide just spiritual guidance; he was in many ways influential and sometimes directly responsible for invoking the laws of the community. One example was the Reverend Jacob Ide, A.M. Pastor of the Second Church in Medway, Massachusetts.

In 1818, the Reverend Jacob Ide delivered two sermons on successive weeks (December 21 and 28) that were specifically directed against dancing. The sermons were also combined and published under the title, "The Nature and Tendency of Balls, Seriously and Candidly Considered" and received a fair amount of distribution. Ide's justification was that it was the role of the religious leaders to decide what was right or wrong for the congregation. He argued

> that religious teachers should carefully examine the nature and tendency of prevailing opinions and practices, and faithfully approve or censure them, according as they agree, or disagree, with the known will of God. These observations, illustrative of the text, show the propriety of making that species of amusement, commonly known by the name of Balls, a subject of our serious and prayerful examination (4–5).

Ide felt that in order to justify his own condemnations he had to explain his reasoning. He expressly stated that he did not dispute any "ancient religious ceremony, in which the people of God, occasionally expressed their pious gratitude and joy, by dancing before the Lord." He also specifically acknowledged the Shakers practice of dancing. He added, "Nor do I feel myself called upon, in this place, to attack the Shakers, who, professedly in imitation of the ancient saints, now make dancing a part of their religious worship" (5–6). Instead, the Reverend Ide aligned himself with the same pattern as outlined by Cotton Mather nearly 120 years before in *A Cloud of Witness Against Balls and Dances* (see Chapter 1). Ide's specific protest was against the practice of attending a public ball to engage in mixed dancing, especially among the "youth."

The Reverend cautioned that, "Balls are, either very good things, or they are very bad things." But he added that the mere existence of a dancing party was solely aimed at attracting the innocent "natural vivacity, and playfulness of youth" (6). Therefore, Ide presented his argument as follows:

> The question, now to be determined, is, whether rational, and accountable beings, capable of the exalted pleasure of serving and enjoying God, destined to a future and an eternal existence, in which they are to receive according to the deeds done here in the body, have a right to spend their precious time, in dancing for mere amusement; in circumstances too, where they are exposed to peculiar temptations; where the mind is necessarily dissipated; where health and property are often wantonly sacrificed; where hours, consecrated, by nature, to silence and repose, are devoted to hilarity and mirth; and where by common consent, and the laws of fashion, serious reflection and fervent piety have no place (5).

He added that although many other religious leaders provided arguments in defense of dancing, Ide claimed that they were "obviously inconclusive" (23).

The Reverend invoked the justification that attendance at a ball was a waste of time and money. His reasoning was that if a person had idle time, then that time should be spent in either working or other things that might "benefit of himself, his family, and the public" (23). Ide recognized that many proponents claimed "there is no harm in dancing." He also presented information that there were counterarguments that the youth needed exercise and that time was needed for amusement. He countered that these arguments were not justification for the purpose of sponsoring a ball. He offered that instead of dancing, amusements could be better afforded and "advantageously conducted" through "reading instructive books...conversing upon important subjects...and in meditating upon what is read, and heard, and seen" (24).

The Reverend Ide did acknowledge that the churches were becoming more tolerant of the practice of dancing. In fact, by his own argument it appears that the toleration might have been almost evenly divided. Ide claimed:

> Besides, if the fact, that these amusements are countenanced by Christian churches, and by ministers of the gospel, is an argument in favour of them; then the fact, that they are opposed by Christian churches, and ministers of the gospel, is an argument against them (30).

Ide cautioned that after "a long course of indulgence" in dancing, the youth would be disappointed as they reviewed their lives in "confusion and regret." At that time, when "their usefulness were destroyed" it would have been "too late to retrace their steps" (36). Therefore, he attributed the attendance at balls to the "alarming degree of stupidity" among the youth in general. He contested that "The minds of youth must be extremely stupid, with respect to their own improvement" (44). He asked,

> Will not a view of the snares, to which youth, engaged in these amusements, are exposed in this life; the anxiety, which they are liable to feel at the hour of death; and the loss of eternal life, which they are in danger of sustaining; fill the minds of Christians with deep solemnity (50).

He concluded and warily cautioned that the youth of his congregation were faced with "the loss of eternal life" if they did not abstain from dancing (50).

THE PHILADELPHIA ASSEMBLY, THE NEW YORK MESCHIANZA, AND AMERICAN FASHION

Before the American Revolution the customary formal ball in the colonies was usually in honor of the birthday of the King, Queen, or Prince of England. After the revolution, a grand American ceremonial ball was held in honor instead for Washington's birthday. In contrast to Europe, though, class rank and social titles were eliminated in America, and invitations to elite balls were based on "professional standing" and wealth. Therefore, the honor of the first dance reserved for the "most important" person was usually also the wealthiest person (Marks 1957, 60–61).

Throughout the American colonial cities, fashionable assembly balls were held similar to those rules laid out in the fashionable London ballrooms. At any of the formal balls, throughout the American colonies, the wealthy and social elite continued to follow the etiquette and rules of the fashionable Assembly rooms such as Almack's in London or Bath, England. The Americans also sought similar instruction from a Dance Master well-versed in the European traditions. In 1738, for example, Theobald Hacket in Philadelphia advertised in the *Pennsylvania Gazette* of August 24–31 to teach "all sorts of fashionable English and French Dances, after the newest and politest manner practiced in London...and Paris" (quoted in Keller, "The Eighteenth Century Ballroom," 1996, 19).

One of the most famous was the Philadelphia Assembly that adopted a set of rules and regulations patterned after England. The first Philadelphia Assemblies were held every two weeks for a subscription price of 15 shillings (about $15) at Andrew Hamilton's house located on the wharf on Water Street. In the same manner of the English ballrooms such as Beau Nash's at Bath (see Chapter 1), the rules of the Assembly and ballroom etiquette were also posted on the wall. The "traditional dances" included the Minuet, Cotillion, Allemande, and Contredanse. The Philadelphia Assembly was held continually from 1706 to 1742. During that same time, the Quaker Society of Friends attempted to ban dancing from Philadelphia. However, in 1742, because of pressure applied by religious leader George Whitfield and the Quakers Society of Friends, the Philadelphia Assembly dancing ball was disbanded (also see earlier this chapter) (Marks 1957, 32–33).

In the winter of 1748, as the religious fervor of the Great Awakening subsided, the Philadelphia Assembly resumed at Hamilton's house with the support of the governor. However, at one event it appears that the governor was snubbed for reasons unknown. On May 3, 1749, the Reverend Richard Peters wrote to his friend Thomas Penn of the incident. Peters described it as follows:

> By the Governor's encouragement there has been a very handsome Assembly once a fortnight [two weeks] at Andrew Hamilton's house and stores…of eighty ladies and as many gentlemen…There happened a little mistake at the beginning, which at some other times might [have] produced disturbances. The Governor would have opened the Assembly with Mrs. Taylor, but she refused him…After Mrs. Taylor's refusal, two or three other ladies, out of Modesty and from no manner of ill design, excused themselves (Wharton 1893, 201).

It is not known how the escapade transpired, but it is known that the ball continued, not only through the season but also in the ensuing years. In addition, dancing was not the only entertainment at the Philadelphia Assembly. A separate room was also set aside for cardplaying and socializing.

In the following years, it appeared that the Philadelphia Assembly also revised the rules for admittance. In 1771, for example, a notice was placed in the *Pennsylvania Journal* that stated the following:

> The [Philadelphia] assembly will be opened this evening, and as the receiving money at the door has been found extremely inconvenient, the managers think it necessary to

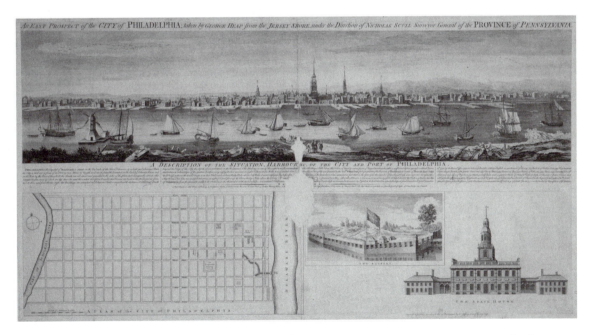

An illustration of the City of Philadelphia looking across the Delaware River from the shores of New Jersey. The illustration provides a good example of the American Colonial city and the reliance on waterways and ships. George Heap created the illustration under the authorization of the "Surveyor General of the Province of Pennsylvania" and was engraved by Thomas and published, "according to an Act of Parliament," in London, c. 1768. Library of Congress, Prints and Photographs Division LC-USZ62-3282.

give the public notice that no person will be admitted without a ticket from the directors, which (through the application of a subscriber) may be had of either of the managers (Wharton 1893, 209).

It is quite possible that the Philadelphia advertisement was simply following the lead of a similar 1769 advertisement placed by Almack's in the *London Daily Press* (see earlier this chapter). In the following years, admission to the Philadelphia Assembly was based on membership with a subscription ticket. Guests were allowed, but only if invited by a subscription holder. In 1772, the venue was changed to the Freemason's Lodge and the dances were held on Thursday evenings from January through May. Rules stipulated that the event begin promptly at 6:00 P.M. and end at exactly at midnight (Wharton 1893, 206–207).

During most of the Revolutionary War years (1775–1783), however, the "official" Philadelphia Assembly was held intermittently. Attempts were once again made to suspend not only the Philadelphia Assembly but all dancing. On October 12, 1778, the Continental Congress met and held business in Philadelphia. However, in response to a lobbying contingent of delegates from New England, composed of Puritan and Calvinistic delegates, the Congress adopted a resolution restricting amusements and entertainment. The New England delegation claimed that the amusements, such as dancing, were a distraction to the American Revolution. Maybe in deference to the Revolutionary spirit, the governor of the city disregarded the Continental Congress and sponsored a ball that included dancing (see earlier in this chapter) (Cole, "The Puritan and Fair Terpsichore," 1942, 25).

A short time later, Philadelphia was subject to British occupation. During the occupation, the British filled their idle time with dancing. One British supporter (known as Tories) named Miss Franks wrote to her friend,

> You can have no idea of the life of continued amusement I live in.…I am dressed for a ball this evening at Smith's where we have one every Thursday.…I spent Tuesday evening [with British General William] Howe where we had a concert and Dance (Wharton 1893, 219–220).

Around 1780, the British evacuated Philadelphia. By that time, it was also obvious that the war and politics were intertwined with the social amusements of the Philadelphia Assembly. During the winter season of 1780 to 1781, for example, the Assembly was "officially" reinstated; however, "the Tory ladies [were] publicly excluded" (Cole 1942, 28).

The Marquis de Chastellux of France provided a contemporary account. During 1780 to 1782, Chastellux traveled the American colonies and kept a journal of his accounts and observations. On December 14, 1780, he recorded that he attended "an assembly in Philadelphia." Of particular interest were the Country-dances named after the ongoing Revolutionary War. He wrote:

> These dances, like the "toasts" we drink at table, have a marked connection with politics: one is called "the success of the campaign," another "Burgoyne's defeat," and a third, "Clinton's retreat" (Rice 1963, 177).

It is quite possible that Chastellux's description of "the success of the campaign," was actually "A Successful Campaign," a Country-dance that was very popular at the time (see earlier in this chapter).

With the war over, the dance assembly continued uninterrupted. From 1784 to 1789, for example, the *Pennsylvania Journal* noted that they were held at the City Tavern. During the 1790s, the Philadelphia Assembly was moved to Oeller's Hotel, which had a ballroom over 60 feet square. Oeller's ballroom was also decorated in contemporary French wallpapers and similar fashion to the London Assembly rooms. At about the same time, a second competing assembly was organized and also held a biweekly series of dancing separate and apart from the Philadelphia assembly. In 1800, they were merged and continued as one elite society. In 1802, the dances were held at the Francis Hotel on Market Street. It was suspended once again briefly during the War of 1812 and revived shortly thereafter. It continued through the twentieth century (Wharton 1893, 206–207; Buckman 1978, 111).

In all cases, the rules of dance etiquette and proper ballroom manners were visibly posted and the subscription requirement remained. A contemporary account by a French visitor to Philadelphia named Moreau de Saint-Mery noted, "This is particularly noticeable at balls. There are some balls where no one is admitted unless his professional standing is up to a certain mark." However, Saint-Mery, who traveled extensively throughout America from 1793 to 1798, expressed dislike to the subscription policy, which he described as "great snobbery in Philadelphia" (Roberts and Roberts 1947, 333).

The tradition of the European assembly carried over into all the American colonies. One direct example was in the city of Boston, which named its assembly "Almack." Similar to the other assemblies, Boston's Almack was limited to only about 100 well-to-do Boston subscribers. However, one contemporary account provided a striking contrast to the "great snobbery in Philadelphia." In 1744, Dr. Alexander Hamilton (no relation to the famed statesman) noted upon a visit to Boston:

> Assemblies of the gayer sort are frequent here...the gentlemen and ladys meet almost every week at consorts of musick [sic] and balls. I was present at two or three such and saw as fine a ring of ladys, as good dancing, and heard musick as I had been witness to anywhere...I saw not one prude while I was here (quoted in Nevell 1977, 31).

Throughout the 1760s and 1770s, the society season in Boston held dances every other week beginning in January and continuing through April. Invited guests numbered between 100 and 200 and included the governor and the social elite. Unlike some other contemporary assemblies or the rural dances that had maybe one fiddler and another musician, the Boston assembly balls usually had between five and ten musicians. Many of the dances were held in a place called Ransom's located near the Boston State House. The dancing usually started at 7:00 P.M. and lasted until 2:00 A.M. A unique feature of the third floor ballroom at Ransom's was a specially constructed "spring floor." The device softened the stamping of feet against the floor, and not only was it less tiresome, it also was "intended to expedite the rhythm of the dance" (Daniels 1995, 116).

During the War of 1812 with England, the official Boston assembly balls were suspended. From 1813 until 1817, a series of "cotillion Parties" supplemented the lack of an official assembly ball. Despite the war, one Boston socialite informed a friend, "In the regions of fashion dancing still continues the rage. Private balls are numerous, and little cotillion [sic] parties occur every week." In 1818, after the cessation of hostilities with England, Bostonians celebrated with a "Peace Ball" and the official assembly was revived (Cole 1942, 19–21).

Numerous other cities around the New England area had similar balls. In 1787, for example, the city of Hartford, Connecticut, noted that a dancing master from New York City had set up shop. He tallied 90 pupils taking up to three lessons per week in the graces of "four different kinds of minuets; also Cotillions, minuet Cotillions, Country-dances and the Hornpipe." There followed a series of "cotillion parties" and eventually by 1790, Hartford sponsored a local assembly hosted by the governor's daughter that were held every two weeks for a ten-week winter season. The first session was attended by George Washington (see earlier in this chapter). It ran annually until 1813, when it was also disrupted by war (Daniels 1995, 116; Cole 1942, 20).

As early as 1736, dances and balls were given in the Black Horse Tavern in New York City (see Chapter 1). Throughout most of the eighteenth century, the Black Horse Tavern continued as host of many dances and assemblies. In New York, however, the assembly balls were not just limited to one place. In 1747, in New York City, for example, it was noted that assemblies were given and even divided between the young set and the old set. However, most took lessons from a Dance Master. In 1759, for example, the *New York Gazette* of September 24 listed an advertisement for the dance instruction services of one "Mr. Hulet." The account noted that Hulet "would attend them in their own homes" for dancing lessons. By 1770, he opened his own Public Dancing School and taught afternoon and evening classes in the Minuet and in English Country-dances for both young men and women. He even offered private lessons for "gentlemen only" in the Hornpipe (Marks 1957, 39).

One elite New York assembly ball was known as the Meschianza. According to author Anne Hollingsworth Wharton in *Through Colonial Doorways* (1893), "The names by which this *fete* is known, Meschianza and Mischianza, are derived from two Italian words,—*mescere*, to mix and *mischiare*, to mingle." The first Meschianza was most likely held in May 1778 and continued through the nineteenth century (Wharton 1893, 27–28).

Similar assembly balls were also held in the South. In 1783, for example, the Richmond Assembly in Virginia was held every two weeks. Some of the specific rules set the minimum age of entry for a young lady at 13 and the gentlemen at 18. In similar fashion, a notice of the rules and etiquette were not only posted on the walls but also printed on a flyer. For example, one notice listed as the *Rules of the Richmond Assemblies, November 1790* set the dance to begin with Minuets but limited them to no "more than four." Any additional "fancy dances" such as the French Allemande, was limited to "half an hour" and "to be succeeded by country dances." The rules were actually numbered and a sampling was as follows:

6th That the couple which may have led a dance, must thereafter stand at the bottom, and no couple may call two dances.

7th No gentlemen shall dance in boots, or without gloves.

8th If any person dance out of turn without permission, they shall not dance again that evening.

The assembly rules in other cities were quite similar with only slight variations (Keller and Fogg 2003, 4–6).

In 1790, the rules of the Assembly in Savannah, Georgia, added, "No lady shall call more than one dance, and the figure which she sets shall be observed through the whole without variation, unless altered with her consent." In 1791, the Baltimore Assembly prescribed that after one lady had called a dance and led it from the top of the set she was required, with her partner, to take a place at the bottom of the set (Keller and Hendrickson 1998, 109).

An integral part of dancing at a formal assembly ball was formal attire. After the French Revolution in 1789, European fashions changed drastically. One noticeable example was that the powdered wigs of the Royal Court were eliminated (see Chapter 1). Similarly, Americans did the same. After 1800, American fashion followed the European trend in Neoclassicism as the dress styles and hair styles alluded to the fashions of the ancient Greeks and Romans. In a few short years, women's dress waistlines rose a little bit higher, thereby slightly raising the skirt hem above the floor. The shortened skirts were also "A-shaped," and the dress sleeves were puffed. Shortly after 1820, the waistlines were once again lowered closer to "the natural waistline of the female body." At the same time the skirts were also cut a bit more fuller. After that and for the remainder of the nineteenth century, the fashions reverted back to the French styles from Paris.

On the other hand, the gentlemen's attire remained virtually unchanged. *The Ball-Room Guide, a Handy Manual* recommended "a black dress suit in the evening, only allowing him a white waist-coat as an occasional relief to his toilet." Between 1800 and 1820, knee-breeches were slowly phased out and gentlemen wore close fitting pantaloons, which at about that time were soon called "trousers." Although in separate publications in 1808 and 1816 venerable Dance Master Thomas Wilson declared that the pantaloons were not "considered proper dress" for dancing in the ballroom, the pants style became standard attire for men. And with very little change they remained the standard attire for the remainder of the nineteenth and twentieth centuries (Aldrich 1991, 24–25, 33–34).

A basic necessity (and even required for many events) was gloves. However, in the strictest sense of the changing values in society that although face-to-face dancing was slowly accepted, the touching of each other's bare skin was definitely not acceptable. After 1800, many etiquette manuals of the day stressed the necessity of not one—but two pairs of gloves. The reason was twofold. The glove was first and foremost, at least in the described etiquette, to prevent the gentleman's perspiration from "soiling" the lady's dress. Second, a common reason given was that just in case the gentleman soiled his gloves while preparing a drink of punch, he would therefore have a second "clean" pair (Aldrich 1991, 35).

THE VILLAGE ASSEMBLY, DANCING IN RURAL AREAS, WEDDINGS, AND TAVERNS

From 1793 to 1798, during his extensive travel of America, Moreau de Saint-Mery witnessed firsthand dancing at formal assemblies and also among poorer city dwellers and among the rural countryside residents. In many cases, American colonists in a small town or village would also sponsor a community "Village Assembly" for dancing and enjoyment. In contrast to the formal assembly balls, Saint-Mery observed that many of the "plainer folk" in all of America danced just for fun and were not necessarily concerned about the strict formalities. Saint-Mery added,

> I have already said elsewhere that dancing for the inhabitants of the United States is less a matter of self-display than it is true enjoyment. At the same dance you will see a grandfather, his son and his grandson, but more often still the grandmother, her daughter and grand-daughter. If a Frenchman comments upon this with surprise he is told that one dances for his own amusement, and not because it is the thing to do (Roberts and Roberts 1947, 290–291).

Although in similar fashion to the fashionable assembly balls of the wealthy, the "plainer folk" also dressed their best when attending a dance.

In the rural areas, they would also gather together and dance on the occasion of a "bee" or a "frolic." The bee or frolic usually followed a combined family or community work task such as husking, harvesting, quilting, or even barn building. A contemporary account in the journal of John De Crevecoeur described his elation of the purpose of music and dancing in America. He wrote:

> I really know among us of no custom which is so useful and tends so much to establish the union and the little society which subsists among us. Poor as we are, if we have not the gorgeous balls, the harmonious concerts, the shrill horn of Europe, yet we dilate our hearts as well with the simple Negro fiddle (95–96).

For many of the dances whether by the social elite or the "plainer folk," music was usually provided by an African American. And in some cases, African Americans also taught dancing. On October 14, 1775, for example, the *Virginia Gazette* reported that the recent arrival of a slave ship contained a "dancing master" (Marks 1957, 41; footnotes 51 and 53).

Dancing in the American colonies was also associated with other festive occasions such as weddings. According to historian Bruce Daniels, in *Puritans at Play: Leisure and Recreation in Colonial New England* (1995), "The quiet feasting era of wedding celebrations began to end in the 1730s and 1740s; by mid-century, the boisterous and lavish reception had emerged" (118). After 1740, it was quite common and respectable for a wedding celebration to last two or more days and also include games and music.

Historian Jane Carson in *Colonial Virginians at Play* (1965) noted that at colonial weddings in Virginia dancing was intermingled with games. Carson wrote,

THE VILLAGE ASSEMBLY

American colonists dance at a "Village Assembly." The illustration is actually a caricature created in England of a "stately dance" in the American Colonies c. 1776.   Library of Congress, Prints and Photographs Division LC-USZ62-59606.

> Dancing began immediately after the meal and lasted until dawn. If a tired dancer tried to hide out for a brief nap, he was hunted up, paraded on the floor, and required to dance to a special tune, [titled] "Hang Out till Morning" (21).

Carson noted, regardless of the Virginian hostess's graceful capability of sponsoring a wedding reception, "all of them loved to dance, and they gave formal balls on the slightest excuses—or none at all."

In 1774, Philip Fithian, traveling from his home in New Jersey, noted in his journal that he had attended a dance at Lee Hall in Virginia that lasted four days. The dancing included Minuets, Reels, Country-dances, and Jigs. Fithian expressed utter astonishment because he was unaccustomed to the long-lasting revelry. The revelry continued with a breakfast in the morning followed by some other activities including cardplaying, music, and conversation during the day. The evening continued with a supper and followed by dancing once again in the evening (Carson 1965, 22–23).

In comparison with New England, which preferred more Country-dances, Fithian remarked that Virginians preferred Minuets and French dances. On December 15, 1781, at a ball in Williamsburg, Virginia, he noted in his journal the following:

> The fair sex in this city like Minuets very much. It is true that some of them dance them rather well, and infinitely better than those up north; to make amends for this, the latter

dance the Scottish [reels] better. All of them like our French Quadrilles, and in general, they find the French manners to their taste.

Fithian also noted that on that same night French General Rochambeau also attended the dance (see earlier in this chapter) (Fithian "Journal," 1953, 213).

Earlier, in 1774, Fithian had also written of another ball he had attended that had more than just dancing. He added:

> About Seven [p.m.] the Ladies & Gentlemen begun to dance in the Ball-room—first Minuets one Round; Second Giggs [Jigs]; third Reels; And last of All Country-Dances.... But all did not join in the Dance for there were parties in Rooms made up, some at Cards; some drinking for pleasure (Keller and Hendrickson 1998, 13).

"Drinking for pleasure" was an increasingly common occurrence among common folk and laborers in both rural areas and the cities.

In the bigger cities, such as New York, for example, some of those included "Negro Dance Cellars" (see earlier in this chapter) that afforded an opportunity for drinking, cardplaying, listening to music, and dancing. Throughout the

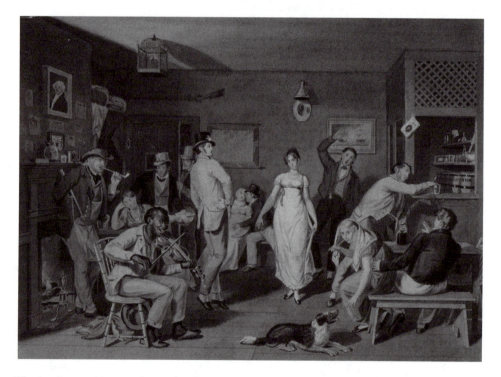

The drawing provides a good example of Americans partaking in the fun and merrymaking in a local tavern. "The simple Negro fiddle" provides music, and a man and woman dance in the center. The woman's dress waistline is indicative of the time period as it rose a little bit higher, thereby slightly raising the skirt hem above the floor, and the dress sleeves were shorter and puffed. The man is wearing "pantaloons," c. 1820.   Library of Congress, Prints and Photographs Division LC-USZ62-94848.

American colonies, similar entertainment was had in taverns. One of the earliest records of dancing in taverns appeared at least as early as 1651 recorded by Nathaniel B. Shurtleff, editor of the *Records of the Governor and Company of Massachusetts Bay in New England*. Prior to the Revolution, because of the combination of alcohol and dancing, many of the colonial cities and towns simply outlawed any dancing in taverns. Shurtleff noted that in Boston, the General Court of Massachusetts issued an edict to end the practice by instituting a fine of "five shillings" for any individual who danced in a tavern (Cole 1942, 17).

However, during the Revolution, most likely as a diversion to the war, many taverns offered dancing with little or no interference. After the revolution, many taverns offered one of the few opportunities to meet and mingle. Not unlike the formal Assembly balls, the taverns included a combination of drinking, listening to music, cardplaying, dancing, and, in general, just plain having fun and "merry-making" (Daniels 1995, 115–117).

AMERICAN DANCE MASTERS, JOHN GRIFFITHS, AND DANCING AS EDUCATION

The nature and acceptance of dance among Americans as part of the social fabric was evident by numerous advertisements and articles in contemporary newspapers and journals. In July 1785, for example, a popular monthly journal, *The Lady's Magazine*, published a series of articles titled "A New Treatise on the Art of Dancing." The article, published in six installments from February through July, was addressed "To the Editor" by an anonymous author. The author wished to provide "some useful instructions never before published" regarding dancing and also commented "on the different Manner of Teaching this Art, interspersed with some Observations on dancing Masters in General" (44).

It was certainly evident that the author definitely approved of dancing. In regards to dancing and social acceptance, the author provided the following argument:

> It has been universally allowed that *Dancing* is one of the most useful accomplishments a well-bred person can be possessed of. No gentleman or lady can be said to be qualified for a court, an assembly, or even any public life, without some knowledge of this art: a man or woman, cannot even walk with any degree of the graces (as the late lord Chesterfield terms it) without having been taught at least the rudiments of Dancing (45).

This statement is actually paraphrased from a well-known contemporary English etiquette expert named Lord Chesterfield (see later in this chapter).

The author, however, implied that it was the contemporary method of dance instruction as taught by Dance Masters that was rigid and awkward, resulting in a "stiff gait, so resembling the *monkey who had seen the world*" (a title of a 1724 fable). The reaction was also strongly against the rigidity of the five positions of the feet and the Minuet style, claiming that the "rise and sink" of the forward Minuet step was "an *unnatural* form" and the "bow" as a "ridiculous movement." The criticism continued, adding:

These are the movements which ever after constitute that abominable stiff and unnatural gait, which we see in the generality of Dancing-masters; and the more the scholar imitates the master, the more affected he appears (47).

Considering the article was written in 1785, an air of American loyalty and anti-British sentiment might have been evident as the contention was that the unnatural appearance was a direct result of European Dance Masters. The reasoning applied was, "Our English teachers have in general, no conception of it, and the greatest part of the foreigners murder it with unnatural and ungraceful movements" (46–47).

A knock was also placed squarely against the French cotillion, claiming that they were performed without vitality.

The *cotillion* must be considered, as it really is, a French country dance, and consequently should be danced, as already said, with uncommon vivacity: for as the French do everything with great spirit, and as we pretend to imitate them, we should not omit the most essential part, which gives life to, and renders their dances any way tolerable.

It was suggested that "They should be danced with great spirit and attention to time, otherwise they are by no means entertaining, and at best fall short of our English country dances" (48–49).

It is quite possible that the remarks printed in *The Lady's Magazine* were part of a growing sentiment in America. For the most part, dance instruction was still applied in the formal manner; however, some Dance Masters might have felt the need to dispel any reservations that a prospective dance student might have had. On September 25, 1788, for example, Dance Master Simon C. McMahon advertised in the *Virginia Gazette* to teach "elegant, fashionable, tasty, and approved parts in the science of dancing." He proposed to teach both "in private and in publick" on Fridays and Saturdays, Minuets, Allemandes, Cotillions, and Country-dances. He also added to "use all kinds of industry, all manners of decorum, and every specie of attention, that the first rate Dancing Masters are so much praised for" (quoted in Keller and Fogg 2003, 5).

In 1797, another example in the *New Hampshire Gazette* carried the following advertisement:

Dancing School—Messrs. Renard & Barbot Respectively inform the public that they intend opening a dancing school, in which they will teach Country Dances, Cotillions, Minuet, Allemand, and Horn-Pipe. They will neglect nothing to deserve the approbation of those who will trust them with their tuition (Page 1977, 28).

After the Revolution, a notable change was evident in the emergence of American dance masters and publications of American sources. At the time it was common for Dance Masters traveling from town to town to also have either copies of European publications or their own "self-made reference books." One of the traveling Dance Masters was American born John Griffiths (earlier sources list him as "Griffith"). Griffiths taught many of the dances that were popular in

America at the time. However, he also made up and wrote down some dances of his own design (Nevell 1977, 34).

In 1787, Griffiths traveled to Norwich, Connecticut, where he was introduced to a fiddler named John Turner. At the time it was quite common to copy tunes and dance figures from just about any available source. It was apparent that Turner was no different as he borrowed from Griffiths some collections of dances and copied over 100 dance tunes into his own notebook. One of the tunes was an original by Griffiths titled "Griffiths Whim" (Keller, "Early American Social Dance," n.d.).

In 1788, John Griffiths published 29 Country-dances, which is most likely the first American dance publication. Within that publication was "Fisher's Hornpipe" (see earlier in this chapter). Some sources claim that the publication was actually issued earlier in 1786 in New Haven. In 1789, John Griffiths advertised that he was teaching "new cotillions, which have been but four months since invented in Paris; and a Solo-minuet which was never before danced in America." Although Griffiths traveled as far south as Charleston, South Carolina, his publications of at least eight collections of American dances were from New England, including Northampton, Massachusetts; Providence, Rhode Island; and Walpole, New Hampshire (Nevell 1977, 33–34).

In 1794, Griffiths published *A Collection of the Newest Cotillions, and Country Dances; Principally Composed by John Griffiths, Dancing Master. To Which is Added, Instances of Ill Manners, to be carefully avoided by Youth of both sexes.* Sometimes simply known as *Etiquette for Dancemasters* the Northampton, Massachusetts, publication was reprinted on a few occasions between 1794 and 1804. According to dance historian Bruce Daniels, Griffiths's publication was "to help dances and dance schools overcome the last pockets of small-town and rural opposition" (113).

Two publications by the Colonial Music Institute, *John Griffiths, Dancing Master, 29 Country Dances* (1989) by Charles Cyril Hendrickson and *John Griffiths, Eighteenth-Century Itinerant Dancing Master* (1989) by Kate Van Winkle Keller, provided an excellent reference source for John Griffiths. Another publication, *Dance Figures Index: American Country Dances, 1730–1810* (1989), by Robert M. Keller compiled 2,738 American dances from 82 contemporary sources. The compilation was derived from contemporary commonplace books, journals, and published sources in the American colonies.

A wonderful bibliography of sources was compiled by Kate Van Winkle Keller of The Colonial Music Institute that contained almost every known published American source pertaining to dancing in America prior to 1820 (see author's bibliography). The bibliography, available online, in a Web article *Early American Social Dance: A Bibliography of Sources to 1820*, provides an excellent source for dance instruction of the early American colonial period. According to Keller, the bibliography contains, "a list of every book, pamphlet, broadside, periodical or manuscript published or made in North America to 1820." Most of the publications are from 1790 and 1810, which actually correlates to the emergence of the new American nation. Keller also acknowledges the fact that, "Undoubtedly there are more sources to be located, and some that we know about have not been relocated" (Keller, *Early American Social Dance*, n.d.).

A sampling of the titles includes Benjamin Walker's *Orders for a Dancing School* (1784) that included "Rules of school and figures of 26 country dances," published in Lunenburg, Virginia; James Alexander's commonplace book of 1730 that contained the figures for 27 country-dances (see Chapter 1); an interesting London publication edited by Mr. Cantelo, *Twenty Four American Country Dances as Danced by the British during their Winter Quarters at Philadelphia, New York, & Charles Town* (1785); a 1795 New Hampshire publication of a commonplace book, *Square Dances. Manuscript instructions* that contained figures for 54 Country-dances in manuscript form. In 1799, John H. Ives published *Twenty-four Figures of The Most Fashionable Country Dances: Together with Eight Cotillions, for the Year Eighteen Hundred* in New Haven, Connecticut. The following year Pierre Landrin Duport released a New York publication titled *United States Country Dances* (1800). One Philadelphia printer published a collection of works from 1798 to 1804 of Alexander Reinagle's *Mr. Francis's Ballroom Assistant* that included "a collection of the most admired cotillions and country dances with their proper figures annexed. Including a variety of marches, minutes [sic], reels, gavots, hornpipes, &c. The music composed and selected and the whole arranged as lessons for the piano forte by Mr. Reinagle." Another Philadelphia publication, *Elements and principles of the art of dancing, as used in the polite and fashionable circles, also rules of deportment and descriptions of manners of civility, appertaining to that art* (1817) by J.H. Gourdoux-Daux, might have been directly related to the Philadelphia Assembly.

One of the most noted instructional books on manners was by Lord Chesterfield. Originally published in England, the posthumous writings were published in Boston in 1794 under the title *Principles of Politeness, and of Knowing the World, by the Late Lord Chesterfield*. He indicated that the best way to "good-breeding" and "genteel manners" was through dance. Chesterfield proclaimed:

> Now to acquire a graceful air, you must attend to your dancing: no one can either sit, stand or walk well, unless he dances well. And in learning to dance, be particularly attentive to the motion of your arms for a stiffness in the wrist will make any man look awkward. If a man walks well, presents himself well in company, wears his hat well, moves his head properly, and his arms gracefully, it is almost all that is necessary (Trusler 1794, 20–22).

However, not everyone agreed with Lord Chesterfield. One critic, Samuel Johnson, wrote that the advice was the equivalent of "the morals of a whore and the manners of a dancing master" (Marks 1957, 47).

In America, many viewed dancing as part of the education of the youth. It was common that young men were taught the classics, drama, science, arithmetic, fencing, and dancing. As for females, the education was limited. Abigail Adams (wife of president John Adams) stated, "Female education, in the best families, went no further than writing and arithmetic; in some few and rare instances, music and dancing." In 1782, the Reverend John Eliot, also of Boston, countered, "We don't pretend to teach ye female part of ye town anything more than dancing, or a little music perhaps" (quoted in Marks 1957, 38).

In 1792, a Philadelphia publication on education written by a Dr. Blair titled *Sentimental Beauties, and Moral Delineations...Selected with a View to Refine the Taste, rectify the Judgment, and Mould the Heart to Virtue* suggested a different approach. He proclaimed:

> Yet, though, the well-bred woman should learn to dance, sing, recite, and draw; the end of a good education is not that they may become singers, dancers, players, or painters; its real object is, to make them good daughters, good wives, good mistresses, good members of society and good Christians (Marks 1957, 47).

One of the "essential" books for the well-mannered young lady was *Sermons to Young Women* by James Fordyce. Printed in London, by 1814 it was in its 14th edition. Many girl's boarding schools listed it as required reading. Fordyce, on the other hand, was another that stressed the good effects of dancing. He wrote that dancing was well-suited:

> To promote health and good humor, a social spirit, and kind of affections between the sexes...[for] what is dancing, in the best sense, but the harmony of motion rendered more palpable? (Vol. I, 181–184).

On the other hand, in 1788, Noah Webster was one of the early advocates in developing a distinct American cultural tradition. He thought that Americans were continually making mistakes and doing "ill-will to the young lady's" by blatantly following the cultural lead of England and France. Webster said that the European tradition was evident and "illustrated in every large town in America." However, he added that an education in dancing, music, and the arts would drastically alter the domestic duties required of females. Ironically, Webster himself was known to frequent balls and partake in dancing. While in New York he had taken dance lessons from Mr. Hulet (Webster 1788, 339–340; Marks 1957, 53–54).

The idea of dancing combined with education was not widely accepted, especially as it applied to American colleges and universities. In 1722, Benjamin Franklin, for example, satirically wrote that all that a student had learned at Harvard could well have been "which might as well be acquir'd [acquired] at a Dancing School." From 1725 to 1769, during the tenure of president Wadsworth (1725 to 1737) and president Rev. Edward Holyoke (1737 to 1769), Harvard University maintained a strict written policy, "That there shall be no Dancing allow'd [sic] on any part of Commencement Week, either in the College-Hall or Chapel." Although under strict control of "Puritan propriety," one father protested that the students "must not be permitted to have any engagements but with their Books." However, by 1771, John Adams noted that dancing was included as part of Harvard's commencement ceremonies and during the 1770s that the students did partake in dancing (Marks 1957, 56; Cole 1942, 22–23).

By 1815, it was noted that a local dancing school in the Cambridge area was frequented by many a Harvard student. In response, in 1819, Harvard president John T. Kirkland instituted a fine of "five dollars" for any Harvard student who attended a dance in the local Boston area. Throughout, the nineteenth century, dancing was banned at the university. In 1907, Harvard president Charles W. Eliot proclaimed, although a bit sadly, "I have often said that if I were compelled to have one required subject in Harvard College, I would make it dancing if I could" (Cole 1942, 22–23; James 1930, 163).

In 1782, Ezra Stiles, the president of Yale College, approved the hiring of a local Dance Maser to instruct Yale students; however, pressure from "civil authorities" forced the discontinuance of the dance instruction. In 1829, one of the rules defined in the *Laws of Yale College* warned, "If any Student shall attend any dancing assembly, or dancing school in the city of New Haven, in term time, he [Yale was strictly men only] may be admonished, suspended or sent home" (Cole 1942, 21–24).

Princeton also banned dancing among their students. During the 1780s, for example, when told that a French Dance Master held dance lessons in a local tavern, the college administrators forbade any students from attending. However, the student body protested. Not long thereafter the students secured the right to hold an annual ball and by 1786 dancing was a regular occurrence (Marks 1957, 57).

In 1819, at Georgia University, president Moses Waddel instituted a strict ban against dancing. In 1823, for example, a group of students violated the policy and attended a dance. They were fined a very hefty sum of one dollar each. In addition, they were admonished and threatened with worse penalty if the attendance at a "Ball or Dancing party" happened again (Cole 1942, 26, footnote 96). For the most part, however, most of the southern colleges encouraged dancing. According to dance historian Joseph Marks, "Where northern colleges tended to pass laws against dancing and forbid their students to frequent dancing school, the southern colleges encouraged it." In almost all cases, dancing was an integral part of the social life and well-grooming of southern aristocrats. One case in point was the College of William and Mary in Williamsburg, Virginia, that had approved and provided space for local dance instructors (see Chapter 1) (Marks 1957, 59).

JOHN ADAMS, THOMAS JEFFERSON, AND THE PRESIDENTIAL INAUGURAL BALL

From 1760 to 1762, future president Thomas Jefferson was a student at the College of William and Mary in Williamsburg, Virginia. During one winter season, he attended a series of balls at the Raleigh Tavern adjacent to the college. Although he did not dance nearly as much as George Washington (see earlier in this chapter), Jefferson was fond of dancing. Shortly after the death of his wife, Jefferson accepted an appointment as the American Minister (ambassador) to France. During his five-year stay, from 1785 to 1789, Jefferson experienced firsthand all the culture Paris offered. He frequented the Royal Court of Marie Antoinette and King Louis XVI and attended numerous balls. At the same time, he made the acquaintance of an artist named Maria Cosway. Together they were known to frequent and enjoy the salons, parties, and assemblies. By 1789, just prior to the French Revolution, Paris was the center of the dancing world. At the time there were over 700 dance halls in Paris alone (Richardson, 40–42; Clarke and Crisp 1981, 101).

In March 1818, Jefferson, in regards to female education in general, proposed "dancing, drawing, and music." Jefferson was meticulous in scheduling out every waking moment of the day for both himself and his family. For example, he suggested that his daughter Patsy should allow time for dancing lessons from 10:00 A.M. to 1:00 P.M. every other day (Carson 1965, 24).

In contrast to Jefferson's friend and later political nemesis, John Adams was known to deplore dancing. Around 1760, the Revolutionary leader and the nation's second president wrote in his diary, for example, that he "never knew a good dancer good for anything else." Adams, who unlike his compatriot Washington and friend Jefferson, did not himself dance. Adams also confessed in his diary that he knew of knowledgeable people of "sense and learning" who did dance but conceded none of them "had the more sense or learning or virtue for it." He did concede that he did know one Zab Howard who "had the reputation for at least fifteen years of the best dancer in the world. Several attempted but none could equal him, in nimbleness of heel" (*John Adams* 1961, Vol. II, 289; Daniels 1995, 113–116).

In 1778, as John Adams sailed to France as minister to solidify the new ally in the American Revolution, he witnessed dancing onboard his ship. In his diary of March 7, 1778, Adams wrote,

> Then the Captain [Barron] ordered a Dance, upon the Main Deck, and all Hands, Negroes, Boys and Men were obliged to dance. After this the old Sailors set on Foot another Frolic, called the Miller, or the Mill....It is not superiour [sic] to Negro and Indian Dances (Bruccoli et al.,, 372).

On the other hand, his wife Abigail Adams thought dancing to be a necessary part of the education of the young women of New England. Also in contrast to his father, future president John Quincy Adams, while studying law at Newburyport, "was often cavorting in eight or nine hour dancing sessions." In 1783, the younger Adams also joined the residents of Salem, Massachusetts, in celebration of the New Year with five dances in nine days (Cole, "The Puritan and Fair Terpsichore," 1942, 18, 26).

In December 1796, at the end of Washington's presidency, the society elite of Washington, D.C., hosted its first dancing assembly. During the presidency of John Adams, as the first residents of the newly built White House, dancing was not a focus of the social calendar. Actually, it was not until 1809, during the presidency of James Madison and his wife Dolley, that the first "official" inaugural ball was held in Washington, D.C. The event hosted by Dolley Madison became a tradition every four years for all succeeding presidents into the twenty-first century. In 1810, Dolley also purchased the first official White House piano and sheet music from an artisan in Philadelphia. In addition, the winter society season in the nation's capital soon became a series of what seemed like never-ending parties and balls (Cole 1942, 30).

NEW ORLEANS, THE PROJET D'ARRÊTE LEGISLATION, AND CONGO SQUARE'S "LURID REPUTATION"

In December 1803, the city of New Orleans was officially transferred to the jurisdiction of the United States. The city had recently been acquired by President

Thomas Jefferson as part of the Louisiana Purchase from the French under the reign of Napoleon Bonaparte. The French themselves had only recently reacquired it, less than a month before, through a war with Spain. (The Spanish had controlled the area from 1743 to 1803, and the French were in power prior to 1743.) Prior to the transfer of New Orleans from French to American control, the French governor Pierre de Laussat sponsored a lavish ball for over 300 invited guests. The dance was led off by the traditional Minuet and was followed by 12 hours of dancing. Throughout the 12 hours, careful consideration was paid to those "Americans" in attendance as one English Country-dance was played for every three French Quadrilles or Contredanses. In addition, an occasional Waltz was played for those of Spanish ancestry (Needham 2002, 66–68).

In fact, the United States' occupation of New Orleans presented a clash of cultures on the dance floor. The language difference of the French Creole inhabitants (about 90 percent of the population) and the newly arriving English-speaking Americans spread to the main area of public assemblies, which were the dance halls. In January 1804, during the first month of American control, some rumors arose that the new American Governor William C. Claiborne would not allow a continuation of dancing at public balls. The rumor was rampant enough that some influential New Orleans citizens questioned the new American governor.

However, it did not appear that the banning of public dancing at balls was ever considered. Therefore, in order to waylay any apprehensions, American Governor Claiborne made as many public appearances at the dances as possible. In fact, on January 8, 1804, Claiborne attended the same ball as the former French governor Laussat. On that night, however, a disagreement over the style of dancing arose between the French citizens and the Americans. The French Creoles preferred Quadrilles and Contredanses, whereas the Americans preferred English Country-dances (such as the Virginia Reel) and Jigs. Laussat witnessed an incident and noted in his diary:

> Two quadrilles, one French, the other English, were formed at once. An American, taking exception, brandished his stick over a fiddler, and there was at once, great turmoil. [Governor] Claiborne...finally, used more persuasion than rigor to prevail upon the American...The French quadrille was allowed to go on, but the American interrupted it on its second time around with an English quadrille, taking his position on the floor: some one cried out: "If the women have a drop of French blood in their veins, they will not give in!" (Laussat 1940, 138).

But the disagreement was not an isolated incident. Laussat noted that the next public ball, held on January 22, 1804, aroused even more emotions. At that dance, rumors abounded among the French that a local New Orleans resident had been arrested by the American military. Tensions ran high and caused arguments that interrupted the dancing. An American military authority tried to dispel the rumor, but language barriers prevented the resumption of dancing. A fight ensued between the French and the Americans, requiring intervention by the local militia.

The situation was not one to be taken lightly. Newly appointed Governor Claiborne notified Secretary of State James Madison of the circumstances. Reports of the incidents were carried as far away as New York City. The animosity in the culture clash in public places was hinted as a subversive act by sympathizers to Bonaparte. On March 10, 1804, for example, the *New York Herald* newspaper asked:

> What the national consequences of this quarrel will be, God only knows. It is very apparent from the whole, taken together that it is only breaking out of long smothered animosities of which we fear we have not heard the last. Bonaparte has got his millions of our money.

Actually, at that time many Americans thought that the sale of the Louisiana territory amounted to a "swindle" perpetrated by Napoleon against the American people.

Governor Claiborne considered the situation serious enough to enact legislation regulating the sequence of dances played in the public dance halls and at official assemblies. On January 25, 1804, in response "which troubled the public balls last Sunday, the 22nd of this month," he issued a full set of regulations titled *Projet d'Arrête*. The regulations set down a specific rotation of dances representing the three main ethnic citizens of New Orleans, the French, Americans, and Spaniards. The specific ratio of dances included two French Contredanses or Quadrilles for the Creoles, one English Contredanse or English Country-dances and Jigs for the Americans, and one Waltz for those of Spanish ancestry. The English Country-dances were limited to two sets of 12 couples each to prevent any mass intrusions if "as many as will" crowded the dance floor. However, not all the residents agreed with the legislation. One prominent Spaniard expressed some dissatisfaction, declaring, "We have been [in New Orleans] thirty years and the Spaniards have never forced us to dance the Fandango. We do not wish to dance either the reel or the jig."

Some of the other *Projet d'Arrête* provisions required that any person entering a public dance was obliged to leave any weapons at the front entrance. In addition, any person who was deemed to "interrupt any dance or tune" was subject to arrest. For good measure, two police officers were stationed within each of the dance halls. At the first event following the new regulations, Governor Claiborne not only attended but also assigned 15 additional soldiers to ensure compliance. As a gesture of goodwill, Claiborne surrendered his own sword at the door.

The New Orleans *Projet d'Arrête* was not the first and certainly not the last time that dancing was regulated by municipal legislation. According to dance historian Maureen Needham in an article titled "The War of the Quadrilles: Creole vs. Americans," she aptly pointed out it was definitely the first and maybe only "American legislation to set out equal opportunity for dances associated with different ethnic and political groups." Unfortunately, on the other hand, Needham added, it was, in fact, the first time that legislation was enacted "into the United States in which the Anglo-Saxon minority high-handedly refused to permit political power to be exercised by other European settlers who preceded them" (Needham 2002, 57, 66–71).

By 1805, regardless of the legislation, dancing in New Orleans was available at a ball or a public ballroom every night of the week. At that time, the city counted

15 public ballrooms, and the insatiable desire of New Orleans to dance only increased. By 1815, there were at least 30 public ballrooms. Typically a dance or a formal ball began at 8:00 P.M. and lasted until 3:00 A.M. Sometimes a ball would be held after an opera performance or a similar special theatrical event, which might invariably delay the start of the ball. On April 2, 1829, one *New Orleans Abeille* newspaper reporter boasted that visitors observed that the citizens of New Orleans *"on aime passionnément la danse"*—translation: "They passionately love the dance." Many other visitors told similar tales of Creoles of both genders and all ages from children through grandparents who all had an inherent love and desire for dancing (Needham 2002, 59, 66–67).

In contrast to the dancing concerns of the French, Spanish, and American citizens, the preference of dance style for African Americans in New Orleans was strictly segregated. In February 1819, American architect Benjamin Henry Latrobe witnessed and provided a firsthand written account of African American dancing in Congo Square. Latrobe, who was visiting New Orleans, decided upon a leisurely Sunday afternoon walk through the city. During his walk, he "heard a noise" that at first he attributed to "horses trampling on a wooden floor." Upon investigation he ventured into Congo Square and "accidentally stumbled upon an assembly of Negroes." At the time, Congo Square (latter day Beauregard Square on Rampart Street) was a place where African Americans, mostly slaves, but also a few free or former slaves, were allowed to congregate on Sunday afternoons for dancing, playing music, and in general having a good time. All told, Latrobe estimated about 550 to 600 people assembled in the square adding, "All those who were engaged in the business seemed to be blacks" (72–73).

In contrast to the formal balls and public dance halls of New Orleans, the African American gathering appeared informal and nonjudgmental. Unlike the conflict resulting in the *Projet d'Arrête* legislation, there did not seem to be any complaints of the choice of dances among the African Americans. Latrobe astutely added, "There was not the least disorder among the crowd, nor do I learn, on inquiry, that these weekly meetings of the Negroes have ever produced any mischief." The music and dancing was not to Latrobe's liking; therefore, he left to continue his walk (74).

As Latrobe made his return from his walk "after sunset," he once again passed Congo Square and was surprised that the "noise" and dancing was still going on. Latrobe, unfortunately, displayed the inherent social prejudice of the day and added to his dislike as he wrote:

> The amusements of Sunday have, it seems, perpetuated here those of Africa among its inhabitants. I have never seen anything more brutally savage and at the same time dull and stupid, than this whole exhibition (Latrobe 2002, 74).

Unfortunately, it was due to the prejudgment based on European cultural traditions by the likes of Benjamin Latrobe that Congo Square developed a "lurid" reputation.

In 1822, for example, *Paxton's Directory of 1822*, an early travel guide, warned potential visitors to New Orleans about Congo Square. Author John Paxton

African Americans held their own formal assembly balls, but in almost all cases they were entirely segregated. This drawing of a "Negro Ball" provides a good example of the social situation of both slavery in America and acceptance of African Americans as part of society. At the left of the drawing, one white man is shaking an African American's hand indicating acceptance, while another is holding his nose in disgust, c. 1807.   Library of Congress, Prints and Photographs Division LC-USZ62-78129.

suggested that the area be avoided: "on account of its being the place where the Congo, and other Negroes dance, carouse, and debauch on the Sabbath, to the great inquiry of the morals of the rising generation" (40). Paxton also added that many citizens of New Orleans did not approve of the Sunday dancing. The reason was that the white Europeans felt that the Christian Sunday observances of the Sabbath should be substituted instead of the celebration of African ancestry and cultural traditions of music and dancing. But in reality, Sunday was the only time, if at all, that a slave was allowed not to work. As a result of the "lurid reputation" and pressure from the governing body of New Orleans, the dance assemblage in Congo Square ended around 1835. It was revived from time to time until about 1845. According to Needham, "In this case once again…a dominant majority may label dance as subversive political activity and seek to control it" (2002, 58).

In some cases, free Blacks attained a measure of wealth and affluence. However, African Americans were not afforded any degree of acceptance into American society. Therefore, in a fashion similar to other Americas, African Americans held their own formal assembly balls, but in almost all cases they were entirely segregated. They were usually advertised as a "Negro Ball" and held in cities including New Orleans and New York. Dance historian Curt Sachs also offered an explanation of the suppression of ethnic culture. He added:

White men have often become excited over the "shamelessness" of such dances. But the words, which they use to describe their reactions—"indecent," "unbridled," "obscene"—are not objective. For to the primitives it is not a matter of sensation and pleasure, but of life and unity with nature (93).

Sadly, both the municipal legislation of dance places and the suppression of cultural identity in association with ethnic dance traditions also became an "unofficial" American tradition. Throughout American history and into the twenty-first century, the pattern as it applied to social dancing continued.

3

The Buffalo Dance, Cotillions, and the Polka: 1820–1865

Dancing is, of all the fine arts, that which seems peculiarly devoted to cheerfulness and joy.

—Thomas Hillgrove, 1863

The Political, Social, and Cultural Climate

By 1820, the population of the young United States of America was over 9.6 million in 22 states. At the time, the balance of slavery was a tenuous issue as the nation was evenly divided between slaveholding states and free states. But although the importation of slaves was outlawed by the Constitution, slavery and an internal slave trade in America was not. In 1820, with the introduction of Maine as a "free state" and Missouri as a "slave state, a compromise by Congress established the introduction of future states above the 36-30 meridian line as free states and those below the line as slaveholding.

In late 1849, the discovery of gold in California quickly hastened a claim for statehood. California entered the Union as a "free" state, which upset the balance of the slave states and touched off a federal debate. In an effort to settle the slavery issues and preserve the Union, the U.S. Congress adopted a series of compromises that collectively was known as "The Compromise of 1850." Under the compromise that admitted California as a free state, the slave trade was prohibited in the District of Columbia, the return of runaway slaves under the Fugitive Slave Act required the northern states to aid "southern slave catchers to return runaways." In the case of new territories and future states the issue of slavery was left to the "popular sovereignty" of the people (Goldfield, Abbott, et al., 2001, A-28–29).

Throughout the nineteenth century, for the most part, Americans still looked to Europe, especially England, for culture and refinement in manners and etiquette.

However, beginning about 1830 and extending through the nineteenth century, Americans developed a "homegrown" culture that was sometimes known as the American Renaissance. Some, such as artists and painters including Thomas Cole, Asher Durand, Frederick Church, Albert Bierstadt, Thomas Moran, and George Catlin, were collectively known as the Hudson River School of Art. In 1858, Fredrick Law Olmsted and Calvert Vaux created the first urban park at New York's Central Park. The park was actually an invented romantic landscape providing similar imagery of the American landscape painters of the Hudson River School.

Also characteristic of the period was a growing number of American authors including Henry Wadsworth Longfellow, Oliver Wendell Holmes, Nathaniel Hawthorne, Walt Whitman, Ralph Waldo Emerson, Henry David Thoreau, and Harriet Beecher Stowe. In fact, Stowe's famous work *Uncle Tom's Cabin* (1852) dramatized the savage condition of American slavery so vividly that Lincoln was said to have remarked upon meeting her, "So this is the little lady that ignited this great war." During the first year of publication over 300,000 copies were sold. Within a few years, *Uncle Tom's Cabin* sold over 7 million copies. (In comparison, at the same time Herman Melville's *Moby Dick* sold about 50,000 copies.) However, *Uncle Tom's Cabin* was overwhelmingly resented in the South, and raised the moral question about and problems with American slavery. Therefore, it also added to the sectional disputes between the states.

Throughout the 1790s and continuing through the 1830s many religious revivals swept through America. During the period of 1820 to 1840, the revivalism intensified. A major proponent of the evangelical crusade was Charles G. Finney, a former "lawyer-turned-itinerant preacher." In 1826, Finney conducted his first revival meeting in Utica, New York, and traveled throughout most of the northern part of the United States preaching his itinerant message to "obtain salvation." In fact, during a six-month period of the winter of 1830 to 1831, Finney converted almost the entire city of Rochester, New York. Many sources claim that the revivalist momentum launched many "secular reform movements" including temperance, public education, and utopian socialism. Many of the evangelical leaders also promoted the abolition of slavery and helped form the American Anti-Slavery Society (Nash et al., 2003, 341; "Second Great Awakening," n.d.).

Other significant developments included the introduction of Cyrus McCormick's mechanical reaper in 1834, the invention of the telegraph and John Deere's "sod busting" steel plow in 1837, the founding of the Smithsonian Institution in 1846, and the Seneca Falls Convention held for Women's Rights in upstate new York in 1848. Manufactured goods in the form of wallpaper, dishes, and furniture were prevalent, and many adorned the Midwestern farmhouses. Almost all goods, both from and to the interior, were transported through Ohio and into either Philadelphia or New York.

A significant development was the implementation of a transportation network of roads, canals, and railroads that connected the interior production factories and farms with the eastern coastal cities with available seaports for international trade. In 1825, the Erie Canal, constructed in New York between the Hudson River at Albany and Lake Erie at Buffalo provided connection with the Great Lakes, thereby allowing Midwestern farmers access with a continuous water route to New York City and international trade markets. The water route was enhanced by the development of Robert Fulton's steamboat that first traveled from New York City up the Hudson River to Albany in 1807. Within a decade, steamboats traversed the Erie Canal and also the Mississippi River along the major route between New Orleans and Louisville, Kentucky (Marks 1957, 68).

By 1831, steam locomotives traveled the route between Albany and Schenectady. And by 1860, a vast railroad network (mainly in the North) connected farm produce from the Northwest Territories and manufactured goods in the Northeast that reached Midwest markets such as Cincinnati, Ohio, and Chicago, Illinois. The railroad also opened up the vast interior of America to European trade, mainly through the eastern coastal cities.

As a result, the eastern cities experienced a significant growth in population and overcrowding. New York, for example, became the most populous city, rising from 63,000 inhabitants in 1800 to over 700,000 in 1850. Philadelphia, which had been the most populous city with 73,000 in 1800, was second with 450,000 residents. The other most populous cities included Boston (212,000), St. Louis (77,860), Albany (50,700), and Chicago (30,000). In addition, because of the construction of the Erie Canal, cities that were basically nonexistent in 1800, such as Oswego and Buffalo in New York and Cincinnati, Ohio, increased dramatically to populations of 12,200, 42,260, and 115,400, respectively. In 1815, for example, the city of Rochester, New York, was a small village of only about 300 people. However, after 1830, because of its strategic location on the Erie Canal, Rochester ballooned into a thriving city of over 20,000 inhabitants (Glaab 1963, 78; Nash et al., 2003, 341).

An increase in immigration to the cities, particularly among the Irish and Germans, occurred as early as 1815, but a significant number entered the United States during the 1840s. In an American workforce, almost evenly split between farming and industry, almost all the immigrants settled in the North as a source of cheap labor in the rapidly increasing industrialized economy. The southern plantation economy did not accept immigrants in order to preserve the slave-based economy.

From 1840 to 1860, over 4 million northern European immigrants entered the United States. During the years 1845 to 1848, in particular, a potato famine in Ireland resulted in a large influx of Irish immigrants into the United States. A substantial number settled in the cities of Boston, New York, and Philadelphia and worked in menial jobs in the factories, as laborers, or built the railroads. (Prior to the 1840s, most of the factory workers in the Northeast were mostly women and children.) In many of the cities, the newly arrived immigrants, many of whom were Catholic, touched off tensions with "nativists" Irish Protestants leading literally to bloody gang fights in the streets of cities such as New York. The anti-immigrant feelings only contributed to the growing national fervor over individual state's rights and slavery (Marks 1957, 69; Goldfield, Abbott, et al., 2001, A-28–29).

As a result of the overcrowded cities, many Americans looked to the West. However, as early as 1830, in order to move west, President Andrew Jackson and the U.S. Congress authorized the Indian Removal Act of 1830. The United States government offered Native American Indians land west of the Mississippi River.

Many of them accepted, but some did not. In 1832, for example, the Cherokee Nation (composed of the Cherokees, Creeks, Choctaws, Chickasaws, and Seminoles) took the state of Georgia to court. In the case of *Worcester v. Georgia*, the Supreme Court of the United States ruled that the relocation was unconstitutional. However, President Jackson simply refused to enforce the Supreme Court decision and ordered Federal troops to forcibly remove the Cherokee Indians, thereby allowing southern states to continue encroaching on Native American lands.

Between 1835 and 1838, about 16,000 Cherokees were forced west under harsh conditions to the Indian territories of Oklahoma. En route, through Tennessee, Kentucky, southern Illinois, Missouri, and northern Arkansas, eventually into Oklahoma, over 4,000 died, and this route became known as the "Trail of Tears." In 1838, Jackson's successor, President Martin Van Buren also sent the U.S. Army to evict the remaining 18,000 to 20,000 Cherokee remaining in the South and move them to what is today Oklahoma.

By 1840 the western portion of the United States extended from Texas and Louisiana north to Arkansas, Missouri, Illinois, and Michigan. West of those boundaries was land known as the "Permanent Indian Frontier." In the Oklahoma territory were the relocated Choctaw, Chickasaw, Creek, Seminole, and Cherokee. North were the Osage, Ottawa, Arapaho, Cheyenne, Kansa, Delaware, Fox, Pawnee, Omaha, Sauk, and the great Sioux nation. Many of the tribes had been relocated from eastern lands (Brown 1995, 41).

By the 1840s, Americans were fueled with the inherent right and desire to occupy the western lands and the Northwest Territory acquired through the Louisiana Purchase (see Chapter 2). In doing so, indigenous people including Native Indians and Mexicans were displaced, sometimes by force. A growing popular movement supported by Congress and glorified in newspaper accounts supported the westward expansion. In 1845, one New York City journalist provided the movement with its name—Manifest Destiny.

As a result, the internal migration continued into the Southwest. As early as 1598, the Spanish conquest of Mexico spread into the southwest territory of America including southern California, Arizona, New Mexico, and Texas (see Chapter 1). The Spanish controlled the area until the early nineteenth century. In 1821, Mexicans fought a successful revolution of independence against Spain and established the Republic of Mexico. At about the same time, American settlers began moving into Texas. At first, Mexico encouraged them but also demanded that new settlers become Mexican citizens and therefore, respect the Mexican government's abolition of slavery within the territory. For the most part, the settlers ignored the demands, and they continued to settle into Texas, even after the Mexican government tried to stop the migration. By 1835, the 30,000 Americans in Texas outnumbered Mexicans six to one.

In 1836, the Mexican government sent an army into Texas to exercise its authority over the Texans. The Texans revolted and made a stand at the Alamo (a former Spanish mission, see Chapter 1). At the Alamo, a larger Mexican army led by General Antonio López de Santa Anna overwhelmed a small group of Texans. A similar stand was made and also defeated at Goliad. Shortly thereafter, thousands of Texans, aided by numerous volunteers from the United States, fought for independence, rallying under the slogan "Remember the Alamo! Remember Goliad!" In April 1836, an army of Texans and volunteers led by Sam Houston defeated Santa Anna's army at San Jacinto in east Texas. As a result, Mexico was forced to recognize the independent Republic of Texas.

The following year, Texas requested annexation to the United States. The debate over slavery prevented Texas from joining the Union until July 1845. Mexico, however, viewed the annexation of Texas into the United States as a declaration of war. As Mexico prepared for war, President James K. Polk sent troops into the disputed area north of the Rio Grande, and in May 1846, the U.S. Congress declared war on Mexico. In September 1847, an American army drove deep into Mexico and captured Mexico City, forcing Mexico to accept a concessionary treaty with the United States. In 1848, under the Treaty of Guadalupe Hidalgo, Mexico relinquished claim to the areas of Texas, New Mexico, Arizona, California, Nevada, Utah, Colorado, and Wyoming. In essence, the northern third of Mexico had become the southwestern quarter of the United States.

In 1857, as a result of a banking crisis, the United States of America suffered a devastating blow to the economy. Known as the "Panic of 1857," the economic crisis caused a credit crunch in the North. The effect in the South was just as immediate; however, high cotton prices assured a quick recovery. As a result of the nationwide depression, the following year brought another "Great Awakening" or revival (see Chapter 2). It started in the economically strained eastern cities and spread westward. In the western areas, lively and colorful camp meetings sometimes lasted for many days. It was sometimes known as the "Great Revival of 1858" and in many instances the "Second Great Awakening."

At the same time in 1857, the Supreme Court decision in the Dred Scott case effectively nullified Congressional jurisdiction over slavery. (Dred Scott was a slave who sued, claiming that his residence in a free state allowed him freedom.) The decision, as rendered by Chief Justice Roger B. Taney, ruled that an African American was not a citizen (and since Scott was not a citizen could not sue) and added that an American Citizen (slave master) could not lose his property as he traveled from state to state. The ruling also declared that the Missouri Compromise was unconstitutional since it deprived citizens of their property (slaves) without "due process" granted by the Fifth Amendment. The decision was a major issue during the presidential election of 1860.

In 1860, a Cincinnati newspaper parodied the implications of the Dred Scott decision upon the political race for president of the United States through a reference to social dancing. At the time, dancing was such a recognizable aspect of American culture that the American public easily understood both the parody and title of "The Political Quadrille—Music by Dred Scott." The cartoon depicted Dred Scott in the center as the fiddler providing music for a Quadrille dance. The four dance couples were the four presidential candidates dancing with individuals who represented each candidate's political allegiance. In the upper left corner, for example, was Southern Democrat John C. Breckinridge dancing with the incumbent president and political supporter James Buchanan. In the upper right corner was Northern Republican Abraham Lincoln who dances with an African

American slave, in obvious deference to his political stand against slavery. In the lower right corner, is the Constitutional Union party candidate John Bell dancing with an American Indian. In the lower left, is Northern Democrat Stephen A. Douglas dancing with an Irish immigrant.

By 1860, with the American population at 31.4 million, the North (with over two-thirds of the total population) was a firmly established industrialized society, whereas the South was heavily based on the plantation system and the production of cotton. At the time, the South produced about 75 percent of all cotton produced in the world. Ironically, the two were intertwined since a majority of the mills that worked cotton into fabric and clothing were located in the North and, therefore, were dependent on the raw product of "King Cotton" produced in the South.

The production of cotton was almost entirely based on American slavery. Thus, it was Slavery that was the central cause of the Civil War, especially as it applied to the introduction of new states to the Union. Up until that time, a series of compromises had kept the fragile balance of the United States of America together. However, in 1860, the election of Abraham Lincoln as the sixteenth president of the United States prompted a secession of 11 southern states from the Union. By

"The Political Quadrille—Music by Dred Scott," was a parody of the implications of the Dred Scott decision upon the political race for president of the United States. The cartoon depicted Dred Scott in the center as the fiddler providing music for a Quadrille dance. The four dance couples were the four presidential candidates dancing with individuals who represented each candidate's political allegiance. It is believed this illustration appeared in a Cincinnati newspaper, c. 1860. Library of Congress, Prints and Photographs LC-USZ62-14827.

the time of Lincoln's inauguration in March 1861, he was faced with a deeply divided nation. On April 12, 1861, the secession culminated in a civil war as the Confederacy bombarded the Union Fort Sumter in the harbor of Charleston, South Carolina. As a result, from 1861 to 1865, Americans were "engaged in a great civil war, testing whether that nation, or any nation so conceived and so dedicated, can long endure" (to quote Lincoln's Gettysburg Address).

The Civil War bitterly divided the northern United States of America (known as the Union) against 11 southern Confederate States of America (known as the Confederacy). In 1863, Congress enacted a "conscription law" that drafted desperately needed soldiers. Ultimately, immigrants made up over 25 percent of northern forces, as did 10 percent African Americans. During the course of the war, over 600,000 Americans were killed and many more permanently wounded. Most of the southern plantations and cities were left in ruins. Sadly, in April 1865, only one month before the official end of the war, John Wilkes Booth, a southern sympathizer, assassinated Abraham Lincoln.

A major diversion and source of recreation during the Civil War was dancing. In fact, the nineteenth century brought a significant breakthrough in American dance. Although still following the European traditions, Americans embraced the "closed couple" position of the Waltz, Polka, and Mazurka and also embraced the Schottische, Galop, Redowa, and Varsovienne. The Quadrille and Country-dances continued as favorites, but combined with the Waltz and the Polka, group dances, sometimes including party games known as the Cotillion (later known as the German), slowly displaced the Country-dances. For the most part, these dances did not change throughout the century.

The general sentiment among Americans was that dancing was a valuable means of community interaction and also served as an essential function of elegant refinement and social manners. At the time, Americans also developed an attitude that dancing could serve as a means of physical education. In 1863, a New York publication, *A Complete Practical Guide to the Art of Dancing* by Thomas Hillgrove, summed it up. Hillgrove wrote:

> Dancing is, of all the fine arts, that which seems peculiarly devoted to cheerfulness and joy. It is the lively expression of these emotions by gestures and attitudes.... it tends to refine the manners; and to give health, activity, and vigor, as well as graceful ease and elegance to the human frame (14).

However, Hillgrove's summation did not apply to the dances of the Native American Indians or African Americans.

The Dances

To dance the Polka men and women must have hearts that beat high and strong. Tell me how you do the Polka, and I will tell you how you love.

—Perrot and Robert, 1845

INDIAN LAND, GEORGE CATLIN, THE MANDANS, AND THE BUFFALO DANCE

In 1907, Lilly Grove, in *Dancing*, provided a long chapter that included American Indian dances under the title "The Dances of Savages." However, at the time she merely continued the societal misconceptions and prejudice against both Native American Indians and African Americans, whom she grouped together as "savages." As a severe misconception, she also claimed that all of their dances were performed "in a very unsophisticated manner." In specific regards to the Native American Indians, Grove correctly stated that "[dance] plays a very important part in their daily life." Among the dances in relation to the daily life of American Indians, she included courtship, hunting, spiritual, and religious. Unfortunately, once again she arbitrarily grouped them together as "a common subject for exhibition in savage dances." Grove correctly added "his religion is inseparable from his daily life, and in his daily life the dance takes a large share." However, she quickly dismissed the significance of the ritual dances of Native North Americans, claiming "the religion of the savage, like that of the little child, is essentially egotistical" (Grove 1907, 64–67).

In America at the time that Grove added her commentary, the dances among Americans of European ancestry were purely secular and associated with recreation and sometimes courtship. In contrast, the dances of Native American Indians were performed in connection with all aspects of recreation, community, spiritual worship, peace, and even war. Therefore, the view from outside the Indian tribes was usually suspicious and oftentimes misinterpreted. Dance historian Maureen Needham in *I See America Dancing: Selected Readings 1685–2000* (2002) noted that there was a common misconception of American writers in regards to Native American dances. Needham correctly surmised that "Ancient Native American dances were fully integrated, communal ceremonies that combined chants, prayers, and music, as well as ritualistic movement" (16). In support of her statement, Needham astutely cleared up some misconceptions and added a firsthand account written by George Catlin in 1836, *The Manners, Customs, and Condition of the North American Indians* (Needham 2002, 21–25).

George Catlin serves as probably the most accurate representative voice of not only the Buffalo Dance but many other Native American Indian dances as well. Catlin (b. 1796, d. 1872) was an artist and ethnographer who spent many years observing and chronicling, by writing, painting, and line drawing, the Native American Indian tribes such as the Sioux and Mandan. Unlike European civilizations, the Native Indian tribes did not record their history in writing or leave a legacy through architectural monuments. Indian civilization was based upon respecting the land and nature for the sustenance they provided and, in addition, passed on their native cultural traditions through storytelling and dance. Specifically from 1830 to 1836, Catlin lived among the Mandan and Sioux and accurately recorded their lifestyles and culture. Catlin, by his own admission was "describing the living manners, customs, and character of a people who were rapidly passing away from the face of the earth—a dying nation who had no historians or biographers of their own" (Catlin 1975, 89).

Beginning at the time that the very first settlers landed on North America, the Native American Indians were viewed with suspicion. In the Southwest, for example, the Spanish rule was quite harsh and maintained a murderous control over those Indians who did not convert to Catholicism. In New England, the Puritan religion of Calvinists did not open themselves towards acceptance to any form of worship in a manner different from their own. In 1684, for example, Increase Mather (see Chapter 1), in his discourse *An Arrow Against Profane and Promiscuous Dancing Drawn Out of the Quiver of Scriptures*, insinuated that American Indian dances involved "pagan ritual" invoking the spirit of the Devil in performing "Satanical Dances" (1684, 23). In a fashion similar to the Spanish conquest, the British colonists outright rejected the Indians and their worship on a regular basis. Although the Indian tribes were continually harassed and pushed westward, the massive displacement and eradication did not escalate until the mid-nineteenth century.

From the California gold rush of 1849 and just prior to the beginning of the Civil War in 1861, many thousands of Americans emigrated into and through the Indian territories. The settlers went in search of gold, homesteading a farm or establishing a trading post along the well-traveled famous westward Oregon Trail and Santa Fe Trail. However, the migration was in general a violation of an understanding between the Indians and the American government that basically said all the land west "of the big bend of the Missouri [River]" was Indian land. In response, the Indians attacked the white settlers. To safeguard the settlers, the U.S. Army built forts and outposts along many of the trails.

During the course of the Civil War, many of the soldiers were transferred to units in the South fighting the Confederacy. As a result, the Indians attacked the weakened forts and settlements. In 1862, for example, a small group of Sioux Indians attacked a settlement in New Ulm, Minnesota. Within one week, over 700 settlers were killed. An American militia unit from Minnesota captured over 400 Sioux Indians and placed them in captivity in St. Paul. The Indians were tried by a jury, and almost all were sentenced to death. Actually President Abraham Lincoln pardoned all but 38, who were all publicly hanged in Mankato on December 26, 1862. The incident ignited a 25-year battle between the Sioux nation and the United States culminating in December 1890 at Wounded Knee, South Dakota (see Chapter 4) (Dee Brown 1995, 81–83).

For the Indians settled along the Midwest plains from Oklahoma through the Dakotas, the major conflict over the "Indian land," was not the land itself, but the buffalo. During the course of migration, the white settlers killed thousands of buffalo, mainly for sport. To American Indians, the buffalo was not only a source of food and clothing, but it was also a spiritual symbol. Therefore, as a result of the needless slaughter of the buffalo, the life sustenance of many Indians was destroyed. According to historian Dee Brown, "Not only was the buffalo a symbol of food, shelter, and clothing, he was a symbol of life after death." In connection with the successful hunt, the plains Indians held a ritual dance (1995, 78–79).

For the Mandan tribe, in the area of northern Missouri, the buffalo was the primary source of food, clothing, and shelter. Catlin noted that oftentimes the buffalo herds ventured far from the Mandan village. As a result, the small tribe was left "in a state of starvation." Rather than venture far from the protection of the village, Mandan tradition promised that a symbolic dance would bring the buffalo closer to their own village. According to Catlin, by performing the "Buffalo Dance," the Mandans believed they were "inducing the buffalo herds to change the direction of their wanderings, and bend their course towards the Mandan village, and graze about on the beautiful hills and bluffs" (Catlin 1836, 24).

In 1836, Catlin witnessed the Buffalo Dance as performed by the Mandan tribe. He described it as follows:

> The place where this strange operation is carried on is in the public area in the centre of the village, and in front of the great medicine or mystery lodge. About ten or fifteen Mandan's at a time join in the dance, each one with the skin of the buffalo's head (or mask) with the horns on, laced over his head, and in his hand his favorite bow or lance, with which he is used to slay the Buffalo (Catlin, 24).

The Mandans shuffled in a continuous circle, stepping in beat to the pounding of a drum. The dance, however, did not stop until the buffalo returned, and sometimes the dance continued for two or three weeks. Obviously, the dancers could not continue without a break. Therefore, when one of the dancers was "fatigued," he would ceremoniously drop his head. In turn, a waiting brave on the perimeter shot a "blunt arrow" at the fatigued dancer and replaced him in the dance. The gesture symbolically represented the successful hunt of the buffalo. When the actual buffalo returned to the village, all the participants gave "thanks to the Great Spirit" and the dance ended. In specific regards to the Buffalo dance, Catlin was most likely the first European to witness the dance firsthand. At the very least, he was definitely the first to accurately record not only the Buffalo dance, but also other dances and ceremonies of the Mandan and Sioux Indians in northern Missouri and the Dakotas (Catlin 1836, 24–25; Needham 2002, 17).

In 1836, Catlin published *The Manners, Customs, and Condition of the North American Indians,* which contained numerous illustrations of the tribal customs and dancing. Catlin revealed that, unlike the popular American misconceptions of the war-like Indian tribes, almost all the Indian tribes maintained a communal peaceful life. In addition to the Mandans, he observed many other tribes that "lead lives of idleness and leisure." A good portion of that time was devoted to "sports and amusements." Despite it all, dancing maintained the "principal" form of amusement and recreation (22–23).

Catlin continued his work with the North American Indians, and in 1876, he published a two-volume set of his writings, illustrations, engravings, and oil paintings in *Illustrations of the Manners, Customs, and Condition of the North American Indians.* Within the text, Catlin indicated that dancing was not confined to just the hunt, it was an integral part of their native culture. Catlin exclaimed,

Native American Indians of the Mandan tribe perform the Buffalo Dance. The illustration by George Catlin was published in Catlin's *North American Indian Portfolio*, c. 1845.   Rare Books Division, The New York Public Library, Astor, Lenox, and Tilden Foundations. Digital Gallery: 466214.

Dancing...is one of the principal and most valued amusements of the Indians, and much more frequently practiced by them than by any civilized society....These dances consist in about four different steps, which constitute all the different varieties: but the figures and forms of these scenes are very numerous, and produced by the most violent jumps and contortions, accompanied with the song and beats of the drum, which are given in exact time with their motions (I: 243).

Catlin was obviously aware of the American European dance traditions of the day as he compared the Indian dances to the Quadrille and Country-dances. In similar fashion to the eastern ballrooms, both the Mandan and Sioux were often "performing them at their own pleasure...or for their own amusement." In contrast to the formality of the ballrooms, the Indians were a bit livelier. Catlin wrote:

Instead of the "giddy maze" of the quadrille or the country dance...the Indian performs his rounds with jumps, and starts, and yells, much to the satisfaction of his own exclusive self, and infinite amusement of the gentler sex...I saw so many of their different varieties of dances amongst the Sioux, that I should almost be disposed to denominate them the "*dancing Indians.*" It would actually seem as if they had dances for every thing (1836, 22).

Not unlike the ballroom dances, the Indian tribes also had "a set song and sentiment for every dance." In addition to the Buffalo dance, Catlin also observed that they had numerous other dances, including "the boasting dance, the begging dance, the scalp dance, and a dozen other kinds of dances." In fact, each of the dances also had its "peculiar characters and meanings or objects." Each of the songs and dances were "perfectly measured" and kept in time with the beat of the drum. In addition, he observed that each distinct song was also accompanied by gestures particular to the song. Catlin also captured many of the specific dances by drawings and paintings (Catlin 1836, 23).

Catlin's paintings were not only a valuable historical reference, they also became a valuable part of America's art history. Catlin's works are in the collections of the National Gallery of Art in Washington, D.C., The Metropolitan Museum of Art in New York City, and many other notable museums and private collections throughout the United States. However, notable works of art in relation to Native American Indian dancing was not limited to George Catlin. During the 1930s, for example, three notable works included *Buffalo Dancer*, c. 1930 by Monroe Tsa-To-Ke; *Deer Dancer*, c. 1935 by Theodore Suina; and *Taos Turtle Dancer*, c. 1938 by Vincent Mirabel. Other works of art are included as part of the U.S. Department of the Interior, Indian Arts and Crafts Board (DeMille 1980, 2).

DANCING THE SLAVES, THE RING SHOUT, JUBA, AND MINSTREL SHOWS

Similar to the tribal dance customs of the American Indian, African slaves also maintained a tribal custom of dancing. Although the international European slave trade in America ended in 1807, many of the American slaves were born in the "heart of the slave area" in Africa. The African regions that produced almost 40 million slaves, as described by anthropologist Melville Jean Herkovits, included the Gold Coast, Nigeria, Dahomey, and Benin, and the slaves were from many African tribes including Akans, Ashantees, Bakongo, and Ibos. Many Africans from those areas were transported during their "Middle Passage" by ship to North America. During the sea travel the conditions were harsh beyond description and many died. The monetary value of a slave on the auction block, however, was largely based on his or her physical health being in good condition. Therefore, in an attempt to keep the Africans somewhat healthy, the slave traders often exercised them on the ship's deck by forced dancing (Stuckey 2002, 43–44; Allen, "From Slave Ships to Center Stage," n.d.).

One eighteenth century account by Alexander Falconbridge described the practice that was known as "dancing the slaves." The dancing was certainly not for enjoyment. In fact, Falconbridge described the practice as "brutal" and "merciless" since any slave that was deemed to be moving too slowly was "flogged." (A "flogging" was a brutal whipping, usually with a whip supplemented with metal objects to tear the flesh of the person being whipped. The practice of flogging was continued in America, and many slaves bore the brutal scars of numerous whippings.) However, once in America, neither the brutal whippings nor the constant attempt by the white overseers could eliminate the African tribal cultural traditions from being passed on to the children of slaves born in America. One of those African tribal traditions was the "Ring Shout."

During a Ring Shout, the dancers formed a circle and moved counterclockwise. In most cases the rhythm was supplied by "juba." (Juba was a self-devised method of keeping rhythm by clapping their hands and slapping their thighs, or improvising rhythms with their feet.) In some cases, they provided music by a drum or banja (the forerunner of the American banjo—see Chapter 2). Zita Allen, in an article for a PBS documentary *Free to Dance*, described a typical "Ring Shout" as follows:

> Hunched low to the ground, flat feet pounding the earth with rhythmic intensity...a group of men and women wearing the drab, tattered, everyday clothes of southern plantation field hands danced.....Every part of their bodies danced, from their shuffling feet and bent knees to their churning hips and undulating spines, swinging arms, and shimmying shoulders. Even their necks bent like reeds to balance heads rolling from shoulder to shoulder before pulling upright to reveal faces filled with the joy and the ecstasy of dance.

However, in many instances the use of a drum by an African slave was literally outlawed. As a result of the fears of a possible slave revolt, the southern states enacted laws known as "Slave Codes" that restricted the daily life-styles of the slaves. Part of these laws was the prohibited use of drums "for any purpose at all, even for dancing." The penalty for violating a Slave Code was extremely severe and harsh, usually involving a whipping and in some cases even death.

Actually, southern slave owners were fearful that any large gathering of slaves might incite a revolution. Therefore, large gatherings were either outlawed or severely restricted. In 1817, in Louisiana, specifically New Orleans, for example, the municipality enacted a law that limited the slave gatherings only to Sundays within Congo Square (see Chapter 2). Within Congo Square, the slaves were basically free to dance what they wished; however, they were usually "under strict surveillance" by whites. The dances within Congo Square were most often those that were danced in the tribal villages of Africa. In some respects, according to Richard Kraus, "the slaves in the early 19th-century New Orleans were permitted to dance, as a kind of palliative to their subservient condition" (Kraus 1981, 100; Allen, "From Slave Ships to Center Stage," n.d.).

Unbeknownst to the slave owners, the Ring Shout also served as spiritual expression and as a link to African religion. According to historian, P. Sterling Stuckey,

> In fact, dance was the principal means by which slaves, [used] its symbolism to evoke their spiritual view of the world...In an environment hostile to African religion, that denied that the African had a real religion, slaves could rise in dance and, in a flash, give symbolic expression to their religious views (2002, 41).

For the most part, African slaves were able to embody their spirituality within the Ring Shout, since Americans of European ancestry danced for secular celebration and did not associate any dancing with religious connotations. The circular nature of the dance, as with the American Indians and early Medieval peasants, was the symbolic nature of the "spirit of community" (Stuckey 2002, 44).

In later years, the Ring Shout was actually an integral part of Sunday religious church worship among African Americans. In 1899, W.E.B. Du Bois observed a Ring Shout during a religious service at a church in Philadelphia. He briefly described it as follows:

> The whole congregation pressed forward to an open space before the pulpit, and formed a ring. The most excitable of their number entered the ring, and with clapping of hands and contortions led the devotions. Those performing the ring joined in the clapping of hands with wild and loud singing, frequently springing into the air and shouting loudly....This continued for hours, until all were completely exhausted (221–222).

In many ways the Ring Shout was also closely related to the circular choral dancing of ancient Greeks and western Europeans, and the Buffalo dance of the Native American Indians (see Chapters 1 and 2).

However, noted dance choreographer Agnes DeMille described a basic cultural difference between the American Indian and the African slave. She wrote:

> whereas the Indian danced for power and magical assistance, the slave danced for escape and forgetfulness....The Indian danced toward spiritual integration, the marshaling of his powers for endurance and ordeal; the black, however, danced for release, abandon, and comfort (DeMille 1980, 13).

Another difference was that the Indians were kept separate and removed from white Americans, whereas African American slaves witnessed the cultural rituals and dancing of their white masters. In addition, in the case of the slaves, whenever they had any limited time away from actual work, one of the few leisure activities (if that term can even be applied to the life of a slave) was to dance. A time for the most joyous occasion of celebration and dancing on the plantations was Christmas.

In 1859, Anson De Puy Van Buren noted in *Jottings of a year's sojourn in the South* that as Christmas approached the "cotton-picking was over and gone" and the slaves "could revel in fun and frolic for a whole week." Although the statement might have been a bit overzealous, Van Buren added,

> This is literally true of the South. Throughout the [South] country, on every plantation, there is a merry time—a joyous leisure from all work; merry Christmas is with them all. The Negroes whole troops of them mounted on mules, male and female, laughing and singing, go from one plantation to another; thus gathering in jolly groups they feast and frolic and dance the time away (116–117).

Regardless whether it was the wealthy plantation owner and his family or the lowly slave, "all dressed in their best" for the Christmas holidays.

In regards to the dancing during the celebrations, Van Buren observed some of the common contemporary American dances including Hornpipes, Jigs, Strathspeys, and Reels (see Chapter 2). Unlike the stately reserved dances of the ballrooms, the dancing among the slaves was vigorous and exciting. He described that they were

An early eighteenth century illustration of a "Negro dance" on a southern plantation. Although the illustration is a bit idealized, it does provide a good representation of the communal aspect of African American dancing among slaves.   Library of Congress, Prints and Photographs LC-USZ62- 24233.

whirling in the giddy mazes of the dance…each seeming to vie with the other in dancing the most…No restraint of the ettiquettish ball-room, to fetter their actions and motions, but charged like galvanic batteries, full of music, they dance with a vigorous vim (Van Buren 1859, 118).

In contrast to what Van Buren viewed in the "ettiquettish ball-room," he gushed, "This is *dancing*. It knocks the spangles off your light fantastic tripping, and sends it whirling out of the ballroom" (1859, 117–118).

However, the dancing at Christmas time was not confined to just the African slaves. In the larger southern plantations, and for that matter all across the United States, Christmas time meant "large parties, music and feasting, dancing, and cards." In specific regards to the plantation owners, Van Buren noted:

Dancing is not confined to the Negroes alone, the planter's whole household is entirely given up to merry-making during the holidays. The dance and festival is first held at

THE CHRISTMAS WEEK.

An illustration of a card "The Christmas Week" showing African Americans dancing at a Christmas party in Philadelphia, c. 1863. Library of Congress, Prints and Photographs LC-USZC4-2527.

one planter's house, and then at another's; two or three often assembling in one place, where they have what is termed a "storming" (118).

Often times the slaves were forced to learn the American music, for it was usually the house servants (African slaves) who provided the musical entertainment for the dancing.

While dancing among African Americans was not confined to the plantations, most Americans never had the opportunity to actually witness the dancing of African American slaves. Therefore, Americans held misconceptions about African American dancing because of minstrel shows. In 1828, during a stage show at the Columbia Street Theater in Cincinnati, Ohio, a performer named Thomas Dartmouth Rice presented a characterization of a "Negro" slave named Jim Crow. Rice's performance triggered a wide popularity in minstrel stage shows across America. Minstrel performers were typically white individuals who donned "blackface." (Blackface was a method employed by both the black and the white performer to cover his entire face with the residue from burnt cork. In addition, the size of his lips was exaggerated by a combination of a red and white outline around the mouth. The performer was also clothed in "rags.") By the 1840s, the minstrel shows were "the most popular male form of nineteenth-century amusement." The minstrel shows were akin to the early twentieth century vaudeville shows that shared the same stage with a variety of stage acts including music, comedy, and even drama performances such as Shakespeare. By the 1870s, they were housed in their own specialty theaters (DeMille 1980, xii; Erenberg, "Entertaining Chicagoans," n.d.).

In the eyes of the white viewing audience, the minstrel performers supposedly were performing "authentic Negro dances." In reality, the caricature of the African American was completely derogatory and stereotypical. According to historian Lewis Erenberg, "Minstrels portrayed northern 'Zip Coons' as self-indulgent, incapable of self-control and will-power, while plantation slaves were shown as happy because they lived subservient to white owners." Historian Zita Allen added, "Blackface minstrelsy was both a unique form of American entertainment and [sadly] a reflection of the African-American image that white American audiences had come to expect." Hence the character of "Jim Crow" became a term that symbolized the southern segregation laws and attitudes from the early nineteenth century through the twentieth century. Ironically, the caricature was so dominant that the first African American minstrel performer, William Henry Lane, also donned "blackface" when he danced in minstrel shows. By the time Lane (also known as "Master Juba"—see Chapter 2) and other African Americans were regularly performing, the stereotype was so dominant that they also had to perform in blackface and minstrelsy costume (Erenberg, "Entertaining Chicagoans," n.d.; Allen, "From Minstrel Show to Center Stage," n.d.).

Despite the fact that African Americans performed in blackface, they did not conform to the "white" style of dancing. Actually, some sources have pointed to the fact that one of the rea-

The illustration of "G. Swaine Buckley" is a good representation of a minstrel performer in "blackface" and dressed in "rags." This lithograph was published in Boston by Oliver Ditson in 1865. Library of Congress, Prints and Photographs LC-USZ62-31129.

sons that whites initially donned blackface was so that they could perform and dance uninhibited. In either case, both white and black minstrel performers danced versions of the Jig, the Rigaudon, the Hornpipe, the Breakdown, and Clogging (see Chapter 2). In contrast, in almost all cases African American stage performers infused the traditional African tribal dance styles and created unique styles of stage dancing.

THE GALOP AND THE "QUADRILLE OF THE LANCERS"

The Galop dance (sometimes "gallop," or "galopade") first appeared around 1800 and was often described as a simple and sometimes "exhausting" dance. Some claim it was from Hungary, while others place it as German or even Austrian in origin. Others claim that the Galop was simply the final figure in a Quadrille (see Chapter 2) that was speeded up with chassé steps and crossing the dance floor.

One of the earliest recorded occurrences of dancing the Galop was on June 11, 1829, at the St. James's Palace in England. During that same year, it was also introduced in France during a carnival. In either case, it was named after the French word for "gallop," and according to dance historian Peter Buckman, it "was one of the few dances whose name...was an entirely accurate description of its form" (Ferrero 1859, 151; Buckman 1978, 138).

The Galop was danced in 2/4 time, and some dance teachers, especially when teaching it to children, simply had them "galloping like horses about the floor." In fact, in the same manner that a child would mimic a galloping horse, the dance was a simple continuous series of "step-close" chassés. For the dancer, one foot always led with the other foot following behind with a quick close step. (In the case of the Galop, either the left foot or the right foot could serve as the lead foot.) The Galop was often started with two lines of couples facing each other starting in the "Waltz position," and they danced down the floor in straight lines, often turning or zigzagging. Therefore, many times it was mistakenly called a version of the Waltz. Depending on the size of the room and the number of couples, it was also danced in lines or sometimes in a very big or a very small circle (Shaw 1949, 53, 70, 100).

In fact, some sources differentiate the Galop and Galopade as actually two different dances. Whereas the Galopade contained the turning and zigzagging, the Galop was danced in either a continuous straight line or a circle. In some cases, the circle had all the couples facing the same direction, and they danced in a continuous chaîne. Dance historian Lloyd Shaw, for example, claimed that they were, in fact, two different dances. However, he did explain that the Galop and Galopade "are so much alike that you can't always tell them apart." For the most part, however, the Waltz was so dominant (especially before the introduction of the Polka) that in most cases the Galop was the only other dance that offered couples an opportunity to dance in a closed embrace. Shaw added, "Before the Polka came to give variety and relief, it was the Galop and the Waltz alone holding the interest of those who were turning to couple dances" (300).

During the 1830s through the 1890s, the Galop was popular in the American ballrooms and was typically the final dance of the evening. Dance historian Leon Dorfman in *The Cavalcade of American Ballroom Dancing: Minuet to Hustle* (1976) described the American Galop as follows:

> Still in waltz position but to music in 2/4 time, the couples moved in nothing but straight lines, zigzagging down the hall. As the musical momentum increased, the dancers moved faster and faster and practically skipped off the floor at the finish (5).

The *American Ballroom Companion* Web site at the Library of Congress also claimed that the Galop danced in America was a variation of the Galopade. The following is stated:

> It appears to have been a modification of a dance or step called the galopade, which consisted of continuous chasing steps. The galopade took on some variant steps and became the galop. The variant steps, which included the *deux-temps* [see earlier in this chapter], served to reduce the rate of travel, the frequency of turns, and the vigor of

the chase step. As a consequence, the galop was smoothed out and gradually became danced at quicker tempos ("Instrumental Dance Music 1780s–1920s," n.d.).

Although the Galop was, in fact, a simple dance, not all the descriptions were as simple.

A contemporary description of the American Galop was often described either as very simple or sometimes as a predescribed set figure. In 1847, for example, *Leaflets of the Ball Room*, published by New York publishers Turner and Fisher, described it as follows:

All eight promenade a la galopade; first lady advances alone, and retires, (four bars); opposite gentlemen idem, (four bars); top and bottom couples chassez to the couples on their right, and set, (four bars); the four gentlemen, with contrary partners, gallopade open to the top and bottom, and turn both hands half round, forming two lines, (four bars); all eight (in the two lines) advance and retire, (four bars); advance again, and retake partners, turning into places, (four bars) (No page).

Leaflets of the Ball Room was a pocket-size dance instruction manual that, although it did not contain any page numbers, it did contain simple directions for many popular dance of the day including the Waltz, Polka, various Quadrilles, Redowa, and Spanish Dance.

On the other hand, in 1859, Edward Ferrero in *The Art of Dancing; Historically Illustrated* claimed that the Galop "is the easiest of all dances to learn, being, as the name implies, simply a gallop, though rapid in its movements." Ferrero added:

It can be made very pleasing and entertaining by the dancers, in couples, forming a column. The whole party then follow the leaders, or head couple, through a variety of serpentine courses, now winding themselves in circles, and [also] unwinding to create new ones (151).

The Galop actually continued as a simple fun dance and was oftentimes mixed in with Cotillions towards the end of the evening.

In 1868, *Beadle's Dime Ball-room Companion and Guide to Dancing* called the Galop "undoubtedly one of the fastest of dances." *Beadle's*, published in New York by Beadle and Company, was a popular series of inexpensive publications aimed at the mass market. In regard to the dance itself, they cautioned: "The great rapidity of this dance requires the utmost care to prevent...its degenerating into a mere scramble. A good dancer should be able to introduce into the galop every variety of reverse-movement." They did speculate that due to "its life and spirit" the Galop "will long continue to be a great favorite" (31).

In fact, by the early twentieth century the Galop was still in favor at formal dances. In 1905, for example, Edward Scott in his dance instruction book simply titled *Dancing* indicated that the Galop was still recommended; however, it appeared that at formal dances it was danced much slower. In addition, the quick chassé steps were replaced by slower deliberate Waltz steps. However, Scott did offer the "historical" description of the Galop as follows:

> The step used for this dance is simply the *chassé*...Suppose you are going in a forward direction, slide the left foot forward, counting *one*. Bring the right up close behind it with momentary transfer of weight, then immediately slide the left foot again forward and balance the body thereon, counting *and two*. This may be repeated *ad lib*. Remember that in making a *chassé* step forward the same foot is always in front. When you wish to go round, the movements executed to the right and left alternately, and the steps are taken sideways in turning (147).

But Scott did indicate that by the turn of the century, the Galop had changed, both in the step pattern and the speed of execution. He stated:

> Whenever the music of a galop is now played, the people who dance to it generally take their steps as if they were waltzing, counting *one and two, one and two*, letting the second and fifth steps come in at the *ands*. The waltz step, in this instance, is a very great improvement on the *chassé* (147).

A short time later, however, the Galop fell out of favor as a new slew of couple dances were introduced to Americans.

In America, at about the same time as the Galop, the Quadrille was also danced (see Chapter 2). Sometime around 1820 or so, the set figures in the Quadrille dances were regularly "called," usually by one of the musicians and oftentimes by a fiddler. Although an individual step sequence or a set pattern was danced in a specific manner, the caller could rearrange them in any order. Therefore, in the case of any particular Quadrille, the advantage of a "caller" added an infinite amount of variations. The practice of "calling" a Quadrille was the precursor to the twentieth century American Square Dance and became a standard in America but not necessarily in Europe (DeMille 1980, 5).

In addition, to the "calling" some other changes to form developed within the Quadrille. One example was the elimination of an introductory set of eight bars of music. According to *The Database of Recorded American Music* at New York University:

> First, the introductory eight bars were frequently done away with in the following sequences. The first couple often introduced "show-off" steps in the midst of each sequence, challenging the other couples to duplicate or surpass them. "Promiscuous" figures (from other dances) such as the dos-a-dos (or do-si-do) were introduced. And the final or next-to-final sequence was frequently replaced by an entirely different sequence or dance.

Many in Europe thought the American version was "corruptions of the form" of the standard Quadrille. However, at least in America, the changes were often viewed as adding lively merriment more in style with the playful Cotillions and earlier Quadrilles ("Instrumental Dance Music 1780s–1920s," n.d.).

At about the same time, a distinctive version also developed in both Europe and America that was sometimes known as the "Lanciers Quadrille" or the "Quadrille of the Lancers." Some contemporary documents such as *Brookes on Modern Dancing* (1867; first edition in 1836), for example, termed it "Lanciers Quadrille." Other documents, especially in England, named the dance "Quadrille of the Lancers." In later documents, the most common referenced was simply "Lancers" and in a few cases "Lanciers."

All things considered, the Lancers was actually "a very elegant and elaborate form of the Quadrille" and was often described as "particularly pretty and graceful." An English writer named Mrs. Armytage may have invented it in the early nineteenth century around 1817 or 1819. On the other hand, an Irish Dance Master named John Duval claimed to introduce the dance, as well as did a composer named Joseph Hart around 1819. Some sources also claim that it was developed by a Paris Dance Master named Laborde in 1820 and later, in 1836, he introduced the dance to France. Historians Marshall and Jean Stearns, on the other hand, acknowledged that the dance did, indeed, have European origins, but also claimed that the dance might have originated in the West Indies (Harris et al., 2000, 125–127; Buckman 1978, 137; Stearns and Stearns 1994, 15).

It is not definitely known how it originated in America. A contemporary account by Lawrence De Garmo Brookes in *Brookes on Modern Dancing* (1867) claimed that the "Lanciers Quadrille originated in England" and was first "danced in America" about 1825. Brookes might have also been the original source who claimed that it was later on "introduced in France by Laborde" in 1836. In either case, it was definitely danced in America prior to that date since Brookes added, "I have now in my possession a copy of the music published February, 1827, by E. Riley, 297 Broadway, New York" (1867, 38). Nevertheless, after 1850, the Lancers were popular in America, England, and France, and sometimes incorporated steps from

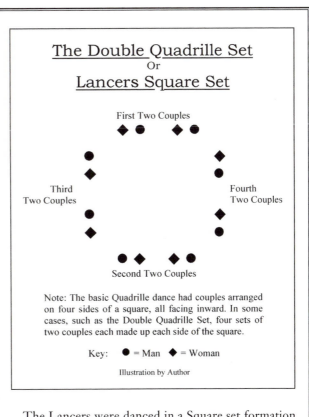

The Double Quadrille Set
Or
Lancers Square Set

First Two Couples

Third
Two Couples

Fourth
Two Couples

Second Two Couples

Note: The basic Quadrille dance had couples arranged on four sides of a square, all facing inward. In some cases, such as the Double Quadrille Set, four sets of two couples each made up each side of the square.

Key: ● = Man   ◆ = Woman

Illustration by Author

The Lancers were danced in a Square set formation either with 8 or 16 couples arranged in a Square set formation (see Chapter 2) that was also sometimes known as the Double Quadrille Set. The unique feature of the dance was a combination of five different dance sequences with each set danced at a different tempo. According to dance historian Peter Buckman, "The steps involved military-style salutes, a progress and retreat across the floor…and ended with a grand march and a waltz." Buckman's description differentiated from the later Lancers, which usually "ended with a Galop" (137). As to the dance posture, Marshall and Jean Stearns added that, in fact, there was a distinction as it applied to Americans of European ancestry as opposed to Americans of African ancestry. They explained, "The custom of holding the body stiffly erect seems to be principally European…African dance is frequently performed from a crouch, knees flexed and body bent at the waist" (15).

the Waltz, Polka, or Galop. They continued through the nineteenth century and into the first half of the twentieth century mainly in rural areas at barn dances and in small towns (Harris et al., 2000, 125–126).

In 1859, Edward Ferrero in *The Art of Dancing; Historically Illustrated* claimed that the Lancers was "but a revival of an old dance, but in its modern shape is a great favorite." As a result of the popularity of the Lancers, he remarked that it had also created a new interest in the older Quadrilles, which by that time he claimed "had almost become extinct" (130). Ferrero explained the appeal of the Lancers as follows:

> It combines all the conveniences for conversation and repose from more exciting dances, which is a characteristic of the plain quadrille, with a greater variety of figures, and employs all the gracefulness of demeanor and elegance of manner which the dancers possess. We have observed that those who participate in its execution, embrace it with a peculiar zest, and generally go through its mazes with the utmost satisfaction (131).

He noted that the dance formation was "the same as the plain quadrille, [with] each figure being danced four times, until all have danced in turn." Ferrero, who termed the entire dance sequence "Les Lanciers," named the five figures as the *Les Tiroirs, Les Lignes, Les Moulinets, Les Visites,* and *Les Lanciers* (131).

Ferrero's instructions for each figure were in similar fashion to the contemporary explanations for the Quadrilles and Country-dances. He described the "First Figure Les Tiroirs," for example, danced in 24 bars of music, as follows:

- First lady and opposite gentleman forward and back; same two forward again, and turn with both hands....8 bars.
- First and second couple cross over, first couple passing between the second; cross back to places, second passing between the first couple....8 bars.
- All balance to corners, and turning with both hands, resume their places....8 bars.

The "Second Figure Les Lignes" also contained 24 bars of music and was described by Ferrero as follows:

- First couple forward and back; forward again, leaving the lady in the centre, with her back to the opposite couple....8 bars.
- Chassez to the right, then to the left, and turn partner to place....8 bars.
- Side couple separate and join hands with head couples, forming two lines; all forward and back; all forward again, and turn partners to places with both hands....8 bars.

The *Les Moulinets*, which was the "Third Figure," contained 16 bars and was described as follows:

- The first lady and opposite gentleman forward and back; forward again, stopping in the centre to bow and courtesy, and then retire to places....8 bars.
- The ladies form moulinet in the centre, giving the right hand to the opposite lady; turn to the left; reverse by giving the left hand back; the gentlemen walk round, outside the

moulinet, contrary direction and reverse; arriving at their places, they give the right hand to their partners, and turn in place.. . .8 bars.

The "Fourth Figure Les Visites" resumed a figure with 24 bars of music in the following manner:

- The first couple visit the couple on their right; all four bow and courtesy, 4 bars; visit the couple on the left, bow and courtesy, 4 bars.. . .8 bars.
- Chassez four, to right and left.. . .4 bars.
- Turn partners to places.. . .4 bars.
- First and second couples right and left, across and back.. . .8 bars.

The "Fifth Figure Les Lanciers," which was the final figure, was also the longest sequence at a total of 48 bars of music. Ferrero described the final sequence as:

- Grand chain (right and left all round), stopping when you meet your partner, to bow and courtesy to each other.. . .16 bars.
- The first couple promenade round the centre of the quadrille, and stop at their places, facing outward; the couple on the right form behind the first, and the couple on the left behind them.. . .8 bars.
- All chassez across and back; ladies to the left, gentlemen to the right.. . .8 bars.
- March round; gentlemen turn to the left, ladies to the right, within the space of the quadrille, and come up the centre; fall back in two lines, facing each other; gentlemen on one side, ladies on the other.. . .8 bars.
- Join hands, forward and back, forward again, and turn partners to places with both hands. Repeat the grand chain until each couple has led off, and finish with the same.. . . 8 bars.

The fifth figure and final figure of the Lancers was a march in 4/4 time. Some sources claim that the fifth figure was the forerunner to the Grand March that was a component of many a late nineteenth century formal dance (see Chapter 4) (Ferrero 1859, 130–132; Harris et al., 2000, 125–127).

In 1867, Lawrence De Garmo Brookes description of his "Lanciers Quadrille," in *Brookes on Modern Dancing*, was almost exactly the same as Ferrero's, with only some slight modifications. For example, rather than naming the five sequences he merely labeled them No. 1, No. 2, No. 3, No. 4, and No. 5. A slight difference was noted by Brookes's figure for "No. 4," which contained only 16 bars of music as opposed to Ferrero's 24 bars. In addition, Brookes suggested a slightly different set figure that did not include a "Chassez four, to right and left." Finally, at the end of the "No. 5" sequence Brookes noted "finish with a Grand Chain, to which is frequently added [a] Polka round the room ad lib" (1867, 37–38).

The variations on the Lancers, Quadrilles, and other ballroom dances of the day were numerous. In 1858, for example, *Howe's Complete Ball-room Hand Book*, advertised "upwards of three hundred dances." A few years later, the book was reissued under a new title *Howe's New American Dancing Master* and contained "Five Hundred dances." Over 50 Quadrilles, 90 "Fancy Dances" (including the Gallopade,

Hornpipe, Waltz, and Polka), 150 Contra Dances, and over 90 Cotillions (known as the German). The publication actually credited famed inventor Elias Howe as the author; however, it appears that the name was applied by the Boston publisher Oliver Ditson to add "credibility" to the mass-market publication ("Nineteenth Century Social Dance," n.d.).

THE WALTZ *À* TROIS TEMPS, THE WALTZ *À* DEUX TEMPS, AND PAPANTI'S BOSTON WALTZ

In reality, very little of the original eighteenth century Waltz compared with the Waltz that was danced during the twentieth century, other than it was in a closed couple's dance position and danced in 3/4 time (see Chapter 2). For that matter, according to dance historian Lloyd Shaw, the eighteenth century Waltz "wasn't much of a dance." In fact, the simple step and constant turning was a hindrance. Shaw noted:

> It had a peculiar and tricky little step that resulted in a continual turning. It was not much like our waltz of today. And its unique step made it impossible for the waltzes to move forward or backward, or in any straight line. They had to whirl continually, moving slowly around the ballroom as they whirled (1949, 53).

In Europe, by the very early nineteenth century, the continual turning of the Viennese Waltz (see Chapter 2) was replaced by a modified French version known as the *Valseà Trois Temps* (translated as "Three-step Waltz").

Similar to the Viennese Waltz, the *Valse à Trois Temps* always turned clockwise as the couple traversed in a counterclockwise position on the perimeter of the dance floor. However, unlike the Viennese Waltz, the *Valse à Trois Temps* changed the rhythm of the constant turning. In lieu of a continual turn, the dancers alternated between a pivot turn and a stepping turn. During one bar of music, one dancer pivoted through one-half turn and the partner stepped through a half-turn at the same time. During the second bar of music they alternated—one stepped while the other pivoted. In this manner, they danced in a spiraling motion using each other's momentum to half turn the other. During the eighteenth century this method was known by many other denominations including the "Modern Waltz," the "French Waltz," or the "Old Waltz." But even though another Waltz version soon replaced it, the *Valse à Trois Temps* maintained a presence in fashionable ballrooms as a way for dancers to "show off" their prowess on the dance floor (Buckman 1978, 131; "Instrumental Dance Music 1780s–1920s," n.d.).

A New York publication, *Beadle's Dime: Ball-Room Companion and Guide to Dancing* (1868) provided a description of the "Waltz *à* Trois Temps," which they carefully noted was the "old waltz." The music was in 3/4 time; therefore, within each bar of music were three beats of music. The Waltz *à* Trois Temps corresponded one step of the dance with each beat of music. The description (described with the left foot for the gentleman) was in a six-count step as follows:

> The left foot was brought backward on the first beat (Count 1). The right foot was brought backward behind the left foot on the second beat (Count 2). The left foot

was brought forward on the third beat (Count 3), thus completing One Bar of music. Beginning on the Second Bar of music, the right foot was brought forward slightly to the right side on the first beat (Count 4). The left foot was brought forward also slightly to the right side on the second beat (Count 5). The right foot was brought forward and at the same time pivoting on both feet on the third beat (Count 6), thus completing *the turn* on the Second Bar of music (Author paraphrased).

At the time, it was stressed that even though it was the "old waltz," in order to provide "a pleasing variety to the dance" the gentleman should have been so well-versed in Waltzing as to also turn his partner in the opposite direction (*Beadle's Dime* 1868, 27).

In 1834, about 20 years after the introduction of the *Valse à Trois Temps* in Europe, the Waltz was introduced in America. That is not to say that Americans had not ever seen the Waltz. In fact, some Americans may have even danced the Waltz prior to its introduction in America. In 1827, for example, American Senator John Tyler while in Europe saw and maybe even danced the Waltz. During that year, he made note of the Waltz in a letter to his daughter. Tyler wrote of a "dance which you have never seen, and which I do not desire to see you dance. It is rather vulgar I think." The speculation that Tyler may have partaken in the Waltz was due to the fact that he was actually an avid dancer. Later as president of the United States from 1841 to 1845 (president-elect William Henry Harrison died about one month after his inauguration; Tyler, as vice-president assumed the presidency), Tyler and his wife held dances at least twice a month in the White House ballroom. Some of his critics charged that his dancing endeavors amounted to "folly and dissipation" and had actually turned the White House "into a great ballroom." Nevertheless, prior to Tyler's presidency, in 1834, when the Waltz was introduced in America, it was introduced as not only the *Valse à Trois Temps*, but also a new version as the *Valse à Deux Temps* (Buckman 1978, 125).

Unlike the *Valse à Trois Temps*, the *Valse à Deux Temps* (translated as "Two-step Waltz") did not require continual turning. (In America, the French spelling was often applied and other times the American application was either the "Waltz *à Trois Temps*" or the "Waltz *à Deux Temps*.") In contrast, to the intricate and "flashy footwork" of the Waltz *à Trois Temps*, the footwork of the Waltz *à Deux Temps* was actually more of a "step-together-step," which was much simpler and danced to a faster music tempo. The combination of the easier step pattern and the energetic pace appealed more to the average dancer to enjoy.

Actually, the Waltz *à Deux Temps* did not even require a complete rotation for the full six counts of the waltz step. According to research in the archives at New York University Library, the simple Waltz *à Deux Temps* was described as follows:

> The *valse à deux temps*, or two-step waltz, was basically a chasing step in which the dancers stepped out in the line of direction on the first beat, waited till the second beat was past to close up the other foot, and stepped out again on the third beat ("Instrumental Dance Music," n.d.).

As a result of the basic step, the couple did not have to dance along the entire perimeter of the dance floor. Therefore, they could dance out of the line of dance and even, if necessary, Waltz within a small area of the dance floor. In some instances, the Waltz *à* Deux Temps was known as the "Modern Waltz," the "Chassé Waltz," and, for unknown reasons, as the "Viennese," or even the "Galop" (Aldrich 1991, 21; Buckman 1978, 131).

In 1834, Dance Master Lorenzo Papanti "officially" introduced the Waltz to America in Boston, Massachusetts. Speculation is that he gave an exhibition of the dance at the home of socialite Mrs. Otis Beacon. At the time, Papanti was a fixture among Bostonian society. As early as 1827, he had established the "Papanti Dance Academy," which was the first fashionable dancing studio in Boston. But Papanti had taught dancing in Boston from as early as 1823. During that year he was also hired by the U.S. Military Academy at West Point to instruct the cadets in dancing. At that time, West Point archives indicate that he was "a famous dance master...from Boston" (see later this chapter). Papanti's academy focused on dance instruction for the wealthy, and he also applied proper etiquette and ballroom manners for fashionable assemblies. In fact, the Boston Assembly was actually held in Papanti's ballroom of the dancing school. According to BostonFamilyHistory.com, Papanti was a "fixture of Boston's social life for...three-quarters of a century" ("BostonFamilyHistory.com," n.d.).

The Waltz that Papanti introduced was the *Valse à Deux Temps*; however, under his direction it was known as the "Hesitation Waltz" or sometimes the "Boston Waltz." Papanti's Boston Waltz was only slightly modified from the Waltz *à* Deux Temps. According to dance historian Peter Buckman:

> This featured a syncopated "hesitation" on the second and third beats, and involved the dancers in "dipping" movements that contrasted strongly with the turns of the rotary waltz. The dancers used the flat part of the foot rather than the tips of the toes, and favored the "American" hold in which they danced hip to hip.

By the 1860s, some dancers began bending their knees during the Boston Waltz, which was known as "dipping." The Waltz steps were the same, but the dipping was oftentimes viewed as "vulgar" (Buckman 1978, 131; Aldrich 1991, 21).

In 1847, *The Drawing-room Dances* by the Frenchman Henri Cellarius served as an important dance reference for Americans. Cellarius offered an introduction on the benefits of dance followed by a discussion of the popular contemporary dances of the day. In prior years, Cellarius taught both the Waltz *à* Trois Temps and the Waltz *à* Deux Temps (his French translation termed it "Waltze À Deux Temps"). In all cases, he preferred to first teach his students the Waltz *à* Deux Temps since it was easier. He did indicate, however, that he had stopped teaching the "old waltze" since it had fallen out of favor. He explained:

> I shall speak of this waltze [sic] without endeavoring to conceal that the waltze a deux temps is now much more generally adopted, and that it has some particular advantages over its elder brother, which suffice to justify this preference (26).

Although it was obvious that the public desired to learn and dance the Waltz *à* Deux Temps, his own preference was for the Waltz *à* Trois Temps, which he thought was "more in harmony with the movement of the rhythm" (26–28).

Cellarius was obviously well versed in the execution of both versions and offered an explanation of the difference between the Waltz "trois" and the "deux." He explained:

> Differing in this from the waltze à trois temps, which describes a circle, the waltze à deux temps is danced squarely, and turns only upon the glissade. It is essential to note this difference of movement in order to appreciate the character of the two dances (34).

Cellarius also noted that, although both were danced in the closed couple "Waltz position," each version required a slightly different posture between the man and the lady. He described the differences in the closed dance position as follows:

> The position also of the gentleman is not the same in the waltze à deux temps as in that à trois. He must not face his partner, but be a little to her right, slightly inclining his right shoulder, which allows him to spring well when carrying along the lady (34).

Plate V.

THE WALTZE À DEUX TEMPS.

An illustration of the "Waltze *à* Deux Temps" from *The Drawing-room Dances* by Henri Cellarius, c. 1847, page 33. Library of Congress Music Division, http://memory.loc.gov/musdi/037/0051.gif.

However, whereas Cellarius simply offered his preference, some others begrudged the simpler Waltz *à* Deux Temps, even terming it the "Ignoramus Waltz."

In 1868, for example, *Beadle's Dime: Ball-Room Companion and Guide to Dancing* expressed a dislike for the Waltz *à* Deux Temps, stating "Unfortunately, there are few dances which have among their pledged admirers such a vast assemblage of bad dancers as the Valse à Deux Temps." *Beadle's* claimed that it was danced too fast, which as a result "induces many to rush into it…dragging their partners round in a wild scramble, with a total disregard of time and step" (28). On the other hand, some attacked the "loose character" of Waltz dancers. One example of these attacks was *The Gentleman and Lady's Book of Politeness*, a translated French work that went through 15 editions in the United States between 1833 and 1872. In regards to the Waltz the critics wrote:

The waltz is a dance of quite too loose a character, and unmarried ladies should refrain from it in public and private; very young married ladies, however, may be allowed to waltz in private balls, if it is very seldom and with persons of their acquaintance. It is indispensable for them to acquit themselves with dignity and decency (quoted in Buckman 1978, 127).

In fact, just about every book on etiquette or dance instruction contained a description of the Waltz.

Some of the most noted and widely circulated dance instruction books of the time included:

- Carlo Blasis's *The Code of Terpsichore* (1830);
- Charles Durang's *The Fashionable Dancer's Casket* (1856);
- *Howe's Complete Ball-room Hand Book* (1858);
- Edward Ferrero's *The Art of Dancing* (1859);
- *Coulon's Hand-book* (1860); and
- Thomas Hillgrove's *The Scholars' Companion and Ball-room* (1857) and also a second publication by Hillgrove, *A Complete Practical Guide to the Art of Dancing* (1863).

Each of the publications contained a description for either the Waltz *à* Trois Temps or the Waltz *à* Deux Temps, and in many cases commented on both. In 1857, in obvious deference to favoring the Waltz *à* Trois Temps over the Waltz *à* Deux Temps, Thomas Hillgrove in *The Scholars' Companion and Ball-room* advised:

If you cannot waltz gracefully, do not attempt to waltz at all. In this dance the gentleman is more conspicuous than in any other. In waltzing, a gentleman should exercise the utmost delicacy in touching the waist of his partner (1857, 25).

In contrast, in 1859, Edward Ferrero in *The Art of Dancing; Historically Illustrated* simply described the dance as "The Waltz," favoring neither the Waltz *à* Trois Temps nor the Waltz *à* Deux Temps. A video clip performance of the mid-nineteenth century Waltz, based on the description in Ferrero's *The Art of Dancing* (1859), is viewable from the Music Division of the Library of Congress online source *An American Ballroom Companion: Dance Instruction Manuals Ca. 1490–1920* (see bibliography).

As a result, cultural historian Charles Panati cited the Waltz as the "first modern fad dance" since it was kept alive by "ordinary folk." Although sometimes condemned by society and rarely equally sanctioned by Dance Masters, it paved the way for the development of the American social dance trends of the twentieth century. During the mid-eighteenth century, however, it did not make all that much difference whether it was the Waltz *à* Trois Temps, the Waltz *à* Deux Temps, or even the Boston Waltz, American ballrooms and dance halls simply danced and danced the Waltz. As a brief reprise, they added Cotillions and dance party games (Panati 1991, 38).

COTILLIONS, "POP GOES THE WEASEL," AND DANCE PARTY GAMES

Many of the Lancers and Quadrilles were each different in the arrangement and set of figures; however, any particular Lancers or Quadrille set of figures was usually danced in association with a specific musical title. In the case of Cotillons, the attachment to a specific piece of music was sometimes the case, but not necessarily the rule. In fact, many of the Cotillon patterns were danced in either a Waltz or Polka rhythm. In 1841, New York publishers Huestis and Craft, in *The Ballroom Instructer*, provided a definition for the difference between a Quadrille and a Cotillion. They offered the following:

> The difference between *cotillons* and *quadrilles is that the former* [Cotillons] *are single figures*, as right and left, forward two,...while the latter [Quadrilles] are more complicated and consist of a number of figures, varying according to the fancy of different teachers, or as the leader of the orchestra may choose to call them (11).

The publication also advertised "A Complete Description of Cotillons and Other Popular Dances" but also stipulated that their dance instruction book was "written and arranged for amateurs in dancing." As a general rule, Cotillons were designed and danced with the sole purpose for the dancers to simply have fun.

One of the Cotillion party dances included "The Sea During a Storm," which was very similar to the late twentieth century children's game of Musical Chairs. Another twentieth century children's game "Pop Goes the Weasel," was also part of a series of Cotillons that was actually danced to the song of the same name. It was initially arranged and danced by adults in a Longways set and performed in the same manner as a Country-dance. In 1859, Edward Ferrero in *The Art of Dancing; Historically Illustrated* described it as follows:

- The couple at the top begin the figure. They go forward within the line and back, and then outside the line and back again....16 bars.
- After which they form a circle of three, with the lady next to them on the line, turn once round to the right and once to the left. Terminating by making the one they have chosen pass quickly underneath their arms to her place—all singing "Pop goes the Weasel."...8 bars.
- They then turn to the other line, and repeat the same figure with the partner of the last selected....8 bars.
- After this, forward and back inside and outside the line, and repeat the same figure with the next couple.

In similar fashion to a Country-dance, each of the couples took turns as the head couple at the top of the set and repeated the same set of figures (Ferrero 1859, 129).

Many of the Cotillions were listed in American dance instruction manuals with both the American and French titles as well as the American spelling of "Cotillion" and the French spelling of "Cotillon." Some examples included over 80 cotillon variations in Henri Cellarius's 1847 English translation of *The Drawing Room Dances* and 78 in William B. De Garmo's 1865 New York publication *The*

Prompter: containing full descriptions of all the quadrilles, figures of the german cotillon, etc. Some of the more popular and interesting "Cotillons" listed by De Garmo included *La Corde* (The Rope), *Le Mouchoir Entortille* (The Twisted Handkerchief), *Les Cavaliers Changeants* (The Changing Gentlemen), and *Le Rond Final* (The Final Round).

The Rope, for example, had two woman standing a few feet apart and holding a rope between them. The idea was for a woman to be on one side of the rope and a few gentlemen on the other side. Each gentleman in turn attempted to jump over the rope and dance one set around with the lone woman. The two women holding the rope decided if they would either simply let him pass or pull the rope up and trip him, thereby preventing him from engaging the woman in dance. In some cases the "merriment" resulted in the "tripped" gentleman crashing down upon the hardwood dance floor. If the gentleman was successful in passing over the rope, he engaged the woman in either a Waltz or a Galop (De Garmo, 46).

On the other hand, *Le Mouchoir Entortille* or "The Twisted Handkerchief" was less likely to cause serious harm. De Garmo simply described it as follows:

> The first two couples start in a Valse [Waltz] or Galop, each gentleman holding in his left hand a corner of a handkerchief, sufficiently raised to be able to pass under at every turn in the Valse. They waltz until the handkerchief is twisted like a cord. This figure may be performed by as many couples as the dimensions of the room will admit (47).

Cellarius described the same dance in almost exactly the same manner, only he simply titled his *Le Mouchoir* "The Handkerchief."

Henri Cellarius in *The Drawing-room Dances* also described "The Cotillon" in both French and English, adding that it was "that essential finale of every ball" (ii). Most of the Cotillons were actually quite simple, such as *Les Echarpes Volantes* (The Flying Shawls), *L'Eventail* (The Fan), *La Colin Maillard* (Blind Man's Buff), and *Les Cavaliers Ensemble* (The Gentlemen Together). The Flying Shawls, for example, was danced in Waltz rhythm as follows:

> In preparation, two shawls were crossed over and tied together in the center of a ring of four couples. Each of the four gentlemen held one corner of the tied shawl with their left hand and held it above their own head. While holding the shawl, each gentleman danced a turning Waltz with their partner, carefully trying to all keep the same distance from each other. At a pre-described signal they stopped waltzing and returned to their original positions (Cellarius 1847, 108–109).

The Fan involved only three people, one woman and two gentlemen. It also was danced to Waltz music, but in some instances it was also danced to Polka music. In the Fan,

> Within the center of the room three chairs were placed in a straight line. With the one chair in the center in the opposite the direction of the outer two chairs. One couple starts a Waltzed around the chairs. As they approached the center chair the gentleman seated the lady. He proceeded to escort two other gentlemen to each of the outer chairs. The lady, chose one of the gentlemen to dance with and offered her fan to the other. As the new couple danced, the lone gentleman was required to follow them

around the room while "hopping" and fanning them at the same time (Cellarius 1847, 109).

Blind Man's Buff was a popular dance game played by adults that also in later years continued as a popular game among schoolchildren throughout America. Cellarius described it as follows:

> Similar to the Fan, three chairs were placed in the center of the room in a straight line, but all facing the same direction. One couple Waltzed around the chairs. The couple separated and the gentleman dancer selected another gentleman and placed him in the center chair and blindfolded him. The lady dancer selected another gentleman and placed him in one of the chairs as she sat in the other. The first dancing gentleman encouraged the blindfolded gentleman to select either the right side or left side. The gentleman removed the blindfold and had to dance with whomever he had chosen while the first dancer danced with the other. Therefore, one gentleman danced with a lady while the other gentleman danced with a gentleman (Cellarius 1847, 109–110).

Video clip performances of the mid-nineteenth century Cotillion dance games Blind Man's Buff, as well as The Fan and The Rope, are viewable from the Music Division of the Library of Congress online source *An American Ballroom Companion: Dance Instruction Manuals Ca. 1490–1920* (see bibliography).

The *Les Cavaliers Ensemble* or "The Gentlemen Together" was an uninhibited fun dance that began with two couples of men and two couples of women each dancing with a partner of the same sex until signaled to change partners and join together as a couple with a man and a woman. Cellarius described it as follows:

> The two first gentlemen, each choose a gentleman to waltze with them, and the two ladies, each select a lady to waltze with them. At a given signal, the four gentlemen stop and form a round while the ladies form another. Two ladies in advancing to the gentleman's circle, pass under the arms of the other two ladies, and enter it, forming a round à l'envers, when each gentleman waltzes with the lady before whom he finds himself. This figure may be performed by three or four couples (111).

At the time, society did not view a man dancing with a man or a woman dancing with a woman as anything other than just dancing and partaking in merriment.

The Cotillions were usually enjoyed by all in attendance and lasted for an hour or so. In order to end the cotillions one final dance was chosen. Many of the Cotillion party dances had only a few specific dances that signified the end of the sequence of party dances. De Garmo, for example, listed only nine variations for the last Cotillion. One example was *Le Rond Final* (The Final Round), which he explained in the following manner:

> All form a general round. The conductor and his lady separate from the circle (which is immediately reconnected) and perform a Valse or Galop in the midst. At a signal, he stops, and his lady passes, out of the circle. He chooses another lady, with whom he also dances within the circle. He passes out of the circle in his turn, and the lady chooses another gentleman, and so on for the others. When only two or three couples remain, all the couples join in the Valse (74).

The Cotillion was also often ended with everyone in attendance partaking in a Galop, a Waltz, or even a Polka.

THE POLKA, JAMES K. POLK, AND POLKA MADNESS

The Polka was a nineteenth century dance believed to originate around 1830 in the Bohemia Region of Europe in the modern day Czech Republic and Slovakia. (In Czech *Pulka* translates to half step for "the rapid shift from one foot to the other." However, in Polish, "polka" means "Polish women.") Some evidence also exists that in 1822, a Czechoslovakian poet named Celakovsky wrote a dance named the "Cracoviacs" that was almost identical to the Polka (Hinckley, "Eclipsing the Waltz, Polite society discovers polka, 1844," n.d.).

However, one story of the Polka's origin has been repeated so often that it is hard to separate whether the story is fact or legend. Many sources simply retell the story of a young Bohemian peasant girl named Anna Slezak, who around 1830 "began making up a little tune in her head." In response, she "skipped" around in time to the musical tune with a dance that she made up. Slezak was observed by a local schoolmaster who wrote down the song and the dance steps, and within a week he had his students dancing in the same manner as Anna. Supposedly, in 1835, it was seen by a military officer named Joseph Neruba who introduced it as the Polka in Prague. In 1839, it was danced in Vienna. In 1840, a dance master from Prague reportedly introduced the Polka in Paris, where it quickly became a popular dance in the Parisian dance academies and ballrooms. Some other sources trace the Polka to a small village in Hungary and say that in 1844 a retired Hungarian Army officer introduced it to America society. In either case, in 1844, the Polka quickly spread across Europe and America. In early 1844, it was "officially" danced at Almack's in London (Shaw 1949, 68–69; Sachs 1963, 435; Panati 1991, 40; "Polka History of Dance," n.d.).

According to dance historian Joseph Marks, the Polka was first danced in America on May 10, 1844 at the National Theater in New York City by noted dance instructor Lawrence De Garmo Brookes and Mary Ann Gammon. It appears that an American working in Europe for the newspaper the *New York Daily Aurora* saw the dance and notified his editor, who in turn passed it on to Brookes. Later that same year, in 1844, Gabriel De Korponay and Pauline Desjardins introduced the Polka as a social dance to American society. The following year, famed American dance instructor Allen Dodworth (see Chapter 4) was the first dance teacher in America to regularly teach the Polka to his students in New York City (Marks 1957, 75; Hinckley, "Eclipsing the Waltz," n.d.).

In a very short time, Americans of all classes embraced the lively Polka. As a dance, the Polka was actually less inhibited that the strict "carriage" and closeness of the Waltz. Although it was mainly taught and danced in the closed dance position, it was also danced in the side-by-side position. Cultural historian Charles Panati noted, "For sheer delight, the Polka was the darling dance of its day, infecting all levels of society with its quickening pace" (40). Dance historian, Lloyd Shaw said,

It was madness. It swept the ballrooms of the world. It combined the straight line [of the Galop], and the whirling curve [of the Waltz], and the joy and the laughter, and the high spirits that could not be denied (53).

During the 1840s, the Polka was so widespread that many newspapers and publications commented on the dance. In 1845, publishers Perrot and Robert, for example, praised the vibrancy of the dance. In one newspaper publication they exclaimed, "To dance the Polka men and women must have hearts that beat high and strong. Tell me how you do the Polka, and I will tell you how you love" (Sachs 1963, 434). During the same year, the *London Times* described the Polka as combining the "intimacy of the waltz…with the vivacity of the Irish jig" (quoted in Shaw 1949, 67).

The Polka was so popular that after 1845 almost every published dance instruction book contained instructions for it. In 1847, *The Drawing-room Dances* by Henri Cellarius offered an introduction on the benefits of dance followed by a discussion of the popular dances of the day. At the time, to quote Cellarius, "the most popular of these [dances]" was the Polka, which he observed had "become so indispensable" in the ballroom (6). Cellarius claimed that much had been written about the origins and mass popularity of the dance that he only had "to occupy myself with the fundamentals, and…with the technical part of the dance." But in regards to the refinement of the Polka, Cellarius, in an obvious thoughtful sense of national pride added, "in spite of its foreign origin [the Polka] may now be considered as French, for it is to France that it owes its fashion and character of universality" (20–21). At the time, France was still the cultural center of social dance among Europeans and Americans.

The nineteenth century Polka was a couple's dance that progressed counterclockwise around the perimeter of the dance floor in a quick rhythm employing a simple step pattern of "step, close, step, hop." Cellarius described that the Polka began in the same closed dance position as the "ordinary" Waltz, but he carefully warned against any improper dance position. However, the careful warning of the dance position might have been in obvious deference to the possibility of a very close objectionable embrace. Cellarius cautioned,

The gentleman should hold the lady, neither too close nor too far from him. Too close an approximation would be alike opposite to the laws of grace and of decorum; too great a distance would render very difficult, if not impracticable, the turns and evolutions, that form so considerable a part in the execution of the dance.

Similar to the etiquette decorum that was redefining the roles of domesticity of women in society, the man was required to lead the Polka. In that manner, the concept of lead and follow was essential in requiring submission by the lady to the lead of the gentleman. Cellarius warily advised, "A lady is considered the better dancer or waltzer in proportion as she yields with confidence and self-abandonment to every impulse of her partner" (21–22).

The Polka step, as detailed by Cellarius, was danced in slow march-like 2/4 time divided into three measures. As was the standard of European and American closed couple dances, the man began with the left foot and the lady began with the right foot. He described the basic step as follows:

> For the first, the left heel should be raised to the side of the right leg without passing it behind, and so as to slightly touch the calf. In this position you jump upon the right foot, in order to give the spring to the left, which makes a glissade forward, in the fourth position.
>
> The second and third times are composed of two short steps made lightly by either foot, care being taken that both feet should find themselves nearly in the same line.
>
> At the second short step, the right leg is raised, the heel being near the lower part of the left calf...[pause slightly]. You then recommence with the other foot, and so on with the rest.

Cellarius reminded the gentleman that, in addition to the basic Polka step, it was also his responsibility to lead the lady through a variety of steps and also to vary the turning steps both to the right and also to the left.

In situations where the ballroom was either small or crowded, the gentleman was required to add a variation to the turns and "make his partner pivot on the same spot." He suggested that some other variation of steps included the Bohemian (which was a double Polka step) and "the old allemande." However, Cellarius added "that these variations are entirely left to the [discretion of the] gentleman." He did not necessarily preclude any variations, as long as they were performed with "distinction and elegance" (Cellarius 1847, 23–25).

At the same time that the Polka was so prevalent in the fashionable ballrooms, Cellarius confirmed that it was also widespread among the masses. (Although he did suggest that the masses had "travestied and disfigured" the Polka by dancing it at "inferior assemblies.") In addition, Cellarius also indicated that some Waltz aficionados resisted dancing the Polka and some even "despise the polka," and he predicted that it was "only a transient prejudice...[and the Polka was] sure to maintain its place in the ball-room" (Cellarius 1847, 25).

During the first few years, the Polka contained only about ten figures of which about five were regularly danced in the ballroom. They included the *Promenade Valse* (a turn similar to the Waltz); *Valse à rebours* (a reverse Waltz turn); *Valse roulée* (lady turns to the right and man progresses backward); and the *Pas bohemian* (a rapid heel-toe movement). In a few years, many couples employed "vigorous hopping and leaping" and also added many step variations. During the course of the dance, the Polka was versatile enough to change dance positions from arm-in-arm, side-by-side, face-to-face, or even circling one partner. In doing so, the partners could also dance in a straight line, do turning circles, or even have the man lead backwards. The basic step pattern also allowed one to either move the feet quickly in a rapid rhythm within one bar of music or slow down the same step and execute it within two bars of music (Sachs 1963, 437; "Instrumental Dance Music," n.d.).

At the time, it was apparent that since the Polka was danced in many variations and among all classes in a lively jubilant manner, it was not in keeping with the proper decorum of the fashionable ballroom. Therefore, some dance publications suggested a slower version of the Polka. In 1859, Edward Ferrero, for example, in

The Polka was versatile enough for partners to change dance positions. In this contemporary print from 1848, the couple at the far left is arm-in-arm, the two couples in the center are face-to-face, and the couple at the far right is side-by-side.   The Granger Collection, New York, ID: 0073790.

The Art of Dancing; Historically Illustrated provided instruction for a slow version of the Polka. He offered that when "performed slowly and with its proper accentuation...[it was] decidedly a graceful and pleasing dance." The reason that he offered a slow version was that in Ferrero's opinion the Polka "savored too much of the stage to be adopted in private circles without being remodeled to suit the popular taste of this country."

The music was the same in 2/4 time, and the step description was basically the same. However, Ferrero felt that the variations and figures were so "numerous" and the steps "complicated." Therefore, he suggested that the Polka be "reduced to a single step." He described the basic "remodeled" Polka step as follows:

> The left foot must be raised to the side of the right ankle; springing on the right foot at the same time, slide the left foot forward (counting one). Draw the right foot close behind the left, in the third position (count two). Spring out on the left foot, raising the right, as in the first movement (count three)...you pause one for the fourth. Recommence the step with the other foot, using each alternately to commence the step.

Although Ferrero reduced the step to one, he did not restrict the direction of the dancers. Actually, he suggested that the direction of the Polka "should be varied as much as possible" (144–145).

Nevertheless, whether danced slow or fast, the Polka remained quite popular. In response to the demand for Polka music, hundreds of songs were written specifically for the Polka. One example was "The Jenny Lind Polka" written by Allen Dodworth in 1844. In 1846, Dodworth also wrote the "Cally Polka" in honor of his wife. Typically, the songs were arranged and composed for the piano and sold as a few sheets containing only one song. In some cases, sheet music contained more than one song. The *Drawing Room Polkas* published in Boston by Oliver Ditson around 1860, for example, contained a series of Polkas compiled in one bound volume. *Drawing Room Polkas* was also typical of many sheet music publications that also provided a cover illustration of a man and woman dancing.

Although the Polka quickly replaced the Waltz in popularity in all classes of American society, as with most new dances, it also had its critics. In 1845, the *New York Herald* newspaper, for example, called the Polka

Sheet music cover of "Drawing Room Polkas" published in Boston by Oliver Ditson around 1860. The cover illustration shows a man and a woman dancing the first step of the Polka as described by Henri Cellarius in *The Drawing-room Dances* (1847). Library of Congress, Prints and Photographs Division LC-USZ62-119856.

the lowest and most vulgar movement danced in the villages of Hungary... the indecency of the Polka as danced at Saratoga [New York] and Newport [Rhode Island]...outstrips the most disgraceful exhibitions of the lowest haunts of Paris and London (quoted in Dannett and Rachel 1954, 41–42).

During the same year, one southern socialite, Mary Cosby Shelby (granddaughter of the governor of Kentucky), while visiting New York was told by her friend Georgia Edwards of the new popularity of the Polka. Miss Edwards encouraged her friend to take a Polka dance lesson (most likely at Allen Dodworth's Dance Academy—see Chapter 4); however, Shelby was not impressed. She wrote in her journal:

At nine Georgia Edwards came around, said she intended taking a Polka lesson, & would be glad for Sue & I to go with her. It seems to be greatly in vogue here. I never before saw it danced. It is a graceful pretty dance, and Georgia danced it very gracefully. But I have the same objections to seeing a Lady and gentleman dance it that I have to the waltz. And nothing would induce me to learn it (Shelby, 36–37).

It also appears that the Polka caused a stir in Washington, D.C.

In late 1844, the election of James K. Polk as president of the United States caused a few to speculate that the dance was named after him. But it definitely was not, and President Polk actually bore the brunt of many a "Polka" joke. In fact, during the end of 1844, Julia Tyler (wife of president John Tyler) had introduced the Polka in the ballroom of the White House. After the Tylers left the White House, so did the Polka. In early 1845, Polk continued the tradition of the presidential inaugural ball. However, Polk created the unusual situation of two separate presidential inaugural balls. The first one was a highly priced private ball for 900 select committee members and special privileged guests. (The suggested contribution price was $10.) The second ball, at less than half the contribution price, was open to the public and was attended by over 3,000 people. But Polk's wife thought the new dances of the day, especially the Polka, were not suited for public display. Therefore, upon residency in Washington, she banished all dancing from the White House (Dannett and Rachel 1954, 40; "White House History," n.p.).

For the most part, the Polka remained popular through the end of the nineteenth century. Within the private wealthy ballrooms, the Polka was often danced a bit slower than among the public dance halls of the working class. In 1906, for example, dance historian Thomas Reginald St. Johnston's description of the Polka (which he called "La Polka") was quite similar to Edward Ferrero's slow version. He suggested the same music in 2/4 time with "the accent on the 2, to be played not so fast as the Galop." St. Johnson offered the following description for the basic Polka step:

> We commence with the first and most general.—At the one, hop on the right leg, lifting or doubling the left at the same moment: at two, put your left leg boldly forward on the ground: at three, bring your right toe to the left heel: at four, advance your left foot a short step forward. Now is the "one" in the next bar or measure of the tune. Hop on the left leg, doubling or lifting up your right leg, and so on—proceeding in this step with your arm circling your partner's waist round the room.

St. Johnson cautioned that the Polka was "a noiseless dance," and therefore, he strongly warned against any stamping of the feet or any kicking out of the legs (St. Johnston 1906, 151).

Shortly after St. Johnston's publication, the Polka almost disappeared from the American ballrooms. The disappearance was due mainly to the emergence of Ragtime music and the public's new desire for Animal Dances. The Polka did enjoy a revival after World War II; however, the lively dance barely resembled the nineteenth century American Polka. The late twentieth century Polka was danced in either a similar closed dance position or side-by-side in similar 2/4 time. However, it was danced in a rhythm of 1,2,3 and 4,5,6. The basic step for the man started with the left foot with a slight hop (count 1) followed by quick short *chassé* steps right foot (count 2), and left foot (count 3), the pattern repeats with the right foot with a slight hop (count 4) followed by quick short *chassé* steps left foot (count 5), and right foot (count 6).

THE MAZURKA, THE POLKA MAZURKA, THE REDOWA, THE POLKA REDOWA, AND THE VARSOVIENNE

As a result of the mass popularity of the Polka, American dancers (and to some extent European dancers) actively sought other progressive round dances that engaged one couple of a man and a woman. In quick succession, other dances similar to the Polka were actively danced in the ballrooms, including the Redowa and the Mazurka.

The Mazurka (sometimes *mazurek* or *mazourka*) was Polish in origin and was even danced in Russian courts. It originated in the Mazurs region of central Poland during the sixteenth century. During the early nineteenth century in Europe, it developed as a couple's ballroom dance and in France as a Quadrille. In some cases it was danced by just one couple, whereas other times it was danced in a circle by either four or eight couples. In 1845, it followed the Polka into the American ballrooms where it was most often danced by couples in a circle executing many different figures, often improvised, and the figures accentuated by foot stamping ("Mazurka," n.d.).

As best as could be determined, most danced the basic Mazurka in 3/4 time with a slight leap step and a glide. However, according to dance historian Lloyd Shaw, "The published descriptions that reached the United States were so unclear that no one could quite figure it out, except that, since the mazurka had stamps and leaps, it must be like a polka, but in 3/4 [time]" (239). Dance historians Sylvia Dannett and Frank Rachel described the Mazurka as "the couples follow the leader, turning from right to left in a circle or in an oval; sometimes the woman kneels down while her partner executes a chasse around her and then the maneuver is reserved" (43). Dance historian Curt Sachs added, "Its step pattern has a good deal of latitude; the only characteristic steps are the stamping of the feet and the striking together of the heels." Sachs's research indicated that during the first basic step the striking of the heel is done once, during the second basic step twice, and during the third basic step three times. This observation led Sachs to believe that the Mazurka might have developed from an ancient choral dance known as the *Siebensprung*, translated as the "seven jumps" (440).

In 1847, Henri Cellarius in *Drawing Room-dances* provided a description for the Mazurka. However, Cellarius realized that most of the Mazurka was improvised at the whim of the dancers. An implementation that he called "altogether independent and truly inspired, [but] which has no rule." As a result, he said, "Only one part of the Mazurka can be taught; the rest is invented, is extemporized, in the excitement of execution." Despite the wanton improvisation of the dance, he offered four basic steps that he considered "fundamental" to the Mazurka. They were the *Pas glissé*, the *Pas de basque*, the *Pas boiteux*, and the *Pas polonaise*.

The *Pas glissé* was the basic step and sometimes simply called the Mazurka step. During the *Pas glissé*, the right foot springs slightly forward with a leap (count 1) with the left "gliding" (or *glissé*) past the right foot and placing it in front (count 2).

The left foot is lifted and placed behind the right (count 3). The pattern is reversed with the left foot springing slightly forward with a leap (count 4) with the right "gliding" (or *glissé*) past the left foot and placing it in front (count 5). The right foot is lifted and placed behind the left (count 6). The basic "Mazurka Step" was repeated as often as necessary. The *Pas de basque* was similar to a "ronde," which had the foot swing and included a leap and a glide. The *Pas boiteux* was a step close with a click of the heel. The *Pas polonaise* was a three-step figure that employed the left foot to "strike the right heel...for the first beat." The second step was a "slide with the left foot and close the right foot next to the left foot on the third step." The other basic figures could be danced at the desire of the dancers; however, Cellarius indicated that a promenade "is indispensable, before each figure." The promenade portion, which he termed "the foundation of the mazurka," was performed as the gentlemen went around with the lady in place (Cellarius 1847, 52–55; Shaw 1949, 239–240).

A hybrid of both the Polka and Mazurka was also danced and was aptly named the Polka Mazurka. Dance historians, such as Lloyd Shaw, suggested that the Polka Mazurka may have even been an unsuccessful attempt by a Dance Master to actually teach the Mazurka. He reasoned that in the absence of any written descriptions, the dance was misinterpreted and taught with "a *lot* of polka steps." In fact, the Polka Mazurka that was danced shortly after 1845 did combine steps from both the Polka and the Mazurka. In a fashion similar to the Mazurka, a significant number of figures were also improvised (Shaw 1949, 239–240).

In 1859, Edward Ferrero in *The Art of Dancing; Historically Illustrated* described it as "a very graceful dance . . . [with] a combination of the polka and mazourka steps." He described the basic Polka Mazurka step as follows:

> Slide the left foot forward (count one); bring the right foot up to the left; at the same time raise the left foot, extending it, pointing the foot down (count two); bring the left back close to the right, at the same time springing on the right foot without touching the left on the floor (count three); then execute the polka Redowa step (count three). Commence the whole with the right foot; the mazourka part is executed forward without turning; then turn half round with the polka Redowa step; repeat, and you make the whole round.

Ferrero suggested that the dance in 3/4 time "being rather slow" was not as often requested as the fast dances (148–149).

All in all, both the Mazurka and Polka Mazurka were often included on just about every dance program from 1859 through the 1890s. After that, the dance simply disappeared from the dance floors. However, the *Pas de Basque*, which was one of the basic steps described by Cellarius, evolved into another contemporary dance the Redowa. In turn, the Redowa was the forerunner of the twentieth century Waltz step (Dorfman 1976, 9).

In order to satisfy the insatiable public desire for round dances, in a similar fashion dance instructors introduced the Redowa and Polka Redowa. The Redowa was actually a Waltz-type movement that was used within the steps of the Polka. It incorporated the couple turning to the man's left for three measures of music and turning in the opposite direction for one measure of music. Most of the time the Redowa was repeated in this same pattern for the entire song (Sachs 1963, 435–436).

In 1856, Charles Durang in *The Fashionable Dancer's Casket* claimed that the Redowa was a waltz step that was part of the second figure of a French Mazourka Quadrille from about 1847. (At the time, American dance instructors still followed the lead of Europe, but mainly France.) Therefore, Durang provided the same description for the Redowa. However, unlike most authors of dance instruction manuals throughout history, Durang actually described the steps for "the lady to commence" beginning with her right foot in the "third position." (Almost all dance instruction books described the step patterns for the gentleman and then merely suggested a form, such as the lady repeats the same steps in the opposite foot pattern beginning with the right foot.)

The basic Redowa began with the Lady standing in the "Third Position" and was danced in 3/4 time as follows:

> The right foot was brought forward with a slight hop and placed down behind the left foot, at the same time the left foot was raised slightly (count 1). The left foot slid forward with the left knee slightly bent (count 2). A hop with the right foot was repeated similar to the first step (count 3). The left foot was brought behind the right foot with a slight hop of the left and the right foot was raised slightly (count 4). The right foot slid forward with the right knee slightly bent (count 5). Once again, the left foot was brought behind the right foot with a slight hop of the left and the right foot was raised slightly and keeping it forward, (count 6).

The gentleman performed the opposite foot pattern beginning with the left foot. Durang also suggested that in order to provide variety "the reverse turn may also be used." He simply added that the reverse turn step was "almost the same form as the *pas de Basque:* the only difference is the hop" (Durang 1856, 77–79).

In 1868, *Beadle's Dime: Ball-Room Companion and Guide to Dancing* also provided a step description for the basic Redowa. Although it was described as "somewhat difficult," the instructions were actually quite brief. The basic "movement" was simply described as follows:

> Gent takes one hop on left foot and lady upon right simultaneously. Gent then takes one hop upon right foot, which has been passed behind, and to right of the left, which movement will turn gent to right, turning lady, who makes the movement in two running hops. This is continued alternately, one hop in time of partner's two running hops, care being taken to keep in perfect time with the music (31).

The Redowa was actually quite popular and also spawned an offshoot known as the Polka Redowa. The difference was that the Polka Redowa, although danced in the same step pattern, was danced in 3/4 time as opposed to the 2/4 time of the Polka.

Another dance that joined the Mazurka, the Polka Mazurka, the Redowa, and the Polka Redowa on the American dance floors was the Varsovienne. The Varsovienne (sometimes "Varsouvianna") was danced in 3/4 time and was basically a combined Mazurka, Polka, and Polka Redowa; it was first danced in America about 1853 or 1854. Dance historian Lloyd Shaw said the Varsovienne was "one of the loveliest and one of the best-loved of all the old-time dances" (Shaw 1949, 245).

Shaw described the Varsovienne pattern (which he called "Varsouvianna") as a combination of two patterns of a series of a "Sweep, glide, close" and a series of "Sweep, glide, cross, step, point." The "Sweep, glide, close" was described for the gentleman as follows:

1. Sweep left foot back and over the right instep.
2. Glide forward on the left foot.
3. Close right foot to the left.

The "Sweep, glide, cross, step, point" was described as:

1. Sweep left foot back and over the right instep.
2. Glide forward on the left foot.
3. Step on right while crossing partner over in front of you.
4. Step on left as you finish crossing her to your left side.
5. Point with the right toe barely touching the floor in front of you and a little to the right.
6. Hold this point.

Shaw described that the two patterns were put together for "Varsouvianna" in the following sequence:

Sweep, glide, close, Sweep, glide, close, Sweep, glide cross, step, point.
Sweep, glide, close, Sweep, glide, close, Sweep, glide cross, step, point.

Sweep, glide, cross, step, point, Sweep, glide, cross, step, point,
Sweep, glide, cross, step, point, Sweep, glide, cross, step, point.

The pattern was repeated once again, and upon completion of the second sequence the couples proceeded to Waltz (Shaw 1949, 249–250).

However, in regards to the rhythm of the dance, the steps were not danced with the phrasing and beat of the music. Actually, it was danced off-phrase. Shaw offered the following explanation:

The interesting thing about the music is that, like the Mazurka, it begins on the last beat of a measure, and the unit or three-beat phrase of the dance falls on this third beat together with the first two beats of the next measure. This is apt to confuse some persons if the dance is described so far as the phrasing of the steps is concerned (247).

The Varsovienne was also danced in the Southwest. In Texas, for example, it was called "Little Foot" and in Spanish California it was called *La Varsouvianna*. However, among Mexican Americans in the Southwest and New Mexico, it was danced a bit faster incorporating more leaping and improvisation (Shaw 1949, 246–247).

Video clips of the Varsovienne from the mid-nineteenth century are viewable from the Music Division of the Library of Congress online source *An American Ballroom Companion: Dance Instruction Manuals Ca. 1490–1920*, as well as

Sheet music cover for "The Celebrated Varsovienne" published in Boston by Oliver Ditson in 1857. The cover illustration shows a man and a woman in a closed dance position. Each is dressed in fashionable ballroom attire typical of the 1850s. Library of Congress, Prints and Photographs Division LC-USZ62-17451.

Dancetime Publications *500 Years of Social Dance: Volume I: The 15th to 19th Centuries* (see bibliography).

THE VIRGINIA REEL, THE SCHOTTISCHE, AND THE MILITARY SCHOTTISCHE

Although the round dances such as the Waltz, the Polka, the Mazurka, the Redowa, the Varsovienne, the Galop, and the Cotillion were the favored dances of the day, the Quadrille was still danced alongside them. Among the Quadrilles, the most well-known and also the apparent favorite was the Virginia Reel. The dance dates to the early seventeenth century as an English Country-dance by the name of "Sir Roger de Coverly" (see Chapter 1). It continued in America as the "Virginia Reel" from the very early part of the eighteenth century through the nineteenth century. For the most part, the patterns remained the same and were danced in the Longways set, oftentimes for "as many as will." For example, the music continued until each couple in the Longways set had a turn leading the dance as the head couple at the top of the set (see Chapter 2). As with other Country-dances in a Longways set, the gentlemen lined up shoulder-to-shoulder spaced a few feet apart on one side and the women in similar fashion facing their male partners. Some instruction manuals recommended that each set be limited to six or eight couples. However, oftentimes the lines extended to 12 or more couples.

In 1885, Allen Dodworth in his famous work *Dancing and Its Relations to Education and Social Life* provided the Virginia Reel as a reference for a dance that could both be "fun" and reach across the social divide between the wealthy and the poorer classes. Dodworth remarked:

> It has been said, and is a truth, that at no time is the difference between those who are, and those who are not accustomed to refining influences so strongly marked as when they are in their merriest moods. If that should be during the enjoyment of a lively dance, the wide separation between the motions and manners of the two classes is curiously obvious (135).

He also reminded the reader that the dance was also valuable to impart upon children. In doing so he claimed that the "impression may last."

Dodworth's firsthand experience with the Virginia Reel began around 1835. At that time, he had attended the Governor's Inauguration Ball in Hartford, Connecticut. At the inauguration were "assembled nearly all the dignitaries of the state" of which almost all danced and participated in the dancing fun. Dodworth recalled that the "popular dances were such as the Virginia Reel...and other country or contra dances, all quick, spirited, and full of action." He remembered that

> The impression made was that this was a company of happy humanity, as merry as they could well be, yet their merriment was a beautiful expression of refined jollity, indicating the presence of cultivated people in their merriest moments, when least occupied with thoughts of motion or manner.

In contrast to the 50 years between the Governor's Inauguration Ball in Hartford and the time of his publication in 1885, Dodworth observed that the dignitaries of the late nineteenth century did not participate in dancing with the same fun and vigor as he had remembered at the Governor's Inauguration Ball at Hartford, Connecticut. He wrote, "more than fifty years ago... many more of them [participated] in the amusements than would do so at the present time" (Dodworth 1885, 135–137).

The Virginia Reel may have continued as an old favorite, but it was joined by a new favorite known as the Schottische. The Schottische (sometimes "Schottisch") might have originated around 1844 from a Bavarian dance

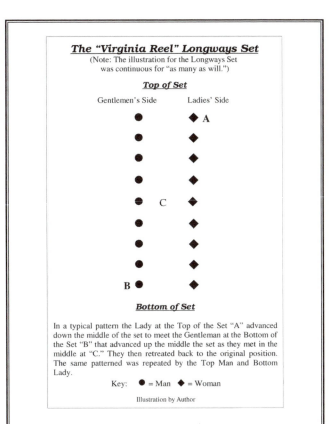

The "Virginia Reel" Longways Set
(Note: The illustration for the Longways Set was continuous for "as many as will.")

Top of Set

Gentlemen's Side   Ladies' Side

Bottom of Set

In a typical pattern the Lady at the Top of the Set "A" advanced down the middle of the set to meet the Gentleman at the Bottom of the Set "B" that advanced up the middle the set as they met in the middle at "C." They then retreated back to the original position. The same patterned was repeated by the Top Man and Bottom Lady.

Key: ● = Man ◆ = Woman

Illustration by Author

In a typical pattern of the Virginia Reel, the lady at the top of the set "A" advanced down the middle of the set to meet the gentleman from the bottom of the set "B" as he advanced up the middle of the set and they met in the middle at "C." They then retreated back to the original position. The same pattern was repeated by the top man and bottom lady.

One of the favorite patterns was the top gentleman meeting his partner at the top of the set where they held hands in a face-to-face position and chasséd sideways down to the bottom of the set and repeated the pattern back in the other direction up the middle of the set and returned to their original positions. Other patterns included the top couple passing each other in the middle and weaving in and out of the entire Longways set as they made their way to the bottom of the set. As they took their place at the bottom, the former second couple took their place at the top of the set. The Virginia Reel remained quite the favorite among Americans through the end of the nineteenth century. In almost all cases it was danced in rural areas and did maintain a presence at some fashionable dances.

known as the "Rheinlaender" that was also known as the "Bavarian Polka." As a result, some speculated that it might also have predated the Polka. It is hard to determine the origin of the name of the dance, but the spelling "Schottische" is the German word for "Scottish." Therefore, some have speculated that the dance came from Scotland; however, most agree that it developed in Bavaria in Germany. On the other hand, according to the English Folk Dance Society in London, the Schottische might trace its roots about 100 years earlier to a dance known as the Ecossaise that was similar to a Scotch Reel. In the case of the Ecossaise, it is quite possible that the Germans named their dance the Schottische, since both dances incorporated quick changing of the weight between the feet, stamping of the heels, and similar pointing of the toes. In *The Social Dances of the Nineteenth Century in England*, dance historian Philip Richardson claimed that the Schottische was first introduced in England around 1848. It was "in vogue" among the upper classes and the fashionable assemblies. At about the same time it was introduced in America (Richardson 1960, 102–103; "Instrumental Dance Music 1780s–1920s," n.d.).

In 1859, Edward Ferrero in *The Art of Dancing* added a contemporary description of the "Schottisch." However, he thought that the dance was "too slow in its movement to suit the popular taste." Therefore, he provided two descriptions—one in the "slow" fashion and the other "accelerating the movement," which he thought would be more to the liking "among rapid dancers." The basic step was divided into two parts. In the first part, the dancer would slide the left foot forward, close the right foot behind the left, slide the left foot forward, and hop forward on the left foot and close the right foot behind the left at the same time. The pattern was repeated with the other foot. After the first part was danced twice the second part started with hopping twice with the left foot, while at the same time keeping the right foot on the floor. The left foot was brought down with the toe pointed to the left and made a half-turn. The pattern was repeated with the right foot and "turning half round, which completes the whole step of the schottisch." As with other round dances of the day, the direction of the dance could be varied at the whim of the dancers either "forward and back, or across the room, as you please." In order to make the dance "more lively," Ferrero suggested replacing the second part of the dance with the Waltz *à* Deux Temps (Ferrero 1859, 146–147).

A video clip performance of the Schottisch, based on the description in Ferrero's 1859 description from *The Art of Dancing*, is viewable from the Music Division of the Library of Congress online source *An American Ballroom Companion: Dance Instruction Manuals Ca. 1490–1920* (see bibliography). At about the same time, the Schottische was commonly danced to a song "Dancing in the Barn" by Turner and Orrin. The song and dance was so popular together that the Schottische was commonly called "The Barn Dance." ("Instrumental Dance Music 1780s–1920s," n.d.).

The Schottische was one of the most popular dances of the time. It also was danced among all classes of society. In the rural areas the Schottische was often danced with vim and vigor, incorporating the leaps and hops. However, the dance instruction books of the day were geared towards the fashionable ballrooms and also the use of etiquette and manners. Therefore, most of the publications recommended a toned-down version of the Schottische. In 1868, for example, *Beadle's Dime Ball-Room Companion and Guide to Dancing* suggested, "The slower the time is played, in moderation, the more pleasing the effect." They added that the "hopping or jumping movement is singularly ungraceful." In addition, they objected to any "kicking out" of the heels, which they termed vulgar and an "inconvenience of other dancers" (29–30).

In the 1870s, there were a number of variations on the schottische, the best known being the Military Schottische. The Military Schottische started with the dancers facing forward in side-by-side. In the side-by-side position the man's right hand was placed behind the lady's back at waist level. The lady placed her left hand lightly upon the man's right shoulder. Care was taken to ensure about one foot of space between the man and the lady. The first part was a simple Waltz step with a hop for two bars of music. The second part was danced face-to-face in Waltz position. The lady started with her right foot with a slight leap from the left foot to the right foot (count 1), followed by a slight hop on the right foot (count 2), and a slight leap from the right foot to the left foot (count 3), followed by a slight hop on the left foot (count 4). The pattern was repeated once. The man performed the same pattern beginning with the left foot (Dick and Fitzgerald 1878).

EL BORREGO, EL COYOTE, EL JARABE, THE SPANISH WALTZ, AND THE SPANISH DANCE

In all likelihood, the earliest written account of dancing in the Spanish southwest area of California (see Chapter 1) is a copybook by Maria Garcia Joseph in Chalco, Mexico. The handwritten manuscript, dated from 1772, was written in Spanish but contained information on 298 music melodies for dancing, 76 descriptive figures of Country-dances, and a few Minuets. The account is very similar to the contemporary copybooks and diaries that were kept by individuals in the British colonies at about the same time. In turn, the collection is a combination of English, French, and Spanish dances (Keller, "Early American Social Dance," n.d.).

Other Mexican folk dances that might have existed at the same time included the Chipanecas, Bamba, and Alegrias. The Alegrias was a Spanish Gypsy dance, usually performed solo by a woman, that mimicked the movements of a bullfight. The Bamba was a flirtatious couple courtship dance that involved using their dancing feet to literally tie a sash in a knot. The Chipanecas, from the Mexican province of Chiapas, allowed the audience to interact with the dancers as they clapped hands in 3/4 time (Arthur Murray, "Dictionary of Dance," n.d.).

Although exaggerated, historian Lucile Czarnowski in *Dances of Early California Days* (1950) quoted an early nineteenth century contemporary account by Walter Colton who said, "A Californian would hardly pause in a dance for an earthquake, and would renew it before the vibration ceased" (18). At the time, the Californian in reference was of Spanish ancestry. Dances obviously were plentiful, and the dances of the early Spanish years (before the 1840s) also included dance games such as *El Borrego* (The Lamb) and *El Coyote* (The Coyote).

The dance *El Borrego* was an interpretation of the song of the same name. During *El Borrego*, a man and a woman, or a boy and a girl, performed a mock bull fight with the male as the bull. Each held a red kerchief; however, the kerchief belonging to the girl was large, about two feet square, and the one held by the boy was purposely much smaller in mock humor. They stood only a few feet apart and the steps were simply walking steps with a brief "bull run" at the point in the song when the word "Borreguito" was sung. The boy lowered his head like a charging bull and the girl darted her kerchief in playful anticipation as the matador. Later during the dance, they exchanged places, and the girl charged as a bull when the word "borreguita" was sung. Some accounts claimed than the girl sometimes darted her skirt rather than a kerchief.

El Coyote was another dance game, but played in Waltz rhythm. During the dance, any amount of couples joined hands in a circle around; however, one solitary person or "coyote" stayed in the middle. The group circled right for eight measures of music and left for another eight measures of music. They continued to change direction in the circle every eight measures until there was a break in the music. As the music stopped, the person in the center quickly chose a dance partner from the outer circle. At that point, all the others turned and tried to quickly secure a dance partner as all the couples Waltzed counterclockwise in a continuous circle. Therefore, the person left without the partner took a place in the center of the circle as the "coyote." The group repeated the pattern of joining hands and danced in a circle. According to Lucile Czarnowski, "In the haste to secure a partner it sometimes happens that a man will take a man, or a woman a woman for a partner, which is all part of the fun and adds to the jollity of the dance" (Czarnowski 1950, 33–36).

Both *El Borrego* and *El Coyote*, as well as other similar dance games, were also played during Carnival and Cascarone Balls (see later in this chapter). In addition, there were also similar type couple's dances, dances with sets for couples, group dances, and demonstration dances. Some set dances included *Las Pollitas* and *El Pollito*. The *El Pollito* was originally from Argentina and quite similar to *Las Pollitas*, which was danced to an accompanying song also called "*Las Pollitas.*" Both were danced, sometimes also singing the words, with improvised dance steps imitating a chicken. Other folk dances included the *El Jarabe*, the Fandango, and the Bolero.

In 1829, in San Diego, for example, Alfred Robinson recalled seeing the *El Jarabe* danced at a festive occasion in relation to "the blessing of Don Juan Bandini's house" (see later in this chapter). The *El Jarabe* was actually a common Mexican folk dance that involved a man and a woman mimicking flirtatious gestures. It was danced in 3/4 time similar to the Mazurka, and in later years in America it was sometimes known as the "Mexican Hat Dance." Robinson recalled that the pair "kept time to the music by drumming with their feet on the heel." His contemporary description provides an eloquent depiction of the dance. He noted:

> The attitude of the female dancer was erect, with her head a little inclined to the right shoulder, as she modestly cast her eyes to the floor, whilst her hands gracefully held the skirt of her dress, suspending it so as to expose...the execution of her feet. Her partner ...was under full speed of locomotion and rattling along with his feet with wonderful dexterity. His arms were thrown carelessly behind his back, and secured, as they crossed, the points of his "serape," that still held its place upon his shoulders.

In fact, the woman also lifted her dress slightly "above the ankle" so that she could perform the rapid foot movements without stepping on her own dress (quoted in Czarnowski 1950, 19–20; "Arthur Murray Dictionary of Dance," n.d.).

The *El Jarabe* was similar to other Spanish dances, most notably the Flamenco and the Fandango. The Fandango was danced by both a man and a woman in 3/8 time. The musical accompaniment was often supplied only by wooden castanets played either by the woman or sometimes by both of the dancers.

During the early nineteenth century, however, the sentiment of the United States of America towards Californians of Spanish ancestry was very similar to that of Native American Indians and African Americans. In similar fashion some of the prejudice was evident in the contemporary dance manuals. In 1831, for example, in *The Code of Terpsichore, The Art of Dancing,* Carlo Blasis displayed a hint of the times as he provided a thorough written description of both the Fandango and Bolero. Blasis recognized that the Fandango, as "a highly boasted dance, [was]...the leading dance of Spain." He did acknowledge that the dance exhibited "remarkable" grace and balance. However, he added, "the majestic movements express those feelings which determine the national character; namely, hauteur, pride, love, and arrogance" (32).

Blasis also claimed that at one time, the Fandango was once danced "by persons of quality" with "more dignity [and] more formality." That dancing, however, was supplemented by the "lower orders" whom "by the slightest movement...could give offence to modesty, or shock good taste." He also included:

> The lower orders...in high request, accompany it with attitudes which savour of the vulgarity of the principal performers, and their extravagant movements never slacken, never cease, till they are fairly tired out (33).

Blasis claimed that a common feature of all the Spanish was characterized by "different gradations" of passion. He provided a long description of the various emotions and passion as follows:

> In the execution of the Spanish dances, the arms are always expanded, and their movements...always undulating. They at times represent the generous sentiment of an absolute protection of the object beloved, at other times they describe with vivacity the tender feeling it inspires, and the sincerity of the avowal. The eyes, oftentimes directed towards the feet, glance over every part of the body, and testify the pleasure which symmetry of form inspires them with. The agitations of the body, the footing, the postures, the attitudes, the waverings, whether they be lively or dull, are the representatives of desire, of gallantry, of impatience, of uncertainty, of tenderness, of chagrin, of confusion, of despair, of revival, of satisfaction, and, finally, of happiness.

In defense of Blasis, the 1866 edition (and possibly the 1831 edition) released by the Parisian Roret Publishing company claimed Blasis as the author. Although the publication did include a reprint of Blasis's 1830 *Code of Terpsichore*, the publishing company did take liberties without Blasis's permission. Italian-born Carlo Blasis (b. 1803, d. 1878) was a famed dancer, choreographer, and teacher. His most noted accomplishment was the founding of the Italian style of ballet that eventually led to the basic ballet form and technique widely practiced throughout the world and America well into the twenty-first century. Blasis's two books, *An Elementary Treatise upon the Theory and Practise of the Art of Dancing* (1820) and *The Code of Terpsichore* (1830), are considered the first detailed instruction manuals applied to ballet techniques ("Nineteenth Century Social Dance," n.d.).

In contrast, Blasis claimed, "The Bolero is a dance far more noble, modest, and restrained, than the Fandango" (33). The Bolero was also danced mainly as an exhibition dance by a man and a woman. It was danced to a variety of music in 2/4 time and sometimes 3/4 time. Blasis described the steps as follows:

> It is composed of five parts, namely—the paseo, or promenade, which is a kind of intro-
> duction; the traversias, or crossing, to alter the position of the places, which is done
> both before and after the differencias, a measure in which a Change of steps take place;
> then follows the finales, Which is succeeded by the bien parado, a graceful attitude, or
> grouping of the couple who are dancing.... The steps of the Bolero are performed terre
> à terre; they are either sliding, beaten, or retreating, being always, as it were, clearly
> struck out (34).

In addition to the Bolero and Fandango, other couple's dances included *La Yucca*, the *La Camila*, *La Varsouvianna* (Varsovienne), and the Spanish Waltz (Czarnowski 1950, 36, 55).

At about the same time that Lorenzo Papanti in Boston "officially" introduced the Waltz in 1834 (see earlier in this chapter), a regional version developed near the Los Angeles area. Often described as the "Spanish Waltz," it was danced in a fashion similar to the closed dance position in 3/4 time. The Spanish Waltz began as individual couples danced in the closed dance position around the room in similar Waltz fashion. They finished the Waltz in the side-by-side position holding hands facing another couple in the same position, thereby forming a set of two couples. Each woman dropped her right hand and maintained contact with her left hand joined with her partner's right hand. Each woman circled their own partner counterclockwise in four Waltz steps. As the woman circled, during the second Waltz step, she made a complete left turn under the joined raised arms of both her and her partner. At the same time, the man performed the same amount of Waltz steps in place. When the woman returned to the original position she joined right hands with the opposite man under their left arms and all remain joined together. The two woman proceeded to exchange places and the two couples set all joined hands in a star pattern and circled eight Waltz steps to the left. At the completion of the star pattern, all raised hands, and each woman returned to her original partner with two Waltz steps (Czarnowski 1950, 64).

A contemporary account of the Spanish Waltz was provided by Alfred Robinson during a dance at Don Juan Bandini's house. Robinson noted,

> The waltz was now introduced and ten or a dozen couples whirled gaily around the
> room, and heightened the charms of the dance by the introduction of numerous inter-
> esting figures (quoted in Czarnowski 1950, 20).

The "interesting figures" described by Robinson were obviously the intercon-
nected four set couple dancing around their partners.

However, in a fashion similar to the rest of the country at the time, most of the "padrones" of the Spanish Missions placed a ban on dancing both the Waltz and the "Varsouvianna" because of the embrace in the closed dance position. At the time, the cultural traditions of the Spanish settlements and ranches were extremely patriarchal and deferred to the hierarchy of the immediate family. Prior to 1831, for example, a young man did not dance until his parents granted permission. At the time deference was given to the older adults who began the dancing, and usually no young individuals danced unless they were married. Young people danced only after their elders had left the dance floor. However, in most cases, the younger generation continued only until about ten or eleven o'clock. Both the Waltz and Varsouvianna dances were not readily accepted until the mass influx of "Americans" after 1849, with the discovery of gold in California. As a result, a change in the Spanish traditions was noted, particularly in the dance styles, including the introduction of the Schottische, Polka, Mazurka, Lancers, and variations on the Spanish dances. By the mid-nineteenth century, the Spanish Dance was a common dance in the ballrooms throughout America (Czarnowski 1950, 25).

Although many contemporary accounts likened the Spanish Dance to the "Saraband [sic] of Spain," the American ballroom version hardly resembled late sixteenth century Sarabande (see Chapter 1), nor did it hearken back to any Mexican American folk dances. In fact, as danced in the eastern ballrooms, it most closely resembled a Virginia Reel, Contra Dance, or a Country-dance. In 1847, *Leaflets of the Ball Room*, for example, explained the dance formation as follows:

> Danced in a circle or line by twenty or thirty couples. All the gentlemen arrange on one side—their partners opposite; the first, or leading gentleman, must stand on the side of the ladies, and the leading lady at the head of the gents' line; this position must be observed by every couple arriving at the top.

The step pattern for each figure was described similar to the set figure patterns for the Quadrilles and Country-dances. It was explained in *Leaflets of the Ball Room* in the following manner:

> The top couple pass into the second couple's places, (four bars, waltz time): cross over to partner's places, (four bars); take top corners, (four bars); return to places, (four bars). This figure repeated, joining hands four; or hands across, (sixteen bars); poussette two couples, which leads to next couple; the second lady and gent are thus left at top, the same as in a contra dance. The first lady and gentleman then go through the same figure, with the third couple, and so proceed to the end of the dance (No page number).

In 1859, Edward Ferrero in *The Art of Dancing; Historically Illustrated* described the Spanish Dance almost exactly the same way. Ferrero noted that it was "formed by any number of couples...forming a straight line, or circularly around the room." He did add one bit of clarification that each couple continually repeated the dance pattern "until all have danced with each other" (Ferrero 1859, 130).

Even after American annexation and statehood, California and the American Southwest maintained a strong presence of the Spanish and Mexican dance traditions. In a fashion similar to the societal factions of dance styles in the eastern ballrooms, there was also a noticeable difference in Spanish California. Many accounts noted a distinct contrasting style between the smooth and graceful movements of the "dons" and "senoritas" that was in stark contrast to the vim and vigor of the "cowboys" (Czarnowski 1950, 44).

The Places to Dance

Were people to dance a little more in this world the cares of life would not weigh so heavy on them.

—*Boston Times* editorial, 1847

Dancing…flourishes most in this country when religion prospers least, and then declines again as vital piety prevails.

—Catharine Beecher, 1851

It is improper also for two gentlemen to dance together when ladies are present.

—Thomas Hillgrove, 1863

SPANISH CALIFORNIA, BAILES, FANDANGOS, CARNIVALS, AND CASCARONE BALLS

In the early days California consisted mainly of Spanish settlements composed of a chain of 21 missions (the Spanish reign extended from 1768 to 1821—see Chapter 1) ranging north from San Diego (founded 1769) to Monterey (1770), San Francisco (1776), Santa Barbara (1782), and eventually to Sonoma (founded 1823). Almost all of the missions were military outposts termed "presidios." Some of the early nonmilitary settlements included San Jose (1777), Los Angeles (1781), and Santa Cruz (1781). In 1821, Mexico fought the War of Independence from Spain and, therefore, gained control of the area until 1844, when the land area was ceded to the United States after a war with Mexico. Therefore, the native Californians were mainly of Spanish and Mexican ancestry. Regardless of territorial control, at the remote outposts and settlements, the arrival of a ship was usually cause for celebration of either a *meriendas* (picnic) or a *bailes* (dance) (Czarnowski 1950, 17).

Removed from the missions, presidios, and settlements were larger farms and ranches sustained by agriculture and cattle. They were known as "ranchos" and were mostly family owned and, therefore, displayed an air of communal life. Regardless of the size of the rancho or, for that matter, the missions, presidios, and settlements, any celebration contained an important component of communal dancing. A typical grand celebration was usually held on an occasion such as a birth of a child, a baptism, a religious holiday, or a wedding. But even if there was no cause for "grand celebration," dancing served as a regular way to occupy an evening. In an early nineteenth century contemporary account, Platon Vallejo remembered:

> The evenings were given over to pure merriment. Every hacienda [house] had its stringed band of several pieces, the harp, guitar, and violin—once in a while a flute. And every night rain or shine—except at times of death or sorrow, there was a baile [dance]. In this every one had his part. The elder people stepped the stately Contra-danza. The budding generations enjoyed the Waltz and the beautiful Spanish folk dances to the accompaniment of the castanetas, and even little ones had their own figures to romp through…everyone enjoyed themselves (quoted in Czarnowski 1950, 19).

During the dancing, custom prevailed that the oldest generation danced first, followed in descending order of age. The evening dancing often occurred only after partaking in an evening meal. After the meal, the dancing often lasted late into the night, sometimes past midnight (Czarnowski 1950, 18–19).

The predominant religion of Americans of Spanish and Mexican ancestry was Catholic. Therefore, an important component of that religion included weddings, baptisms, or the "blessing" of new homes, which were occasions for all-day festive celebrations. (In some cases the baptism celebration lasted for more than one or two days. Weddings could last from three to seven days with a combination of music, merrymaking, and dancing.) In 1829, in San Diego, for example, Alfred Robinson recalled one such festive occasion in relation to "the blessing of Don Juan Bandini's house." During the blessing of Bandini's house, the "padre" went from room to room sprinkling Holy Water and said a blessing in Latin. When the ceremony was completed, musical instruments were brought out and the festivities and dancing began. The afternoon dance celebration was short, as preparation began for a larger nighttime celebration termed a "Fandango." Although the name "Fandango" was also applied to a specific dance (see Chapter 1), historian Lucile Czarnowski explained:

> the term fandango had a unique meaning at this time. It was not only the name of a Spanish dance which some performed, but it was likewise the name given an informal dancing party; in fact, in the early days of the ranchos any entertainment in which dancing was a major event was called a fandango (19–22).

In later years the "Fandango" referred to the dance of the poorer people, and the "Bailes" represented dances of the wealthy and larger lavish affairs. A Bailes typically included invitations and formalities similar to an Assembly Ball (see Chapter 2), whereas a Fandango was usually open to all. A traditional wealthy dance was run by an *El Tecolero* who acted in similar fashion to a traditional Master of Ceremonies. Therefore, *El Tecolero* served in the same manner of introducing the men and woman for dancing as well as coordinating and directing the musicians.

Many of the wealthier Rancho owners also built a specific room for dancing within their houses that was known as a "sala." The *sala* usually contained benches on either side, an area set aside for the musicians, and plenty of open space for dancing. The *sala* in Don Juan Bandini's house, for example, was about 50 feet long and 20 feet wide. Sometimes the dancing was held outdoors, and in some cases if the guest numbered a lot of people, a special "Ramada" was built in a prominent location near the main house.

The Ramada was most often a simply constructed roofed three-walled arbor-like structure. The open side had a simple post type fence that served as a barrier, mainly to prevent riders on horseback from closing in on the dance area. The walls of the Ramada were cheerfully decorated and seating areas were installed on the three walled sides. Custom of the day dictated that men were separated to one side of the Ramada unless dancing with a woman. Men on horseback viewed the festivities from the open side with the barrier. If one of the men wanted to dance, he dismounted, removed his spurs, and entered the dance space with sombrero in hand. Once inside, *El Tecolero* introduced a suitable young lady for dancing. At the conclusion of the dance, the man returned the lady to her seat, and he remounted his horse (Czarnowski 1950, 18–23).

Another cause for celebration was a Carnival or a Cascarone Ball. Described as "distinctly Californian," Cascarone Balls were colorful festive social events that included merrymaking, music, and dancing. They were usually held between November and the Catholic religious observance of Lent during the Spring months. The Cascarone Ball in the Monterey region of California, for example, was celebrated well into the twentieth century. In fact, a "cascarone" was actually a brightly colored decorated egg that was drained on the inside and filled with decorative elements and colorful paper. During the festivities it was a common gesture for a young man to approach a young lady (sometimes in courtship) and in turn, broke the "cascarone" in her hand. Sometimes the lady would return the favor, or in some cases initiate the egg breaking. The Cascarone was also included as part of the Carnival event just prior to Lent (Czarnowski 1950, 23–24).

Carnival was part of a weeklong grand celebration before the Catholic religious observance of Lent and could also include the tradition of the *cascarone*. The Carnival ball was often the highlight of the social life for Spanish Californians. The festivities included frolicking and revelry, and usually lasted all night. The carnival, however, could also be cause for other types of celebrations such as a visit from a special guest. In 1891, Brigida Briones wrote a firsthand account in *Century Magazine* of one such celebration of "A Carnival Ball at Monterey in 1829."

In 1829, Briones was 18 years old and described herself as "Senorita Brigida Canes," thereby indicating that at the time she was unmarried. She indicated that she "was invited by a friend in Monterey [California] to visit her." As was the custom of the day, her friend welcomed her guest by giving a Carnival ball. Actually, it turned out that it was the very first Carnival ball that Briones had ever attended. She described her arrival as follows:

> On our arrival at the ranch near Monterey where the festivities took place we found every one already dancing. The assembled guest, rushing up to us, lifted us from our horses and led us in, smearing our faces with more paint and breaking cascarones [eggs] over our heads with much laughter....On this occasion they all had red, black, and green paint (for the most part colored earths, powdered), and cascarones egg-shells filled with finely cut gold and silver paper), and vials of different colored liquids, all harmless (468).

The festivities and dancing were part of an afternoon celebration that concluded only so that the guests could wash the paint off their hands and faces in preparation for a "banquet in the old adobe." Upon completion of the meal, the guests resumed dancing until late in the evening. The evening dancing was in stark contrast to the "wild revel of the earlier part of the ball." Briones indicated that the evening ball and dancing observed "the most courtly behavior" (Briones, "A Carnival Ball at Monterey in 1829," 1891, 468–469).

"A SOLEMN WARNING TO DANCERS," BRIGHAM YOUNG, AND AN "INNOCENT RECREATION"

During the 1820s and culminating in the 1830s, organized religious opposition to social dancing in general intensified, and, similar to the Great Awakening of almost 100 years before, social dancing was pushed deeply into the background of society. Dance historian Richard Nevell in *A Time to Dance: American Country Dancing from Hornpipe to Hot Hash* (1977) claimed that the religious opposition maintained a fundamental belief that social dancing among other cultures such as African slaves, American Indians, or even the Appalachian mountain regions were an affront to Christian morals. Nevell wrote:

> All of them held a common belief that the mountain people were fundamentally backward, sinful creatures in desperate need of salvation, an attitude that had usually been reserved for American Indians and for black slaves from Africa. But eventually all of these poor people, the "hillbillies," Indians, and blacks, were lumped together as those who were not "saved." These were also the people who generally still danced and held respect for their ancestral traditions, much to the dismay of the invading missionaries (Nevell 1977, 44).

The organized opposition even included attacking the places where the people assembled to dance.

The Reverend Joel Hawes, for example, was a noted "crusader for moral reform" who held strong opposition to balls and social dancing. In one instance in 1825, he reportedly accepted an invitation to a ball in Hartford, Connecticut; however, he had no intentions of dancing. Once he was at the dance he dropped to his knees and called for all the other dancers to join him in a repenting prayer against the "evils of dancing." Apparently, no one else joined him in prayer, but his actions were obviously disruptive as the music stopped and many dancers simply left the building. Hawes jubilantly reported "the dance was broken up, the fiddler disappointed, [and] the devil routed" (Kazlitt Arvine, *Cyclopedia of Moral and Religious Anecdotes*, New York, 1881, 66–67; quoted in Cole 1942, 6–7).

Regrettably, the Reverend Joel Hawes was neither an isolated incident nor was he alone in his actions. In 1825, the formation of the American Tract Society took up the cause of the moral crusade against the "sins" of "Fashionable Amusements" that included cardplaying, drinking alcohol, and social dancing. One of their very first publications (possibly published around 1825 or 1833) was a pamphlet titled *Dancing, as a Social Amusement by Professed Christians or their Children.*

The opening salvo in *Dancing, as a Social Amusement by Professed Christians or their Children* warned that anyone who participated in "social dancing" was a "sinner" and therefore was "on the way to hell" (2). In order to define their position, they sought to distinguish that whenever dancing was mentioned in the Bible, such as Exodus 15:20, 1 Samuel 18:6, 2 Samuel 6:14, Psalm 30:11, and Jeremiah 31:4, it was associated with "a *religious act*, expressive of grateful joy for some signal deliverance, and in the performance of which the sexes did not unite." They decried that any other instances of dancing mentioned in the Bible were in negative references as a "*social amusement*." Therefore, they chastised that during any of those instances "a religious service had been perverted; and those were deemed vile and impious who indulged in it" (7). In summation of their evaluation of references to dancing in the Bible, they concluded:

> For the only instances of social dancing to which the Bible alludes are so mentioned as never to indicate approval, but usually distinct disapproval...therefore, "God's word pointedly condemns dancing as a *social amusement* (8).

Therefore, the American Tract Society proposed that in order to "abstain from all appearance of evil" the time should be well spent "dedicated to the Lord's work" (1–8).

The American Tract Society was actually quite a formidable opposition in its organized attacks against dancing. A significant weapon was the establishment of a publishing house at 150 Nassau Street in New York City. The publications (about 40 each year) were widely circulated among religious organizations and churches throughout America. By 1832, there were over 280 different pamphlets in publication with over 20 devoted specifically to the "social amusements" and dancing. As an organization, the American Tract Society continued its crusade and continued to publish similar pamphlets well into the twentieth century (Wagner 1997, 122).

The American Tract Society was not the only publisher of anti-dance literature. The Tract Society of the Methodist Episcopal Church also published similar publications. One example was a short four-page pamphlet *A Solemn Warning to Dancers* (published in New York sometime between 1824 and 1832). Similar to the American Tract Society argument, *A Solemn Warning to Dancers* condemned the practice of social dancing. It warned that all dancing was "evil" and that the time spent dancing took time away from the application of the mind for "spiritual thoughts":

> dancing is not only a notorious conformity to the world, but is directly calculated to divert the mind from every thing of a serious nature, and, by the manner in which it is conducted, tends to awaken in the breast of youth every unhallowed passion, and to set on fire of hell the whole course of nature.

The condemnation was quite harsh, but the Society members added that it was the Scriptures that "condemn the practice of dancing." Therefore, they cautioned, "you must either abandon it, or acknowledge yourself guilty in the sight of God and of course no Christian" (1–2).

The question of dancing was not left without posing the question of teaching dance to children. They cautioned that the practice of either employing a dance master "into your house" or sending children to "dancing school" was also ill-advised. The Society members asked those "who are parents" to consider the ramifications for those who say "there can be no harm in teaching your children to dance." They asked,

> Would you have your child, when grown to manhood, go in the way of dancing? And suppose he was to step from the dancing room into eternity? Would you have the consolation of reflecting that he had gone to heaven! What would he do there? He has not learned the employment of that society.

However, the accusation of eternal damnation was professed as one that could be ably avoided. Therefore, they decried, "Fly, then, from the dancing room, as you would from devouring fire" (2–3).

In 1832, the annual *Religious Monitor and Evangelical Repository* noted the dangers that dance applied to "Christian morality." The publication cited as one example the Boston *Banner of the Church* that claimed dancing was pursued only "for the simple purpose of pleasure [casting] a shade of dullness and disgust, over the solid and serious objects of human life." In 1836, the *Philadelphia Presbyterian* decried, "[Dancing] creates a taste which is not easily satisfied, and which when indulged, inevitably leads to criminal expenditure of time, exposure of health, and dangerous associations" (Cole, "The Puritan and Fair Terpsichore," 1942, 5).

The following year a crusading group known as the *Advocate of Moral Reform* provided a tract that was quoted in the *Religious Monitor and Evangelical Repository* in Philadelphia:

> Such then are balls, with all their glory and disgrace; and such they stand, the abhorrence of heaven and the joy of hell. In the grand arsenal of Satan, there are no more formidable armor, for the destruction of the souls of young unsuspecting females; and in the dread solemnities of the judgment day, the ruined votaries of balls, will stand in trooping multitudes, before the throne of the Eternal cursing their own destructive folly, and calling on the crumbling universe, to conceal their shame and guilt, while the wailings of their endless woe, will swell the undying tortures of eternity (quoted in Cole, "The Puritan and Fair Terpsichore," 1942, 5).

The threat of "eternal damnation" was a common application by the religious opposition to social dancing. However, one denomination actually encouraged social dancing.

In April 1844, a letter to the editor of the official Mormon publication *Times and Seasons* asked for the following explanation in regards to Mormons and dancing:

> I should be very much gratified by your informing me, and not only me, but the public, through the medium of your valuable paper, the *Times and Seasons*, what your views are in regards to balls and dancing, as it has lately existed in our city.

Considering the united religious objection to social dancing, the response from the editor, John Taylor, might have surprised some. Taylor replied:

There existed on the minds of the religious community, a great deal of unnecessary superstition in relation to dancing...but like all other athletic exercises, it has a tendency to invigorate the system and to promote health...enabling...a more easy and graceful attitude...There certainly can be no harm in dancing, in and of itself...certainly no one could object to it...we have no objections to [dancing] (Hemoni, "To Parents," *Times and Seasons* 5, 1 April 1844: 486).

Although most religious denominations certainly "objected" to all forms of social dancing, the Mormons did not (Miller 2000, 14–15).

In all fairness, the Mormons did not necessarily believe in going to public dance halls, but they certainly encouraged dancing within their own community. In October 1844, a few months after Mormon founder Joseph Smith was killed, new leader Brigham Young warned his followers to avoid intermingling with non-Mormons. In *Times and Seasons* he also reminded his followers "not to mingle in the vain amusements and sins of the world." He did offer that as long as they mingled among the congregation "if they wish to exercise themselves in any way, to rest their minds and tire their bodies, go and enjoy yourselves in the dance" (*Times and Seasons* 5, 1 October 1844: 668–670; Holbrook 1977, 12).

In American society at the time, church sponsored recreation simply did not exist. In 1830, when the Mormon Church was formed, it also began what is most likely the first form of church sponsored community recreation. (The idea of church sponsored recreation among most of the other denominations in America did not begin until around the 1870s and 1880s.) One of the main aspects of community recreation was social dancing. According to Leona Holbrook in *Dancing as an Aspect of Early Mormon and Utah Culture*, Mormon dancing was "an outward manifestation of an inner joy...expressing itself in group response and group participation...employed dancing as one of their sociological-cultural patterns" (5–6).

In later years, the Mormons sought an exodus to Utah, establishing a religious community separate and apart from the rest of America. In transport from the Midwest to Utah, during the winter of 1846 to 1847, Brigham Young and his followers encamped. In a fashion similar to the eighteenth century revolutionary encampments of George Washington (see Chapter 2), they danced to relieve the tribulations of winter and also to maintain moral and body exercise and circulation. Young reportedly told his congregation, "I want you to sing and dance and forget your troubles" (Miller 2000, 11).

Upon settlement in Utah, at Brigham City, they built a schoolhouse and instituted community recreation by opening "a dancing school." The following winter almost all of the 19 Mormon schoolhouses had dancing schools. In March 1852, Brigham Young made a clear distinction between the social aspect of dancing and the religious worship as it applied to Mormons. He stated that "fiddling and dancing are no part of our worship." However, he did explain that dancing served an important purpose. In regards to himself, Young said he danced so "that my body may keep pace with my mind...[giving] me a privilege to throw everything off, and shake myself, that my body may exercise, and my mind rest" (Holbrook 1977, 9–11).

On January 1, 1853, a large "Social Hall" was opened in Salt Lake City. The opening dedication was marked by a "grand ball" with invitations in the name of Brigham Young. Balls and dancing continued on a regular basis in the Social Hall. However, the dances were mostly Country-dance and cotillions as round dances such as the Waltz and Polka were not allowed. The Mormons only permitted dances that expressed the communal nature of their society and, similar to other denominations, objected to the close public embrace exhibited in the round dances. For that matter, even in the Country-dances any embrace such as "waist swings" were substituted by holding hands at arms length (Holbrook 1977, 6, 11).

In 1854, a visitor who attended a Mormon ball hosted by Brigham Young remarked, "the utmost order and strictest decorum prevailed. Polkas and waltzing were not danced; country dances, cotillions, quadrilles…were permitted." He also recalled that he was impressed by "Governor" Young's dancing. He added,

> At the invitation of Governor young, I opened the ball with one of his wives.…An old fashioned cotillion was danced with much grace by the lades and the Governor acquitted himself very well on "light fantastic toe."

In fact, a defining trait of Mormon worship that set it apart from other religious sects in America was the ability for one man to have more than one wife. As it transposed to the dance floor, one French visitor in 1860 noted that during the Quadrilles, the Mormon man had two ladies as partners for each dance. The French traveler indicated that the Mormons had invented "a new type of dance," which he termed the "Double Quadrille" (*Millennial Star* 14, 13 November 1852: 601; Holbrook 1977, 6–12).

In keeping with their creed that permitted social dancing, but at the same time did not approve of going to public dance halls, the Mormons sponsored and built their own community halls and pavilions for dancing. In the years after the Civil War, they built a series of large "bathing resorts with dance floors" including Garfield Beach (1875), Lake Shore (1878), Lake Park (1886), and Saltair Pavilion (1893). Other dance halls were built at Lindsay Gardens (1865) and Calder's Park (1865) (Holbrook 1977, 11).

Despite the Mormons' limited acceptance of dancing, most other religious denominations continued their complete disdain against all forms of social dancing. In 1847, for example, the Reverend Nathan Lewis Rice of the Central Presbyterian Church in Cincinnati, Ohio, added to the list of anti-dance publications with *A Discourse on Dancing*. His publication proposed to "prove the impropriety of dancing" (9). In 1849, the Reverend B.M. Palmer of the Presbyterian Church in Columbia, South Carolina, also published an essay against dancing. In a recount of a sermon that he had delivered in June of that same year, Palmer's self-descriptive title proclaimed *Social Dancing Inconsistent with a Christian Profession and Baptismal Vows*. At about the same of the publications by Rice and Palmer, one of the most profound anti-dance publications was written by Jonathan Townley Crane.

In 1849, Crane's *An Essay on Dancing* was in its ninth edition. Unlike some of the earlier publications, his discourse contained well over 100 pages. He commented on the history of dance from Biblical times through his present day. As with all the other anti-dance condemnations, Crane imparted his reasons that Christians should not dance. In Chapter IX, which he analyzed a "Practical Application of the Whole Subject," he wrote,

> There has been no design to charge any particular person with having advocated what he knows to be sin. If dancers consider the question of morality at all, it is probable that they believe, or try to believe, that their favourite amusement is a harmless one. And some may even marvel that it should be opposed (119).

Crane claimed that there had been enough evidence submitted against dancing as "an unmixed moral evil." He damned that dancing was most certainly a "dangerous amusement" that most simply participated in since they were delusional. In an obvious outward display of pious compassion, he invoked a prayer for those who danced "under the delusion that they are right." He added, "Father, forgive them, they know not what they do!" (120).

Crane's appeal to a higher authority did not end with a simple recount of a New Testament proverb. As he imparted the following reasoning, Crane bellowed:

> If you will close your eyes and stop your ears; if you will not listen to the voice of God or of reason; if you are governed by blind impulse alone, all reasonings upon the subject will be of none effect. Nothing can be done for you by any agency, save an omnipotent one. But if you are really desirous of choosing the right way; if you have resolved to be led by reason and conscience, instead of irrational inclination, be entreated not to resist, in any degree, the conclusion to which your mind is now tending, that the pleasure-dance is foolish, dangerous, and, consequently, morally wrong (Crane, 120–121).

Crane's comprehensive attempt to discount dancing also invoked the contemporary prejudice against the American Indians. In his discourse, he claimed that dancing among Native American Indians "appeal[s] directly to the brutal passions of the savage" (39).

At the time, a few other religious groups also embraced the value of dancing both as a communal activity and as a means of physical education and recreation. In Ohio, for example, in a fashion similar to the Shakers in New York (see Chapter 2), a religious sect known as the Schismatics incorporated dance as part of their religious worship. The Schismatics actually broke from the larger congregation of the New Lights—mainly over the disagreement of incorporating dancing as part of their religious ceremony. In *The History of the Chillicothe Presbytery*, historian R.C. Galbraith explained the difference. He wrote,

> the principal thing that distinguished the Schismatic worship from that of the New Lights, was their taking privilege of exhibiting, by bold faith, what others were moved to by a blind impulse. This they considered a great advancement in the spirit of the revival; and upon this principle, the voluntary exercise of dancing was introduced as the worship of God.

As a result, according to Galbraith, the Schismatics encouraged "one another to praise God in the dance" (22–23).

Some religious leaders such as Unitarian minister W. E. Channing of Boston, for example, accepted a limited form of social dancing. On one hand, he was totally opposed to dancing when it was a "social pleasure" within a formal ball that exhibited wealth and opulence. However, Channing was not opposed to communal social dancing as an "exercise and exhilaration" if it did not require any special preparations or extravagance of fashion or expenditure of vast sums of money. In fact, Channing felt that dancing among the working classes was merely "an innocent amusement" (Marks 1957, 70).

On the other hand, by 1847, progressive social reformers such as Dr. Sylvester Graham actively rebutted the anti-dance publications and praised dancing. In February 1847, he wrote in the progressive journal titled the *Regenerator*,

> The religious prejudice against dancing, is altogether illfounded; for it is entirely certain that [dancing]...is more favorable to good health, sound morality, and true religion, than perhaps known in society...dancing when properly regulated, is one of the most salutary kinds of social enjoyment, ever practiced in civic life (*The Regenerator*, February 22, 1847, 380; quoted in Cole 1942, 11).

Other publications joined in the rebuttal and proclaimed the positive benefits of social dancing. In March 12, 1847, for example, the *Boston Times* newspaper also commended dancing. The editors proclaimed,

> A good dance with a pleasant partner...is a very pleasant thing, for it gives circulation to the blood and a flow to the spirits...were people to dance a little more in this world the cares of life would not weigh so heavy on them (1).

Jane Swisshelm, editor of the mainstream newspaper *Pittsburgh Saturday Visiter* also challenged the religious pious objectors, claiming that not one single "text of scripture...either directly or indirectly condemns dancing." Swisshlem wrote:

> nothing appears better calculated to contend with the hard, money-loving spirit of our age than music and dancing. It tends to melt the hard crust which the dust of ledgers forms around the hearts of our people, and there is no place to which we should go... with more hope of success, than a social party when all were dancing to the music of two good violins and a trombone (*Pittsburgh Saturday Visiter*, September 13, 1851, 134).

At the time, Swisshelm's reply was reprinted in many other newspapers, including the *Cleveland Plain Dealer* and the *Ohio State Journal* (Cole 1942, 11–13).

One of the most interesting statements in favor of social dancing was supplied on April 11, 1857, in a page one editorial in the *New York Ledger* newspaper. The editors simply titled their article "A Physical and Innocent Recreation." They wrote:

> Dancing has at times met with strong opposition, but has gradually overcome its opponents. There are but few now who oppose it, and they belong to a class of beings who cannot appreciate the bright side of life. Even in the earliest histories of the world, we have the recorded fact, that the best and greatest of men and women were in favor of

this recreation. Socrates and Cato were among these. Pintarch, Sallust, Lucian, and many others of their period, commended dancing.

The editors added another individual who was in favor of dancing, "the Father of his Country on dancing"—George Washington (see Chapter 2).

But the summation of the debate between the anti-dance crusaders and the writers in favor of social dancing might have been easily summed up by a brief lesson in American history. In 1851, noted author Catharine Beecher provided what might have been the most poignant statement in regards to the American view on social dancing. In her well-respected *A Treatise on Domestic Economy*, she steadfastly decried:

> Dancing…flourishes most in this country when religion prospers least, and then declines again as vital piety prevails (248).

A WOMAN'S DOMESTICITY, ETIQUETTE BOOKS, FASHION, AND THE "CAVALIER"

During the time between 1840 and 1860, the role of a woman in society changed. As a result of the increased immigration, especially from Ireland, the cheap labor forced both women and children out of the workplace. In almost all cases, women were now excluded from industry and agricultural work. Therefore, the role of a woman in society was redefined as a domestic caretaker. At the time, according to architectural historian Spiro Kostof,

> The most influential designer of this domestic environment was a woman—Catharine Beecher,…[who] believed in and strongly advocated the strict social separation of American life into the male world of work and aggressive competition and a pious, tranquil, female-operated home environment, preferably suburban (32).

In 1869, Beecher cowrote *The American Woman's Home* with her sister Harriet Beecher Stowe. Catherine Beecher's other writings included *A Treatise on Domestic Economy* (first published in 1841 with 15 editions), *The Duty of American Women to their Country* (1845), and *Common Sense Applied to Religion* (1869). However, *The American Woman's Home*, in particular, was a major influence in defining a woman's role in American society.

In association with working with American architect Andrew Jackson Downing, the Beechers redefined both the basic arrangement and aesthetics of the typical American house. On the exterior the house promoted the "picturesque" in the form of landscaping and architectural decorations. Within the home, improved methods of heating and ventilation were proposed and implemented. The most significant changes within the American home, as applied by the Beechers, were in the kitchen. They actually collaborated on an extremely efficient streamlined kitchen design (that they termed a "workroom") that, according to Kostof, "became accepted as the national model by thousands of families" (33–34).

Similar to the Beecher's publication, the redefined domesticity role of a woman was constantly reinforced through many of the etiquette manuals of the day. Some of the many etiquette books included the following:

- *Madame Celnart's The Gentleman and Lady's Book* (Boston, 1833);
- *The Laws of Etiquette, by a Gentleman* (Philadelphia, 1836);
- *The Young Lady's Friend* (Boston, 1836);
- *Female Beauty; as Preserved and Improved by Regimen, Cleanliness, and Dress* (New York, 1840);
- *Etiquette for Gentlemen, By a Gentleman* (Philadelphia, 1844);
- *The Art of Good Behaviour* (New York, 1845);
- *True Politeness, a Hand-Book for Ladies, By an American Lady* (New York, 1846);
- *True Politeness, a Hand-Book for Gentlemen, By an American Gentleman* (New York, 1847);
- *Miss Leslie, The Behaviour Book* (Philadelphia, 1853);
- *The Illustrated Manners Book* (New York, 1855);
- *The Gentlemen's Book* (Boston, 1860);
- *The Habits of Good Society* (New York, 1860); and
- *Mixing in Society* (New York, 1860).

At the time, the etiquette manuals provided information including "the proper fork to use while eating, the correct mode of delivering calling cards and issuing party invitations, and the right way to give parties and balls." Many of them were termed "self-helpers" that contained exhaustive lists of "rules" for acceptable behavior in "good society."

In some cases, such as Mrs. Edna Witherspoon's *The Perfect Art of Modern Dancing* (1849), the domesticated etiquette manuals included not only information on how to properly prepare and attend a ball, they also included such domesticated duties including "canning, preserving, pastimes for children, and nursing for invalids." Emily Thornwell's *The Lady's Guide* (1857) also included tips on dressmaking as well as suggested topics for conversation at a dance party. In most of the publications, the most evident change was in fashion as it applied on the dance floor ("Nineteenth Century Social Dance," n.p.).

In 1836, for example, Mrs. John Farrar in *The Young Lady's Friend* reproached young American ladies to be wary of what they wore. She warned:

> Whatever the fashions may be, never be induced by them to violate the strictest modesty. No woman can strip her arms to her shoulders and show her back and bosom without injuring her mind and losing some of her refinement; if such would consult their brothers, they would tell them how men regard it (368).

In 1840, in *Female Beauty; as Preserved and Improved by Regimen, Cleanliness, and Dress*, Mrs. A. Walker indicated that low-cut dresses were no longer in vogue. She wrote:

> It was formerly the custom to wear ball-dresses so low in front, as almost to amount to indecent exposure of those charms which cease to be attractive when unblushingly obtruded. The fashion has changed, and the ball-room no longer presents a collection of semi-nude female figures (Walker 1840, 356).

Their roles became even more defined as fashion required dependence upon others.

Many of the formal dress styles were designed to make the woman's waist appear as small as possible. In order to do so, they required tightly laced corsets under the dresses that also required another individual to help pull them tight. As a result, some of the illustrations of the day appear almost surrealistic, but in fact, some of the corsets were so tightly laced that not only did the waist appear very tiny, it also restricted a woman's breathing. In many cases, the tightly laced corsets caused a woman to "faint," adding to the idealized notion of the so-called "weaker sex." However, in reality, it certainly was not that they were the "weaker sex" as they were so often called but simply that they could not *breathe* (DeMille, 10–11).

By the 1850s, however, the "frail look" of the previous decades was slowly replaced by wider flounced skirts. By the 1860s, dresses had elaborate trains and fuller bustles. The increased size of the dresses actually slowed down the dancing and the turning and gyrations of the Waltz and Polka for fear of the lady stepping on her own dress. In the case of the Waltz, the larger dresses limited the dance to a "pendulum-like box-step" (Aldrich 1991, 26–30).

In regard to the complete fashionable attire for the "lady," Charles Durang, for example, listed a series of suggestions for the proper attire at a dance, which was collectively termed "The Toilet." At the time, Durang was a well-known dance instructor in the Philadelphia area. He was also the son of the famous American dancer John Durang (see Chapter 2). In 1856, he published *The Fashionable Dancer's Casket; or, The ball-room instructor. A new and splendid work on dancing, etiquette, deportment, and the toilet.* (The book was later released with the simple title of *Ball-room instructor.*) Durang's manual, however, was mostly a compilation of other published works on dance instruction, mainly from England and France.

Within *The Fashionable Dancer's Casket*, Durang included the requisite gloves and fashionable ballroom attire. He wrote,

Ladies...should remember that gentlemen look more to the effect of dress,

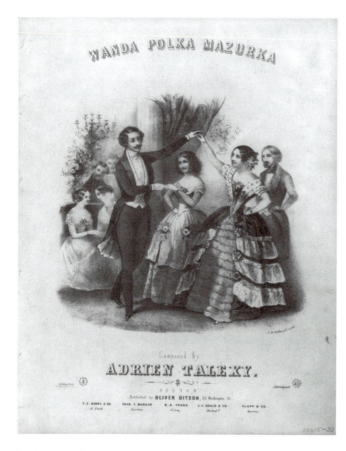

By the 1860s, dresses had elaborate trains and fuller bustles. This cover illustration from the sheet music for the "Wanda Polka Mazurka" shows a variety of dresses worn for dancing. The man is dressed in a black jacket, pantaloons, and contrasting white shirtwaist. Library of Congress, Prints and Photographs Division LC-USZ62-66777.

in setting off the figure and countenance of a lady, than its cost. Very few gentlemen have any idea of the value of ladies' dresses (1856, 13).

Because the hat was almost completely out of fashion, in almost all cases a head-dress was worn. During the 1840s, an evening hairstyle "was lopped over the ears or worn in ringlets," and the hair in back was "wound in a knot." At about the same time, women also applied a significant more amount of "paints and powders" to their face (Aldrich 1991, 26).

Durang reminded the fairer sex that, "Tall ladies should avoid wearing anything across the head, as that adds to the apparent height. He suggested that for a woman with "beautiful hair" all that was needed was a "simple flower." At the time, women also adorned their own hair with a decorative wreath that was known as a "chaplet" or a "drooping wreath." Durang suggested that for those young ladies who were "less gifted" with beautiful hair "wreaths are generally thought becoming" (Durang 1856, 13–14). In regards to the selection of the appropriate dress to wear for an evening of dancing, Durang actually included a "selection of colors" for the lady to keep in mind as she selected the appropriate color to match both "her figure and her complexion." He suggested that "very light colors" were agreeable with a "slender and sylph-like" figure. However, if the woman was not slender, the light colors "should be avoided, as they have the reputation of apparently adding to the bulk of the wearer." In regards to the "complexion," Durang suggested the following:

> Pale colors, such as pink, salmon, light blue, maize, apple green, and white are most in vogue among the blondes, as being thought to harmonize with their complexions. Brilliant colors are more generally selected by the brunettes, for a similar reason. Harmony of dress involves the idea of contrast. A pale girl looks more wan, and a brunette looks less dark, contrasted with strong colors. But as the blonde and the brunette are both beautiful in themselves, when the contour of the countenance and figure is good, a beautiful young girl, blonde or brunette, may without fear adopt either style, or both, for a change (12).

To match the color of the dresses, Durang added, "White satin shoes are worn with light colored dresses; and black or bronze with dark ones" (1856, 12–14).

Although the fashion of the day continued that the lady wear long dresses, it was customary to pay particular attention that the hemline should not completely touch the ground. It was important to have the hem slightly above the floor, so that during an evening of dancing the lady did not step on her own dress, and therefore be "apt to be torn before half the evening is over." Durang cautioned, "It is almost impossible to thread the mazes of the dance without such an accident, if the dress should sweep the floor, except with a careful and accomplished cavalier." At the time a debonair gentleman was often referred to as a "cavalier." In later years, the term was often used for a man who was disreputable (Durang 1856, 13).

For the gentleman cavalier, Durang also included a subject heading "Ball dress for Gentlemen." In a fashion similar to the previous years, Durang noted the "Gentlemen's ball attire varies but little, as they generally appear in black." He added, "Showy colors [and] gaudy patterns should be avoided...a black [dress] coat is always 'in keeping.'" The black attire consisted of pantaloons and a long length jacket. He did note that the contemporary trend was to also wear a "black neckerchief" contrasted with a white waistcoat. However, if the gentleman chose instead to wear a white neckerchief, Durang reminded them that "black or dark waistcoats prevail" as well as boots. At a formal ball as an invited guest, it was appropriate to wear patent leather boots." Shoes were no longer acceptable, except at rare formal occasions such as "State balls, where court dresses are worn." The gentleman's attire was completed by "white or lemon-colored gloves" (Durang 1856, 14, 188).

Throughout the nineteenth century, however, the only socially acceptable way for a man and a woman to embrace was during a dance. In the pre-Victorian days, although face-to-face dancing was in vogue, touching of each other's bare skin definitely was not. Therefore, in almost all cases gloves were worn by both men and women, and in some cases the bare flesh was separated by a decorative handkerchief. In fact, many etiquette manuals of the day continually stressed the need of not one, but two pairs of gloves. The reason as it applied to the gentleman was not only to prevent perspiration from soiling the lady's dress, but also to be prepared in case the gloves became soiled while pursuing the gentlemanly act of fetching a drink of punch for the lady (DeMille 1980, 10; Aldrich 1991, 35).

Durang was careful to caution the gentleman of certain inappropriate fashion items "which well bred persons are unwilling to depart, and which polished society inflexibly adheres to." In all cases, for example, the gentleman was reminded to remove his outer coat (or "frock coat") before entering the ballroom. Durang claimed "we shudder at the appearance of a man in a ball-room, wearing a frock coat." In addition, he suggested, "Jewelry may be worn in moderation, (the less the better;) an ostentatious display of chains, rings, and pins, is a personification of vulgarity." As for the accruements of the lady, Durang simply added,

> Gallantry therefore, forbids that, we should intrude in any further remarks to the belle of the ball-room; being convinced of the truth of the adage: Beauty unadorned, is adorned the most (1856, 188).

ETIQUETTE OF THE BALLROOM AND DANCE CARDS

In the case of applying manners and etiquette within the ballroom, American social custom dictated that each individual exhibit only the most impeccable behavior. In 1868, *Beadle's Dime: Ball-Room Companion and Guide to Dancing*, for example, explained the following:

> It is in the ball-room that society is on its best behavior. Everything there is regulated according to the strictest code of good-breeding, and as any departure from this code becomes a grave offense, it is indispensable that the etiquette of the ball-room should be thoroughly mastered (5).

All the other contemporary etiquette manuals and dance instruction books agreed, including Charles Durang's *The Ball-room Instructor*, Edward Ferrero's *The Art of*

Dancing, Thomas Hillgrove's *A Complete Practical Guide to the Art of Dancing*, and Hillgrove's *The Ball-Room Guide, a Handy Manual*, to name but a very few. (At the time many of the dance instruction manuals hyphenated the spelling as "ball-room.") In addition, just about all included directions for and explanations of contemporary dances, information regarding the rules of etiquette, suggestions for planning a private dance party or a formal ball, fashion hints, music suggestions, information about flooring, and instructions for other special arrangements such as refreshments, decorations for the ballroom, and the proper format for invitations.

Unlike the formality of the eighteenth century Assembly balls coordinated by a Master of Ceremonies, the nineteenth century formal balls and assemblies usually dispensed with a Master of Ceremonies. In some cases a floor manager was employed, but usually with the sole purpose of maintaining order in regards to maintaining decent public behavior. *The Ball-Room Guide, a Handy Manual*, for example, noted:

> Formerly, at balls, a Master of Ceremonies was considered indispensable; but this custom is going out, and his duties are performed by the [floor] "Managers," who are often distinguished by a tiny rosette, or arrangement of a single flower and a ribbon in the button-hole. These superintend the dances (13).

The floor manager also arranged for the musicians. A large party in excess of 100 guests usually employed four musicians—typically a piano, cornet, violin, and violoncello. In some smaller dance parties, the cornet was not employed, and a violin and piano was often enough. However, no matter how small the dance party, a piano was the recommended instrument. (In rural areas the violin or "fiddle" was the essential instrument.)

Written invitations to a ball were de rigeur, and social decorum suggested that they be sent out at least ten days before the scheduled event. However, in no case whatsoever was an invitation to be verbal. If the dance was in a private home, the invitation was sent out in the name of the "lady of the house." Normally the number of invitations was limited in order not to overcrowd the ballroom. But it was always suggested that a few extra invitations be sent out since it was unlikely that all would accept. Also, the list of invitations was careful to plan for an equal number of gentlemen and ladies, with a deference towards inviting more men (*Ball-Room Guide*, 5–7).

In regards to the invitation, *Beadle's Dime: Ball-Room Companion and Guide to Dancing* suggested a simple handwritten or preprinted invitation as follows:

> Monday, Jan. 1st.
> Mrs.—requests the pleasure of Mr.—'s company at an Evening Party,
> on Thursday, Jan. 11th.
> "An answer will oblige."

Upon receipt, an immediate reply was required "within a day or two." A simple written reply was suggested as follows:

> Wednesday, Jan. 3d.
> Mr.— has much pleasure in accepting Mrs.—'s polite invitation
> for Thursday evening, the 11th inst.

There were also stringent behavioral rules on attending a ball. Charles Durang in *The Ball-room Instructor* (1856), for example, advised the following:

> Go to a private ball at an hour suited to the habits of those that invite you. It is extremely inconvenient, however, to be too early, as you very much disconcert your friends. To a public ball, ten o'clock is quite early enough (188–189).

Etiquette also dictated that about one week after the dance of a private party an acknowledgment in the form of either a written "thank you" or a calling card delivered to the house was required (*Beadle's*, 15).

All agreed that the ballroom be a well-lit and well-ventilated area. It was also suggested that light color curtains replace any dark curtains. On the other hand, *The Habits of Good Society* went so far as to suggest the "best color" as a "very pale yellow." A careful inspection of the ballroom floor was also advised so any irregularities or rough surfaces could be eliminated. Most of the manuals suggested that prior to the event the floor receive a good scrubbing. *The Ball-Room Guide*, for example, suggested "scrub the boards with very hot water, and then pour a quantity of milk over them before they are perfectly dry." The desired effect was a highly polished clean ballroom floor (Aldrich 1991, 116; *The Ball-Room Guide*, 17–18).

In the case of all formal balls, private parties, and assemblies, or for that matter any "socially accepted" dance, it was common to preselect the order of dances and the accompanying music. The order of dances certainly could be adjusted as the host saw fit; however, all social decorum booklets dictated that the specific dances should be arranged beforehand. Most of the contemporary etiquette manuals and dance instruction books suggested about 18 to 21 dances with at least one "Intermission" break for either supper or refreshments at about the halfway point. (Some of the more elaborate dances scheduled an intermission after every four or five dances).

A "Social Assembly" given by Lorenzo Papanti on Thursday evening, December 5, 1850, for example, listed the following program and order of dances:

> INTRODUCTORY MARCH.
> 1. Sicilian Circle, 2. Cotillon, 3. Waltz Quadrille, 4. Cotillon,
> WALTZ and POLKA
> 5. Cotillon, 6. Merry Dance, 7. Cotillon, 8. Cotillon,
> WALTZ and SCHOTTISCHE
> 9. Cotillon, 10. Ladies' Triumph, 11. Waltz Quadrille, 12. Cotillon,
> WALTZ and POLKA,
> 13. Cotillon, 14. Hull's Victory [a Country-dance], 15. Cotillon, 16. Cotillon.

Music was provided by the Wiggins and Lyon's Quadrille Band, and three floor managers were employed and noted as E.W. Nevers, D.W. Gilbert, and Fred A. Howard. Around the 1860s, a typical suggested list of dances included a sampling as follows:

This photo of a ballroom within a statehouse in Charleston, South Carolina, restored to its original pre-1865 condition, is a good example of a highly polished wood floor and neoclassical interior that was typical of the time in a wealthy home.   Photo courtesy of Thelma Lynn Olsen.

1. Quadrille, 2. Polka Redowa, 3. Lanciers, 4. Waltz, Galop, or Polka, 5. Quadrille, 6. Redowa, 7. Mazurka, 8. Polka Redowa, 9. Quadrille,
10. Schottische, 11. Lanciers.
INTERMISSION.
12. Quadrille, 13. Varsovienne, 14. Polka Redowa or Galop, 15. Polka, 16. Lanciers,
17. Waltz, 18. Quadrille, 19. Polka, 20. Lanciers, 21. Quadrille.
HOME.

The music and dances were not continuous, as proper time was needed both before the dance to properly escort the lady to the dance floor and upon completion to return a lady to her seat or offer refreshments. Sometimes the break between dances lasted as long as ten minutes.

In all cases, the order of dances was preprinted on a program. In regards to the program and specific order of dances, *Beadle's Dime: Ball-Room Companion and Guide to Dancing* (1868), for example, suggested the following:

It is convenient and inexpensive to have them printed on their cards, the numbered dances on one side, and numbered lines for engagements on the other. A better plan is to have a card of two pages, with dances on one page, and spaces for engagements on the opposite one (10–11).

The preprinted program was known as a "Dance Card."

Some of the more elaborate Dance Cards provided a small booklet that contained a number of pages. The front cover was of a heavier stock, sometimes of fabric, and was embossed with a decorative element such as a rose. The first page listed items such as the name of the event, time, and place of occurrence. The following pages contained the name of the orchestra and a list of the music and names of the songs that accompanied each scheduled dance of the evening. The center section was reserved for the list of the dances and a blank line for the lady to write down the name of her gentleman dance partner. The pages following the list of dances usually listed the names of the individual or the members of the sponsoring dance committee. In lieu of an embossed cover (which was also costly) the front cover contained the name of the event and the back cover the name of the sponsors. In turn, many young ladies saved the dance cards both as a memento and as an indication of their social standing. In some cases other items were employed to serve as a program and dance card. One example was a paper fan on which the order of dances was printed. The fan, given only to the ladies, was practical in an age before air-conditioning but did not prove practical for writing down an engagement for a dance (*Beadle's*, 10–11).

In many cases, a small plain card about 3.5 inches by 5 inches or a smaller version at 2.5 inches by 4 inches with a single page insert was sufficient as a Dance Card. One of the Dance Cards was suggested to be given to each guest as he or she arrived, but in most cases it was given only to the lady. Therefore, the Dance Card was a convenient way for the lady to keep track of whom she had promised dances to during the course of the evening. In most cases the lady reserved both the first and the last dances for the gentleman who had brought her to the dance. In order for the lady to write down an engagement for a specific dance, a pencil was also provided. Various methods were employed to attach a pencil to the dance card, such as attaching a ribbon to the card, threading a cord through a small pinhole in the pencil, or even providing a paper sleeve within the card itself. However, the attachment of a pencil proved unreliable. *The Ball-Room Guide, a Handy Manual*, offered the following suggestion:

> No reliable method has yet been discovered of including the pencil to cleave the cord, so that it is safer for gentlemen to be provided with a pencil of their own (20–21).

In other cases, the gentleman often carried his own pencil in a small case kept in an inner jacket pocket. Some of the cases were elaborate and sometimes made of silver or gold (Beadle's, 20–21).

Although the contemporary dance instruction books listed many different types of dances, most of them were reserved for the dancing schools. In many cases, the books were reprints that in some cases were 10 or 20 years old, and many of the dances might have also been obsolete. Therefore, dance cards of the actual events served as a good case study of the popular dances of a particular time period. However, that particular case study can be applied only to the fashionable dances.

Although similar dances were often done in rural areas, most of the dance halls in cities and towns, especially in rural areas, did not conform to the strict formality of a specific dance card and ballroom etiquette associated with reserving a dance "in writing." Dance Cards remained in fashion all through the nineteenth century and lasted until the 1920s. At that time, with the introduction of dances such as the Charleston and Lindy Hop, the ballrooms were less formal; the dance cards were associated only with formal balls and cotillions.

The Dance Card was only one part of a series of rules of manners and etiquette for the ballroom. The rules also included how to escort the lady to the cloak room, how a gentleman should deposit his own cloak and hat, how the lady waited for her gentleman escort, how to enter the ballroom, and more—all these rules even before they actually began to dance. In *A Complete Practical Guide to the Art of Dancing* (1863), for example, Thomas Hillgrove clearly defined the manner that was required of a gentleman immediately upon entering the building. Hillgrove suggested the following:

Most Dance Cards contained the name of the event on the front cover, such as the one in the lower left from a "Social Assembly" given by Lorenzo Papanti on Thursday evening, December 5, 1850, or as the one in the upper left from the Epsilon Sigma Fraternity for Friday, March 1, 1912. In the upper right is a listing of the "Order of Dances" with a corresponding blank line for the lady to write in the name of a gentleman partner. Some of the more elaborate Dance Cards, such as the one in the lower right from about 1880, were small booklets that contained a number of pages with the front cover of a heavier stock. A pencil attached by a cord was provided for the lady to write down an engagement for a specific dance.   Photo courtesy of Thelma Lynn Olsen.

> When a gentleman accompanies a lady to a ball he will at once proceed with her to the door of the ladies' dressing-room, there leaving her; and then repair to the gentlemen's dressing-room. In the meantime, the lady, after adjusting her toilet, will retire to the ladies' sitting-room, or wait at the door of the dressing-room...After the gentleman has divested himself of hat...and after arranging his toilet, he will proceed to the ladies' sitting-room, or wait at the entrance to the ladies' dressing-room for the lady whom he accompanies, and with her enter the ballroom (Hillgrove 1863, 26).

Prior to entering the ballroom, the gentleman was required to be fashionably attired and most importantly wearing gloves (see earlier in this chapter). In fact, both the gentleman and the lady were required to be properly "gloved" before entering the ballroom.

In some cases, upon entering the ballroom, the guests were announced by name. This practice was usually reserved for wealthy parties or for a larger social gathering of political importance. A servant located by the front entry typically announced the names of the guests preceded by "Mr. and Mrs." for a married couple, "Mr." for an individual gentleman, and "the Misses" for an unmarried young lady and her chaperone. Once inside the ballroom, the guests proceeded directly to the host of the party and politely thanked him or "the lady of the house" for the invitation. After the exchange, they were obliged to acknowledge any friends or acquaintances. After the proper acknowledgments, they were allowed to dance. In the case when a gentleman escorted a lady to a ball, it was suggested that he offer her the first dance of the evening. After the first dance, they were obliged to dance with others. The same social decorum applied to any invited individuals, including a gentleman who arrived alone (Hillgrove 1863, 21).

It was acceptable for a gentleman to go to a ball alone, but it was not acceptable for a lady. A lady was required to be escorted either by her husband or, if unmarried or widowed, by a chaperone, who was usually her mother. Although the gentleman was allowed to enter the ballroom by himself, he was not allowed to indiscriminately ask a lady to dance. Social conditions still strictly defined how a person, especially a lady, danced with another person in public. Therefore, in order for a gentleman to dance with a lady, certain rules of behavior were prescribed.

Immediately upon entering the ballroom, the gentleman was required to introduce himself to either the host or floor manager, who in turn would introduce the gentleman to a lady for a particular dance. In a similar fashion, a chaperoned lady would also be introduced, but by the chaperone to the floor manager. In all cases, the gentleman was first introduced to the lady for a dance, and not the lady first introduced to the gentleman. In addition, it fell upon either the host or the floor manager to know beforehand that any introduction was agreeable to both parties. The formalities of introduction were strictly observed at a public formal ball. Although at a small private ball within someone's home, the mere fact that one was invited usually precluded the formal introductions. However, whether at a private ball or a public formal dance, the rules of etiquette still applied (Hillgrove 1863, 19).

Once introduced, the gentleman would politely ask the lady to dance. A simple suggestion included, "May I have the pleasure of the next dance?" or "Will you dance this Waltz with me?" In response, the lady was obliged "if she be not already engaged," to dance with the gentleman. To accept the dance a simple reply of "Thank you" was sufficient. However, if she refused to dance, "she must beg to be excused, as politely as possible"; the simple accepted reply was, "Thank you, I am engaged." If, in fact, she was not scheduled to dance, due to a written engagement on her dance card, or was asked by another gentleman more to her liking, it was completely unacceptable to dance that same dance that she was previously asked by the first gentleman. *Beadle's*, for example, suggested "it is in better taste for her not to dance at all in that set" (13). But, in all cases, a refusal was viewed as "a breach of the law of good manners." In addition, it was not good manners for a gentleman to ask the same lady to dance more than two dances in a single evening (Durang 1856, 16–17).

This illustration, "The Last Ball of the Season," appeared in *Harper's Weekly* on February 20, 1858. It is a good example of a formal dance in a "well-lit" ballroom. In the foreground, the floor manager, denoted by "a single flower" on his lapel, is arranging an introduction for the lady to dance with a gentleman partner.   Library of Congress, Prints and Photographs Division LC-USZC2-6400.

In contrast, a lady was "not entitled" to the same privilege of either asking a man to dance or, for that matter, asking the floor manager for an introduction to a gentleman. (In some cases, the decorum was broken; however, it was considered quite scandalous for a lady to ask a man to dance.) In the case of ladies sitting idly while waiting to dance, the responsibility rested entirely upon the host, the floor manager, or the properly introduced gentleman to make sure "that ladies shall not sit long waiting for partners." A severe breach of good manners was for any gentleman or group of gentlemen to "stand idling whilst ladies are waiting to be asked [to dance]" (Hillgrove 1863, 31–32).

Outside the ballroom, social conditions certainly precluded any interaction between a married individual and an unmarried person of the opposite gender, but not within the ballroom. Most, if not all the etiquette dictums of the day agreed that it was noticeably impolite for one couple to dance only with each other. In fact, most etiquette manuals suggested that no husband and wife dance together at all, but rather intermingle and dance with the other guests. Charles Durang, for example, wrote:

> Married couples ought not to dance with each other: there is, perhaps, no positive impropriety in it, and deviations from the rule may sometimes be either expedient or unavoidable; but it is more generous, and therefore more polite, for wedded gentlemen to dance with other ladies (21).

The practice in regards to married couples was usually strictly applied. However, in the case of a gentleman, the rules were sometimes less stringent.

A gentleman either married or unmarried was allowed to ask an unmarried lady to dance, and she was obliged to dance. However, that was not the case in regards to a married lady. Although a gentleman may have been properly introduced into the ballroom setting, he was still obliged to ask the husband for the honor of dancing with a married woman. Thomas Hillgrove warned,

> It is not considered proper to ask a married lady to dance, when her husband is present, without having previously ascertained whether it be agreeable to him (36).

In similar fashion, personal preference or favoritism towards a dance partner was frowned upon. In the same manner any couple engaged to be married or even courting was required to maintain the dance floor etiquette as prescribed to married couples. Durang added,

> Perfect politeness conceals preferences, and makes itself generally agreeable. Favoritism is only suitable for private life. Lovers are apt to forget this in the ball-room, and make themselves disagreeable, and sometimes particularly offensive, by their exclusive devotion to one another. The ball-room is not the proper place for making love, but for general and agreeable association (17–18).

However, a lady was expected to maintain the utmost strict decorum, lest she lose her social standing. Charles Durang, for example, warned, "Ladies especially ought to remember this, as no lady, however beautiful, accomplished, dignified, or opulent, can afford to lose the good opinion of the society in which she moves" (18).

Introduction for a dance and actually dancing were not the only functions pre-described by the manners and etiquette of the ballroom. In fact, the list of rules of manners and etiquette seemed endless. Some of the dance instructors recognized the exhaustive list. Edward Ferrero, for example, in *The Art of Dancing* offered the following advice:

> We are perfectly conscious of our inability to offer any fixed and definite rules for the guidance of dancers, in matters of etiquette, for there are so many and such a variety of circumstances in which another course of action would be required...[therefore] We can only hint at certain violations of etiquette which are practiced (91).

Others, including *The Ball-Room Guide, a Handy Manual,* Durang's *The Ball-room Instructor,* Hillgrove's *A Complete Practical Guide to the Art of Dancing, Beadle's Dime: Ball-Room Companion and Guide to Dancing,* and Ferrero's *The Art of Dancing,* to name but a very few, all contained very similar long lists of rules and acceptable behavior in the ballroom. A sampling of the long list of etiquette rules aimed specifically at the gentleman included the following:

- Never become involved in a dispute, if it be possible to avoid it.
- If a gentleman should ask a lady to dance, and receive a polite refusal, let him not exhibit any symptoms of dissatisfaction if he see her dancing with another; but he is certainly justified in never afterwards repeating the request.
- Give your opinions, but do not argue them.
- Never lose control of your temper.
- Gentlemen should endeavor to entertain the ladies who dance with them with a little conversation, more novel than the weather and the heat of the room.
- Be careful not to speak upon subjects of which you are ill-informed.
- Do not speak in a loud tone, indulge in boisterous laughter, nor tell long stories.
- Confess ignorance rather than pretend to know what you do not.
- Never repeat in one company any scandal or personal history you have heard in another.
- If you have in any manner given offence, do not hesitate to apologize. A gentleman on accidentally touching you, or passing before you, will ask pardon for the inconvenience he causes.
- Never forget that ladies are to be first cared for, to have the best seats, the places of distinction, and are entitled in all cases to your courteous protection.
- Do not cross a room in an anxious manner, or force your way to a lady to merely receive a bow, as by so doing you attract the attention of the company to her.
- The gentleman who dances with a lady in the last dance before supper, conducts that lady to the supper-room, attends on her while there, and escorts her back.
- If a gentleman be introduced to a lady at a ball, he is not thereby entitled to claim her acquaintanceship afterwards. All intimacy should end with the dance.
- No gentleman should offer his services to conduct a lady home, without being acquainted with her, or requested so to do by the host or hostess.

The list of rules specifically for the lady was just as long. A sampling of the etiquette requirements directly applied for the lady included the following:

- On no account should a lady parade a ball-room alone, nor should she enter it unaccompanied.
- On entering a ball-room, all thought of self should be dismissed. The petty ambition of endeavoring to create a sensation by either dress, loud talking, or unusual behavior, is to be condemned.
- It is not well to dance every dance, as the exercise is unpleasantly heating and fatiguing.
- While dancing, a lady should consider herself engaged to her partner, and therefore not at liberty to hold a flirtation with another gentleman.
- A lady should recollect that it is the gentleman's part to lead her, and hers to follow his directions.
- At a private ball or party, a lady should not manifest preference for a particular partner, but should dance with any gentleman who properly asks her company.

- At a public ball, if a gentleman, without a proper introduction, asks a lady to dance, she should positively refuse.
- When a gentleman, having been properly introduced, requests the honor of dancing with a lady, she should not refuse without explaining her reason for so doing.
- Ladies should take special care not to accept two partners for the same dance.
- A lady should not accept refreshments from a stranger who dances with her.

The exhaustive lists of rules might appear tedious and, in some cases, self-explanatory, but all agreed that these "rules" were essential for the ballroom. Edward Ferrero, for example, offered that the basic rules were "among the most important rudiments of the Terpsichorean art. A proper knowledge of them is indispensable to both sexes." Ferrero even recommended that the long list of manners and etiquette could even be applied in "every-day life, and among all classes of the community." In many cases, the manners and rules of etiquette often included an "old fashioned" Bow and Curtsy (Durang 1856, 17–33; Ferrero 1859, 92–118; Hillgrove 1863, 18–25; and *Beadle's*, 5–15).

LEARNING TO DANCE WITHOUT A DANCE MASTER

In 1847, Henri Cellarius in *The Drawing-room Dances* noted an apparent change in the manner of dancing and type of dances in the ballrooms. He wrote:

> If we compare the appearance of a ball of the present day with the assemblies of only five or six years ago, we can not fail to be struck by the favourable [sic] change, which has been introduced into the habits, and, if I may venture so to say, into the manners of the dancers (iv).

The "favourable change" was the introduction of round dances such as the Waltz *à* Deux Temps, Polka, Mazurka, and Redowa (see earlier in this chapter). These dances provided an impetus on the ballroom dance floor that Cellarius called a "revival of the modern dance" (6–8).

On the other hand, the popularity of the new dances might be attributed to the fact that they were quite easy to learn. As a result, many disregarded the importance of attending a "dancing school" and learned the social dances either by watching or by reading a dance instruction manual. (Not to be discounted was also the fact that the dances were also popular among the working and middle classes, who could not necessarily afford dance classes in either time or money.) Therefore, as a result of dances such as the Waltz and Polka, the importance of a Dance Master decreased. In fact, at the time the profession of Dance Master changed to that of a dance teacher or a dance instructor. (However, the term "dance master" was often used until the end of the nineteenth century.) The major difference was that in the past the Dance Master taught not just dance steps, but mainly grace, manners, and deployment of the body. Dance teachers, on the other hand, taught the basic steps to the dances to the simple Waltz and Polka (Marks 1957, 76).

Henri Cellarius agreed that social dancing could not be learned by merely reading the step descriptions within a book. He favored lessons by a qualified dance teacher combined with the pupil observing the actual dance. He explained,

"Dancing, as may be imagined, can scarcely be explained by word; it is made much less to be apprehended by the mental eye than by those of the body" (6). But, on the other hand, Cellarius disagreed with the formalities of the strenuous attention to the nondancing details of bows, curtsies, body posture, walking, and sitting. His basic understanding was that any individual who could capably dance the Waltz or Polka also obviously knew "how to walk." In that regard, Cellarius added, "The [dance] master has little or nothing to do with these details" (14–15).

In regards to the difference between a Dance Master and a dance teacher, Allen Dodworth in his famous dance treatise *Dancing and its Relations to Education and Social Life* (1885) offered the following explanation:

> These [dances] were so easily learned that the education in motion was deemed unnecessary; simply to make the motion required was quite sufficient, manner becoming entirely secondary…they were, therefore, simply dance teachers, not teachers of motion and manner, which is the definition of dancing-master as the term was formerly understood (15–16).

Many of the older Dance Masters, however, complained that the whirling and quickness around the floor was without the necessary grace, refinement, and manners that was such an integral part of the total teaching method that was employed in the past. In turn, they often criticized the newer instructors since they taught only the steps of the dance.

As can be expected, the Dance Masters who made their livelihood by teaching promoted the necessity of proper dance instruction. In 1859, for example, Edward Ferrero in *The Art of Dancing* asserted, "Dancing…can never be acquired by means of books alone, although they are of great utility in refreshing the memories of those who have obtained some knowledge of the art from a professor" (115). In a similar argument, Thomas Hillgrove agreed with Ferrero. In *A Complete Practical Guide to the Art of Dancing* (1863), he said, "Books alone are not sufficient to teach our art. Personal instruction and discipline are indispensable." Hillgrove added that learning to dance with others present "has the advantage over most other exercises, in being social" (16).

THE GRAND BALL IN NEW YORK, "ROWDY" DANCE HALLS, AND "49ER DANCE HALLS"

The "social dance" as described by Hillgrove was basically that of an elegant formal ball. At the time, social dancing was basically divided between private balls and public balls. In the case of the elegance of private balls, for example, Edward Ferrero exclaimed:

> It may be prejudice, perhaps, but we know of no more pleasing spectacle than a well appointed ball; we, of course, allude to select private assemblies, where refinement and courtesy prevail; where elegant dressing and fine taste are apparent, and where grace and easy carriage are the predominating characteristics (74).

For the most part the same idea was applied to public balls where admission by a ticket was usually required. In lieu of an invitation to a private ball, admission to a public ball was regulated by a prepurchased ticket. In addition, the behavior at a public ball was expected to follow the same manners and etiquette as prescribed for the private balls and assemblies. In that same manner, the public balls also employed a floor manager. The public balls were given in honor of many occasions, including a charity ball.

On February 19, 1831, the *New York Mirror* newspaper reported that many of the formal assemblies and balls were for charitable functions such as raising money for the local fire departments. By that time, for example, in New York City "the annual Firemen's Ball had become a regular institution" and drew crowds in excess of 2,700 people. In addition, throughout New York City dances were held for occasions such as St. Valentine's Day, as was a Bachelor's Ball, a Patriarch's Ball, and just about any other occasion. In January 1841, a group of unmarried ladies and gentlemen even revived the New York City Assembly ball. At the time, in New York City it was reported that there were dance balls "five nights a week, in perhaps twenty public ball-rooms, beside a multitude of private parties, where dancing is the chief amusement." One contemporary observer, Thomas L. Nichols, in *Forty Years of American Life* noted, "If there is anything New Yorkers are more given to than making money it is dancing" (Nichols 1864, 279–280; Cole 1942, 27).

In 1860 in New York City, one of the "grandest" of all the balls honored the Prince of Wales. The Grand Ball, held on October 12, 1860, at the New York Academy of Music, was a lavish affair hosted and attended by the wealthy socialites of the city. During that year, on a celebrated tour of the United States, Edward VII, the Prince of Wales (and future King of England) was touted by a series of balls honoring his presence. The Prince was known to have a fond affection for dancing and even for affecting fashion in the ballroom. On most occasions, the Prince did not wear gloves in the ballroom, much to the disdain of the American teachers of manner and etiquette (Cole 1942, 27–33).

At the same time as the elegant fashionable balls, social dancing also crossed over as a commercial proposition accessible to the working class. The "Negro dancing cellars" still offered the combination of alcohol, dancing, and, in many cases, prostitution (see Chapter 2). However, in many of the ethnic immigrant neighborhoods, business owners combined the local ale house or saloon with an opportunity for dancing as a viable commercial proposition. In many commercial dance halls the women were admitted free of charge and the men were charged an admission fee, usually around 25 cents. Most, if not all, of the women were young, unmarried, and poor. Some, such as those working in the growing seamstress trade in New York, sat for long hours at work. In turn, they sought some relief and activity at the neighborhood dance hall and saloon. However, at the time a woman of any class unescorted in public was still viewed as unacceptable. Also, although the young women did not venture out alone, the working class dance halls received an unsavory public reputation. One example was John Allen's Dance House at 304 Water Street on the lower east side in New York City. One widely distributed illustration of the day, for example, captioned "The Wickedest Man

The Grand Ball, held on October 12, 1860, at the New York Academy of Music, was a lavish affair hosted and attended by the wealthy socialites of the city. During that year, on a celebrated tour of the United States, Edward VII, the Prince of Wales (and future King of England) was touted by a series of balls honoring his presence. Grand Ball, New York Academy of Music.   The Granger Collection, New York, ID: 0018259.

in New York," depicted John Allen's Dance House as a rambunctious dance hall devoid of the socially acceptable etiquette and manners of the day (Burrows and Wallace 1998, 816).

A similar image was portrayed in other cities within America. During the 1830s and 1840s, for example, Chicago was basically "a male frontier town." In Chicago, and for that matter all frontier towns in general, the entertainment offerings were severely limited. In almost all cases the saloon served as the central meeting place that also offered music, dancing, and sometimes a stage show or concert. In addition, in places such as Chicago, they were often heavily populated by males, and women were scarce. Therefore, according to historian Lewis Erenberg, the absence of women, "diminished controls of class, family, and culture, leading to a rowdy, male-dominated" environment. As a result, the saloons were often loud, boisterous, and unruly, and therefore "had a poor reputation" (Erenberg, "Entertaining Chicagoans," n.d.).

At the time, the American frontier towns were somewhat limited in number. However, beginning in 1849, with the discovery of gold in California, hundreds of thousands of speculators and prospectors traveled to the west coast of the American continent. The large majority of the speculators and prospectors were

In an illustration captioned "The Wickedest Man in New York," John Allen's Dance House is portrayed as a rambunctious dance hall devoid of the socially acceptable etiquette and manners of the day, c. 1850 to 1870.   Library of Congress, Prints and Photographs Division LC-USZ62-2162.

poorer working class Americans and immigrants. Those who could scrape together enough money, arrived by a sailing ship to San Francisco. Many others chose the long overland arduous trip by wagon across the continent. In the process, hundreds of frontier towns were established along the routes. Within those towns social dance traditions were also established. According to dance historian Richard Nevell,

> the new settlers brought music and dances with them to these new frontier outposts and mining communities. Generally the miners were not of the genteel type, and dancing in the West during its early days was vigorous and earthy (50).

Most of the dances in the west included the Cotillion, Quadrille, and Jigs.

The Quadrille was a particular favorite since it was easy, did not always require a female partner, and was helped along by a "caller" who called out each figure of the dance. It was at that time that the method of continually calling out the figures for the Quadrille became standard. (However, the idea of "calling" was frowned on in Europe and never quite caught on in the eastern American cities.) In the West the job of "calling" a set of dance figures usually fell to a solitary fiddle player. Unlike the delicate instruments of the ballroom, such as a piano or cello, the fiddle was an easy instrument to carry around. In addition, as historian Richard Nevell added, "These western callers were not in the least bit interested in the deportment and gentility of the city dances from back east" (50).

Most of the frontier dances were often described as "vigorous, rowdy affairs"; however, the tremendous number of people entering the western regions also enticed wealthy entrepreneurs to migrate into cites such as Denver, Colorado, and San Francisco, California. By 1861, for example, Denver was a combination of the "rough and rowdy" settlers with an influx of entrepreneurs from the eastern cities. The easterners sought the "genteel manners" and refined dances of the ballrooms back east, and the speculators and prospectors sought the simple Quadrilles. In a situation similar to that of New Orleans at the turn of the nineteenth century (see Chapter 2), the city of Denver offered a compromise. The social dance event sponsored by the "Masonic fraternity" of Denver was held at the Broadwell House. In an advertisement in the *Rocky Mountain News*, they announced the following:

> A capital arrangement has been adopted for the dancing exercises at the Broadwell, on Friday night. The lower room will be set apart for the quadrilles, and the upper room for Fancy dances. Both rooms are to be decorated in a magnificent style surpassing anything of the kind ever before seen in this region.

By all accounts, the dance was held without any incidents or complaints. The following day the newspaper reported that the social dance event at Broadwell House "was by far the most brilliant affair ever witnessed in Denver. The attendance of the ladies was very numerous, and the display of elegant and costly apparel equal to any seen on any similar occasion in the leading cites of the Western states" (Nevell 1977, 50–51).

For those in the "gold rich" area of southern California, San Francisco was the most notorious. For entertainment, many of them congregated near the docks and piers of the arriving sailing ships, an area known as the Barbary Coast. It is not sure how the Barbary Coast got its name, but one writer simply described it as "three blocks of solid dance halls, there for the delight of the sailors of the world." The dance halls were very similar to those of the frontier towns. They were loud and boisterous with music, dancing, drinking, and "whatever," attracting "sailors, gold prospectors, and wayfarers" (Cressey 1969, 179).

In San Francisco and around the area were also a series of dance halls known as "49er Dance Halls." The dance halls were named after the "49er Camps" that developed in response to the California Gold Rush of 1849. (Since gold was discovered during that year, the nickname "49ers" was applied to all those speculators and prospectors who hurriedly went there in search of fortune.) Sociologist Edgar Thompson described a '49er Dance Hall as follows:

> It occupied a separate tent, to which admission was charged. On the inside was a little raised platform on which the local boys were invited to dance with the girls attached to the show. At the end of the platform stood a little bar which dispensed everything the law allowed—but at double prices.

In later years traveling carnivals and shows often had a "49er Camp" that offered dancing. At the close of each dance the manager usually enticed the crowd to buy a drink by announcing, "Up to the bar, boys! Just as in the days of '49" (quoted in Cressey 1969, 25).

"DANCING AS A MEANS OF PHYSICAL EDUCATION" AND DANCING AT WEST POINT

Prior to the 1820s, America did not promote much in the way of basic public education for its inhabitants. However, at about that same time Europe introduced new developments in the principles of basic public education combined with the idea of physical education. Shortly thereafter, Americans followed the European idea of both public education and physical education. Most sources claim the "birthplace of physical education in America" as the Round Hill School in Northampton, Massachusetts. It was opened in 1823 and based the ideas of physical education on the European model (Marks 1957, 79).

During that same time, the University of Virginia opened and promoted the idea of state supported secular higher education. In a curriculum designed by former president and statesman Thomas Jefferson, a student was freely able to pick his or her own major area of study. As part of all program areas of study was a promotion of physical fitness. The most common method of promoting physical education and fitness was through the introduction of dancing. In 1830, the *Philadelphia Journal of Health* proclaimed:

> We have said that dancing in moderation is a salutary exercise, but it is only when every limb and muscle is allowed to participate naturally and without constraint that the motion is thus communicated to the body (*Journal of Health:* Philadelphia, 1830 Vol. I, 133).

In 1850, John L. Blake in *The Farmer's Every-Day Book* stressed the importance of the inclusion of dancing in the curriculum "in every country school" under the direction of the schoolmaster. Blake recommended:

> let half an hour be spent in this fascinating exercise [of dancing], as a reward of good conduct as scholars…Besides, it will refine the manners and the temper of the minds beyond calculation. Instead of diminishing progress in study, it will increase it…It is simply to give them a healthful exercise; for boys instead of playing ball—and girls, instead of romping (165).

However, dancing was not immediately accepted within higher education. At the time, most of the colleges and universities in America still formulated their curriculum based on training for the ministry. In 1834, for example, one Harvard student, James Henley Thornwell, by way of South Carolina was a self-proclaimed "avowed enemy to the sport [of dancing]." He claimed, "It [was] an insult to God, who has made us beings of an intellectual dignity; it is an abuse of our own persons, and a prostration of our own powers" (Cole, "The Puritan and Fair Terpsichore," 1942, 23).

In 1851, in *Dancing, as a Means of Physical Education*, Mrs. Alfred Webster broached "the most delicate portion" of her subject. Webster asked, "Why is Dancing so deprecated on religious grounds?" Webster sought to disavow the religious objections. She suggested, "If we inquire what Dancing is, we shall find that it is merely the natural movements of the body subjected to rhythmical restraint, as sound becomes music under similar control" (3). In support of her defense of the innocent amusement and valuable means as physical education, Webster cited the writings of the Reverend James Fordyce. In his *Sermons to Young Women* (1794), Fordyce had defended the practice of social dancing. He said,

> I freely confess that I am one of those who look on with a very sensible satisfaction, well pleased to see a company of young persons joyful with innocence and happy with each other. It seems to me there can be no impropriety in it...What is Dancing, in the most rigid sense, but the harmony of motion rendered more palpable.

Webster added that dancing also served as "forming a social amusement when friends and neighbours meet together" (Webster 1851, 53–54).

Webster explained that dancing and education maintained an inseparable relationship, and in that same sense, she added that dancing as a means of physical education was especially necessary for females. Webster argued that many "daughters" were compelled in an education involving a significant amount of time in sedentary studies including writing, reading, drawing, and "sitting at the piano." Therefore, as a counterbalance to the education of the mind, but inactivity of the body, Webster provided the simple answer of engaging females in physical education of dancing. Webster was only one of a growing trend of writers promoting the benefits of social dancing as an acceptable means of physical education (Webster 1851, 6–9).

In 1836, in *Exercises for Ladies*, Donald Walker agreed with Mrs. Alfred Webster's suggestion to offset the sedentary education of females. Walker claimed, "Dancing is an excellent exercise for females, because it powerfully counterbalances the injurious effects of their sedentary occupations." However, in obvious deference to the supposed frailty of females (an idea that was prevalent in American society), Walker cautioned against the lively energetic popular dances such as the Waltz and the Polka. Walker cautioned,

> There are, however, several dances that should be abandoned by very delicate women, on account of their causing too violent emotions, or an agitation which produces vertigo and nervous symptoms. Dances which require these violent shocks and the forcible employment of the muscles, are obviously unsuitable to females, in whose movements we look for elegance instead of strength.

On the other hand, that same advice to avoid certain rigorous dances was not considered for men (Walker 1836, 116, 144–148).

In 1853, T.S. Arthur in *Advice to Young Men on their Duties and Conduct in Life* steadfastly exclaimed "By all means, take lessons in dancing" (69). However, in contrast to the advice given to the "delicate women," Madame Lola Montez in *The Arts of Beauty* (1858) provided different advice for young men. Montez advised,

> Dance with all the might of your body, and all the fire of your soul...and you need not restrain yourself with the apprehension that any lady will have the least fear that the violence of your movements will ever shake anything out of your brains (113–114).

Overall, at the time, the mind-set in regards to the benefits of social dancing as a means of physical education was changing.

At Vassar College, for example, founder Matthew Vassar added physical exercise as part of the curriculum. He stated:

> Years ago I made up my judgment on these great questions in the religious point of view, and came to the decision favorable to amusements. I have never practiced public dancing in my life, and yet in view of its being a healthful and graceful exercise, I heartily approve of it, and now recommend it being taught in the College (1869, 45).

Nationwide, colleges slowly incorporated social dancing as part of the physical education curriculum, including the United States Military Academy at West Point.

In 1802, the United States Military Academy was officially established at West Point in New York. Prior to that time, the area was occupied as a fortified garrison by the United States and was also of strategic importance during the Revolutionary War. On May 31, 1782, West Point had the distinction of hosting a ball in honor of the French allies that was attended by French General Lafayette and American Generals Henry Knox and George Washington. The dance was held under a specially constructed arbor that was located on the site of the present day parade ground at the academy. The following year, Washington's German military advisor Baron von Steuben recommended the formation of a national military academy (see Chapter 2). Within the organization, von Steuben suggested instruction in horsemanship, fencing, music, and dancing.

In 1817, at the request of the cadets, a voluntary class in dance instruction was offered and taught by the resident sword master Pierre Thomas. In 1823, instruction in social dance was made a compulsory requirement for the third and fourth year classes as part of the official summer encampment. During the summer, from July 4 to August 28, cadets were instructed in daily lessons lasting for 45 minutes. During that same year, the well-known Lorenzo Papanti of Boston was hired as the first official West Point dance instructor. (In 1827, Papanti opened Boston's first dancing studio and in 1834 introduced the Waltz to America at his fashionable dancing school in Boston on Tremont row—see earlier in this chapter.) Papanti served as the West Point dance instructor until 1839 (*The Centennial of the United States Military Academy at West Point* 1904, 908).

One cadet remembered that throughout his four years at West Point he participated in "regular dancing lessons." During that time, the dance instruction was led by Lorenzo Papanti whom the cadet described as "the celebrated dancing master of Boston." During the summer lessons, Papanti's wife, an accomplished singer, occasionally accompanied him to the obvious delight of the cadets. The cadet also recalled,

> She occasionally joined in our dancing lessons, much to our enjoyment, and during my cadetship, I think she was the only lady, with a single exception, who ever joined us in a dance at any time (Rapp 1978, 34).

Because of the remote location of the summer encampment, female partners were not readily available, so the cadets practiced dancing with each other as partners. According to West Point historian Kenneth W. Rapp,

Initially, the cadets were taught the part of the gentleman, or "lead," in dancing, and then the part of the lady. This method enabled them to dance with each other, and they took alternate parts each day (40).

Rapp's book, *West Point: Whistler in Cadet Gray, and other Stories about the United States Military Academy* (1978), contained an entire chapter "The History of Dancing at the U.S. Military Academy."

As for practicing without a female partner, one cadet wrote, "it was rather a dry business dancing without ladies; however, we cannot complain for the want of them in the evening." In 1824, Eliza Leslie wrote of regular dances held at the academy. She was often invited to dances at the homes of either the officers or one of the professors. In one case she accepted a dance that was given "by the Corps of Cadets and held in the Mess Hall." For the occasion the hall was "decorated for the occasion." Leslie was taken aback and impressed by the scene of neatly polished cadets and officers in military dress uniforms ready for the dance. The dance in the Mess Hall known as a "Cadet Hop" became a regular occurrence that lasted well into the twentieth century.

At the time, many wealthy individuals also left the city during the summer months to avoid the unsanitary conditions caused by the heat. In 1832, for

A "Cadet Hop" at the United States Military Academy at West Point, New York, c. 1859.   Library of the United States Military Academy at West Point.

example, a cholera epidemic in New York City "had driven legions of girls" out of the city. In search of an uncrowded urban environment, the "girls" flocked to homes in and around the West Point area. Many were the daughters of wealthy socialites and were accustomed to dances and assembly balls. Therefore, they "very willingly" attended the Cadet dances (Rapp 1978, 35).

In 1839, after Papanti left the academy, the dance instruction still continued. That same year, a new instructor, John Nevere, was hired; however, it is not known how long he was employed at West Point. It is known that sometime prior to the Civil War the famous dance instructor Edward Ferrero was hired. In 1859, Ferrero authored a noted dance instruction manual *The Art of Dancing*. But, Ferrero's services were soon ended, as was the dance instruction for the cadets. With the onset of the Civil War, Ferrero served as a colonel with the 51st New York Infantry. He rose through the ranks and was promoted to Brigadier General, seeing action at the battles of Bull Run, Antietam, and Fredericksburg. At the end of the war he returned to teach in New York City.

After the Civil War, the dance instruction at West Point was also reinstated with various dance instructors. In 1879, Louis W. Vizay was appointed to the position of dance instructor and stayed on until he resigned in 1898. Earlier in 1883, Vizay's son Rudolph was hired as an assistant dance instructor. Rudolph Vizay continued on for an uninterrupted tenure of 52 years as dance instructor at West Point until his death in 1935. During the Vizays' tenure, they applied similar regimentation to the dance instruction as did the military academy. The cadets not only marched both to and from the dance lessons, they also lined up in military ranks. In addition, Vizay taught the cadets the proper manners and etiquette of the ballroom. Historian Kenneth Rapp explained,

> Since the Military Academy was and still is an institution devoted to turning out not only capable Army officers but also polished gentlemen, "dancing and ballroom etiquette" was of primary concern to the Vizays (1978, 38).

At one point, the Commandant of Cadets issued a written commendation to Rudolph Vizay for the military precision of the dancing. The Commandant noted, "your usually fine instruction in dancing has aided in creating the rhythmic beauty of their marching, which is so universally recognized" (Rapp 1978, 40).

After Rudolph Vizay's death, Mr. and Mrs. George H. Roberts of Tulsa, Oklahoma, were hired as dance instructors. The Roberts' instruction continued until it was suspended in 1941 due to America's entry into World War II. In 1943, Barbara F. Cation resumed the dance instruction on a voluntary basis. During the 1950s, William Lewis, a West Point academy physical education instructor, reinstituted the dance lessons. Lewis, an accomplished square dancer and ballroom dancer, instructed the cadets in the Fox Trot, Polka, Cha-cha, Jitterbug, and Waltz. The Waltz was of utmost importance since it was danced to the music of *Army Blue*, which was the traditional song to end an evening of dancing at a cadet hop (Rapp 1978, 33–42).

By the 1860s, many of the dancing schools sought to capitalize on the growing trend to promote dancing as a means of physical education and exercise. In Boston, for example, a March 30, 1861, advertisement by a "Mr. Wm. N. Bell," for

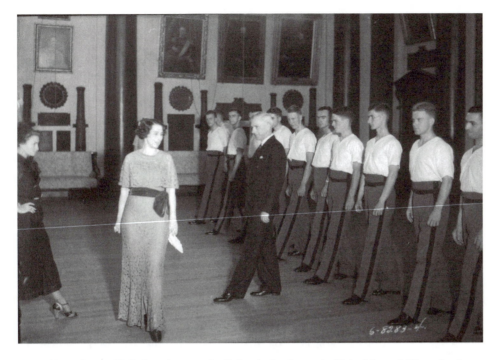

Mr. and Mrs. George H. Roberts instruct the Cadets in dancing at the United States Military Academy at West Point, New York, c. 1937. The Roberts were hired as dance instructors at West Point after the death of Rudolph Vizay in 1935. Vizay had served as dance instructor at West Point for 52 years. Library of the United States Military Academy at West Point.

example, promoted "Dancing and physical exercise" at his new dancing school at the corner of Court and Hanover Streets. Bell offered 24 lessons on "Wednesday and Saturday, at 3 o'clock, P.M." for the tuition price of $6. He promised to teach the "latest and most fashionable dances of the day." Bell's date of opening, however, coincided with the beginning of the American Civil War.

"THE MISCEGENATION BALL" AND DANCING DURING THE CIVIL WAR

At the time of Abraham Lincoln's inauguration as president on March 4, 1861, the American nation was divided as 11 southern states had seceded from the Union of the United States of America. Lincoln's inauguration was, indeed, overshadowed by an impending civil war; however, in the tradition established by George Washington, an inaugural ball was held (see Chapter 2). Despite the apparent optimism of welcoming the new president with a traditional dance, the nation was soon engaged in a civil war. In fact, during the course of war the North and the South were not as clearly divided over the slavery issue as many might think.

Although the cause of the northern states was directly linked to the abolition of slavery, the main reason for the American Civil War was to preserve the Union. Throughout the northern states many individuals supported abolition, but they also believed in segregation and were totally opposed to any intermingling of the races. In fact, during the wartime presidential campaign of 1864, some northern opponents openly attacked Lincoln's stance on the abolition of slavery and played upon the actual "Northern fears of racial intermingling." At that time, the political cartoon was an influential public media tool and many opponents used that source to attack Lincoln's reelection bid.

The widely read *New York World* newspaper of September 23, 1864, for example, published a political cartoon captioned, "The Miscegenation Ball" that showed whites and blacks openly dancing with each other. ("Miscegenation" was a term applied to the intermarriage of the races and was illegal in the Confederacy and in most northern states.) Therefore, the artists' depicting an actual dance was one that almost all Americans understood as an integral part of American culture. In addition, at a time when strict decorum within the ballroom was maintained between the mere intermingling of gender, it was obvious that the intermingling of the races through the medium of close couple dancing would ignite societal emotions.

The location of "The Miscegenation Ball" was parodied as if it were actually held at the New York City Headquarters of the Lincoln Central Campaign Club at the corner of Broadway and Twenty-Third Street. However, accounts of the day indicate that the drawing was a "perfect facsimile" of the actual room in New York City. The *New York World* actually concocted an explanation of the event that read almost like an actual news account of the day. In the foreground was a formal dance ball, and in the background was the musicians' stand. Above the musicians was a portrait of Abraham Lincoln. The text of the caption below the drawing read as follows:

> No sooner were the formal proceedings and speeches hurried through with, than the room was cleared for a "Negro ball," which then and there took place! Some members of the "Central Lincoln Club" left the room before the mystical and circling rites of languishing glance and mazy dance commenced. But that many remained is also true. This fact We Certify, "that on the floor during the progress of the ball were many of the accredited leaders of the Black Republican party, thus testifying their faith by works in the hall and headquarters of their political gathering. There were Republican Office-Holders, and prominent men of various degrees, and at least one Presidential Elector On The Republican Ticket."

In reality, no such "Miscegenation Ball" was ever held, but the illustration attempted to ignite northern fears of race mixing.

Despite the outrageous falsehoods and waylaid fears, Lincoln was reelected President of the United States. In 1865, the second inauguration of Abraham Lincoln was held in the ballroom of the White House. During the course of the American Civil War, both sides continued dancing. On February 22, 1864, in Washington, D.C., for example, a grand ceremonial ball was held in honor of George Washington's birthday. During that same year in New Orleans, from January 1 through March 12, the military mayor issued over 150 permits for various dances, including balls and private parties (Gushee, "The Nineteenth-Century Origins of Jazz," 1994, 6).

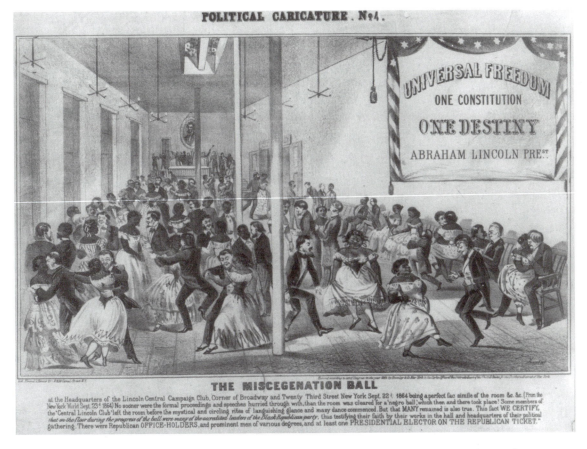

POLITICAL CARICATURE. No 4.

THE MISCEGENATION BALL

at the Headquarters of the Lincoln Central Campaign Club, Corner of Broadway and Twenty Third Street New York Sept. 22 ª 1864 being a perfect fac simile of the room &c. &c. [From the New York World Sept. 23 ª 1864] No sooner were the formal proceedings and speeches hurried through with, than the room was cleared for a 'negro ball;' which then and there took place! Some members of the 'Central Lincoln Club' left the room before the mystical and circling rites of languishing glance and many dance commenced. But that MANY remained is also true. This fact WE CERTIFY, *that on the floor during the progress of the ball were many of the accredited leaders of the Black Republican party,* thus testifying their faith by their works in the hall and headquarters of their political gathering. There were Republican OFFICE-HOLDERS, and prominent men of various degrees, and at least one PRESIDENTIAL ELECTOR ON THE REPUBLICAN TICKET."

A political cartoon captioned, "The Miscegenation Ball" published in the *New York World* newspaper of September 23, 1864, was a parody that played on the northern fears of racial intermingling. In the foreground, whites and blacks openly dance with each other and in the background above the musicians' stand is a portrait of Abraham Lincoln.   Library of Congress, American Political Prints.

But the "Grand Balls" were not necessarily the common dances of the day. Throughout the Civil War, soldiers on both sides danced as a viable means of recreation, as a way to bide time, and as a diversion from the harsh realities of war. In 1862, for example, during the Christmas holidays in Murfreesborough, Tennessee, Confederate General Braxton Bragg settled in with a large force. According to historians William Cullen Bryant and Sydney Howard Gay in *A Popular History of the United States*,

> There were wedding festivities, at one of which the warlike Bishop Polk officiated, and the guest danced upon a floor where the hated Union flag served for a carpet, that it might be literally and boastfully "trampled upon."

However, shortly after the New Year of 1863, the Confederate forces were once again engaged in battle (Bryant and Gay 1881, 535).

A reception in the White House Ballroom in honor of the second inauguration of President Abraham Lincoln, c. 1865. By the 1860s, formal dresses worn for dancing had elaborate trains and fuller bustles.   Library of Congress, Prints and Photographs LC-USZC2-2046.

In between battles, the armies on both sides passed the time with music and dancing. Within the military encampments, each regiment had a commissioned band; therefore, a musician was always available. In many cases, one of the soldiers was also fiddler and played for the enjoyment of his comrades. In turn, other soldiers would likely dance the Jig, Clog, or Reels. In the dire absence of females, the soldiers often held "Stag Dances." A Stag Dance simply meant that the soldiers danced as "couples" with each other.

In many cases to support the ongoing war effort, the once private ballrooms and fashionable assembly rooms were often employed to entertain soldiers with dances. Apparently, soldiers from different regions of America also had a different understanding of the acceptable social decorum as applied to behavior within the ballroom. At the time, these social dances were one of the few instances where

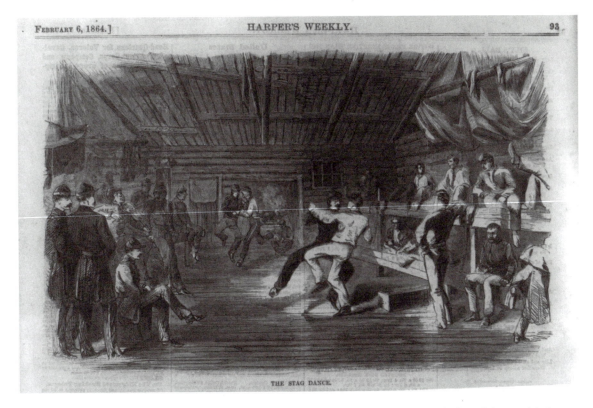

THE STAG DANCE.

In the absence of female partners, soldiers often held "Stag Dances," during which they simply danced the couple's dances with each other. This illustration appeared in *Harper's Weekly* on February 6, 1864, page 93.   Library of Congress, Prints and Photographs Division LC-USZ62-66765.

soldiers interacted with females. And, as with all wars, many of the soldiers were away from home for the first time. As a result, the social intermixing of culture, class, and gender from different regions of America was not always agreeable. Therefore, in 1863, during the Civil War, Thomas Hillgrove published *A Complete Practical Guide to the Art of Dancing*.

Hillgrove's book was obviously written in reaction to the "ballroom manners" observed during the Civil War. He added some new items to the long list of the etiquette and social manners described during the 1840s and 1850s. Hillgrove's volume cautioned that the "practice of chewing tobacco and spitting on the floor… [is] strictly forbidden." He claimed that the practice was "not only nauseous to ladies, but is injurious to their dresses." He also advised against unusually loud conversation, the use of profanity, and loud stamping of the feet in time with the music. In obvious deference to the common encampment practice of Stag dancing, Hillgrove politely stated, "It is improper also for two gentlemen to dance together when ladies are present" (22–29).

Hillgrove's dance book was certainly a reflection of the time and, therefore, serves as a valuable study of the changing behavioral patterns on the social dance floor. However, some later dance historians, such as Lloyd Shaw, did not

SOLDIERS' BALL AT HUNTSVILLE, ALABAMA—DANCING THE "VIRGINIA REEL."- [See Page 235.]

In this illustration for a Soldier's Ball at Huntsville, Alabama, c. 1863, the women line up to dance the Virginia Reel with soldiers in uniform. One woman at the top of the set wears a "mourning" shawl, as does a woman at the far right who is speaking with a wounded soldier.   © Corbis.

necessarily arrive at any specific conclusions for the behavioral change on the dance floor. Shaw, on the other hand, posed an interesting observation. He asked:

> Does that account for a certain roughness that entered the ballroom? Or had the war, like every war, mixed the social classes so that people untrained in etiquette, danced side by side with those who preserved the old traditions? Or had the dance spread so widely that rougher characters were taking part in it, and the elegance of the old ballrooms was lost?

In either case, another deference to the war was that young girls were encouraged to dance only with young men in uniform (Shaw 1949, 38).

During the American Civil War, in many cases the prevalent thinking was for the young lady to shun the young male who was not in uniform. The practice was actually encouraged by the governments on both sides as a means of recruiting young males into military service. Many of those "young" females themselves were also widowed wives of either Union or Confederate soldiers. With the continually mounting casualties during the Civil War, the number of widows increased. (All told, over 600,000 Americans died during the conflict.) The social decorum of

One of the most endearing and famous movies in Hollywood history is *Gone With the Wind* (1939). In this photo, the widow Scarlett O'Hara (actress Vivien Leigh), dressed in "mourning black," is dancing the Virginia Reel with the dashing Rhett Butler (actor Clark Gable). Rhett and Scarlett are at the top of the set holding hands in a face-to-face position and preparing to chassé sideways down the middle of the set to the bottom and repeat the pattern back to the top of the set.   Brown Brothers.

the day did not prevent the young lady from attending a ball; however, it was appropriate to signify that she was in mourning. In many cases, the widow simply wore a black shawl that was either handmade or presented to her. However, many chose to wear dresses that were made of all-black material (Cave, "Uncle Sam Wants You," 2005, WK3).

Hillgrove's book also acknowledged the fact that so many widowed women also attended dances. Therefore, he slightly modified a passage copied almost entirely from Charles Durang's 1856 Philadelphia publication of *The Fashionable Dancer's Casket*. In the case of a widow attending a fashionable ball, Hillgrove advised the following:

Mourning—even half-mourning—has always a sombre [sic] appearance, and is, therefore, unbecoming in a ball-room; but since decorating it with scarlet has come into fashion an air of cheerfulness has been imparted to its otherwise melancholy appearance....A lady may wear a black dress with scarlet flowers and trimmings (Hillgrove 1863, 18–19; Durang 1856, 14).

Although it was unclear exactly what "half-mourning" implied, the general appearance of a widow dressed in black at a dance was a common occurrence.

One of the most endearing and famous movies in Hollywood history is *Gone With the Wind* (1939). The movie set in the South during the American Civil War provided a romanticized portrayal of dancing. One of the most indelible moments in the movie depicted the widow Scarlett O'Hara (actress Vivien Leigh) dressed in "mourning black" dancing the Virginia Reel with the dashing Rhett Butler (actor Clark Gable). The women were dressed in fashion somewhat similar to the ball gowns of the period, and most of the men were dressed in military uniforms.

Because of the Civil War, some dancing academies either curtailed their business or suspended business indefinitely. In Boston, Brown's Dancing Academy was opened for business both prior to and after the start of the Civil War. In fact, a placard of December 4, 1861, advertised a full range of dance classes including afternoon and evening sessions. The classes offered instruction for "Young Ladies, Misses, and Masters," as both beginners and experienced "scholars" of social dancing. The beginning classes were taught Cotillons, the Waltz, the Spanish Dance, Waltz Quadrilles, Contra Dances, and Polka Quadrilles. The advanced "scholars" were taught "in the modern style of Dancing" that included all of "the fashionable fancy Waltzes and Dances." The "fashionable fancy" dances included the Polka, Schottische, Polka Redowa, Varsovienne, and Mazurka. Brown also advertised that he offered the most up-to-date fashionable newer dances as those "danced at the best French Academies, in New York and Philadelphia, and at Nahant, Newport, and other fashionable watering places during the last summer." Shortly thereafter, as the

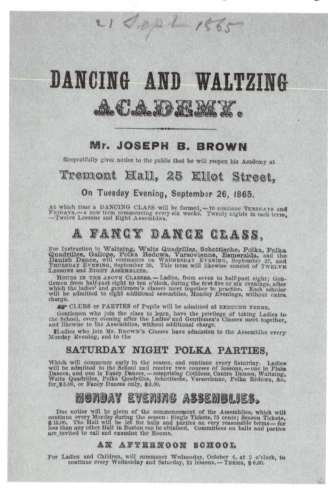

A placard advertising the reopening of Joseph Brown's Dancing and Waltzing Academy in Boston dated September 26, 1865. Because of the Civil War, some dancing academies either curtailed their business or suspended business indefinitely. Library of Congress, American Memory Collection.

228

war intensified, the desire to attend dancing classes was severely curtailed, and Joseph Brown closed his dancing school.

In due turn, when the Civil War ended in April 1865, some of the dancing schools once again opened for business. In September 1865, for example, Mr. Joseph B. Brown served public notice to reopen his *Dancing and Waltzing Academy* at Tremont Hall, 25 Eliot Street, on "Tuesday evening, September 26, 1865." The advertisement announced a continuing twice-a-week six-week series including "Twelve Lessons and Eight Assemblies." Brown suggested that during "the first five or six evenings," separate instruction was required for ladies at 7:00 P.M. to 8:30 P.M. and gentlemen from 8:30 P.M. until 10:00 P.M.. After those first sessions, Brown combined both the ladies and the gentlemen to "meet together to practice."

Brown offered instruction for "A Fancy Dance Class," including instruction for the Waltz, Waltz Quadrilles, the Schottische, Polka, Polka Quadrilles, Gallop, Polka Redowa, the Varsovienne, Esmeralda, and the Danish Dance. He also taught afternoon dance instruction classes for ladies and children. A total of 24 afternoon classes at a total cost of $6 were scheduled for Wednesdays and Saturdays at 2 o'clock P.M. In connection with the dance instruction, Brown advertised Monday evening dance assemblies and "Saturday Night Polka Parties." The Monday assembly required an admission price of a single ticket at 75 cents or a season subscription ticket for $12.00.

4

The Ghost Dance, the Cakewalk, and the Two-Step: 1865–1900

I went up to heaven and saw the Great Spirit…He gave me a dance to give to my people.

—Wovoka, 1890

The Political, Social, and Cultural Climate

In 1870, the total population of the restored Union of the United States of America was 39.8 million in 37 states. However, after the American Civil War, the southern states were literally in ruins, and the northern states were faced with the political, social, and economic problems to restore the Union of the United States of America. During the years 1867 to 1877, in order to readmit the former Confederate States to the Union, the United States Congress passed four Reconstructive Acts. During that time, the South was under the jurisdiction of Federal troops and the Reconstructive Acts divided the South into five Military Districts, required new state constitutions, made the African American slaves citizens, and disfranchised any loyal Confederates.

By 1877, a compromise plan, with both the election of Rutherford B. Hayes as president and the need for troops to deal with the "Indian problem" in the west, removed the Federal troops from the Military districts. With the troops gone, and a promise by Congress not to interfere, the southern states restored most of their prewar government. Each of the southern states enacted a series of "Black Codes" that became known as "Jim Crow Laws" (in essence they were basically the same Slave Codes that existed before the Civil War). At the time, because of resentment of the northern interference with the slavery issue, the formation of the Ku Klux Klan terrorized African Americans and "enforced" the Jim Crow laws.

In 1896, with the Supreme Court decision of *Plessy v. Ferguson*, the South was legally segregated, which further intensified the racial issue.

The Homestead Act, passed in 1862, promised free land in the western territories to white settlers. During the years 1870 through 1890, there was a great westward migration of white settlers into the Indian frontier. Although President Rutherford B. Hayes recognized in his annual address in 1877, "The Indians were the original occupants of the land we now possess," the westward migration continued. During those years, the population west of the Mississippi River expanded from less than 7 million during the Civil War to over 16 million by 1890. Historian Dee Brown called it, "The story of the advancing frontier and the retreating Indian" (1995, 78).

In July 1874, Lieutenant Colonel George Armstrong Custer, searching for gold and other minerals, led an unheralded expedition into the sacred Indian burial grounds in the Black Hills of South Dakota (the present day location of Mt. Rushmore). In response, thousands of prospectors, in violation of the Fort Laramie Treaty, rushed into the Great Sioux Reservation. After a failed attempt to displace the Sioux nation, the United States Government declared war on the Indians. In June 1876, Custer and the 7th Cavalry met their fate at the Little Big Horn at the hands of Cheyenne and Sioux warriors led by Chiefs Sitting Bull and Crazy Horse. The attention of the so-called "massacre" provided by the newspapers and magazines "told and retold the story," igniting an American hostility towards all the Indian tribes.

From 1876 to 1890, the "Sioux campaign" became the last in a series of battles to rid the West of the "Indian problem," thereby opening the territory to unhindered settlement, farming, cattle procurement, mining, and railroad expansion. In 1890, as a last resort to thwart the white settlers, Indian Chief Wovoka spread a message of hope among the Native American Indian tribes. Wovoka told them:

> I went up to heaven and saw the Great Spirit...He gave me a dance to give to my people....When you get home you must make a dance to continue five days.

It was the Ghost Dance, and it promised to rid the territories of the soldiers and their weapons. However, in December 1890, that hope was crushed forever, as the last of the Sioux warriors were killed by the U.S. Cavalry at Wounded Knee in South Dakota (Brown 1995, 195).

As the Sioux battled Custer at the Little Big Horn, the American Centennial Exhibition opened on May 10, 1876 in Philadelphia in celebration of the 100th year anniversary of the ratification of the Declaration of Independence. In Philadelphia, the Centennial touted American industrialization as an "Age of Progress." The exhibition featured, among others, the rudimentary telephone, a typewriter, linoleum floor covering, the Otis elevator, steam engines, the railroad, and information on the opening (and conquering) of the West. During that same year, Centennial celebrations were held throughout the United States in both towns and cities (*This Fabulous Century: 1870–1900*, 1970, 26–28).

The western territories were expanding due to increased settlement and the building of the railroad. Oftentimes, the history of the area was dominated by stories of Indians and "cowboys," as well as tales of the cattle drive. The cowboy and the cattle industry, both in reality and in American folklore, simply did not exist prior to the American Civil War. However, during the 1870s, massive cattle drives from the Texas panhandle through the Great Plains states to "cow towns" in the Midwest became a big business. By 1884, over 800,000 head of cattle per year were shipped from cow town cities such as Abilene, Kansas, and Dodge City, Kansas, by railroad to cities such as Chicago and others on the east coast. In these cow towns, the cowboys often celebrated the end of a long arduous cattle drive with a bath, new clothes, a drink of whisky, and a dance in a hurdy-gurdy house. However, the era of cowboys and the cattle business simmered down after the introduction of refrigerated railroad cars (Brown 1995, 195).

In 1869, the opening of the railroad link between the Central and Union Pacific Railroads at Promontory Point in Utah connected both coasts of the continental United States. As a result, a coast-to-coast trip could be had in seven days. In prior years, an overland crossing by a stagecoach could take over a month, by a wagon train five months, and by sailing ship from an east coast port such as Baltimore, Philadelphia, Boston, or New York traveling around the Cape Horn of South America as much as six months. By that time, railroads were economically powerful, and they could make or break a town. In a scant ten years from 1870 to 1880, for example, Denver, as a result of a railroad center, grew in population from 5,000 to over 35,000 people; by 1890, the population passed 106,000. By that time, four different railway companies had transcontinental lines, and the United States possessed more than half of the world's mileage in rail lines (*This Fabulous Century: 1870–1900*, 1970, 25–26).

The rapid westward expansion of settlers and the rapid buildup of the railroad added seven new states: Colorado in 1876; North Dakota, South Dakota, and Montana in 1889; and Washington, Idaho, and Wyoming in 1890. At the time, the population reached 62.9 million people. However, by the time Utah was admitted as the 45th state in 1896, the population approached 76 million, and over 60 percent of the workforce was in industry (Goldfield, Abbott, et al., 2001, A-28–29).

At the same time, the U.S. economy was shifting from an agricultural-based economy to an industrial base. With that shift came a new influx of massive wealth for the industrialists involved in businesses such as the railroads, the steel industry, and the oil business. In 1894, at Corsicana, Texas, a routine well drive for water unexpectedly hit petroleum. It was the first "oil boom" in the West and began the production of American petroleum. A few years later in 1901, just outside of Beaumont, Texas, the Spindletop gusher was "the most famed well in the history of Western petroleum." Before long the oil boom spread throughout eastern Texas and into Oklahoma. In 1898 after war with Spain, America annexed the territories of Hawaii, Samoa, Guam, Cuba, the Philippines, and Puerto Rico. By 1900, the United States was both a major military and industrial power as well as the world's largest consumer of manufactured goods (Brown 1995, 158; *This Fabulous Century* 1970, 30).

During the 1890s, the United States was rapidly expanding as an industrialized nation and, therefore, required a large workforce. As a result, a massive influx of new immigrants entered America, mainly from areas of southern Europe including Italians, Hungarians, and Russians who settled in the industrialized cities. By the end of the nineteenth century, all the cities throughout the nation (although mostly east of the Mississippi) experienced a tremendous population boom. New York was not only the most populous, but also the most crowded. In 1870, New York had over 940,000 people (Brooklyn had 396,000). By 1890, New York had 1.5 million (not including over 1 million combined in Brooklyn, Bronx, Queens, and Staten Island). By the time the five boroughs incorporated into the city of New York in 1898, the population was 3.4 million people. By comparison, Chicago's inhabitants numbered 1.7 million and Philadelphia's 1.3 million people. The next three most populated cities were St. Louis, Boston, and Baltimore, which each had over 500,000 people (U.S. Bureau of the Census, Table 10, 12, 13).

The 1890s produced an upsurge in the amount of "new wealth" among an enlarging class of millionaires. The *New York Tribune* newspaper, for example, touted a count nationwide that located 4,047 millionaires. Manhattan had 1,103, Chicago numbered 280, Brooklyn counted 155, and San Francisco had 145. At the time, economist Thorstein Verlben defined this new "Leisure class" as most evident by their "conspicuous consumption." The flaunting of wealth was most conspicuous through the sponsorship of a lavish ball that included dancing (Panati 1991, 9; Wallace et al., 1986, 34).

On March 26, 1883, for example, a grand ball given by Mr. and Mrs. William K, Vanderbilt signified their entrance to the top of New York society. Within the Vanderbilt's opulent Fifth Avenue mansion, hundreds of guests danced in a grand ballroom 65 feet long, 20 feet wide, and 16 feet high decorated with European tapestries and ornate decorations. Not to be outdone, the Bradley Martin Ball on February 10, 1897, was held at the famed Waldorf Astoria in New York City. The ballroom was decorated in similar fashion to the grand palace of Versailles, France. Guests were adorned in gold and diamonds worth thousands of dollars. Americans sought to establish themselves as "Society," and the *London Chronicle* applauded the triumph of New York Society (Dannett and Rachel 1954, 50–51).

In America up until the 1890s, all of the mainstream dances of society were of European origin—mainly French or British. During the 1880s and 1890s, other than the Quadrille and Cotillions (which were the most popular), Americans danced the Waltz, the Polka, the Virginia Reel, and even an occasional Minuet. By the same time, however, a homegrown tradition was developing at the same time among the African American slaves, indigenous Native American Indian tribes, Creoles in Louisiana, and the mountain regions of the Appalachians, among others. By 1890, American music in the form of John Philip Sousa's marches and syncopated Ragtime music also brought new dances such as the Two-Step.

The 1890s were termed by many historians as the "Gay Nineties." The term, however, was changed during the late twentieth century and is most often known as the Gilded Age. Throughout most of the written history of America from the earliest days until well into the twentieth century, the word "gay" was often applied to dancing. In fact, the word as a reference to homosexuality did not become common until the 1970s. Prior to that time, it simply meant happy or joyous. And as it applies to American social dancing of the time—it certainly was true.

The Dances

No matter what teachers of dancing may assert, the most expedient and certainly best way to learn to dance is to stand up and try it; no one can ever learn by sitting quietly and looking on.

—George Wilson, 1884

THE GHOST DANCE AND THE "DISCONTINUANCE OF CERTAIN SAVAGE CUSTOMS"

Prior to 1870, estimates claimed that as many as 4 million buffalo roamed free along the Great Plains of America. Regardless of the actual numbers, there were certainly plenty of buffalo and other game to satisfy the American Indian's need for food and sustenance for many centuries. However, in a systematic fashion, as more and more white settlers moved west, as more cattle were driven north from Texas, and as the railroads crisscrossed the continent, the source of food supplies for Indians was greatly diminished. As a final desecration, with the consent of the U.S. government, between the years 1871 and 1875 almost all the buffalo were systematically slaughtered. U.S. Army General Phil Sheridan, who saw it as a viable means to "subdue the Indians," condoned the slaughter. As a result, the elimination of the food source practically wiped out the American Indian civilization of the Great Plains (Brown 1995, 274).

In 1870, an Indian chief named Tavibo made a pilgrimage into the mountains among the Paiutes in Nevada. He returned with a tale of a "vision" of a land that once again belonged to the Indian tribes filled with buffalo, fish, and game—devoid of the "white invaders." Tavibo did not convince many other Indian tribes, but did pass on his vision to his 14-year-old son Wovoka. After Tavibo died, Wovoka was taken into the home of a white farm family and assumed the family name of Jack Wilson. However, a few years later Wovoka had a similar vision as his father. In a statement to the Indians, later transcribed as "The Messiah's Letter," Wovoka proclaimed:

> I went up to heaven and saw the Great Spirit and all the people who had died a long time ago. The Great Spirit told me to come back and tell my people they must be good and love one another, and not fight, or steal, or lie. He gave me a dance to give to my people.

The dance that Wovoka was given was the Ghost Dance.

Wovoka told other Indians that if they eliminated any violence against the white man and performed the Ghost Dance, the Great Spirit would come and wash away the plague of the invading white man among the plains of America. He explained the Ghost Dance to other Indians as follows:

> When you get home you must make a dance to continue five days. Dance four successive nights, and the last night keep up the dance until the morning of the fifth day, when all must bathe in the river and then disperse to their homes. You must all do in the same

way....I want you to dance every six weeks. Make a feast at the dance and have food that everybody may eat. Then bathe in the water. That is all.

Wovoka also indicated that the Ghost Dance must be maintained as a secret ceremony. He added, "Do not tell the white people about this" (Brown 1995, 365; "Wovoka's Message: The Promise of the Ghost Dance," n.d.).

During the late 1880s, his message spread, and Wovoka was viewed as a "Messiah" among his followers and believers. Apparently, in January 1889, the first known Ghost Dance was performed on the Walker Lake Reservation in Nevada. Historian Dee Brown described it as a simple ceremony as "the Indians forming into a large circle, dancing and chanting as they constricted the circle, the circle widening and constricting again and again" (366). As part of the ceremony, the Indians wore shirts decorated with spiritual symbols. Wovoka promised that the "ghost shirts" would prevent any of the "white man's bullets" from harming them. Within a few weeks, the news spread to neighboring tribes of the Rocky Mountain region. Soon many others joined in, and others traveled from as far away as the Dakotas. In the spring of 1890, the Shoshones, the Cheyenne, and the Sioux embraced the new religion and actively danced at the Pine Ridge Reservation in South Dakota. The Sioux added new symbols and colors to the ghost shirts that were destined to protect them from the white man's bullets.

The U.S. Army soon heard of the "new religion" and the American government became fearful when the great Indian Chief Sitting Bull joined the religious ceremony. Sitting Bull, who had led the Sioux nation and defeated Custer at the Little Big Horn, had long ago surrendered and was living under the agreements of a treaty on the reservation. A former Indian Agent Valentine McGillycuddy was dispatched from Washington to investigate the potential for serious trouble. McGillycuddy actually recommended that the Ghost Dance remain unhindered. In a report to Washington, D.C., he wrote:

> The coming of the troops has frightened the Indians. If the seventh-Day Adventists prepare the accession robes for the Second Coming of the Savior, the United States Army is not put in motion to prevent them. Why should not the Indians have the same privilege? If the troops remain, trouble is sure to come.

However, rather than let the religious ceremony continue, the U.S. Army, still fearful of a "Sioux uprising," ordered the arrest of Sitting Bull.

The arrest order was sent to U.S. General Nelson Miles stationed in Rapid City, South Dakota, a few hundred miles from the Pine Ridge Reservation. Although sympathetic to the Sioux cause, General Miles claimed, "The Ghost Dance craze has reached such proportions that it's now entirely beyond [our] control." Therefore, on the morning of December 15, 1890, General Miles dispatched over 40 Indian police with orders to arrest Sitting Bull. They surrounded his cabin, and in an ensuing melee Sitting Bull was killed. As a result, the remaining Sioux Indians fled the Pine Ridge Reservation, seeking safety in the Badlands and Black Hills of South Dakota. Niles was given orders to return the fleeing Sioux Indians to the reservation.

On December 28, a detachment of the U.S. Cavalry intercepted and surrounded the Sioux at their camp in Wounded Knee Creek. The small group of Sioux Indians numbered 120 men and 230 women and children. On the following morning of December 29, 1890, the soldiers searched the camp for weapons. According to an eyewitness account by Lieutenant James D. Mann,

> While this was going on, the medicine man, who was in the center of the semi-circle of (warriors), had been going through the Ghost Dance.

Apparently, the soldiers were unaware of the religious belief of the Ghost Dance and became unsettled. The Indians, on the other hand, strongly believed that the ghost shirts and dance protected them from the soldier's rifles and Hotchkiss machine guns.

In the next few moments, "things" happened quite fast—gunshots were fired. Not sure who had fired first, the surrounding Cavalry fired their Hotchkiss machine guns into the camp. In a very short time, 31 soldiers and 128 Sioux were dead including men, women, and children. Many more of the Sioux were wounded

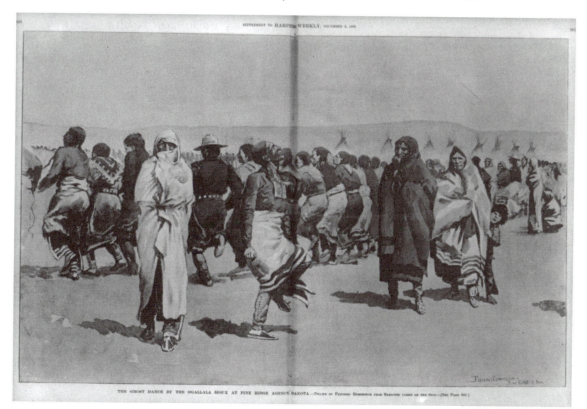

The Ghost Dance performed by the Sioux on the Pine Ridge Reservation in South Dakota. This illustration that appeared in *Harper's Weekly* on December 6, 1890, was drawn by Frederic Remington from sketches that he prepared on the spot. Library of Congress, Prints and Photographs Division LC-USZC2-99404.

and later died. To the U.S. Government, the "Battle of Wounded Knee" was hailed as a "suppression" of a potential uprising and signified the end to the American Indians resistance to the takeover of the western plains of America. On the other hand, to Native American Indians the "Massacre at Wounded Knee" represented a massacre not only of the human kind but also of their culture (Lewis 1999, 452–456; Brown 1995, 366–373).

During that same month of December 1890, ethnologist James A. Mooney was also dispatched by the Washington Bureau of American Ethnology to investigate and chronicle the Ghost Dance. He not only witnessed the Ghost Dance, he also saw many other Native American Indian Dances—and he also participated. During the course of his campaign, he also obtained a transcribed version of Wovoka's message to the Indian people regarding the Ghost Dance. Known as "The Messiah Letter," it was written by "a joint Cheyenne-Arapaho delegation that visited Wovoka in Nevada in August 1891." During the three-year period from 1891 to 1893, Mooney recorded a 32,000-mile journey, observed 12 different tribes, and photographed and illustrated over 70 Ghost Dance images. (The images are held in the National Anthropological Archives of the Smithsonian Institution.) However, historian Thomas W. Kavanagh of the University of Indiana presented evidence that the images might have been retouched and, therefore, might not be a totally accurate representation of the actual ceremonies. Nevertheless, Mooney's illustrations and firsthand accounts do serve as a valuable historical resource in regards to late nineteenth century Native American Indian dances and tribal customs (Kavanagh, "Imaging and Imagining the Ghost Dance," n.d.).

Despite Mooney's exhaustive work, Bureau of Indian Affairs Commissioner W.A. Jones decreed that the Native American Indian dances and tribal customs were "hindrances to civilization." Therefore, Jones petitioned the U.S. Secretary of the Interior for the "discontinuance of certain savage customs prevailing among Indian tribes." Those "certain savage customs" were, of course, dancing—specifically the Ghost Dance. In his petition, Jones claimed,

> Dances that are degrading and so-called religious rites that are immoral, though gradually disappearing, still prevail…It will be extremely difficult to accomplish much toward the civilization of the Indians while these adverse influences are allowed to exist.

The Secretary of the Interior and others in Washington obviously agreed with the request. On October 16, 1902, Commissioner Jones issued the following directive to all Indian agents on the reservations:

> Indian dances and so-called Indian feasts should be prohibited. In many cases these dances and feasts are simply subterfuges to cover degrading acts and to disguise immoral purposes. You are directed to use your best efforts in the suppression of these evils.

In fact, from 1902 through the 1930s, the Bureau of Indian Affairs continually prohibited the Ghost Dance and all other American Indian Dances (quoted in Needham 2002, 36–38).

In 1907, Lilly Grove, in a well-respected publication *Dancing*, included a chapter "The Dances of Savages." A hint of contemporary prejudice might well have been apparent as she wrote, "The dance among savages may be considered a just indication of their character." At the time, the prevalent thought throughout not only America but also most of the Western world was to term any tribal groups as "savages." But Grove did recognize the importance of the dancing as it applied specifically to the American Indian. Grove offered a brief explanation and offered a suggestion to her readers. She explained,

> However strange some of the dancing customs of savages may appear to us, they are not consequently to be condemned. The advance of civilisation [sic] tends to weaken the picturesque aspect of life and to reduce everything to a smooth uniformity.

Grove added that, unlike those of European ancestry, for Indians dancing was "a very important part in their daily life" (65).

During the 1920s, some Native Indian tribes once again publicly displayed some of the tribal dances. In order to avoid trouble with the government, a delegation of Tewa and Pueblo Indians from the southwest areas of New Mexico, traveled to Washington, D.C., to secure legal rights to maintain their village rituals—mainly the dancing. However, Bureau of Indian Affairs Commissioner Charles H. Burke refused and suggested that the Native American Indians stop the "evil [and] foolish things." In fact, he specifically "insisted" that the dances "should be stopped." Therefore, Commissioner Burke reissued a directive indicating that Indian dance rituals be discouraged or if possible outright banned (Sweet 1985, 41; Needham 2002, 19).

In 1923, in response to Commissioner Burke's decision, columnist Elizabeth Sergeant in the *New Republic* magazine offered an explanation as to the adamant suppression of the Indian dances by the United States Government. She explained:

> The reason why certain powers…are out to "get" Indian dances is not that they are harmful, but that so long as they continue, the Indian cannot be transformed into a white man…with the dances, will die Indian costume and handicraft and decorative symbolism, Indian rhythm and music and song…Then will every Indian surely prefer the Y.M.C.A to the kiva, the cornet to the tumble, and the movies to the Deer Dance.

Unfortunately, the suppression of Native American cultures continued well into the twentieth century (quoted in Sweet 1985, 41).

However, similar to Pueblo Indians in the face of suppression by Spanish rule in 1689 (see Chapter 1), the Native American Indian dances were kept hidden and survived through the oral tradition. Open invitation to powwows did, in fact, begin in the late 1920s, but they were not widespread or openly accepted until the late 1970s. At that time, after a series of protests by the American Indian Movement, including an occupation of the Bureau of Indian Affairs in Washington, D.C., Mount Rushmore, and Wounded Knee, in South Dakota, Congress passed the Indian Self-Determination Act. In 1976, the Congressional Act finally gave Indians control of their own education and continuation of tribal customs that included the tribal dances. Even in the late twentieth century, many Americans did not know that social dancing was such a strong part of their cultural traditions. Even if they did know, most Americans were oblivious to the fact the first Americans to participate in social dancing in North America were the indigenous Indian tribes.

THE GRAND MARCH, THE NINE PINS, AND THE GERMAN "THE MOST SOCIAL OF DANCES"

In a fashion similar to the seventeenth century Pavane and eighteenth century Minuet, during the late nineteenth century, all of the formal dances opened an evening of dancing with a Grand March (also known as The March, Polonaise, Grand Promenade, or Opening March). In a fashion similar to the European courts of the eighteenth century, the most prominent couple led the march and the other guests followed in line as they traversed the ballroom one or two time. Sometimes it was a simple march keeping the steps in time with the music. But more often than not, the wealthier classes maintained an even more stringent approach to the formalities and processions of the Grand March. Instead of normal walking steps, emphasis was placed on a great variety of spatial patterns that involved some set figures such as interweaving the lines.

Allen Dodworth in *Dancing and Its Relations to Education and Social Life* (1885, revised 1900), for example, described the Grand March as a "ceremonious procession most frequently used in opening the state balls of European courts." He described the basic "motions" as follows:

> The master of ceremonies takes command and conducts the dancers through various evolutions. For example, after marching round the room, and then up the centre, at the head the gentlemen turn to the left, ladies to the right, marching round so as to meet again at the bottom of the room, when partners are resumed; or while marching round the room, at a signal (clapping hands) each gentleman disengages his partner's hand, pauses a moment, allowing the next lady behind to overtake him, when they proceed together.

Dodworth explained that The Grand March was also a "ceremonious procession most frequently used in opening the state balls of European courts" (1900, 138–139).

In 1896, E.H. Kopp in *The American Prompter and Guide to Etiquette* termed the March as the "Grand Promenade." He described the basic "March in File," as follows:

> Make a complete circuit around the room, continue [until the] foot of the room is reached, march up middle to [the] head of the room, gentlemen to the left, ladies to the right, in single file. At [the] foot of the room files pass to left of each other, continue [the] circuit to [the] head, when partners join and march in couples to right.

Kopp also described a few variations including a spiraling and reversing Serpentine March, a March in Columns, in Platoons, through Arches, and as a Crisscrossing pattern (15–18).

Other sources that described the Grand March and the variations of figures included E.B. Reilley's *Amateur's Vademecum: A Practical Treatise on the Art of*

Dancing (1870); *Dick's Quadrille Call-Book and Ball-Room Prompter* (1878); *Cartier and Baron's Practical Illustrated Waltz Instructor* (1882); Professor M.J. Koncen's *Quadrille Call Book and Ball Room Guide* (1883); *Wehman's Complete Dancing Master and Call Book* (1889); L.H. Elmwell's *Prompter's Pocket Instruction Book* (1892); and Frank Leslie Clendenen's *Fashionable Quadrille Call Book* (1899). Video clips of a demonstration of the Grand March are viewable from the Music Division of the Library of Congress online source "An American Ballroom Companion: Dance Instruction Manuals Ca. 1490–1920"; as well as Dancetime Publications' "500 Years of Social Dance: Volume I: The 15th to 19th Centuries" (see bibliography).

Cotillions were also popular within the fashionable set. One of the most popular figures of the time was the "Nine Pin." In 1878, *How To Dance: A Complete Ball-Room and Party Guide* noted that the "Nine Pin [had] become quite fashionable of late, affording more amusement probably than any of the other dances" (14). (Interestingly enough, the quote from *How To Dance* was copied verbatim from page 20 of the 1868 publication of *Beadle's Dime Ball-Room Companion and Guide to Dancing*.)

In the Nine Pin, a circle of an equal number of men and ladies (but usually four couples) form around one "extra gentleman" who takes a lone place in the center. Therefore the set comprises "nine" people. (Sometimes it was danced in the square set Quadrille formation.) The gentlemen and ladies perform a Grand Chain weaving in and around the Nine Pin. The men pass the lone gentleman, and the Nine Pin alternately moves in and out of the circle turning each lady. When the music stopped the gentlemen moved to the lady on their right. The lone gentleman without a partner became the new Nine Pin. In other instances, the leader called out any number of movements that required the dancers to separate and come back together. The Nine Pin was actually quite similar to the Spanish dance performed in the American southwest known as El Coyote (see Chapter 3).

The Nine Pin was also danced in rural areas. A contemporary account of the Nine Pin was offered by Mrs. Rose Williams, who recalled dances that she attended as a young girl in the Glendale and Ridgewood area of Long Island. At the time, around 1880 or 1885, the area was quite rural. Williams described it as follows:

> all this district was farm land....Our roads, and the lanes leading to the scattered farm houses, were unlighted at night. When we went out after dark we used to carry lanterns, burning coal oil or candles. On Central Avenue...there was a little country school house—a frame building.

The schoolhouse also served as a community building that sponsored local dances. Williams fondly recalled:

> In those days we used to have the old-time square dances; the Polka, quadrilles, the Virginia Reel and several others. There was one dance in particular that gave us a great deal of fun. It was called the "Nine Pins."

Williams's description of the Nine Pin was basically the same as some of the contemporary written descriptions. However, she did add a bit more flavor as she described the dance as follows:

The part of the [Nine-Pin] was played by one of the men, who would be either a volunteer or a chap who yielded to persuasion. He had to fill the role for the duration of one dance, after which he was relieved by some else.... [He] had to stand in the center of the floor, within close range of the dancers, who would get as near to him as they possible could. The caller would yell out, "Take hold of the Nine-Pin's nose," or, "Take hold of the Nine-Pin's ear," or "Take hold of the Nine-Pin's right hand,"...or of his left hand, his thumb, his shirt-collar, his beard—if he had one, or any part of the chap which might embarrass him the most and afford the greatest amount of merriment for the dancers (Williams, "Old Glendale," 1938).

Cotillions continued in popularity; however, by the late nineteenth century in the fashionable ballrooms they were toned done and known as "The German."

Sometime after the Civil War in America, the Cotillion was renamed "The German" and was a very popular part of society dance balls during the 1880s and 1890s. (It is not known exactly how the name change came about, but many speculate that it was named after the country Germany where the dance form might have originated.) Many of the figures in The German were the same as the mid-nineteenth century Cotillions such as The Rope, The Fan, and Blind Man's Buff, which involved dance games or couple mixers (see Chapter 3). Sometimes, The German was intermittently dispersed throughout the evening's program of dances. Other times a series of them were grouped together near the end of the evening. At the fashionable dances, however, the "dance games" of The German were often led by an "official" Master of Ceremonies. In addition, the props were a bit more elaborate as were the party favors and gifts for "winning" the dance.

In 1899, the influential Marguerite Wilson in *Dancing*, published in Philadelphia, exalted over the sociability of the dance, calling The German "the highest evolution of the art of dancing." She explained her reasoning as follows:

> The constant interchange of partners renders this the most social of dances, and the element of refined humor entering into many of the figures gives an additional zest to the enjoyment of the dance (1920, 131).

For most of the figures, chairs were arranged on the perimeter of the dance floor. The dancers sat in the chairs, sometimes with an assigned number. The lady was always seated at her partner's right side. Sometimes the figures were improvised, but in most cases, Wilson suggested a "programme" of the scheduled order of figures. One particular figure that Wilson was particularly fond of was "The Waltz Favor." She described it as follows:

> [As] one coupled danced the Waltz around the room. They picked up a favor from a table. They proceeded to Waltz towards another seated couple. There they pinned the favor, (sometimes a flower or decorative paper) on the jacket and dress of each of the couple. The second couple follows the lead by also waltzing and doing the same with a favor for a third couple. The figure was enhanced as the lady partner was presented to two gentlemen and she in turn would select one to dance with.

Similar to the mid-nineteenth century Cotillions, most of the figures in The German ended with one or two couples either Waltzing or doing the Polka. By the time that Wilson's publication was reprinted in 1920, however, The German was long out of style (Wilson 1920, 131–135).

In 1887, Mrs. Mary Elizabeth Sherwood in *Manners and Social Usages* also praised The German, calling it "the most fashionable dance in society." She added, "It ends every ball in New York, Washington, Boston, Philadelphia, and Newport." At the time, the cities listed by Sherwood were the areas where only the wealthiest of society danced. However, Sherwood was aware that the dance involved intermixing of couples, she wrote, "No lady can refuse to dance with any gentleman who is brought to her in the German." Cautious of the intermixing of the dancers, she added, "Therefore the German must only be introduced at select assemblies, not at a public ball."

Sherwood acknowledged that there were many different figures to the dance. Therefore, she listed only a select few. One "favorite figure" named *Les Drapeaux* was described by her as follows:

> Five or six duplicate sets of small flags of national or fancy devices must be in readiness. The leader takes a flag of each pattern, and his partner takes the duplicate. They perform a tour de valse. The conductor then presents his flags to five or six ladies, and his partner presents the corresponding flags to as many gentlemen. The gentlemen then seek the ladies having the duplicates, and with them perform a tour de valse, waving the flags as they dance.

The figure was repeated by all the other couples. Sherwood avoided listing too many figures. She added, "We might go on indefinitely with these figures, but have no more space" (153–157).

The German was so popular that many of the dance instruction books either included it within the title or devoted an entire book to the dance figures. A sampling included the following:

- William B. De Garmo's *The Prompter: containing full descriptions of all the quadrilles, figures of the German cotillon, etc.* (1864, reissued in 1865, 1866, 1868, and 1884).
- William B. De Garmo's *The Dance of Society: a Critical Analysis of all the standard quadrilles, round dances, 102 figures of le cotillon "the German"* (1875);
- Dick and Fitzgerald's *The German. How to Give it. How to lead it. How to dance it. By two amateur leaders* (1879 and 1895);
- Cartier and Baron's *Practical Illustrated Waltz Instructor, Ball room Guide, and Call Book. Giving ample directions for dancing every kind of square and round dances, together with cotillons—including the newest and most popular figures of "the German"* (1879).
- Allen Dodworth's *Dancing and Its Relation to Education and Social Life. Dancing and its relations to education and social life, with a new method of instruction for a complete guide to the cotillion (German) with 250 figures* (1885);
- J.H. Wehman, *Wehman's Complete Dancing Master and Call book: containing a full and complete description of all the modern dances, together with the figures of the German* (1889);
- Harris B. Dick's *How to Lead the German* (1895).

Some of the other sources that provided numerous figures and explanations for The German and described the Grand March and the variations of figures included

Dick's Quadrille Call-Book and Ball-Room Prompter (1878), C.H. Cleveland's *Dancing at Home and Abroad* (1878), *Prof. M.J. Koncen's Quadrille Call Book and Ball Room Guide* (1883), C.H. Rivers's *A Full Description of Modern Dances* (1885), Judson Sause, *The Art of Dancing* (1885), and *The Perfect Art of Modern Dancing* (1894).

Besides the German, other fad dances of the time included the Butterfly Dance, the Carlton, the Danish Dance, the Esmeralda, the Loomis' Glide Mazurka, the Cross Step Polka, the Waltz Cotillion (also known as Waltz Quadrille or the Eugenie), the Waltz Minuet, and the Zingirella, among others. Video clips of a demonstration of most of the dances, including The German, are viewable from the Music Division of the Library of Congress online source *An American Ballroom Companion: Dance Instruction Manuals Ca. 1490–920*, as well as Dancetime Publications' *500 Years of Social Dance: Volume I: The 15th to 19th Centuries* (see bibliography).

DANCE INSTRUCTION BOOKS AND "HOW LONG WILL IT TAKE TO LEARN TO DANCE?"

After the Civil War, with the popularity of the Quadrilles and Cotillions, many of the dance instruction manuals listed the many different figures for the dances. In the case of *The Prompter*, by William De Garmo, for example, it was first published in 1864 and was reissued in 1865 with the addition of 87 Cotillon figures. Subsequent editions in 1866, 1868, and 1884 provided additional information for the Quadrilles, Cotillions, and The German. Some of the other popular dance instruction manuals during the 1860s included:

- *The Ball-Room Guide* (1866);
- Professor C. Brooks, *The Ball-Room Monitor* (1866);
- Lawrence De Garmo Brookes, *Brookes on Modern Dancing* (1867);
- *Beadle's Dime Ball-Room Companion and Guide to Dancing* (1868).

Many of these publications freely borrowed from other similar publications. They usually included a section on ballroom etiquette and description of the "popular" ballroom dances including the Cotillion, Quadrilles, Polka, Redowa, Mazurka, Galop, Schottische, and the Waltz ("Nineteenth Century Social Dance" n.d.).

By the 1870s, there was a proliferation of self-instruction dance manuals. These publications often presented the reader with the "promise" that they could learn to dance without a dance master. Some also listed the extensive figures for the Quadrille and Cotillions (which by this time was called "The German"). A sampling of some of the popular dance instruction manuals during the 1870s included:

- *Ball-Room Dancing without a Master* (1872);
- Eugène Coulon, *Coulon's Hand-book* (1873);
- *The Dancer's Guide and Ball-Room Companion* (1874);
- William B. De Garmo, *The Dance of Society* (1875);
- Henry Gass, *The Waltz* (1876);

- *Dancing Without a Master* (1876);
- *How To Dance: A Complete Ball-Room and Party Guide* (1878);
- C.H Cleveland, *Dancing at Home and Abroad* (1878);
- *The Prompter's Own Book; or, Rowe's Calls for the Ball Room Contains all the Latest and Best Calls necessary for an all night party* (1878);
- *Cartier and Baron's Practical Illustrated Waltz Instructor, Ball room Guide, and Call Book* (1879).

At the time, most of the dance instruction manuals either eliminated the sections on Ballroom Etiquette or provided only a brief outline. It was not that ballroom etiquette was dismissed; on the contrary, etiquette was even more impressed upon the formal ballroom than ever before. At the time, there was also an exhaustive list of "pure etiquette manuals" (see later in this chapter) that applied not only to the ballroom, but also to all other aspects of the late nineteenth century society ("Nineteenth Century Social Dance," n.d.).

In 1875, in *The Dance of Society*, for example, William B. De Garmo provided a "much more comprehensive volume" than in *The Prompter*, which he said "was a mere manual." Within *The Dance of Society*, De Garmo provided more detailed descriptions on how to execute the steps of the dances. He explained,

Beadle's Dime Ball-Room Companion and Guide to Dancing was a popular dance instruction book that was often copied. Published in New York by Beadle and Company, 1868. Library of Congress, Music Division, http://lcweb2.loc.gov/musdi/101/0001.gif.

I have endeavored to give as complete a dissertation upon Time and its accentuation, Position, Attitude, Carriage and Style, as was possible for me, with a large amount of other relative matter (10).

Although he did not totally disregard the manner of ballroom etiquette, De Garmo was "as brief as Possible" (10). One of the brief mentions of etiquette involved the manner of the "proper distance" maintained during the closed dance position, as well as the lady's submission to the lead of the gentleman. De Garmo reminded the dancers:

> The gentleman is at all times, responsible for the guidance of his partner, and should therefore use the greatest precaution against colliding with other couples. He should regulate the proper distance to be maintained between himself and his partner, neither holding her so close as to impeded [sic] her freedom of action, nor so far aloof as to prevent him from rendering her sufficient and necessary support. The lady should allow herself to be entirely guided by her partner, without in any case endeavoring to follow her own impulse of action (66).

However, unlike most of the other "How to Dance" manuals, De Garmo suggested a combination of instruction from a dancing school and, of course, his own manual. In regards to the most often asked question of "How long will it take to learn to dance?" De Garmo's answer was not as direct as an impatient student would have liked. He suggested, "As a rule, the best dancers are those who have attended dancing school several terms." But he did stipulate that there were also many variables. The answer to the question also depended upon "the aptitude, the patience, the perseverance and attention of the pupil as well as the ability of the teacher." He added,

> The most inapt are usually the most impatient. They become discouraged in two or three lessons, because they cannot accomplish without practice what has cost more apt, more persevering, more attentive and more patient persons a considerably longer time.

De Garmo warned that it would be a total misconception if either a dance instructor promoted or a potential student thought that "all the fashionable dances may be acquired in four or five lessons" (De Garmo 1875, 15).

In 1878, *How To Dance: A Complete Ball-Room and Party Guide* noted that at the time dancing was such a popular activity that "scarcely a social gathering is held at which dancing...does not take place." In order for any individual who wanted to learn "How to Dance," the publishers proudly promised its readers the following:

> We confidently state that by perusing its pages carefully, following the directions, and practicing the examples found therein, that any of our readers will be able to figure with as much grace and self-possession the ball-room as if they had just emerged from the tuition of some celebrated dancing-master (3).

Most of the book, which was published in New York by Tousey and Small, was basically a copy of Beadle and Company's 1868 publication *Beadle's Dime Ball-Room Companion and Guide to Dancing* and some other etiquette manuals of the 1840s and 1850s.

Although hundreds of self-help dance instruction books were available, one of the most widely circulated was *Dick's Quadrille Call-Book, and Ball-Room Prompter* (1878). Distributed by Dick and Fitzgerald, the subtitle explained the calls and figures for the Quadrille, as well as many other ballroom dances. Another publication, *Cartier and Baron's Practical Illustrated Waltz Instructor, Ball room Guide, and Call Book* (1879), gave "ample directions for dancing every kind of square and round dances." Numerous other "prompters" provided a listing of the figures to aid in the "calling" of the Quadrille. *The Prompter's Own Book of Rowe's Calls for the Ball*

Room (1878) included the Virginia Reel, Fisher's Hornpipe, Hull's Victory, and the Portland Fancy.

At the time two "radical additions" to the Quadrille (which at this time was often called the "Square Dance") was the Caller and the "waist swing." At first the waist swing was a simple "swing" as partners crossed left hand to left hand and placed right hands on their partners left shoulder. This "braced position" allowed the couple the momentum and "balance" to swing around. In some parts, the right hand was placed around the partner's waist and behind the back. This eventually gave way to the swing in the closed Waltz dance position, which many considered unacceptable. Eventually the "balance and swing" found its way into the genteel Quadrilles of the fashionable ballroom. Most, if not all, of the fashionable dance instructors and etiquette manuals considered the "balance and swing" as immoral and, therefore, could not be taught in society (Nevell 1977, 56–58).

As a result, two organizations of dance teachers formed in an attempt to regulate the so-called "corruption of the dance positions." In 1879, one such organization was the Society of Professors of Dancing. In 1883, the American National Association of Masters of Dancing was formed mainly to eliminate such dance styles as the "balance and swing" and to eliminate a Caller within the ballroom. According to dance historian Richard Nevell,

How To Dance: A Complete Ball-Room and Party Guide "confidently" promised its readers that they could learn how to dance. Published in New York by Tousey and Small, Publishers, 1878. Library of Congress, Music Division, http://lcweb2.loc.gov/musdi/098/0001.gif.

> The dancing masters of the day were horrified by this low-class verbalization because it was felt to be unattractive, not to mention threatening to them since their purpose was to teach the dances until the dancers knew the movement by heart (1977, 58).

In regards to the formation of these two societies, dance historians Sylvia Dannett and Frank Rachel claimed that "dancing for a time lost a good deal of its

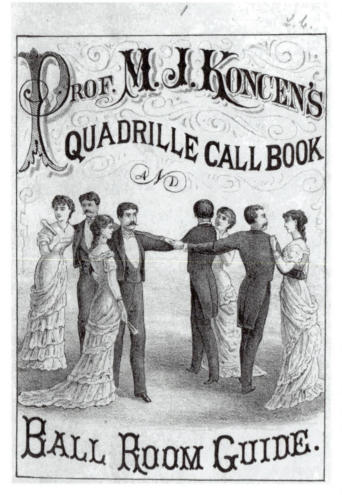

Prof. M. J. Koncen's Quadrille Call Book and Ball Room Guide contained 125 pages that included descriptions for the Grand March, the Waltz, the Boston, numerous versions of the Quadrille, 68 figures for The German, and some newer dances including the Glide Waltz. Published in St. Louis by S.F. Brearley and Co., 1883. Library of Congress, Music Division, http://lcweb2.loc.gov/musdi/109/0001.gif.

originality'' (1954, 56). During the 1880s, most of the numerous pamphlets and books published basically standardized the teaching of similar dances.

In 1884, however, George E. Wilson disagreed with attending dancing school. In *Wilson's Ball-Room Guide and Call Book* (1884), he wrote:

> No matter what teachers of dancing may assert, the most expedient and certainly best way to learn to dance is to stand up and try it; no one can ever learn by sitting quietly and looking on …attend a few good balls or parties with the theory in your mind, a good partner by your side, and you will become a finished dancer before those in the school have made their first attempt (1884, 11–12).

Similar to the 1878 Tousey and Small publication *How To Dance*, during the 1880s many other publications basically copied from previous dance instruction books. In 1883, for example, *Prof. M.J. Koncen's Quadrille Call Book and Ball Room Guide* by Mathias J. Koncen contained 125 pages that were basically compiled from other sources. Published in St. Louis by S.F. Brearley and Co., Koncen's instruction book included descriptions for the Grand March, the Waltz, the Boston, numerous versions of the Quadrille, 68 figures for The German, and some newer dances including the Glide Waltz.

Some other popular dance instruction manuals published during the 1880s included:

- C.H, Rivers, *A Full Description of Modern Dances* (1885);
- Elias Howe, *The Pocket Ball-Room Prompter* (1886);
- Edward Scott, *Dancing and Dancers* (1888);
- William E. Greene, *The Terpsichorean Monitor* (1889);
- Judson Sause, *The Art of Dancing* (1889);
- L.F. Segadlo, *Course of Instruction in Dancing* (1889);

- Herman À. Strassburg, Jr., *Call Book of Modern Quadrilles* (1889);
- *Wehman's Complete Dancing Master and Call Book* (1889).

Although the term "dance master" was sometimes applied to those authors, it was not in the same sense of the pre-nineteenth century usage.

At the time, similar to *Prof. M. J. Koncen* many of the dance teachers were simply called "Professor." In Brooklyn, for example, "Professor" J. L. Hartman was sometimes known as the "Dancing Professor." An article in *The Brooklyn Eagle* on September 8, 1889, for example, reported:

The Dancing Professor, He is Sure the Glide Waltz Will Hold Its Own.

Some of the other dances that were listed as favorites included the Glide Polka, Boston dip, the Newport, the Columbia, Court Quadrille, Waltz Lanciers, Saratoga Lanciers, and Quadrille variations, including the Society Quadrille and the Waltz Quadrille. He added, "we have a number of new dances this season...what is more they will be graceful and attractive." One of the new dances was the American Gavotte that simply started with a Galop step, followed by a Polka step, and a March step, all within 32 bars of music. Professor Hartman proclaimed,

I think I may safely say that dancing will be a far more important element in social life than ever before. The prejudice against dancing which was so prevalent a few years ago has now almost entirely disappeared. To be able to dance well is now an almost indispensable accomplishment for any young man or young woman who intends to enter society.

The professors, such as Hartman, who received newspaper attention also were those who taught the ballroom dances and the proper manners of the ballroom to the wealthy of society (*The Brooklyn Eagle*, September 8, 1889, 10).

By the 1890s, the majority of dances included the Two-Step and the Waltz as well as new music, marches from John Philip Sousa and Ragtime. At the time, a major technological breakthrough with the development of the Home Music Box and Thomas Edison's "Talking Box" allowed the public to hear Sousa's marches and Ragtime within the comfort of their own homes. In an age before radio and twentieth century developments in sound recording, the Home Music Box (which originated in Switzerland) had changeable cylinders, which produced musical sounds. The music box was self-contained within a large wooden cabinet, which served as an additional piece of furniture in a parlor or sitting room. The affordable music box was well within the price range of the middle class and some working class individuals. The music cylinders were also adapted for player pianos both in the home and in smaller dance venues such as a saloon. The music cylinders were sold in lots rather than as individual tunes. A contemporary mail-order catalog by Montgomery Ward Company, for example, advertised, "A very pleasant selection [of] hymns, popular airs, sets of quadrilles, Polkas, [and] Waltzes."

Soon thereafter, Thomas Edison conceived the idea of a "talking box" to reproduce the sound of a person's speaking voice. It was not considered as a replacement to the Home Music Box; however, the fact that it could reproduce the human voice, rather that musical notes, is what set it apart from the Home Music Box and the Player Piano. A short time thereafter, Edison combined the reproduction of both the voice and music on one phonographic record playable on a Victrola (Panati 1991, 17).

In addition to the musical advances was the advent of photography. In regards to social dancing, it meant that photographs could supplement the illustrations within the dance instruction books. One example was Melvin Ballou Gilbert's *Round Dancing* published in 1890 ("How to Read a Dance Manual," n.d.). Other popular dance instruction manuals during the 1890s included:

- Charles Link, *Unique Dancing Call Book* (1893);
- Edna Witherspoon, *The Perfect Art of Modern Dancing* (1894);
- F.L. Clendenen, *Fashionable Quadrille Call Book and Guide to Etiquette* (1899);
- Marguerite Wilson, *Dancing* (1899, reissued 1920).

However, of all the nineteenth century dance teachers and dance instruction books, none was more influential than Allen Dodworth's 1885 publication *Dancing and Its relations to Education and Social Life*.

ALLEN DODWORTH AND "DANCING AND ITS RELATIONS TO EDUCATION AND SOCIAL LIFE"

Allen Dodworth (b. 1817, d. 1896) was born in Sheffield, England, and in 1826 immigrated with his family to New York. In 1832, his father Thomas J. Dodworth, Sr., a highly trained musician, formed the National Brass Band, which was the first of its kind in America. The band included Allen and his brothers Charles, Thomas, and Harvey. Each of the boys was taught and played numerous instruments. Allen at the age of eight, for example, learned the piccolo. In his teens he also played trombone, cornet, and violin. By the time Allen was 25, he composed and arranged most of the bands repertoire, and he was also playing in the Philharmonic Orchestra. The band was soon renowned throughout America and was more commonly known as the Dodworth Band. The band played at presidential inaugurations including those of Van Buren, Harrison, Polk, Tyler, Buchanan, Lincoln, Grant, Garfield, and Cleveland. Later, Harvey succeeded his father as bandleader and instituted the idea of playing band concerts in public parks. During the Civil War, they formed a regiment band and set the standard for all future Brass Bands. The Dodworths also expanded their business to include managing other bands and orchestras and also arranging and publishing music.

It is not known when Allen first became interested in social dancing or when he first became intrigued with the idea of teaching dancing. Some indications are that he started during the mid-1830s. In either case, it is known that in 1842, Allen Dodworth left the band and opened his first dance studio, known as Dodworth's Dancing Academy, at 448 Broome Street at the corner of Broadway in lower Manhattan. A few years later, he opened a second Manhattan location at 806 Broadway and a branch school at 137 Montague Street in Brooklyn under the direction of his son Frank Dodworth. At the time that he opened his first academy, Dodworth almost immediately became the "most fashionable" dance teacher not only in New York but also in America. (The quick accession was most likely due to his family's prominent notoriety.) He was also joined by his wife Cally, for whom, in 1846, he wrote the "Cally Polka" (see Chapter 3). Cally Dodworth assisted her husband at the academy and was described as having "a wonderful business sense" (Richardson 1960, 114; O'Neill, "The Dodworth Family and Ballroom Dancing in New York," 1943, 48–54).

It was also no coincidence that the location of Dodworth's dance studios also coincided with the "fashionable part" of New York City. As industrialization changed the face of the urban city, so did the vast amount of wealth. As a result, many individuals of both "old money" and "new money" sought to separate themselves into "fashionable society." One method was to build large homes within prestigious neighborhoods of Manhattan, which, during the 1830s and 1840s, was the lower west side of Manhattan. However, as the lower portions of Manhattan became increasingly crowded because of immigration, the wealthy moved away to more prestigious uptown locations. In doing so, they also sought the refined manners of social dancing that individuals such as Dodworth provided. Therefore, as society moved

Sheet music cover of "The Cally Polka," written in 1846 by prominent dance instructor and musician Allen Dodworth in honor of his wife and business partner Cally Dodworth. Library of Congress, American Memory Collection, http://memory.loc.gov/music/sm2/sm1846/792000/792200/001.gif.

uptown, so did Allen Dodworth. In addition, the Dodworths, according to biographer Rosetta O'Neill, "were well aware of the social pattern of the city" (52). As a result, each summer the Dodworths also traveled to Europe and brought back the latest in European culture, fashion, and dances.

During the late 1850s, they moved the Dodworth Dancing Academy uptown to the corner of 26th Street and Fifth Avenue. (This location at 26th Street was later taken over by the fashionable Delmonico's restaurant—see later in this chapter.) At the time, Dodworth was still involved in the music business, and he published the influential *Brass Band School* (1853), which was basically an instruction manual on forming brass bands. By the late 1870s, he relocated once again to 681 Fifth Avenue near 54th Street. It was at this location that Dodworth installed a unique parquet floor inlaid with black squares and lines to facilitate the teaching of the placement of the dance students' feet. In 1885, with his nephew and assistant T. George Dodworth, he bought a building at 12 East 49th Street. According to O'Neill, it was turned into "one of the most beautiful rooms in the city." After Allen Dodworth's death in 1896, Mr. and Mrs. T. George Dodworth continued to operate the business in the same traditions as Allen and Cally until 1920 (O'Neill 1943, 52; Wright 1926, 169).

Mabel Osgood Wright, in her memoirs *My New York* (1926), recalled her "most joyful periods of youth" were during her two years at Dodworth's Dancing Academy at 26th Street and Fifth Avenue. Wright, who attended from 1869 to 1871, fondly described the building with "Broad steps with a deeply porticoed main entrance over which the letter 'D' was carved." Once inside, she said, the ballroom "which seemed immense" was lit mostly by natural light from "long square-topped windows" on two sides. As to the floor, she described it as, "A parquet floor smooth as ice." Prior to entering the ballroom, the students waited in a lobby. During the weekday afternoon sessions, Dodworth let the children in promptly at 3:00 P.M.—and not a moment earlier. She described him as "the courteous gracious gentleman" of medium height, with slender muscular build, hair slightly graying, a mustache, and as impeccably dressed. His dark-haired wife, Cally, was "shorter by more than a head" and also impeccably dressed in "black velvet with a stately sweep of skirt" (164–165).

The young girls dressed alike in white dresses "with ribbon sashes and shoulder knots, long white stockings and heelless black kid ankle ties." (The ankle ties prevented the shoe from flying about, "preventing a wild kick.") Most also had a small bag hung from their wrist to hold "gloves or a handkerchief." As the dance students entered the ballroom, musicians played, and the children walked both "singly and in pairs" directly to the Dodworths. In turn, each child, as the gender required, executed either a bow or a curtsy. They walked to assigned places along the wall (a seating area was reserved for parents). According to Wright, "walking was the inflexible rule" as the temptation to run and slide across the highly polished dance floor was quite tempting to the 10-year-old children or young teens. Occasionally, one would think that Dodworth was not looking and enjoy a slide. However, Dodworth always caught "the culprit." Without a word he clapped his hands, the music stopped, and the culprit was required to reenter the ballroom and "walk" to the appropriate place (165–167).

In fact, in *Assistant for A. Dodworth's Pupils*, a booklet written for and distributed only to his students, clear guidelines were listed for "entering the room." He explained, "To Those Who Attend the Afternoon Classes," as follows:

> Upon entering the room make your salutation to your teacher. Never run, but always walk across the room: and let your capability for refinement show itself in your walking (1878, 6–7).

The "walking" was actually an integral part of Dodworth's approach to elegant dancing. Wright added, "To see Allen Dodworth walk was in itself an education in motion and spoke of something more than mere technical training" (165).

The children were grouped in four classes depending upon their level of ability and learned Cotillions, Lancers, Quadrilles, the Polka Redowa, the Waltz, and even the Minuet. According to Mabel Osgood Wright, "perfecting" the Minuet was often "the climax of the season's work." In all classes, however, Dodworth tested his students in the dexterity of the Waltz. Wright described the test as "the waltzing of a single couple at a time, in a figure eight about two chairs in the middle of the hall, reversing frequently without change of direction." In dance class, especially when tested under the watchful eye of Dodworth, students such as Wright wished "for a well-balanced partner," which she described as follows:

> He must be a bit taller yet not too tall. He must be able to hold you lightly but firmly, without pressure, for not only was this a forbidden thing in the school, but being hugged made graceful reversing impossible.

However, Wright did not always get the "perfect partner" (171–172).

During her time at Dodworth's, she was frequently partnered with one youngster whom she nicknamed "Teddy Spectacles," a young boy who did not seem intent on perfecting his dancing skills. Instead, he always seemed to enjoy either tempting the old dance master or antagonizing his female partner, and Wright was not quite sure which Teddy Spectacles enjoyed most. Either during his daring slide across the highly polished "smooth as ice" parquet dance floor or during a dance, he did not miss an opportunity to give her "a quick but decisive kick under the ankle bone." During the years after dancing school she certainly did not miss that particular youngster. In fact, she basically lost touch with all her fellow dance students. However, in 1903, Wright received an apologetic note from "Teddy Spectacles." The short note simply stated,

> I am much amused to think that I should have met you at Dodworth's in the old days. Even now I remember how dreadfully I danced—T. R.

The return address was the White House, and the "T.R." was President Teddy Roosevelt (Wright 1926, 167–169).

Actually, despite the attempts of the young Teddy Roosevelt, Dodworth continually emphasized, "The dancing school is not a place of amusement." In the 1878 edition of *Assistant for A. Dodworth's Pupils*, Dodworth also strongly advised that each of his students demonstrate kindness and manners during social dancing. He added:

> At all times let there be an emulation of kindness to each other among the pupils. If nature has denied gracefulness or ready imitation to any, do not allow that to be a cause for unkind ridicule, but rather let your good nature prompt you to aid such, as it is they who require most assistance (7).

All told, eight editions of *Assistant for A. Dodworth's Pupils* were published during the years 1850 to 1879. The booklets were actually quite small at 2 3/8 inches by 3 3/8 inches and were comparative in size to a Dance Card. They each contained information on fashion, the manners of the ballroom, and hints for the dancers,

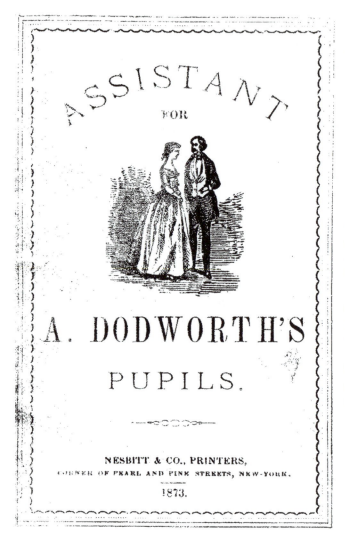

and each revised edition added more information. The 1873 edition, for example, contained 48 pages and the 1878 edition 64 pages.

It should be remembered that any of the potential dancers who possessed the *Assistant for A. Dodworth's Pupils* also had the previous experience of dance lessons with the master himself. Therefore, the written instructions were not as necessarily confusing as might first appear. His instructions for "Holding Partners," for example, was quite detailed and extended over two full pages. The description was for the basic closed dance position, more commonly known as the "Waltz position." At the time, the round dances were the most popular, and in turn the closed dance position was the one deemed most objectionable. However, according to Dodworth, the position required some basic knowledge, which he exhaustively provided. He began the description as follows:

> The gentleman approaches the lady by offering his left hand...The lady places her right hand in that of the gentleman, who then extends his right arm in direct line to the side, the forearm bent so as to form an acute angle. In this angle the lady will place herself, with the centre line of the person opposite the line of the gentleman's right side, both persons on parallel lines, not forming an angle (20).

The illustration above is an 1873 edition of a pamphlet *Assistant for A. Dodworth's Pupils*, printed by Allen Dodworth for the use of his students. The pamphlets were actually quite small at 2 3/8 inches by 3 3/8 inches and contained information on fashion, the manners of the ballroom, and hints for the dancers. Library of Congress, Music Division, http://memory.loc.gov/musdi/012/0001.gif.

The position of the head was important, so that each was "looking over the other's right shoulder." The importance of not being face-to-face was to "prevent all possibility of taking each other's breath." A situation that Dodworth explained "as many ladies have remarked" was, in fact, "rarely pleasant." He was quick to point out that the reason for the unpleasantry was that most young men used a "meerschaum" (a tobacco pipe), and therefore their breath was "positively horrid" (20).

Dodworth continued on with the detailed description for the holding of partners. He was quite conscious of societies' visual imagery of the ideal couple. In fact,
throughout almost all of American cultural history, social custom dictated that the
man always be slightly taller than the woman. Cognizant of that fact, Dodworth
was also aware that the height differential could not be too great. Therefore he
wrote:

> The lady, if not too short, places her left hand, hooked, upon the gentleman's right
> shoulder, the fingers appearing in front. The right hand of the gentleman should rest
> very gently upon the lady's back, as near the waist as possible, so as not to remove the
> upward pressure of the elbow directly under the lady's shoulder, as this is the lady's
> support, and must be held with sure, but gentle firmness (20–21).

It was also of utmost importance that the gentleman's hand "rest very lightly" on
the lady's back. A suggestion that the palm not lay flat on her back "so that the
air may pass between" was accentuated by the caution that such "close contact
induces perspiration, and may leave its mark upon the lady's dress." In the past,
in order to prevent such an occurrence, it was always the custom for both gentlemen and ladies to wear gloves. However, in many cases, most simply did not wear
them. The practice of foregoing gloves dated to 1860, when the Prince of Wales,
Edward VII, made a highly publicized tour of the United States. The Prince was
known for dancing without gloves, and many Americans followed his fashion lead
(see Chapter 3). In fact, Dodworth made reference to the prince, as he conceded:

> What may we expect, therefore, from those young men who, in dancing, recklessly soil
> the beautiful fabrics of women's costumes with perspiring hands, rather than avoid that
> injury by wearing gloves? Their only excuse is that such is the fashion, copied from the
> habits of a dissipated prince (1900, 22).

Nevertheless, Dodworth continually advised that all gentlemen wear gloves as a
consideration to their partner.

Dodworth continued discussing the detailed instructions for the position of
holding a partner. He added:

> Both persons should be slightly bent forward, from the hips upward, so that the shoul-
> ders may be only three or four inches apart, but the distance increasing downward; this
> leaves both parties free in their limbs, so that any contact of person or knees may be
> avoided, and should be so avoided as a most serious mistake. The gentleman's left hand
> holding the lady's right, should be extended downward in a line with the body, the
> hands three or four inches distant from the person, the arms forming a gentle curve
> from the shoulders downward.

In order to aid in the description, in 1885, in *Dancing and Its Relations to Education
and Social Life*, Dodworth included four "Illustrations of Positions in Dancing."
The first was deemed "The proper way." The second illustration was deemed
"not in good taste" since the arms were extended too far and the lady's right hand
was grasping the gentleman's left arm rather than gently placing it upon his right
shoulder. In the third, Dodworth objected that the "lady's head [was] too close"

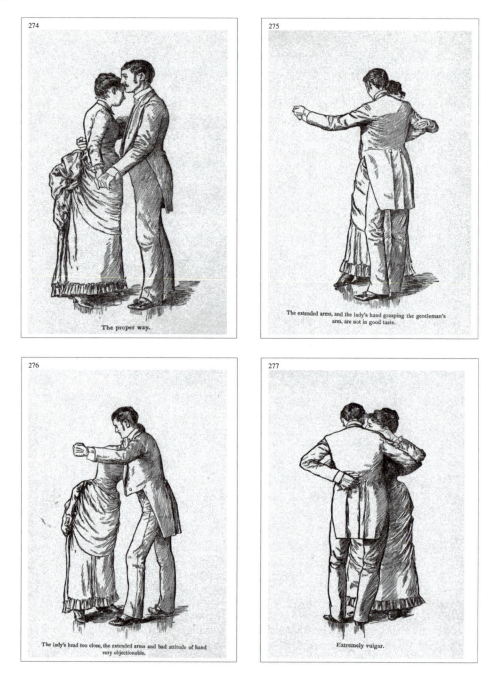

Illustrations from *Dancing and Its Relations to Education and Social Life*, by Allen Dodworth, c. 1900 (274–277), indicated the proper and improper dance positions. The illustration at top left was considered "The proper way." Top right: "The extended arms, and the lady's hand grasping the gentleman's arm, are not in good taste." Bottom left: "The lady's head too close, the extended arms and bad attitude of hand very objectionable." Bottom right: "Extremely vulgar."   Library of Congress.

and the placement of the hand was "very objectionable." The final illustration, which portrayed the couple in a close embrace was simply described as "Extremely vulgar" (1900, 274–277).

Actually, Allen Dodworth's, 1885 publication *Dancing and Its Relation to Education and Social Life* (sometimes simply referenced as *Dancing*) is considered a classic in the study of nineteenth century social dancing. Published by Harper and Brothers in both New York and London, it was not only a dance instruction manual for both theory and practical application, it also encapsulated a history of social dance from about 1830 to 1890. His biographer, Rosetta O'Neill, for example, claimed that in regards to *Dancing*, "A more vivid and concise history of a major development in American social dancing probably does not exist in print" (1943, 48). At first glance, some of Dodworth's discussion might seem out-of-date. However, as dance historian Lloyd Shaw aptly pointed out:

> But he is very emphatic as to how each dance should be done and seems to turn the clock back in some cases to a style that has been dropped for many years. Then you notice his footnotes and under the polka you find "Introduced to my pupils in 1845." You suddenly remember it was only brought to this country in 1844 (Shaw 1949, 45).

In reality, the publication was actually an accumulation of over 50 years of Dodworth's teaching and experience. O'Neill added, "In these writings we have a complete and perhaps the only accurate record of fashionable dancing in New York" (1943, 52).

Dancing and Its Relation to Education and Social Life contained over 300 pages of a detailed analysis of all the facets of social dancing, including manners, posture, positions, and step descriptions. The Table of Contents was quite thorough with the chapter headings titles as follows:

I. Personal
II. Introduction
III. Manners, or Morality Of Motion
IV. Positions And Motions
V. General Directions Applicable To All Round Dances
VI. Galop
VII. Racket and Polka, And The Various Dances Formed From The Same Motions
VIII. Waltz And Knickerbocker
IX. Walking—Salutations
X. Quadrille And other Figure Dances (So-Called Square Dances)
XI. Lancers
XIII. Minuet
XIV. Virginia Reel—Polonaise
XV. Dance Music
XVI. Cotillion or German
Conclusion, To Teachers Of Dancing
Illustrations of Positions in Dancing
Appendix of Additional Dances

Within the chapter "Cotillion or German," for example, he provided a numerical listing and steps for over 250 figures. The German, during the late nineteenth century, was one of the most popular ballroom social dances.

In Chapter IV, "Positions And Motions," Dodworth offered a teaching method unlike any other of the time. Since he was unaware of any similar teaching method, he therefore named it the "Dodworth Method," claiming that it was "the most thorough method yet devised for conveying ideas of motion by language" (26). The Dodworth Method was "six radical motions," which included the change, the slide, the step, the leap, the hop, and the halt. He claimed that every contemporary dance contained at least two of these motions. He explained the following simple observation:

> Every dance now in use is composed of two or more of these radical motions. Knowing these, therefore, enables a learner to comprehend any description by this method without difficulty. Many persons will have difficulty in believing that the waltz and polka, as now danced, are composed of precisely the same three motions; but the fact is easily demonstrated (1900, 30).

With the benefit of his vast musical background, he also corresponded the six motions of the Dodworth Method with music. Above the sheet music staff lines he simply wrote the one word such as "Leap" or "Slide" or "Change" perpendicular to the corresponding musical notes. He also included "six elements" for the "good playing of dance music." They included Speed (the technical term was tempo), Regularity, Distinct Phrasing, Exact Accent, Musical Expression, and Vim. The final part, Dodworth said, was an important element to provide "enthusiasm, energy, excitability, something of the kind almost inexpressible in language but vividly felt when present in a pianist" (1900, 140–141).

In Chapter V under "General Directions Applicable to all Round Dances," Dodworth dispelled the "Absurdity of the Notion that one Cannot Learn without a Partner."

> The belief so prevalent among men that the round dances cannot be learned without the assistance of a partner is simply absurd...nor can any one dance well with a partner until he can dance well alone...not until the learner can move himself has he the right to ask others to move with him (31–33).

The main idea was to produce "self-reliance" and confidence in the proper execution of the particular dance. It was a tactic that was especially geared towards the gentleman. Dodworth added, "It is a curious and suggestive fact that ladies usually learn without assistance of this kind" (31).

Dancing and Its Relation to Education and Social Life was reprinted in revised editions in 1888, 1900, 1902, and 1905. The 1900 edition, published four years after Allen's death, was only slightly revised and contained an introduction by his assistant and nephew T. George Dodworth. (In 1914, George became the first president of the New York Society of Teachers of Dancing.) However, no summation of Allen Dodworth's contribution to nineteenth century social dance was more succinctly stated that by dance historian John Martin. In a preface comment to

Rosetta O'Neill's biographical essay, "The Dodworth Family and Ballroom Dancing in New York" in *Dance Index*, Martin wrote, "It is safe to say that no other figure in nineteenth century America made a greater contribution to the [social] dance than Allen Dodworth did" (1943, 43).

THE CAKEWALK, RAGTIME, AND "THAT TAKES THE CAKE"

The Cakewalk was most popular during the 1890s, reaching its peak around 1896 or 1897, coinciding with Ragtime music. The origin of the Cakewalk (sometimes Cake Walk) traces to African American slaves during the nineteenth century. Most historians agree that the Cakewalk first originated on the southern plantations; however, it is quite possible that it came to America from the Caribbean plantations. In a fashion similar to the development of the Jig, Clogging, and Breakdown (see Chapter 2), African Americans looked at the European American styles and copied some of the elements of the formal dances. Therefore, in the Cakewalk, African American slaves most likely developed the strutting dance to mimic the formal dancing of the wealthy plantation owners. Dance historians Marshall and Jean Stearns speculated that it developed from a dance called the Walk-Around that might have been directly related to the African tribal Ring Shouts. The Walk-Around was often used by African Americans, similar to the Grand March or the Promenade, as the finale to Minstrel shows (see Chapter 3). In either case, the Cakewalk is definitely a hybrid of various forms of dance styles including European, American, and African traditions (Stearns and Stearns 1994, 123).

The Cakewalk more closely resembled a strutting style of walk than an actual dance. In essence, it was basically a "style in walking" in the promenade position. In the dance, a man and a woman stood side-by-side. The man held his hand out, the lady placed a hand in his (sometimes they would interlock arms), and they promenaded. They sauntered and strutted with exaggerated movement of the heads and torso, high stepping in time to the music of a Sousa march, or later syncopated Ragtime music. They sometimes incorporated elements of other dances such as the Two-Step and the Polka. The performances would resemble almost comedic antics involving wobbly knees, tipping high hats, and using a cane as a prop. Sometimes an entire group would do the Cakewalk, en masse, composed of couples and individuals. In 1903, the American Mutoscope and Biograph Company made three film shorts *Cake Walk*, *Cake Walk on the Beach*, and *Comedy Cakewalk*. The film shorts are an excellent sampling from the period and are viewable on the DVD *America Dances! 1897–1948* (see bibliography).

It was also common at an elite formal ball given by whites to have African Americans strut the Cakewalk performance-like for the entertainment of the white elite. Prizes were given to the "best couple," which was usually a cake. Speculation was that the expression "that takes the cake" comes from the prize awarded for the Cakewalk competition. The style of having African Americans perform at formal balls most likely originated in Florida during the 1880s. At the time, Florida was a fashionable winter resort for the wealthy. Dance historians Sylvia Dannett and Frank Rachel claim that Charles Johnson and Dora Dean introduced the Cakewalk in 1893 to the wealthy vacationers (Dannett and Rachel 1954, 65).

In 1897, the first "official" Cakewalk contest, comprising mainly African Americans, was held in New York City at Madison Square Garden (some date it as early as 1892). Similar competitions were held throughout the country in hundreds of Cakewalk dance contests. A 1902 article in *The Brooklyn Eagle*, for example, described one such dance contest held at Coney Island in Brooklyn. They described the Cakewalk as "old-fashioned" and "one time popular." As if to imply the authenticity of the dance, they reported, "Every entry was a real Negro." In reality, the statement revealed the segregation sentiment that existed nationwide ("A Plantation Cake Walk Makes Much Merriment," 4).

At the time, however, racial segregation was prevalent, and Americans maintained an indifference towards African American culture. In one instance, the ultra-wealthy Mr. and Mrs. William K. Vanderbilt hired a noted performer named Tom Fletcher to teach them the Cakewalk in their opulent Fifth Avenue mansion. However, word of the Vanderbilt's learning the Cakewalk prompted criticism. In 1899,

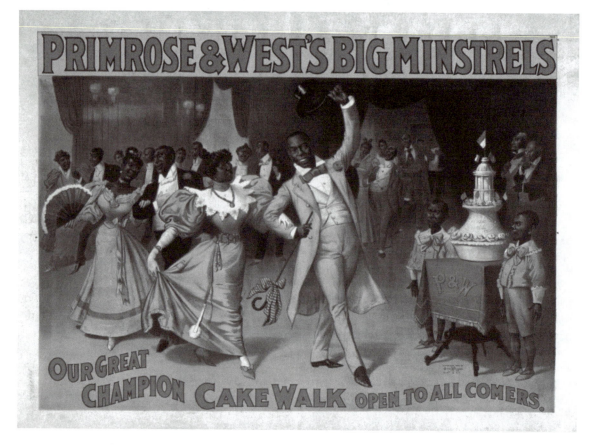

It was common to have African Americans strut the Cakewalk performance-like for the entertainment of whites at an elite formal ball. Speculation was that the expression "that takes the cake" comes from the prize awarded for the Cakewalk competition. This illustration for Primrose and West's Big Minstrels traveling show, advertising a competition for "Our great champion cake walk, open to all comers," is from the Strobridge Lith. Co., c. 1896.   Library of Congress, Prints and Photographs Division LC-USZ62-24432.

the trade magazine the *Musical Courier* provided harsh opposition to both the Cakewalk and, most likely, the Vanderbilts:

> Society has decreed that ragtime and cake-walking [sic] are the thing, and one reads with amazement and disgust of historical and aristocratic names joining in this sex dance, for the cake walk is nothing but an African danse du ventre, a milder edition of African orgies.

The clergy was also particularly harsh when criticizing the Cakewalk. An article in *The Brooklyn Eagle* newspaper on March 22, 1902, for example, reported "Cakewalk Shocked Pastor." The article reported the following:

> Members of the Windsor Terrace M.E. Church attended a social function…and in a moment of forgetfulness started a dance…This dancing which is forbidden to Methodists was so enjoyable that before they knew it the church goers were indulging in a cakewalk.

The Reverend McLean heard of the "dancing" and during a service called on those who danced to "be saved from their evil ways." The so-called "culprits" were members of the church choir and tendered their resignations ("Cakewalk Shocked Pastor," 20).

Nevertheless, by the late 1890s and into the early 1900s, the Cakewalk was a popular fad dance within the wealthy ballrooms. In a similar fashion, wealthy whites often mimicked the Cakewalk style of African Americans and jaunted throughout the fashionable ballrooms. In addition, between 1900 and 1904 famed American musician John Philip Sousa toured Europe making stops in London, Paris, and Moscow. With his American marches, he brought the Cakewalk and introduced it to Europeans (Stearns and Stearns 1994, 122–123).

By the 1890s, elements of syncopated rhythm in the music were combined with the strutting and prancing of the Cakewalk. At about the same time, Ragtime music (sometimes simply referred to as "Rag") developed as a popular American music form. Ragtime music itself was firmly rooted in African American tradition and was soon intertwined with the Cakewalk. Ragtime music had a slightly faster syncopated beat than the Sousa military bands' music. The distinguishing feature between the Sousa marches and Ragtime was the addition of syncopation. Agnes DeMille described syncopation and its relation to dancing. In *America Dances* she writes,

> A new kind of "rhythm" took over in the nation's songs and dances; the accent was placed, not on the downbeat as in European, one-two, but on the upbeat, or offbeat, one-two. This was African but it became American. Rhythmic beats began to be missed, and the accent slipped to unexpected counts….Now the Americans were clapping and stamping their dances on the offbeat (1980, 13).

Syncopation added a beat in between the basic 1-2-3-4 so that the music would be played 1&2, 3&4, or described differently as "ba-da-bump" played within two beats of music.

It is quite possible that in 1897 "Mississippi Rag," composed by William H. Krell, was the first Ragtime song. Later that same year, Tom Turpin composed and released another song "Harlem Rag." Soon thereafter, Ragtime swept America and included songs by Rag composers such as Turpin, W.C. Handy, James Scott, Louis Chauvin, Joseph Lamb, and Scott Joplin. Ragtime was quickly embraced and enjoyed by younger adults, both white and African American, but older adults objected. By the early 1900s, Ragtime was enjoyed by many Americans across ethnic, social, and economic barriers (McCarthy 1982, 9; Stearns and Stearns 1994, 122–123).

The Cakewalk, therefore, represented the first time in American history that both blacks and whites were dancing the same social dance. It also represented the first time that Americans were influenced by an African American trend. Therefore, the Cakewalk represented a "fundamental change" that had a profound affect on twentieth century American social dancing. According to dance historians Marshall and Jean Stearns,

> In the 20th century the dances that the lower classes did would have much more profound an effect on American social dancing than the dances being done by the wealthy. We would look not to the elegant ballroom, but the rowdy dancehall for inspiration.... The form of the blend was largely European, but the music, and especially the dances, were in the American grain (1994, 124).

After the introduction of the Cakewalk, it could not be denied that the development of the most popular American vernacular dances for the twentieth century would be introduced from either African American or Latin American traditions of dance and music.

THE CANCAN AND THE TWO-STEP

Around 1890, a Parisian dance that "caused quite a stir" in America was the Cancan (sometimes Can-Can or Skirt dancing). Most attributed the Cancan to a French dancing master named Chicard who developed it in the Montparnasse area of Paris. Within a few years it was mostly associated with the Moulin Rouge dance hall in that same area. At the time, the French artist Henri de Toulouse-Lautrec made the Cancan dancers a popular subject of his drawings and paintings. Yet others place it as a group dance similar to the Polka, danced as early as 1822. In either case, during the late nineteenth century it was mainly a music hall stage dance performed only by women. At that time it was usually banned in most public places as "against the rules of morals and decency to dance it." In the Cancan, five, six, or more women linked arm-in-arm, facing the audience, raised their skirts with both hands, and alternately kicked one leg high into the air. The music was often fast-paced and lively. In some cases a solitary performer did the Cancan. According to dance historian Curt Sachs, it was the best Cancan dancer "who can knock the spectator's hat off his head with her foot" (Sachs 1963, 440).

Typically, the Cancan dancers wore long black dresses layered with frilly often-colorful petticoats. As the woman lifted and kicked her leg high in the air, she revealed not only her petticoat, but also, black silk-stockinged legs. At a time when

In the Cancan, five, six, or more women linked arm-in-arm, facing the audience, raised their skirts with both hands, and alternately kicked one leg high into the air. The music was often fast-paced and lively. It was the best Cancan dancer "who can knock the spectator's hat off his head with her foot." This illustration is from a poster, c. 1898.   Library of Congress, Prints and Photographs Division POS-TH-1898.P37, no. 6.

merely showing a woman's ankle was considered quite immodest, the Cancan dancer showed the entire leg. Needless to say, it was often considered a risqué dance. In America, the Cancan was a favorite on the stage in frontier theaters in America. A Hollywood movie appropriately titled *Moulin Rouge* (1952) glamorized both the dance hall and the dance. It survived at the end of the twentieth century mainly as a theatrical dance for the stage in showy places such as Las Vegas, Atlantic City, Disney World, and even the original Moulin Rouge in Paris (Dannett and Rachel 1954, 58).

By the late nineteenth century, Paris was still the leader of the social dance world. In America, by the 1890s, the most popular dances were the German (cotillion), the Quadrille, the Polka, and the Waltz—all dances that either originated in Paris or were introduced there. However, in America a new dance was introduced that did not pass through Paris—it was the Two-Step. (The late nineteenth century dance was different from the late twentieth century Texas Two-Step and Country Two-Step.)

An early description of the Two-Step was found in the 1878 publication of *Dick's Quadrille Call-Book, and Ball-Room Prompter*, published by Dick and Fitzgerald in New York. *Dick's* described the Two-Step as follows:

> The "two-step...is nothing more nor less than the old Polka without the hop...The heels must be kept as near to the floor as is possible without touching it, care being taken to overcome the least tendency to hop or leap (149).

At the time, *Dick's* limited discussion of the Two-Step was due in part to the fact that the publishers introduced the new dance as the "latest fad" adding the speculation that "perhaps it will prove to be only a fad." However, they did add that because of its "extreme simplicity" it might "become a lasting favorite" (148–149).

Actually, from 1890 to 1910, the Two-Step became one of the most popular dances in all parts of America. It was as popular at sedate elite formal balls as it was in rural areas during barn dances and community socials. The Two-Step was basically a simple dance that contained some marching chassés steps. Dance historians Dannett and Rachel described it as "a simple dance, not much more than a double-quick march, with a skip in each step, done as rapidly as a couple could go forward, backward, and turn" (1954, 63). *The Complete Book of Ballroom Dancing* described that the Two-Step "consisted of a series of chassés either forward or sideward to 2/4 or 4/4 music...a quick march with a skip in each step." A chassé is three changes of weight alternating each foot with a close of the free foot next to the foot supporting the weight (Stephenson and Iaccarino 1992, 19, 71).

The popularity of the dance coincided with the popularity of the bandleader John Philip Sousa's marches. In 1891, Sousa's "The Washington Post March" was a new musical form that was described as "lively and different with a new kind of beat." The music "caught on immediately," and Americans found that the marching steps of the Two-Step worked well with Sousa's music. In fact, they worked so well together that the dance was often called The Washington Post or even The Washington Post Two-Step. In a short time, Americans cast aside the Quadrilles, Waltzes, and Polkas in favor of the Two-Step. As a result, in rapid succession Sousa wrote over 90 musical tunes with the beat for the Two-Step (Dannett and Rachel 1954, 63).

In fact, the combination of the march rhythms of Sousa's music and the attachment of the simple Two-Step dance was also picked up by Europe. Dance historian Don McDonagh called the Two-Step,

> A simple dance with an exciting beat, it alternated between an open and closed position and became the most popular dance of the Gay Nineties on both sides of the Atlantic (1986, 70).

Up until this time, America had always followed the European tradition of introducing a popular social dance. In Paris, for example, a French publication of G. Desrat's *Traité de la Danse* (1900) provided instructions for the Washington Post Two-Step and the Cakewalk. Both dances were distinctly American and represented a shift that European dances were now imported from America ("Nineteenth Century Social Dance," n.d.).

A video clip performance of the Washington Post Two-Step, danced to John Philip Sousa's "Washington Post March" is viewable from the Music Division of the Library of Congress online source *An American Ballroom Companion: Dance Instruction Manuals Ca. 1490–1920*, as well as Dancetime Publications' *500 Years of Social Dance: Volume I: The 15th to 19th Centuries* (see bibliography).

THE REDISCOVERY OF ENGLISH COUNTRY-DANCING AND THE LEGACY OF CECIL SHARP

During the late nineteenth century, a revived spirit of nationalism swept across Europe. In particular, England was consumed with a predominant obsession of national pride. However, as it applied to social dance, England was totally unaware of its history of the Country-dances. As strange as it may sound, by the end of the nineteenth century, England had basically lost track of the fact that the Playford English Country-dances actually existed and originated in England (see Chapter 1). For the most part, by the mid-nineteenth century in both England and in America, the Country-dances had basically faded from the social dance scene.

In 1915, in regards to the English Country-dance, music ethnologist Cecil Sharp noted, "Up until a few years ago, it was commonly believed that the English race was the only one in Europe that had made no contribution of any value to the universal store of folk-song and dance." In 1878, for example, *Dick's Quadrille Call-Book, and Ball-Room Prompter* had the same misconception, claiming,

> The French Contre Danse became corrupted into the English Country Dance, with that characteristic facility that the English have of calling and spelling foreign words to suit themselves (103).

At the time, even contemporary British works mistakenly credited the French *Contredanses* as the original source and that the English merely copied the form and translated the word to "Country Dances." However, Sharp correctly surmised that, in fact, it was the other way. He wrote:

> So far from deriving our Country Dance from France, it was the French who adapted one particular form of the English dance known as the "Square-eight," developed it, called it Contredanse, and sent it back to England, where in the Quadrille, one of its numerous varieties, it still survives.

Sharp's extensive research presented "conclusive" evidence that England did indeed have a storied history of original social dancing "and in great abundance, [that] cannot longer be disputed." But at first, Sharp actually stumbled upon the Country-dances (Sharp, "English Folk Dance: The Country Dance," 658–659).

As early as 1899, Englishman Cecil Sharp (b. 1859, d. 1924), himself a musician, traveled the English countryside in search of traditional folk music. In Headington, a small town in Oxfordshire, he stumbled upon some musicians playing old country-tunes. In response to the music, a group of villagers danced in a manner that he was totally unaccustomed to. (Sharp's knowledge of social dancing was basically the Waltz and other ballroom dances.) Intrigued, he traveled the English countryside and observed a few other folk dances including the ritual Sword and Morris dances. The dances he discovered closely resembled the English Country-dances within the works of John Playford (see Chapter 1).

As a result, Sharp published some introductory works on the subject including *An Introduction to the English Country Dance* and *The Country Dance Book*, which he continually added to and published in six parts from 1911 through 1922. His publications led in part to a revival of English Country-dancing. In 1911, in order "to preserve intact the traditions," he cofounded the English Folk Dance Society and also started a branch in America. At the Society, he taught and lectured on the English Country-dances. Sharp astutely pointed out, "The revival, it should be pointed out, is not peculiar to this country. A similar movement is being prosecuted, and with a like enthusiasm, in the United States of America" (Sharp, "English Folk Dance: The Country Dance," 1915, 660).

Ironically, it was when Sharp left England and traveled to America that he found an abundance of traditional English Country-dancing that had long been forgotten in his own homeland. In August 1914, his summer classes were interrupted by war in Europe. His son Charles enlisted in the British army, but at 54 years old, Sharp was too old for military duty. The war curtailed his teaching and, therefore, he was out of work. A friend enlisted Sharp to consult on a Broadway stage show in New York, and in December 1914, he sailed aboard the *S.S. Lusitania* to America. (The following year, the *Lusitania* was torpedoed by a German submarine and hastened America's entry into World War I.) In addition to the rehearsals, he lectured on English Folk music in many cities including New York, Philadelphia, Boston, Chicago, and Pittsburgh. Along with his travels, he established the U.S.A. English Folk Dance Society with branches in New York, Boston, Chicago, and Pittsburgh. Somewhere along his travels, he discovered that the English Country-dances had long ago "taken root in America" and were still danced in the remote Appalachian Mountain regions. As a result, he, along with a small group of followers, planned an excursion into those areas (Karpeles 1967, 123–127).

His biographer Maud Karpeles had the unique distinction of accompanying Sharp during his American travels and the excursion into the Appalachians. However, even in the United States, little was known of the "mountain people." In *Cecil Sharp: His Life and Work*, Karpeles recalled, "We were told by our New York and Boston friends that we should find ourselves among a wild and dangerous community" (1967, 146). What they found instead were the roots of English Country-dancing preserved and passed on among the generations. For it was in the American mountain regions that many of the English Country-dances had remained, literally hidden from urban society for almost 100 years. The separation of culture can best be attributed to the fact of industrialization. At the time, both England and America were in the midst of the Industrial Revolution. As a result more industry was centered in urban areas, and less reliance was placed upon the rural areas. In the urban areas, new cultural trends developed and separated themselves from the remote countryside.

Between the years 1916 and 1918, Cecil Sharp and his group spent a total of 12 months in the remote areas of the Southern Appalachian Mountains including the in states of Alabama, North Carolina, South Carolina, Georgia, Kentucky,

Tennessee, Virginia, and West Virginia. They stayed over one month in Tennessee and over three months each in North Carolina, Virginia, and Kentucky. The travel was arduous, oftentimes requiring riding mules "over the mountain passes or along the creeks." In many cases they walked, sometimes 15 or 16 miles in a single day. All told, they visited over 70 "small towns and settlements" (Karpeles 1967, 140–144).

They discovered that, unlike the "invitation only" dances of the fashionable ballrooms, in the mountain regions a dance was an occasion for all to attend. Karpeles noted, "There is no such thing as a private party in the mountains; all come who wish, whether invited or not" (1967, 164). But it was because of the remote location that they found the Country-dances in their purest form, since they had not been influenced by outside sources. In Kentucky, for example, Sharp witnessed the four-couple square formation and named it the Kentucky Running set (see Chapter 2). In the introduction to *The Country Dance Book, Part 5*, Sharp expressed his sheer delight over his anthropological discovery. He described his observation as follows:

> It was danced one evening after dark on the porch of one of the largest houses...with only one dim lantern to light up on the scene. But the moon streamed fitfully in lighting up the mountain peaks in the background and, casting its mysterious light over the proceedings, seemed to exaggerate the wildness and the break-neck speed of the dancers as they whirled through the mazes of the dance. There was no music, only the stamping and clapping of the onlookers...the air seemed literally to pulsate with the rhythm of the "patters" and the tramp of the dancers' feet, while, over and above it all, penetrating through the din, floated the even falsetto tones of the Caller, calmly and unexcitedly reciting his directions (quoted in Karpeles 1967, 164).

As a result, Sharp concluded that the Appalachian Mountain dances were, in fact, the earliest form of English Country-dance. All told Sharp cataloged over 600 folk songs and hundreds of dances (Nevell 1977, 41; Harris, Pittman, et al., 2000, 84–85, 127).

In June 1924, Sharp died in England; however, his dance legacy continued. In June 1930, a dedication ceremony was held for a new building to house the English Folk Dance Society in London at 2 Regents Park Road, NW. 1. The cornerstone of the building was inscribed with the following words:

> This building is erected in memory of Cecil Sharp who restored to the English people the songs and dances of their country.

During World War II, the building was partially destroyed during the blitz of London. In 1951, the building was restored, and at the rededication ceremony Princess Margaret proclaimed that it had been renamed the "Cecil Sharp House: The English Folk Dance and Song Society." The building was still intact at the beginning of the twenty-first century and served as a valuable research center, sponsoring workshops and classes in all styles of English and American traditional dances from the seventeenth to twenty-first centuries. These included American

The Cecil Sharp House, home of the English Folk Dance and Song Society, at 2 Regents Park Road in London. The building shown here was still intact at the beginning of the twenty-first century.   Photo by Thelma Lynn Olsen.

Social dancing, Ballroom, Latin, America-style "Barndances" of Square sets, contras, couples dances, and, of course, English Country-dance.

By the end of the twentieth century, English Country-dancing was still very much alive in America. In 1997, columnist Linda Wolfe, of *The New York Times*, noted, "for several thousand Americans across the country, such dancing is not something that has vanished, but an activity in which they engage regularly." Wolfe imparted a bit of history adding:

> The dances faded into oblivion in the latter half of the 19th century, but they were resuscitated early in the 20th by the English musicologist Cecil Sharp, who studied old dance books, clarified the choreography and founded country dance societies in both England and the United States.

By the end of the twentieth century and into the twenty-first century, reenactments of the English Country-dances known as "Playford Balls" occurred in many areas of the United States. Over one dozen English Country-dance societies in the New York metropolitan area offered workshops, including the Elegant Arts Society, the Metropolitan Dance, both in Manhattan, and the English Country

An English Country-dance Assembly held in a mid-nineteenth century courthouse in Historical Richmondtown. The participants are dressed in period costumes from the eighteenth and nineteenth centuries.   Photo by Thelma Lynn Olsen.

Dancing Assembly of the Staten Island Historical Society (Wolfe, "In Step With Austen: English Country Dancing," 1997).

Throughout the United States over 600 groups participated in English Country-dancing with over 100 societies sponsoring workshop sessions culminating in a dance assembly. They included the Vintage Dance Society in Hartford, Connecticut; the Commonwealth Vintage Dancers in Boston; Mixed Pickles Vintage Dance Company in Philadelphia; the Bay Area English Regency Society in San Francisco; the Louisiana Vintage Dances in Baton Rouge; the Triangle Vintage Dance Society in Raleigh-Durham, North Carolina; the Lexington Vintage Dance Society in Kentucky; and the Grand Traditions Vintage Dance Academy in Ann Arbor, Michigan, to name a few. In Nashville, Tennessee, for example, an annual event attracted many of the regional societies as well as those from Canada, Europe, and Australia. In almost all cases, the participants dressed in period costumes from the eighteenth and nineteenth centuries, and many of the English Country-dances were the same as those Cecil Sharp had prescribed and written down between 1911 and 1922 (Needham 2002, 57; Wolfe 1997).

English Country-dancing was also a favorite at many local branches of the Jane Austen Society of North America. Some were attracted to the dancing by a fascination with the literature of Jane Austen (Austen often made reference to Country-dancing in her novels). Others were enthralled by the numerous television and

Hollywood movies that romanticized the Austen novels. Linda Wolfe of *The New York Times* speculated:

> For many filmgoers and television watchers, the stately dancing in the recent spate of Jane Austen dramatizations stirred a touch of culture envy: a longing for a presumably lost Eden of elegance, for forms of social intercourse less brash and brazen than our own.

A Hollywood film remake of Jane Austen's *Pride &Prejudice* (2005), for example, featured a significant number of English Country-dances.

Others liked the dance style because of the simplicity of the footwork, but the intricate weaving patterns also required a dutiful concentration that occupied the mind and relieved the dancer of any outside thoughts. *The New York Times* columnist Linda Wolfe, for example, was also a participant in English Country-dances. She described her fascination as follows:

> I've never found a form as lifting to the spirit, let alone the feet, as English country.... Partly it's because this is a very social form of dancing; participants dance not just with a partner but also with a group or set of other dancers...And partly it's because English country dancing offers two things that seldom come together in one pursuit: aerobic activity (some dances can be quite strenuous) and intellectual stimulation (the dances are complex, requiring concentration and diligence).

Sharp himself noted: "Every movement should...be executed quietly, easily, and with an economy of motion, and in a simple unaffected manner" (1951, 10).

In 2002, dance historian Maureen Needham called the English Country-dance "the longest-lived ballroom dancing form to survive in North America." However, she noted, as with many styles of dancing, the English Country-dance groups were split into "Traditionalists" and "Revivalists." Needham described the Traditionalists as those who "perform idiosyncratic regional versions of traditional dances." On the other hand, she described the Revivalists as those who "adhere strictly to Sharp's written instructions for these dances" (Needham, 9, 57).

In either case, Cecil Sharp himself knew that if the dances were to remain in existence, the English Country-dances should be easy and fun to dance. In 2002, dance historians Kate Van Winkle Keller and Genevieve Shimer speculated that if the fun was lost, then the English Country-dances "would be relegated to the library shelf once again." They explained that,

> [Cecil Sharp] was committed to making the dances appropriate for an informal setting: not for display, but for recreation. He chose a style adapted to suit the average [person] in the street rather than the dance expert primarily interested in the authenticity of interpretation and steps.

Sharp himself termed the style "gay simplicity"—it was an expression that he found in a nineteenth century dancing manual (Keller and Shimer, 63–64).

The Places to Dance

Dancing has met, at all times, and under circumstances of no ordinary character, with strong opposition; but it has gradually overcome its opponents to such an extent, that they . . . belong only to those classes of people who oppose everything that makes life cheerful.

—Lawrence De Garmo Brookes, 1867

You will, my dear reader, find many very plain things between the two covers of this little book; things which will, perhaps, shock your modesty and probably disgust you altogether.

—Thomas A. Faulkner, *From the Ball-Room to Hell*, 1892

THE FORMAL BALL, WARD MCALLISTER, MRS. SHERWOOD, AND FASHIONABLE SOCIETY ETIQUETTE

After the Civil War, American society was entrenched in a transformation from an agricultural society to an industrialized society. Along with that was also a rise in wealth among a select group of entrepreneurs and business tycoons. By the 1880s, for example, there was a vast disparity of wealth between the very few of the "socialites" of the upper tier versus the millions of poor. For example, in 1880, about 235,000 individuals had a yearly income of over $180,000. In contrast, over 11 million families had a yearly income of less than $1,000. At the time, the heaviest concentration of wealth was within New York City. As a result, a "different" society developed among the ultrawealthy as opposed to the rest of America. "Society" was most visually defined by attending fashionable balls that included dancing during a "society season." A society season was typically during the winter months in the urban areas and during the summer months at fashionable resorts in areas such as Newport, Rhode Island. In New York City, for example, over 600 balls were scheduled during the winter society season of 1865 to 1866 (Erenberg 1981, 12–13; Aldrich 1991, 5; Dannett and Rachel 1954, 49).

In *The Complete Book of Ballroom Dancing*, Richard Stephenson and Joseph Iaccarino noted that, "dancing for 'society' and dancing for the 'working people' were distinctly different" (1992, 9). Among the wealthy, dancing maintained a social prestige, and a select dance instructor (sometimes still called "dance master") played an important role in teaching the fashionably rich. Society in New York held expensive and fashionable balls at hotels such as the Waldorf Astoria and at elite restaurants such as Delmonico's and Sherry's. Each establishment also maintained an accompanying ballroom.

In a fashion similar to Dodworth's Dancing Academy (see earlier in this chapter), the restaurants and ballrooms were also located in the fashionable areas—and even moved when necessary. Prior to the Civil War, Delmonico's restaurant, for example, was located in downtown New York City. In 1860, the restaurant was moved to 14th Street and Fifth Avenue. The new location coincided with society's move uptown. As a result, according to historian Lewis Erenberg,

271

The Fifth Avenue location also marked Delmonico's emergence as a social institution [and] assumed its position as the premier place for fashionable dining...[and was] the center of national political, social, and business life (1981, 10).

At about the same time, they added a French Chef who had no equal in America. (The menu, at over 100 pages and 370 meal offerings, was in both French and English.) As a result, many other organizations held similar affairs "modeled after the ornate official hospitality of Paris."

During the 1870s, Delmonico's marked a breakthrough in society as one of the few public establishments that welcomed unescorted women, only, however, during the day. Evening hours still required an escort. A separate "men's café" was maintained that defined the typical double standard of the time. In 1876, Delmonico's moved to a new location at 26th Street between Broadway and Fifth Avenue. (This location at 26th Street was the former site of Dodworth's Dancing Academy.) At the time, the Waldorf Astoria was located at 35th Street and Fifth Avenue. (In 1930, the Waldorf Astoria moved up town, and the former site was razed for the construction of the Empire State Building.) During the years 1865 to 1895, however, Delmonico's held the distinction as the benchmark not only for elegant French dining in America, but also for hosting the top tier of fashionable balls. During the 1870s, it was Delmonico's that was chosen by Ward McAllister for the exclusive Patriarch Balls (Erenberg 1981, 10–11).

Ward McAllister was considered a "social lion of the late nineteenth century." McAllister (b. 1827, d. 1895), born in Savannah, Georgia, had worked briefly as a lawyer at his brother's law firm in San Francisco. Neither he nor his family possessed significant wealth; however, he did have a yearning toward the life of wealthy society. During the 1850s, he married the granddaughter of a wealthy shipping industrialist and moved to Newport, Rhode Island. It was in Newport, during the winter of 1866–1867, that McAllister caught the attention of the wealthy New York socialite Caroline Astor.

After the 1870s, a "social phenomenon" developed as the men devoted their time to business accumulating more wealth and the women, or more appropriately the wives of the wealthy businessmen, devoted themselves to "the field of culture, social affairs, and leisure." Caroline Astor (nee Schermerhorn) was the wife of wealthy industrialist William Astor, who was brother to John Jacob Astor and co-heir to the famed Astor fortune. In essence,

Delmonico's Restaurant located at the corner of 26th Street and Broadway in New York City. During the years 1865 to 1895, Delmonico's held the distinction as the benchmark not only for elegant French dining in America, but also for hosting the top tier of fashionable balls, including the exclusive Patriarchs' Balls established by Ward McAllister. Library of Congress, American Memory Collection—Detroit Publishing Company no. 016669.

Caroline's extreme wealth literally gave her the influence to "impose her authority on New York society." As a result, Caroline Astor employed Ward McCallister in New York City as a consul for fashionable balls and dancing classes. (McAllister was also a "social advisor" to others of the wealthy elite such as Mrs. Cornelius Vanderbilt II.)

The McAllister Family Circle Dancing Classes, for example, provided dance instruction and parties by "invitation only" for young boys and girls (children of the wealthy) under the age of 12. Young boys were taught the "proper" way to ask a young lady how to dance, and young girls were taught how to curtsy and graciously accept. For the adults, in the winter season of 1872–1873, McCallister created the Patriarchs' Ball. He enlisted the aid, and money, of a select group of 25 wealthy gentlemen including the Astor brothers. Each was responsible for inviting four ladies and five gentlemen of similar class wealth. The gathering of the wealthiest of society also attracted the attention of newspapers, including *The New York Times, Harper's Weekly*, and *Frank Leslie's Illustrated*, that covered each of the events. The written press made "it a matter of public record as to who was in, and who was out" (Stephenson and Iaccarino 1992, 10; Burrows and Wallace 1998, 962–963).

One Patriarchs' Ball held at Delmonico's on December 10, 1894, for example, was a "page one" story of *The New York Times*. The decorum included elaborate dresses, dance cards, and a fashionably decorated ballroom. The following day the décor of the opulent event was described as follows:

> Large cone-shaped gilt baskets, holding ferns and English holly, were suspended by broad red silk ribbons at regular intervals in front of the many mirrors on the walls of the main ballroom. In the halls and other rooms there was the usual array of palms, smilax, and greens of every imaginable variety, some being banked high against the walls, some filling up solitary corners, and other being festooned promiscuously about the doors on the walls and ceiling. The halls and small rooms were veritable fern fairy bowers, but the large ballroom would have been a trifle bare except for the crowd of dancers.

A cotillion ball held on Wednesday evening, February 20, 1895, at Sherry's was described by the *New York Times* with similar fanfare. The report added that the ballroom was "tastefully decorated with flowers and growing palms" (*The New York Times*, December 11, 1894, 1; February 21, 1895, 9).

By that time, the extreme opulence and fashion for a social dance was a regular occurrence. In many instances, however, each succeeding society social dance attempted to outdo the previous one. On January 4, 1901, for example, a fashionable "First Cotillion of the Century" was given by the wealthy W.C. Whitney. (By this time the "Cotillion" signified a formal dance ball and not necessarily the party games of the mid-nineteenth century.) Whitney's guests were treated to an elaborately staged affair within a private ballroom that was decorated in neoclassical European designs.

In other instances, society "stepped out" and organized a social dance event for a charitable cause. On February 5, 1880, for example, New York Society held a "Grand Ball" at the Brooklyn Academy of Music "for the benefit of the Home

MARYLAND—GRAND BALL GIVEN IN THE ACADEMY OF MUSIC FOR THE BENEFIT OF THE NURSERY AND CHILD'S HOSPITAL, BALTIMORE
FROM A SKETCH BY WALTER GLOVER.—SEE PAGE 116.

This illustration of a Grand Ball at the Baltimore Academy of Music appeared in *Frank Leslie's Illustrated Newspaper* on April 24, 1880, page 120. It is a good example of a formal dance and fashion of the time. The men are dressed in black jackets, pantaloons, and shirtwaist. A variety of formal dresses, without the elaborate trains and fuller bustles of the mid-nineteenth century, are worn by the women.   Library of Congress, Prints and Photographs Division LC-USZC2-75200.

for Destitute Children." But Grand Balls were not limited only to New York City. Other major cities, such as Boston, Philadelphia, and Baltimore, although not with the same regularity, held society seasons and sponsored similar lavish balls and charitable events centered on social dancing. In April 1880, for example, a Grand Ball was held at the Baltimore Academy of Music that was attended by the social elite of that city. The charitable event was sponsored to raise money "for the benefit of the Nursery and Child's Hospital" in Baltimore, Maryland. The charity affairs were also occasions for the newspapers to cover the events. The widely circulated mass-market *Frank Leslie's Illustrated Newspaper*, for example, reported on the events in Brooklyn and Baltimore on February 21, 1880, and April 24, 1880, respectively.

Ward McAllister, who also wrote a newspaper society column, reported on these social events. Through his syndicated column he created a short list of "Four Hundred" of the "socially acceptable families." In his later published memoirs, *Society as I Have Found It* (1890), McAllister wryly stated,

Why, there are only about four hundred people in fashionable New York Society. If you go outside that number you strike people who are either not an ease in a ballroom or else make other people not at ease.

Some say McAllister arrived at the "four hundred" number since that was the maximum number of people who could fit in Alice Vanderbilt's ballroom that was located within her Fifth Avenue mansion. It was within Vanderbilt's ballroom that some of the most elaborate social dance events were held, and only those among the select "Four Hundred" were invited (quoted in McDonagh 1979, 11–14).

In regards to McAllister's select "Four Hundred," historian Lewis Erenberg explained,

THE FIRST COTILLION OF THE CENTURY
Given by Hon. W. C. Whitney, January 4, 1901

On January 4, 1901, at the "First Cotillion of the Century," given by the wealthy W. C. Whitney, the guests were treated to an elaborately staged affair within a private ballroom that was decorated in neoclassical European designs. This illustration appeared in *Harper's Weekly*, Vol. 45, January–June 1901, 62–63. Library of Congress, Prints and Photographs Division LC-USZC2-63718.

> The notion of there being four hundred select individuals comprising the social elite of
> New York, while inexact, was perhaps the highest expression of this desire to consoli-
> date society and place its members under formal rules of behavior.

The select group of invitees of the wealthy elite was also expected to comply with the appropriate manners and "civility" applicable to the fashionable ballrooms. As a result, many of the etiquette books were more closely applied to the urban environment of the social elite (Erenberg 1981, 12–13).

Although McAllister's select group of "Four Hundred" was obviously limited to only white individuals of northern European ancestry such as England and Scotland, other ethnic groups copied their social etiquette. One example was a group of a select few African Americans. At the time, nonetheless, regardless of the region, all of the United States was deeply segregated. Within New York City, for example, any African Americans who attained any amount of wealth that enabled them to purchase homes or businesses were limited to areas north of Central Park such as Harlem. In a similar fashion, the social elite among African Americans sponsored a society season. In February 1872, for example, the Skidmore Guard, "a colored military organization," organized a fashionable assembly. The annual event, at the Seventh Avenue Germania Assembly Rooms, was also covered by *Frank Leslie's Illustrated Newspaper* on February 24, 1872.

At the time, American society of all classes received their advice through some of the many handbooks available through mass market publications. Typically a publishing company, such as Beadle's or The Penn Publishing Company, offered a wide selection of titles. Some of the popular handbooks published at the time by Penn Publishing, for example, included:

After Dinner Stories,	*Astrology*,
Astronomy,	*Candy-Making at Home*,
The Care of the Child,	*Conundrums*,
Etiquette,	*The Family Food*,
The Family Health,	*The Family House*,
Graphology,	*Handbook of Pronunciation*,
Home Decoration,	*Hypnotism*,
Journalism,	*Letter Writing Epitaphs*,
Magic,	*Parlor games*,
Physiognomy,	*Practical Palmistry*,
Reading as a Fine Art,	*Ready Made Speeches*,
Socialism,	*Things Worth Knowing*,
Toasts,	and *Ventriloquism*.

Each of the publications was cloth hardcover bound 5 inches by 7 inches in size, at a cost of 75 cents each. Some other publishing companies simply copied other similar types of books. One example was *The Dancer's Guide and Ball-Room Companion*, published in New York by Frank M. Reed in 1875. *The Dancer's Guide* was copied almost verbatim from the 1868 publication of *Beadle's Dime Ball-Room Companion and Guide to Dancing*. Within both publications was a long list of rules and manners for maintaining the proper ballroom etiquette (see Chapter 3). The etiquette books were of particular interest to American society, especially the emerging urban middle class and the wealthy.

Typically, the etiquette books offered advice on how to properly use eating utensils, how to stage a wedding, how to interact with other people, how to publicly mourn, and how to write letters. In addition, these books provided fashion hints, domestic household hints, and suggestions for planning a private dance party or a formal ball, noting special arrangements for refreshments, decorations for the ballroom, and the proper format for invitations. A sampling of the more well-known etiquette books available to the American public included the following:

NEW YORK CITY.—FIRST ANNUAL BALL OF THE SKIDMORE GUARD, A COLORED MILITARY ORGANIZATION, AT THE SEVENTH AVENUE GERMANIA ASSEMBLY ROOMS.

The social elite among African Americans also sponsored a society season. In February 1872, the Skidmore Guard, "a colored military organization," organized a fashionable assembly as an annual event at the Seventh Avenue Germania Assembly Rooms in New York City. This illustration appeared in *Frank Leslie's Illustrated Newspaper* on February 24, 1872, page 380. Library of Congress, Prints and Photographs Division LC-USZC2-115353.

- Robert Tomes's *The Bazaar Book of Decorum* (1870);
- Mrs. H.O. Ward's *Sensible Etiquette of the Best Society* (1878);
- *Manners and Tone of Good Society* (1879);
- John H. Young's *Our Deportment* (1879);
- H.K. Lyverthey's *Our Etiquette and Social Observances* (1881);
- Florence Howe Hall's *Social Customs* (1881);
- *Social Etiquette and Home Culture, By the Lounger in Society* (1881);
- Ingersoll Lockwood's *The P.G. or Perfect Gentleman* (1887); and
- *The Correct Thing in Good Society* (Boston, 1888).

Of all the available etiquette books, however, the most popular and well-known was Mrs. Mary Elizabeth Sherwood's (nee Wilson) 1887 publication, *Manners and Social Usages.*

Manners and Social Usages, as an etiquette book was actually quite extensive. Of the book's 59 chapters and 487 pages, two chapters "The Etiquette of Balls" and "Fashionable Dancing" were devoted to dancing. Sherwood's chapter "The Etiquette of Balls," for example, began with the proper wording and a suggested form for sending out invitations to a formal dance. A sample of the page follows:

---

142   MANNERS AND SOCIAL USAGES.

CHAPTER XV.

THE ETIQUETTE OF BALLS.

A HOSTESS must not use the word "ball" on her invitation-cards.   She may say,

Mrs. John Brown requests the pleasure of the company of
Mr. and Mrs. Amos Smith
on Thursday evening, November twenty-second,
at nine o'clock.

Dancing.   *R.S.V.P.*

Or,

Mrs. John Brown
At Home
Thursday evening, November twenty-second,
at nine o'clock.

Cotillion at ten.   *R. S. V. P.*

But she should not indicate further the purpose of her party.   In New York, where young ladies are introduced to society by means of a ball at Delmonico's, the invitation is frequently worded,

Mr. and Mrs. Amos Smith request the pleasure
of your company
Thursday evening, November twenty-second,
at nine o'clock.

Delmonico's.

The card of the young débutante is sometimes (although not always) enclosed.

A facsimile reproduction from *Manners and Social Usages* by
Mrs. Mary Elizabeth Sherwood, New York: Harper & Brothers, 1887, page 142.

Other chapters included "Letter and Letter Writing," "Chaperones and Their Duties," "Garden Party," "The Fork and the Spoon," "Napkins and Table-cloths," "Summer Weddings," "Autumn Weddings," "Before the Wedding and After," "Mourning and Funeral Usages," "Letters of Condolence," "How to Treat a Guest," and "How to Treat English People." In regards to *Manners and Social Usages,* The Library of Congress noted, "Sherwood's book is an exceptional source for etiquette as it was practiced in the late 1880s." It was published in New York by Harper and Brothers and subsequently went through seven editions between 1887 and 1918 ("Nineteenth Century Social Dance," n.d.).

In the case that the private party was within the home, Sherwood advised, "The first persons asked to dance by the young gentlemen invited to a house should be the daughters of the house. To them and to their immediate relatives and friends must the first attentions be paid" (145–146). However, Sherwood cautioned that the hostess must be careful and "should not overcrowd her rooms." One of the reasons that the rooms were overcrowded was not always because of the number of people, but because of the configuration of the house itself.

As early as 1811, the commissioners of New York City, in preparation for a large influx of immigrants, adapted a narrow rectangular grid street system for the island of Manhattan. The grid system started above Wall Street and extended all the way north to the Bronx. One exception was Broadway, which angled across the grid from east to west running north. The rigid system thereby apportioned many of the lots in 20 foot wide by 100 foot deep segments. In the instances where Broadway intersected the grid, there was a disproportionate series of odd-shaped lots, including triangular ones. As a result, regardless of wealth, many narrow houses were built. To compare, one wealthy home on a narrow lot contained only one family, whereas a narrow lot in a tenement area, such as the lower east side, contained homes for upwards of 15 families.

Therefore, some of the wealthier homes were built on narrow lots, which, in turn, yielded a narrow configuration for all the rooms, including the ballroom.

During the 1850s, the commissioners carved out a large section in the middle of the grid for the construction of Central Park. On the east side of the park, along upper Fifth Avenue, was a series of large urban mansions built by the wealthy of the select "Four Hundred" that included the Astors, Morgans, Rockefellers, and Vanderbilts. Within J.P. Morgan's mansion, for example, was a 3,500 square foot ballroom. Just prior to the end of the nineteenth century, Morgan had added the ballroom especially for the occasion of his daughter's wedding and the expected 1,500 guests. But, not all the wealthy lived in the larger opulent mansions. Therefore, rather than "crowd" too many guests into a narrow ballroom, the wealthy began the practice of giving a ball in a public space (Giordano 2003, 6).

Sherwood claimed that the American "innovation" of giving a ball at a "public room" such as Delmonico's, Sherry's, or the Waldorf Astoria had actually "shocked a French woman of rank who married an American." She quoted the French woman as asking "Now, do you not run great risks when you abandon . . . . . . [your] homes, and bring out your girls at a hotel?" Although the answer in the past was that the young girl was properly protected by the accompaniment of a chaperone, Sherwood posed an interesting caveat. She warned:

> There is something in [the French woman's] wise remarks; and with the carelessness of chaperonage in cities which are now largely populated by irresponsible foreigners the dangers increase.

Sherwood's comment is evidence of not only the separation of economic class in American society, but also the mounting prejudice against the growing number of southern European immigrants, which she termed "irresponsible foreigners" (1887, 146–147).

Although chaperones were a part of all classes of urban society, including immigrants, the main focus of the chaperones among the wealthy was to ensure that the young men, and especially the young women, associated

At the time, the American "innovation" of giving a ball at a "public room" such as Delmonico's, Sherry's, or the Waldorf Astoria was common among the wealthy in New York City. This photo is of the fashionable Waldorf Astoria, located at 35th Street and Fifth Avenue, c. 1901. (In 1930, the Waldorf Astoria moved uptown, and the former site was razed for the construction of the Empire State Building.) Library of Congress, Prints and Photographs Division LC-USZ62-77182.

with only those of the same social class. Among the wealthy, chaperones were still prevalent; however, unlike the customs of Europe, or even years past in America, the practice of a recently married young woman as a chaperone was frequent at society functions. However, Sherwood admonished the practice. In response she wrote:

> The very bad American custom of sending several young girls to a ball with a very young chaperon—perhaps one of their number who has just been married—has led to great vulgarity in our American city life.

Sherwood's answer was that the proper chaperone should be the young woman's own mother. Therefore, Sherwood reminded the hostess that it was "a very poor American custom not to invite the mothers" (1887, 146). She added that the addition of the mother actually added to the décor. Sherwood exclaimed, "A row of well-dressed ladies, in velvet, brocade, and diamonds, some with white hair, certainly forms a very distinguished background for those [daughters] who sit at their feet" (1887, 144).

Attending a society function was also an occasion for fashionable attire. In regards to the fashion, Sherwood dictated:

> It is the height of the gayety of the day; and although dinner calls for handsome dress, a ball demands it. Young persons of slender figure prefer light, diaphanous dresses; the chaperons can wear heavy velvet and brocade. Jewels are in order. A profusion of flowers in the hands of the women should add their brightness and perfume to the rooms.... The present fashion is to have them hung, by different ribbons, on the arm, so that they look as if almost a trimming to the dress (1887, 143).

Men, on the other hand, still dressed mainly in black trousers and jacket, with an appropriate addition of a waistcoat and gloves.

Unlike the fashion of the mid-nineteenth century, the dresses of the late-nineteenth century eliminated the back bustles and bulk of material below the waist, and the skirts were slimmer. But they still covered the ankle and almost touched the ground. Long gloves were still in vogue, although a bit more elaborate and with lots of buttons. A tiny a waist as could be pulled tightly by an hourglass corset was still a must. Hair was "piled high" and wound up above the head. In regards to the fashion of the time, dance historian Don McDonagh wrote, "She was still bundled up to the chin but had very definitely transferred the emphasis from the 'lower back' to the upper torso and in particular the shoulders" (1979, 9).

Regardless of how the woman dressed, Sherwood expressed her desire that all who attended should dance. She added that "no hostess likes to see 'wall-flowers' at her ball: she wishes all her young people to enjoy themselves" (1887, 143). In *The Terpsichorean Monitor* (1889), William E. Greene described a "Wallflower" as follows:

> These are ladies who serve as the drapery to the walls of the ball room, in consequence of, either refusing all invitations to dance, or unfortunately, have never learned the art. Sometimes it is negligence on the part of gentlemen for want of gallantry.

Greene's etiquette manual, although mostly a compilation of other previously published works, was written to discuss the etiquette among those of the wealthy society, which he described as "criteria of good breeding." Greene advised that the responsibility to avoid the accumulation of "wallflowers" at a party fell upon the gentleman. As a solution, he advised,

> Well-bred young men always say to the hostess that they beg of her to introduce them to ladies who may be without partners, as they would gladly make themselves useful to her (25).

Mrs. Sherwood agreed and added, "After dancing with a lady, and walking about the room with her for a few times, a gentleman is at perfect liberty to take the young lady back to her chaperon and plead another engagement" (1887, 143–144).

The "engagement" for dancing usually included round dances such as the Waltz, Polka, Polka Redowa, Polka Mazurka, Lanciers, Quadrilles, and The German. Nevertheless, some of Sherwood's overprotectiveness was obvious in her discussion on the round dances. She warily cautioned,

> It is the gentleman's duty in any round dance to guide his fair companion gracefully; he must not risk a collision or the chance of a fall. A lady should never waltz if she feels dizzy. It is a sign of disease of the heart, and has brought on death (1887, 152).

Sherwood's wildly concocted misconception was most likely the reason that she had suggested that after each dance the gentleman should walk the lady "about the room with her for a few times." Sadly, the supposed "frailty" of woman was not limited to Sherwood's audience; the idea was still impressed among all classes of American society.

In 1896, E.H. Kopp provided a similar account in *The American Prompter and Guide to Etiquette* that was published concurrently in Cincinnati, New York, and Chicago by The John Church Company. Within the introduction, he proudly announced,

> The art of dancing is not only necessary, but indispensable to those that are fond of society (1).

Kopp also provided a section for "Etiquette for the Ballroom." Unlike the very long lists of rules and acceptable behavior in the earlier manuals, however, he provided only three pages. But, he strongly advised,

> Careful study of the three following pages will be extremely beneficial, as the rules of etiquette therein outlined, are everywhere recognized as being eminently proper and correct.

Although not as exhaustive as the etiquette and dance manuals of the 1840s and 1850s, Kopp did repeat many of the same rules. A sampling is as follows:

- Always remember that ladies are to be cared for first, and are entitled in all eases to your courtesy and protection.

- The ladies' dressing-room is a sacred precinct, into which no gentleman would presume to look; to enter it would be an outrage not to be forgiven.
- The first duty of a gentleman after entering the ballroom with his partner is to procure a program for her, and to introduce to her his friends.
- A gentleman should invariably dance the first number on the program with the lady whom he escorts, or at least offer to do so, and see that she is provided with a partner whenever she wishes to dance.
- Should a lady desire to leave before the close of the reception or ball, her escort should cancel her engagements and also his own.
- Do not be guilty of practical jokes in a ballroom.

And a brief list for the ladies included:

- In ascending stairs with ladies, gentlemen should go beside or before them. It is a gentleman's province to lead, and the lady's to follow.
- A lady should never promenade in the ballroom alone, nor enter it unaccompanied.
- Gloves and hats must always be removed at the supper table.

For the most part, it appeared that acting within the guidelines of the acceptable rules of manners and etiquette were more important than the actual dancing (12–14).

In regards to the actual dancing, apparently Kopp was of the opinion that not all society functions paid careful attention to the dance music. He asserted,

> Dancers are often annoyed by the uneven tempos of orchestras. This fault can be attributed almost wholly to the fact that prompters and leaders are usually business managers only, often poor dancers and inferior musicians, without the slightest knowledge of proper tempo for dancing.

Kopp was one of the few writers who acknowledged that the proper enjoyment of each of the round dances required the appropriate music tempo. Therefore, as a solution, he presented a brief listing of the most popular contemporary dances along with the measures of music per minute (mpm).

- Waltz in 3/4 time at 45 to 62 mpm.
- Redowa or Mazurka in 3/4 time at 45 to 55 mpm.
- Newport in 3/4 time at 45 mpm.
- Galop or Two-Step in 2/4 time at 45 to 65 mpm.
- Polka in 2/4 time at 55 to 60 mpm.
- Schottische in 2/4 time at 45 mpm.
- Quadrille in 2/4 or 6/8 time at 58 to 68 mpm.

Kopp was cognizant of the fact that "the tempos of dance music" did, indeed, vary in the different areas of America, but at least he provided a workable guideline (18–19).

The eastern "big city" idea of a "social life" was followed in places as far away as Denver, Colorado, and Portland, Oregon. Although, compared to places such as New York City, the social life of these emerging cities was "rather limited," the main activity was dancing. One young Portland woman, for example, recalled the similar social decorum that was prevalent. She wrote,

> To attend these dances, which were always given in private homes, we always got a special invitation by card. The hostess would send her compliments to you and invite you to attend. She would always name a boy that would come and take you to the party, and would see that you were properly escorted all evening.

Many of the private homes also had ballrooms with luxurious decors. The dances, as well, were also similar, such as the Waltz, Polka, Quadrilles, and The German. But, the few western cities that exhibited such social behavior were more often the exception. Typically, "out west" in the developing rural areas and frontier settlements the social etiquette and ballroom manners were very different and oftentimes rough and tumble ("Girlhood Life in Portland, 1860–76," 1936–1940, 2–3).

THE WESTERN FRONTIER, PUNCHEON FLOORS, AND COMMUNITY SQUARE DANCES

American folklore portrayed the western settlers and pioneering families as entering the western frontier with "a rifle in one hand, and a fiddle in the other." The rifle was necessary to hunt for food and to ward off predators. The fiddle was necessary for music and dancing. Food was, indeed, a necessity, but predators were more often scarcer than most accounts portrayed. On the other hand, the fiddle was always kept at hand, for it was rare that a pioneer turned down the opportunity to dance. For that matter, according to historian Dee Brown,

> Dances were held on the slightest provocation, or none at all. In frontier society where women were scarce, men organized stag dances, either with designated partners or on a solo basis.

Similar to the rural areas of the east coast, the frontier dances were held in a community building, in a small home, in the outdoors, or even in a barn (Brown 1995, 165).

Towards the end of the nineteenth century and into the twentieth century, the term "Barn Dance" was applied to just about any community dance in a rural area. Sometimes it was in celebration of the recently completed barn that was built with the help of the local community. In later years, more often than not, a Barn Dance was held there simply because the barn was one of the few places that had an enclosed open area large enough to accommodate dancing. In most cases, the Barn Dance was open to the entire community. At about the same time, with the introduction of a Caller, the Quadrilles were called Square Dances. The term was most likely applied due to the dances performed in the Quadrille Square set formation (see Chapter 2). In many cases, the term "Square Dance" was often applied to the community dance event itself and sometimes replaced the term "Barn Dance."

(During the late twentieth century, a country-dance known as the Barn Dance served as a mixer that interchanged dance partners.)

Unlike, the eastern rural areas, these dances were often "rough"—mainly because of the surrounding conditions or the state of the dance floor itself. Dancing within the barns, community buildings, and homes was often upon a "puncheon floor." A puncheon floor was simply felled tree logs that were rough hewed as the "finished" floor surface. Since everyone present danced, including children, most of the dances were simple Quadrilles, Jigs, and Reels, and therefore, did not necessarily require such a "smooth" ballroom dance floor. Unlike on the "highly polished" dance floors of the eastern ballrooms, the children did not necessarily have the opportunity to attempt a playful slide across the floor. Whereas in Dodworth's Dancing Academy this action brought on a stern warning from Allen Dodworth, a slide across a puncheon floor could yield splinters. Oftentimes, the youngest children simply played alongside the dance floor, but other times they joined in the frolic. They learned the simple dances by watching and following the instructions of their parents, other older adults, or siblings (Sanders 1951, 23).

In many cases, dances were held in the local schoolhouse. When an area acquired enough settlers to form a town, the first structures built were usually a church and a

In this photograph, mostly likely within a rural house, two dancers are about to begin a dance on a puncheon floor. Two musicians, one fiddle player and one banjo player, are evident in the background, and young children are seen alongside the dance floor, c. 1890 to 1900. Brown Brothers X78.

schoolhouse. In many cases, one building with a large room was built that serviced both needs. During school hours, recess often included childhood games and sometimes dance games such as the Maypole (see Chapter 1). In addition, the "one-room schoolhouse" also served as a community building for meetings and also community dancing. Regardless of where dances were held, an important ingredient was a fiddle player.

Annie Hightower was one of the few women who could hold her own both as a ranch hand and as a fiddle player. (Hightower, born Annie Heckman in 1863, moved to Texas in 1872.) However, it was mainly because of her ability to play the fiddle that she was in demand. Oftentimes, she rode up to 30 miles on horseback to play a dance. At the same time, she noted that some cowboys rode for a distance of up to 60 miles to attend that same dance. Unlike the formalities of the fashionable assembly balls, the cowboys often showed up "dressed in their working clothes" jangling their spurs as they walked and armed with "six-guns."

Queen of the May.

A Maypole Dance held outdoors in a rural area. A fiddler at the base of the tree provided music. The photograph was produced by The Fellows Photographic Company, c. 1891. Library of Congress, Prints and Photographs Division LC-USZ62-100240.

One West Texas ranch hand recalled, "We would civilize up a bit when we went to a dance; that is, we would take off our spurs and tie a clean red handkerchief around our neck" (Sanders, "The Texas Cattle Country and Cowboy Square Dance," 1951, 25).

However, the "social decorum" of the frontier required that all guns remained outside. Hightower recalled:

> That [applied] to me, too, as I wore my six-gun and could use it quite well. While I was never called on to use my gun, in those days one never knew when it would be necessary.

The requirement to "disarm" was readily accepted, since the main reason for the get-together was to listen to music, have fun, and dance. Hightower added, "The dances those days were the big event and all enjoyed the affairs greatly."

The dances were sometimes held in a barn, but more often than not, they were held in a room within a small home. The home of the prairie sodbuster or the Great Plains farmer, however, was drastically unlike the large homes within the cities along the eastern seaboard. Whereas the homes of the wealthy class often had a large ballroom with a highly polished dance floor within a large mansion, the frontier settlers built their own homes that contained only two or three modest rooms with a rough puncheon floor. Therefore, in order to host a dance, one room was cleared of all furniture and placed outside. The "stage" for the musicians was usually a table "arranged in one corner" that also doubled as "the eating table." Hightower remembered playing fiddle upon one such "platform" when she was "just a tot of a girl."

The remote location of the frontier dances also meant that there was a shortage of female dance partners. However, that did not stop the dancing. In order to dance, many of the cowboys simply danced the part of the female. Hightower recalled:

> One of the difficulties the men had to contend with, at dances, was the shortage of women. There were more males than females in the country those days...To meet the uneven number in sex, some men were compelled to dance the female part. The men taking the female part always wore a ribbon to designate their part and were a source of merriment to all those present (1936–1940, 14).

Having men take the "female part" for dancing was quite common in Texas. Typically, a dance was held in connection with just about any celebration. For example, in honor of the opening of the Polk County courthouse in Amarillo, Texas, a "Grand Ball" was held. Over 100 men attended; however, there were only five women in the area, all who attended. But that did not stop the dancing, as some of the men simply wore a "heifer brand." "Heifer brand" was a slang name given to the practice of men tying a bandana on their arms to indicate that they "would dance lady fashion" (Sanders, "The Texas Cattle Country and Cowboy Square Dance," 1951, 23).

Most the dances were usually without incident. In the few instances of a dispute, it was customary to take it outside the house or the barn. Annie Hightower did recall one occasion where two "cowhands" argued over a girl, resulting in tragedy. She described the incident as follows:

> One [cowhand]...it seemed, considered he had the right of a certain girls attention and the other...didn't agree with him. The two did the customary thing by going outside of the house to [settle] the issue...it wasn't long before we on the inside heard shooting ... those who had not already gone to watch the [fight], rushed out with the [sound] of the first shot...when I reached the scene of the shooting, on the ground lay one of the men. He was shot high up in the left breast and bleeding...I wrapped my white handkerchief, and plugged the bullet hole the best I could. That stopped the blood from flowing to a [great] extent. A couple of men started to a doctor with the fellow, but the man [died] before they had traveled very far.

A short time later, Hightower resumed playing the fiddle, and the dancers whirled around the floor. The indifference to the situation, however, was nothing unusual. Hightower explained:

It may seem that the dancers were a hard and cold-hearted lot, but the fact is they were not. Arguments were settled so often with the six-gun in those days that the folks became accustomed to shooting affairs.

At that time, the music and dancing served as one of the very few outlets to deal with the harsh realities of life. Therefore, whenever the opportunity for dancing arose, the frontier settlers enjoyed it to the very end.

For most of the evening, Hightower sat on the edge of the table and played the fiddle. Typically, at the end of the evening's festivities she stood up on the platform and played a favorite song and "poured it on." On occasion, Hightower also entertained the crowd by dancing a Jig—and that was also the time that she earned her pay. She described it as follows:

> Now, I shall tell where my big thrill came [at] the close [of] the dance, the cowboys would say, "now [Annie] stand on the platform and play us your favorite tune." That I would do, and while [I] was playing money would come flying onto the platform.

By 1880, Hightower had married a farmer and as a result had to give up both the ranching and fiddling (Annie Hightower, *American Memory Collection*, 13–15).

Sometimes fiddlers could get the crowd involved immediately simply by playing spirited entertaining music. One Colorado dance hall manager, George Duffy, recalled,

> A colorful fiddler knew how to draw attention to himself and to liven the proceedings by clowning a bit as he fiddled. Some fiddlers could toss their fiddles into the air or flip them upside down without losing a beat. Others made a specialty of waving their fiddles backward over their heads while playing just to prove their complete mastery of the instrument.

Throughout the 1890s, Duffy, a one-time newspaper editor, managed and operated dance halls on a full-time basis. Other times he managed individual dances as a fundraiser for fraternal societies, charitable organizations, church groups, and other community organizations (Duffy, "Old Time Dance Calls," 1938, 4–5).

Prior to the 1890s, the fiddler usually doubled as a Caller. However, around that time Callers emerged as separate individuals who did not always play the fiddle. Some Callers also played the fiddle, but after the 1890s, it was the experienced Caller who was in demand, so the fiddle player often served as a backing musician. Therefore, it was an experienced Caller who kept the crowd dancing.

In 1890, in Nebraska, Charles Weaver was typical of an experienced Caller of the time. During the late 1880s and through the 1890s, Weaver, who started as a farmer, was a Deputy Sheriff in four counties of Nebraska. As a "sideline vocation" he managed dance halls within the community and also was a Caller at Square Dances. But simply calling out the figures of a Square Dance was not always enough—experience was advantageous. By the time he was calling dances, Charles Weaver, was a third generation Caller. He recounted his family tradition as Callers. He said,

Calling square dances or quadrilles had not only been a tradition of three generations standing in our family but has served as a more or less sideline vocation. My grandfather, [Thomas] Weaver, first learned the calls which he handed down to my father Joseph Weaver, who passed it on to my brother Lewis and I.

The experience not only placed Weaver in high demand (he called dances as far away as Wyoming and east to the Mississippi River), it also served him well to improvise in regards to the dance environment.

In order to get the crowd involved in dancing right from the very beginning, an experienced Caller started with an "icebreaker" as the first dance. An icebreaker was usually a simple dance that all in attendance knew and oftentimes was a mixer that involved changing partners. Weaver, for example, rationalized that an icebreaker was an advantage for not only himself, but also the dancers. He explained,

> This gives all of them a chance to find out who is a good dancer and who is not. It also livens up the dance at the beginning for the caller may call any number of different ways to mix the dancers up. There are no set rules for this dance.

Weaver noted that he regularly called an icebreaker known as a Circle Two-Step that was known in many of the surrounding communities. He described a Circle Two-Step as follows:

> The gentlemen choose their partners and the dance is opened with a two-step. At any time the caller may call out, "All join hands and circle left. Now a right and left." When he sees they are sufficiently mixed up he calls "Everybody two-step" and you dance with the partner that you are then changing hands with.... Another call that they use in this dance is to have the ladies on the inside and the gents on the out—or visa versa—circle left and everybody two-step with the partner in front of them.

There were many variations to the Circle Two-Step as it did not have "any set rules." In addition, depending on the skill of the caller, numerous other types of icebreakers were employed. Actually, Weaver added, "He may call anything but the idea is to get people acquainted and in a friendly mood."

After a fun icebreaker, the dancers were ready to continue in all sorts of Square Dances. Typically, the dance figures were not written down, as the Caller recited the different Square Dances from memory. At the time, all the "old time calls" did not always have specific names. In fact, an experienced caller like Weaver often improvised and put together his own set of figures, sometimes in advance, and sometimes during the dance. One of the unnamed "old time calls" that he remembered was listed as follows:

SQUARE DANCE CALL
    [Allamand] left with the left hand partner with a left hand round
    Right hand to your partner and right and left around the ring
    [Meet] your partner and grand promenade
    Everybody swing
    First couple out to the right
    And three hands round

Lady promenades, open the door and circle the four
Ladies do and the gents so low
Then on to the next and then to the third
Right on home and a grand promenade.
(This is repeated until all four couples have followed suit of the first.)

Weaver remembered that on many occasions, depending on the size of the hall, he would have to adjust his calling.

Sometimes it meant adjusting the number of figures corresponding to the physical amount of square sets that the building could comfortably accommodate. He said, "In some halls eight sets can dance at one time and in others more may participate." Another problem he encountered was simply being heard. In the days long before electronic amplification, a Caller's biggest problem was being heard during the assemblage of a large crowd in a community building or barn. Weaver indicated, "My hardest problem to tackle during all these years in this line was to make myself heard to a [large] crowd." Sometimes the "large crowd" was at an open-air dance pavilion, which made it even harder. Unfortunately, an acceptable solution was not always available. Despite the shortcomings, Weaver was not deterred. Of his many years as a Caller, Weaver fondly said,

I can't say I made any amount of money out of it, but I did, and still do have plenty of fun and feel that it's all worth the effort.

In 1939, at the time that Weaver made the preceding statement, his experience as a Caller spanned over 50 years (Weaver, "Mr. Charles Weaver Square Dances or Quadrilles," 1939).

Throughout the rural areas, Square Dancing was extremely popular as a community dance. It was also popular in many of the cities where they were still known as Quadrilles. However, unlike the impromptu calls of the rural Callers, for the most part within the cities the Quadrilles were predetermined set figures interspersed throughout a set program of dances. A Programme of December 13, 1883, for the Annual Ball of the Mohawk Association, for example, started with a "Grand Entrée" (which was a Grand March), followed by 13 dances and an intermission, and concluded with another 13 dances. The dances were a mixture that included six Lanciers, eight Quadrilles, two Polkas, two Schottisches, two Galops, and six Waltzes, one of which concluded the evening of dancing to the song "Home Sweet Home."

A similar program on Friday evening, September 4, 1896, for the North Easton Baseball Club, for example, held its "First Annual Dance." The "Order of Dances" also included a "March and Circle" followed by ten dances and intermission and concluded with ten more dances. The list of set dances included two Lanciers, four Quadrilles, one Polkas, two Schottisches, two Galops, and four Waltzes. By this time, the program had the addition of one Two-Step and fad dances that included two Portland Fancy, one Caprice, and the Danish dance. The last dance of the evening was also a Waltz to the tune of *Home, Sweet Home*.

Once again, unlike the rural areas, the Quadrilles included within a set list program usually did not include a Caller. In those instances, the particular set figure was expected to be known by all in attendance. For those who did not have the experience of learning the Quadrilles from watching, numerous instruction books were available. They included the following:

- Dick and Fitzgerald, *Dick's Quadrille Call-Book, and Ball-Room Prompter* (1878, reprinted in 1923);
- Luis Papanti, *De Witt's "Ball-Room" Call Book* (1878);
- Mathias J. Koncen, *Prof. M.J. Koncen's Quadrille Call Book and Ball-Room Guide* (1883);
- Herman Strassburg, *Call Book of Modern Quadrilles* (1889);
- Charles Link, *Unique Dancing Call Book* (1893);
- Prof. F.L. Clendenen, *Fashionable Quadrille Call Book and Guide to Etiquette* (1895).

At the time, in some of the nonrural areas the dancers were aided by people calling out the Quadrille figures, but they were known as "Prompters." In fact, some of the instruction books such as *Dick's Quadrille Call-Book, and Ball-Room Prompter* were mainly for Prompters of Quadrilles. Another book written mainly for Prompters was Charles Link's *Unique Dancing Call Book*. This instruction manual was actually "unique." In order to make it easier for the Caller, the Quadrille figures were printed in an extra large typeface ("Nineteenth Century Social Dance," n.d.).

MINING TOWNS, "HURDY-GURDY" HOUSES, CATTLE DRIVES, AND "CALICO QUEENS"

The western regions were not limited to just frontier settlements such as farms. Many of the written accounts of American western folklore told tales of rugged cowboys, nuisance Indians, arduous cattle drives, courageous lawmen, and notorious outlaws. But, although the written accounts were somewhat true, most of the folklore was basically fictionalized and exaggerated. This is not to discount the fact that the frontier life in the western territories was unusually hard, unsettled, and very often without law and order. Law, for that matter, was often dispensed by vigilante town committees. Noted historian of the American west, Dee Brown retold a story of one Montana resident who described the "law" in the mining town of Helena. For those lawbreakers who committed crimes such as murder, horse theft, or even lesser crimes, justice was served by a "hanging tree" within the town. The Helena resident described the end result for one lawbreaker as follows:

> There was suspended on the limb of a tree a man hung by the Vigilante committee the night before, the eight specimen of similar fruit encases in leather boots that tree had borne in so many months.

The word "fruit" was a slang term for a lynched victim (Brown 1995, 164).

A significant number of settlers, such as those in Helena, entered the area in search of gold and silver. Hundreds of mining towns were scattered throughout the American territories of Arizona, Colorado, Montana, South Dakota, and Utah. During their peak, the mining towns contained as many as 10,000–15,000 people. Two of the most "famous" mining towns were Deadwood, South Dakota (gold), and Tombstone, Arizona (silver and copper). Their notoriety was mainly because of late nineteenth century mass-market novels and mid-twentieth century Hollywood movies. Unfortunately, for many speculators, frequently the mines simply did not yield enough precious minerals and often proved "a bust" and closed. As a result, so did the towns. By the late nineteenth century, the resultant "Ghost Town," therefore, became another part of American folklore. As with the entire western frontier, the western folklore of America included music and dancing, both of which were also common among the mining towns. One hard luck prospector remembered "it was easier to make a stake with my violin than by hard work in the diggings" (Brown 1995, 347).

A good example of a typical contemporary mining town was Helena, Montana. As a result of mining, about 3,000 people congregated and quickly built the small town of Helena. In July 1865, it was described as a "lively camp"—lively mainly because of music and dancing. In 1867, in his memoirs, *Beyond the Mississippi: 1857–1867*, Albert D. Richardson provided a contemporary account of a similar mining town in Virginia, Montana, which he described as the "remotest Territory of the United States—farthest both from New York and San Francisco." The closest town was Helena (the future capitol) over 125 miles away and Salt Lake City, Utah, at over 160 miles. In 1865, the town was virtually nonexistent; however, a short time thereafter, the discovery of silver in the area caught the attention of thousands of speculators and prospectors. Silver mines quickly sprouted up throughout the area and, in response to the mining activity, so did the town of Virginia. By 1867, the amount of activity was such that a mail coach traversed from Salt Lake City to the Montana town. The town contained a few general stores, a hotel, a theater, but the town was mainly filled with numerous saloons and "Hurdy-Gurdy" dance houses (1867, 479).

A Hurdy-Gurdy was basically a lively rowdy dance hall that sold alcohol and offered gambling. It is not sure exactly how the term "Hurdy-Gurdy" came to apply to the dance halls of the American west. The hurdy-gurdy was actually a medieval French instrument that vaguely resembled a violin, but also had keys and a wheeled crank. The term was also often applied to a barrel organ and a piano. Therefore, it is quite possible that since the fiddle, and sometimes a piano and other instruments, was the main source of music in these frontier saloons that the term was subsequently applied ("Hurdy-Gurdy," n.d.).

Regardless of how the term originated, "Hurdy-Gurdy" was a common term throughout the western frontier, and all understood what was offered within them. In 1867, Richardson described one Hurdy-Gurdy in Virginia, Montana, as follows:

At one end of the long hall, [was] a well-stocked bar, and a monte bank [gambling] in full blast; at the other, [was] a platform occupied by three musicians…The orchestra leader shouted "Take your ladies for the next dance!"…Half-a-dozen swarthy fellows fresh from the diggings, selected partners from the tawdry, bedizened women who stood in waiting. After each dance the miners led their partners to the bar for whisky or champagne; then after a short pause, another dance; and so the sorry revelry continued from nine o'clock until nearly daylight, interrupted only by two fights. For every dance each masculine participant paid one dollar, half going to his partner, and half to the proprietor.

At the time, the price of "one dollar" for a dance was an exorbitant sum of money. But overall, having a good time in a Hurdy-Gurdy was not cheap. According to Richardson, "whisky was sold at fifty cents a drink and champagne at twelve dollars per bottle." In addition, many a miner lost an entire year's worth of digging (at the time, the miner's currency was "gold dust") in one evening at the gambling tables. But in comparison to the hard work of "digging" for gold, paying the extravagant price for a dance with a woman was somewhat justified. Richardson explained,

> Publicly, decorum was preserved; and to many miners, who had not seen a feminine face for six months, these poor women represented vaguely something of tenderness and sacredness of their sex (480).

It was mainly the availability of female companionship for dancing that kept the Hurdy-Gurdy houses filled to capacity. Searching for female companionship for a dance was also an integral part of the legendary cattle drives (Richardson 1867, 479–480).

Shortly after the Civil War, with the advantage of the railroad and the insatiable American desire for beef, cattle could be shipped from the slaughterhouses of Chicago to the lucrative markets in the east coast cities, such as New York and Philadelphia. But before arriving in Chicago, most of the cattle drives began from ranches located in West Texas. It was during the late 1860s through the 1870s that large herds of cattle were driven north from West Texas through the Great Plains. The region of West Texas was distinctly different from those known for cotton production in East Texas and for farming in the adjoining Great Plains states such as Oklahoma and Nebraska. The large flat open prairies of West Texas were conducive to raising large herds of cattle, and the amount of land appeared limitless. As a result, some of the cattle ranches were quite vast. In some cases, a ranch hand needed one or two days to ride from one end of a ranch to the other.

Because of the extreme remoteness of locations, the social gatherings were infrequent. When social gatherings were held, it was usually during the winter months, as the cattle were basically waiting for transport north during the spring months. But, when a social gathering occurred, it always involved dancing and often lasted for two or three days, or sometimes longer. At the Matador Ranch in West Texas, for example, the social dances held during Christmas week were legendary. Unlike for the eastern balls, there were no written invitations, and the dances were open to all comers. Usually mounted cowboys simply rode throughout the area to spread the news. As the news was spread, the riders did not even dismount. A typical invitation was shouted by the rider from atop the horse: "There's a dance over to Johnson's [Ranch] on Friday—everybody invited and nobody slighted." As a result, participants often traveled from as far away as 75 miles. One attendee at a Matador Ranch Christmas dance recalled, "We'd dance for a week, and if it got to snowing we'd stay two weeks" (Sanders, "The Texas Cattle Country and Cowboy Square Dance," 1951, 22–23).

As spring approached, the cattle were "fattened up" in preparation for market. In order to deliver the cattle to market, the ranch owners enlisted the aid of cowboys who rode the cattle herds north along established routes such as the Chisholm Trail or the Sante Fe Trail. The established routes were across the open range of

THE HURDY-GURDY HOUSE, VIRGINIA, MONTANA, PAGE 480.

This illustration of a Hurdy-Gurdy in Virginia, Montana, is typical of the dance halls in the mining towns scattered through the American West during the late nineteenth century. In the background is a "well-stocked bar"; to the right, also in the background, is a "monte bank" gambling table; and to the far right is "a platform occupied by three musicians." Lively dancing among the "swarthy fellows" and the "tawdry, bedizened women" occurs in the foreground. This illustration, although accurate, may have also been published as a warning against such unruly behavior. Evidence of two pious individuals, at the far right foreground, stand in the shadows, possibly in judgment. The clock on the rear wall indicates the late hour of the evening. The cat appearing to pounce is a late nineteenth century artist's depiction of a "trap" about to be sprung.   Brown Brothers B0975.

the prairies and were littered with enough grass to serve as a food source for the cattle herds. Ultimately, after many weeks and sometimes months on the trails, the cattle drives ended in towns in Wyoming and Kansas. Those cattle towns included Abilene, Ellsworth, Caldwell, Wichita, Newton, Hays, Miles City, Cheyenne, Ogallala, and Dodge City (Lewis 1999, 171).

Dodge City, Kansas, was probably the most well-known of all the cattle towns. In 1871, about five miles west along the Santa Fe Trail, near the U.S. military outpost of Fort Dodge, the only "sod house was erected." Because the area was in a strategic geographic location, the following year the railroad arrived. The location of this railroad link to Chicago, therefore, made it a desirable location to deliver a cattle herd. Dodge City was basically a railroad-shipping town that provided holding pens on the receiving end of the overland cattle drives as they were sold and loaded onto railroad cars heading north to the Chicago slaughterhouses. At its peak, over 800,000 head of cattle passed through the holding pens each year. Along with the cattle that passed through were also thousands of cowboys, causing Dodge

City to earn the nickname the "Cowboy Capital of the World." As a result, in a very short time there was a general store, six saloons, and three dance halls (Brown 1995, 275).

After the completion of the long arduous cattle drive, the happy cowboys often drove their cattle right through the center of the town as they hurriedly herded the cattle into the holding pens. Once the cattle were counted and within the holding pens, the cattle drive was over, and the cowboys had free time. Typically, when the cowboy took his pay, he usually got a haircut, had "his mustache or beard properly shaped and blacked," bought new clothes including a hat, and ate a good meal. At that time, according to historian Dee Brown, the cowboy "was ready for fun and frolic." Invariably that "fun and frolic" included female companionship, either for sexual relations or for dancing, or sometimes both. The most obvious place was a saloon or a Hurdy-Gurdy dance hall.

In an 1874 published memoir, *Historic Sketches of the Cattle Trade in the West and Southwest,* Joseph McCoy recounted his life working for the railroads and eventually opening a stockyard in Wichita, Kansas, where he had the opportunity to witness the cowboy's actions. Of the dancing, McCoy wrote,

> Few more wild, reckless scenes of abandoned debauchery can be seen on the civilized earth, than a dance hall in full blast...To say they dance wildly or in an abandoned manner is putting it mildly...The cowboy enters the dance with a particular zest, not stopping to divest himself of his sombrero, spurs or pistols...A more odd, not to say comical sight is not often seen than the dancing cowboy: with the front of his sombrero lifted at an angle of 45 degrees, his huge spurs jangling at every step or motion, his revolvers flapping up and down...his eyes lit up with excitement, liquor and lust, he plunges into it and "hoes it down" at a terrible rate in the most approved yet awkward country style, often swinging his partner clear off the floor for an entire circle...with an occasional demonic yell near akin to the war whoop of the savage Indian. All this he does entirely oblivious to the whole world and the rest of mankind. After dancing furiously, the entire "set" is called to "waltz to the bar," where the boy is required to treat his partner and, of course, himself also; which he does not hesitate to do time and again, although it costs him fifty cents each time (quoted in Lewis 1999, 176; Brown 1995, 199).

The cowboy's dance partner was a woman who worked in the Hurdy-Gurdy or saloon and was known as a "Calico Queen."

Within the cow towns such as Dodge City, many of the women who either were brought in or came on their own were mostly dance-hall girls or prostitutes, and in some cases they were both. In either case, the cowboys were more than happy to see them, and the dance-hall women were known as "Calico Queens." The Calico Queens earned money in different ways. Most of the time the first instance was to dance with a cowboy—for a price. After the dance they often encouraged the cowboy to either buy drinks at the bar or try his luck at the gambling table. In most cases, the Calico Queen later received a small commission from the dance-hall owner.

The cowboys who drove the cattle into the Kansas trail towns such as Abilene, Newton, and Wichita were often simply called "Texans." Many of those Texans were often either Confederate war veterans or men still sympathetic to the southern cause of the Civil War. Therefore, the introduction of the impassioned "Texans" into the Midwest cities and towns was often a volatile combination. Sometimes the mixture of unruly dancing, rowdiness, alcohol, and former confederates led to angry disputes and fistfights. In some cases, the anger led to gunfights and even murder.

In 1873, for example, one newspaper account described an altercation and shooting during a "heated battle" between the U.S. Army and the Texans. At the time, Custer's 7th Cavalry was also stationed outside of Wichita, Kansas. (Typically, as in Fort Dodge, an army outpost was located close to the cow town to prevent interference by Indians.) On the occasions that any of the U.S. Cavalry had leave, they often frequented the same Hurdy-Gurdy dance halls as the Texas cattle trail drivers, and they often engaged in disputes. In one "heated battle" at a dance hall known as Red Beard's, a fight apparently started after one cavalryman tried to cut in on a cowboy who was dancing with one of the Calico Queens. A gunfight erupted during which one soldier was killed and two others wounded. Accounts told that almost all of the Texans "were Confederate veterans, and they disliked the blue uniforms of the army" (Brown 1995, 211).

Many stories of the American west contained a least one tale that involved the common components of a saloon, music, and dancing. Quite a few of the stories were also factual. The notorious outlaw William H. Bonney, better known as "Billy the Kid," for example, was known to favor the Mexican *bailes* "dances" (see Chapter 3) both in Mexico and in the American territory of New Mexico. Another actual legendary character was Bat Masterson, who had been an army scout and a buffalo hunter, and later went on to become a well-known lawman of the West. Masterson had a limp that he acquired from a gunfight in Mobeetie, Texas. Apparently Masterson was in a dance hall enjoying a dance with a young woman, much to the jealously of a U.S. Army sergeant. It might have occurred in Perry Tuttle's dance house, which was also frequented by the cowboy cattle drivers. In either case, it is known that the dismayed sergeant shot and wounded Masterson and in the process also shot and killed the Calico Queen. In response, Masterson fired back and killed the sergeant (Lewis 1999, 217–218; Brown 1995, 281–282).

However, the cattle drives in the American West that produced the factual accounts of the cowboys and their exploits were short-lived. By the late 1870s, the railroad network increased dramatically, and by the 1880s, the railroads extended closer to the cattle ranches thereby making the long arduous cattle drives unnecessary. By the 1890s, the introduction of refrigeration and refrigerated railroad cars ended the cattle drives completely ("Railroads in the United States," n.d.).

"FROM THE BALLROOM TO HELL" AND DANCING AS A "SOCIAL VIRTUE"

In 1869, William Cleaver Wilkinson, a self-professed "advocate" of social dancing, provided an interesting addition to the list of social dance books. In *The Dance of Modern Society*, Wilkinson did not provide any written dance instruction, nor did he provide any examples of etiquette or discussions of the ballroom. Instead, he proposed "an unusual compliment to the dance—I propose to discuss it."

Wilkinson's publication was obviously in response to the long history of written attacks on social dancing. Although he made a strong argument "to vindicate for [the dance] a dignity all its own," Wilkinson was actually against social dancing for reasons that applied to contemporary society. He listed the following order of problems with contemporary social dancing as follows:

I. The bearing of the dance upon the Health;
II. Its relation to the economy;
III. Its Social Tendency;
IV. Its Influence upon Intellectual Improvement;
V. Its Moral or Religious Aspects.

Wilkinson's list of anti-dance sentiment set the pattern for many of the late-nineteenth century anti-dance crusaders (Wilkinson 1869, 5, 24–25).

During the 1860s, the common attack against social dancing was mainly as a "Popular amusement." At the time, social dancing was often grouped with the likes of cardplaying, billiards, gambling, and the theater as social amusements that were deemed "evil" by many of the clergy. Some of the anti-dance publications included the following:

- The Reverend John G. Jones, *An Appeal to all Christians, especially the members of the Methodist Episcopal Church, against the practice of social dancing* (1867);
- Hiram Mattison, *Popular Amusements: An Appeal to Methodists, in regard to the evils of card-playing, billiards, [and] dancing* (1867);
- The Reverend James H. Brookes, *May Christians Dance?* (1869);
- American Tract Society, *Dancing As A Social Amusement* (1870);
- The Reverend C.W. Andrews, *The Incompatibility of Theater-Going and Dancing With Membership in the Christian Church* (1872).

By the 1870s, however, the premise of the attack against social dancing shifted.

During the 1870s, the basic premise for the anti-dance attacks was focused on the fashionable dances of wealthy society. In 1872, for example, Robert Laird Collier, in *Every Day Subjects in Sunday Sermons*, made a distinction between dancing as a general social amusement and social dancing in the wealthy fashionable ballrooms. He proclaimed, "Dancing is beautiful and recreative; and yet promiscuous ballroom dancing is a fearful abuse of a true and good thing" (43). Other contemporary anti-dance tracts also wrote on the same theme as Collier's, but also added a new twist that applied to the health of the individual.

In 1879, in *A Time to Dance: A Sermon on Dancing*, the Reverend J.R. Sikes, for example, proclaimed that prior advocates of dancing who had instituted Biblical passages in favor of dancing had actually "perverted" the Scriptures. Sikes exclaimed,

For every passage of Scripture that you will present that sanctions the practice of dancing as performed in modern balls, I will furnish two passages that sanction the taking of human life—or murder, if you please. Now let us try and see how your system of interpreting or rather of *perverting* Scripture will work (3).

INSIDE HARRY HILL'S DANCE-HOUSE.

During the 1860s, the common attack against social dancing was mainly as a "Popular amusement." At the time, social dancing was often grouped with the likes of cardplaying, billiards, gambling, and the theater as social amusements that were deemed "evil" by many of the clergy. In this 1869 illustration of Harry Hill's Dance House on Houston Street near Broadway in New York City, social dancing is enjoyed along with other popular amusements including drinking.   Picture Collection, The Branch Libraries, The New York Public Library, Astor, Lenox, and Tilden Foundations. Picture Collection ID: 805680.

Sikes's publication was actually a revised 2nd edition that was first issued in 1867.

Overall, Sikes preached that visiting ballrooms provided only a bad association with "wicked men and women that seek their pleasure there." In addition, he stated that attending a dance was injurious to an individual's health and the "excessive exercise" led to the development of "disease." In support of his misleading statement, the Reverend Sikes presented "evidence" of individuals who supposedly had "died" from engaging in social dancing. He also invoked another common anti-dance theme of religious "conscience." He correlated the imposed "fear of death" into a theoretical question posed to his congregation. He asked them the following:

Another evidence that your conscience condemns it, is found in the fact that you are not willing to die in the ball room. I have asked a number of persons this question,

> "Would you be willing to die in the ballroom, and go to judgment from it?"...and I
> have not yet found the person that was willing to go from this place of *innocent* amuse-
> ment to the bar of God.

The wild accusations were often without rebuttal (Sikes, 4).

Among the few who countered the accusations was Lawrence De Garmo
Brookes. In 1867, in *Brookes on Modern Dancing*, Brookes simply wrote:

> Dancing has met, at all times, and under circumstances of no ordinary character, with
> strong opposition; but it has gradually overcome its opponents to such an extent, that
> ...[the opponents] belong only to those classes of people who oppose everything that
> makes life cheerful (3).

Regardless of the simple disclaimer provided by Brookes, the common theme of
dancing as "injurious to health" was echoed by many other anti-dance activists of
the nineteenth century.

In 1879, for example, the Reverend George C. Heckman, in *Dancing as a
Christian Amusement*, also warned of the "Effect of Dancing on Bodily Health."
Heckman limited his anti-dance tract to three subject headings as follows:

1. "Its Criminal Waste of Time and Money,"
2. "The Evil Associations of Dancing,"
3. "The Injurious Effects of Dancing upon Mind and Heart."

Actually, Heckman went a bit further than Sikes and proclaimed that dancing was
not only a health danger, but also a hindrance to Christian society. He asserted,

> I deem it at least questionable, as a barrier to the progress of Christian society, as
> unfriendly to virtue and grace, and as a leaven of individual and social corruption....
> Yet I must unhesitatingly declare dancing in its most popular forms all eminently dan-
> gerous exercise (2).

Heckman also echoed Sikes's theme of "death" caused by social dancing.

Actually, Heckman had the audacity to claim that just during the six months that
it took him to write his tract, he had counted at least "six cases of sudden death by
dancing." His unfounded description of the fatal "dancing disease" listed the
symptoms and effects as follows:

> The physical effects of dancing...are great bodily debility, undue excitement and reac-
> tive prostration of the nervous system, poisoning and obstruction of the lungs and
> throat, often resulting in hemorrhages and consumption, palpitation and other diseases
> of the heart, frequent headaches...and internal injuries of various kinds (3).

If the wild claim of "six deaths" caused by social dancing was not enough,
Heckman boasted that during the very first time that he preached his anti-dance
sermon a funeral procession passed carrying the remains of a young social dancer.
He added,

While preaching on this subject recently at Hanover [College], a funeral procession passed the church, following the remains of a young woman who died of rapid disease caused by dancing (2).

At the time, the Reverend Heckman was also the President of Hanover College in Pennsylvania.

Some of the other late-nineteenth century anti-dance publications that were written on the same themes as Heckman and Sikes included the following:

- The Reverend E.W. Borden, *Dancing as Piety. A Discourse Showing the Incompatibility of Dancing With Spiritual Religion* (1875);
- William Herman [pseudonym], *The Dance of Death* (1877);
- The Reverend George C. Heckman, *Dancing as a Christian Amusement* (1879);
- G.F. Pentecost, *The Christian and the Ballroom, or the Essential Evil of the Dance of Modern Fashionable Life* (1879);
- J.W. Lowber, *"Is It Wrong to Dance?" The Devil in Modern Society* (1888);
- T. DeWitt Talmage, *"Dancing," Social Dynamite* (1888);
- T.J. Bailey, *The Modern Dance* (1889);
- The Reverend E.L. Powell, *Perils Of The Dance* (1891);
- R.E. Brown, *A Treatise on the Elements of Dancing. By T. Erp. Sichore* [pseudonym] (1891);
- The Reverend William W. Gardner, *Modern Dancing: in the light of Scripture and facts* (1893);
- The Reverend T. DeWitt Talmage, *"The Wicked Dances" Sin—A Series of Popular Discourses* (1897);
- Jennie C. Rutty, *Letters Of Love And Counsel For Our Girls* (1898);
- The Reverend George Davis, *An Account of the Trial of Social Dance* (1899).

However, not since the incredulous writings in 1684 of Increase Mather's *An Arrow Against Profane and Promiscuous Dancing Drawn Out of the Quiver of Scriptures* had any single publication professed such a brutal attack on social dancing as did the two late-nineteenth century notorious publications by Thomas A. Faulkner and M.B. Williams.

In 1892, Thomas A. Faulkner's *From the Ball-Room to Hell*, published in Chicago by The Henry Publishing Company, and in 1896, the subsequent Faulkner-inspired *Where Satan Sows His Seed* by M.B. Williams, published in Chicago by the Fleming H. Revell Company, were each particularly harsh in the condemnation of social dancing. Unfortunately, despite unsubstantiated wild accusations and outrageous falsehoods, both publications received wide mass circulation. Faulkner's *From the Ball-Room to Hell* was reissued both in 1916 and 1921, and he wrote two other widely circulated anti-dance books, *The Gates of Death; or the Ball-Room Unmasked* (1899) and *The Lure of the Dance* (1916).

Unlike the clergy of the previous writings, Thomas A. Faulkner was actually a self-professed born-again Christian who revealed that he had been a former "dancing master" and proprietor for six years of the Los Angeles Dancing Academy on the Pacific Coast. He said that he had learned to dance at the age of 12 and subsequently frequented "the dancing parlors and academies." He boasted that on more than one occasion he had won "the championship of the Pacific Coast in fancy and round dancing." At some point, he had a revelation and went through, in his own words, a "conversion from a dancing master and a servant of the 'Evil One' to an earnest Christian and a servant of the Lord Jesus Christ." As his mission, he sought to repent "in the service of the Lord" to abolish social dancing, which he identified as "an evil which I know have been the ruin, both of soul and body, to many a bright young life" (5–7).

Faulkner's *From the Ball-Room to Hell* relied mainly on instilling the shocking fear in the reader that the end result of participating in social dancing was "death"— and death at an early age no less. In particular, he prudently warned that any "lady who danced to excess, [did not] live to be over twenty-five years of age." As for men, he added, "The average age of the excessive male dancer is thirty-one." His diagnosis as to the cause of the death: "It is not the exercise which harms the dancers in mind and body, but the coming in such close contact with the opposite sex... [and] the inevitable end is death" (24, 39).

For many readers, Faulkner's statement was quite shocking. Actually, within his introduction to the book, he forewarned his readers that the contents of his "little book" would, indeed, prove shocking. He proclaimed,

> You will, my dear reader, find many very plain things between the two covers of this little book; things which will, perhaps, shock your modesty and probably disgust you altogether (3).

In fact, some of Faulkner's chapter headings themselves were rather direct and questionable. They included "From the Ball-Room to the Grave," "Abandoned Women the Best Dancers," and "The Approval of Society is no Proof Against the Degradation."

In Chapter II, "From the Ball-Room To The Grave," for example, Faulkner told a fictitious story of a 19-year-old "handsome blonde" country girl who apprenticed in the "big city" of Los Angeles. He said that on one night in December 1891, she decided to take part in the "selfish pleasure and sinful indulgence" of social dancing—that had tragic results. Within an unnamed dance hall, she was befriended by an amorous city man, who Faulkner termed a "professional seducer." He described their amorous dance encounter as follows:

> Her bare arm is almost around his neck, her partly nude swelling breasts heaves tumultuously against his, face to face they whirl on, his limbs interwoven with hers, his strong right arm around her yielding form, he presses her to him until every curve in the contour of her body thrills with the amorous contact... the soft music fills the room, but she hears it not; he bends her body to and fro, but she knows it not; his hot breath, tainted with strong drink is on her hair and cheek, his lips almost touch her forehead, yet she does not shrink;... She is filled with the rapture of sin and in its intensity; her spirit is inflamed with passion and lust is gratified in thought. With a last low wail the music ceases, and the dance for the night is ended, but not the evil work of the night (14).

Faulkner added that after the dancing was over the young woman was returned "to her home that night robbed of that most precious jewel of womanhood—virtue!"

As a result, Faulkner claimed that she was relegated to life as "a brothel inmate, the toy and plaything of the libertine and drunkard" (14–15, 23).

At the time, moralists and progressive reformers had a real-life fear of the "big city" and urban life, mainly among the newly arriving European immigrants. Many newspapers and mass-publication magazines told false stories of the evils of urban life and the ruination of young unmarried woman. Theodore Dreiser's *Sister Carrie* (1900), was one example that told of the downfall of one such "country-girl" who went to Chicago and was seduced and "ruined" by lowly immigrants. In addition, mainly because of the advocacy of individuals, such as Margaret Sanger's promotion of birth control, moralists were also concerned about the supposed promiscuity of urban females (Giordano 2003, 9).

A promiscuous young woman was one, therefore, who was "ruined" in society. In turn, Faulkner played on this same fear and added, "It is a startling fact, but a fact nevertheless, that two-thirds of the girls who are ruined, fall through the influence of dancing." However, some disputed the claims of both the moralists and Faulkner that the number of pregnancies was not evident among unmarried woman in

This illustration of "A Victim of One Night's Pleasure," portraying a 19-year-old woman just prior to death caused by her participation in social dancing, is from Thomas Faulkner's *From the Ball-Room to Hell*, c. 1903, page 55.

urban society. Actually, Faulkner said that he was often asked, "If what you say be true, why do not more of the dancing girls become mothers?" His response, as incredulous as it sounds, was simply, "I will tell you why. It is because they dance away all fear of maternity" (22–24).

Throughout his publication, Faulkner continually pronounced that the "gates of hell" waited for any "dancing woman," especially any woman who was "ruined." But, on the other hand, he did not admonish the "dancing man." For instance, he warned all young women,

> It is a noticeable fact that a man who knows the ways of a ball-room rarely seeks a wife there. When he wishes to marry he chooses for a wife a woman who has not been fondled and embraced by every dancing man in town (22–23).

Faulkner's own misinformation was actually a result of an inherent "double-standard" in American society. In fact, throughout all facets of American society was a continued pronunciation among all levels of social, cultural, economical, and political aspects of a double standard as it applied to both men and women. A woman in society was expected to maintain her virtue, marry, and ultimately bear children.

In a fashion similar to Faulkner's *From the Ball-Room to Hell*, in 1896, Evangelist M.B. Williams, in *Where Satan Sows His Seed: Plain Talks on the Amusements of Modern Society*, also relied on society's fear of a ruined woman. In fact, Williams also told a tale of "The Life of a Fallen Woman." In order to support his claim, Williams quoted from Thomas Faulkner's speculative ad-hoc survey citing the cases of 200 "fallen" young girls. Of the 200, Faulkner claimed 7 came upon ruination due to "poverty and abuse" and 10 by "willful choice"; 20 were driven by "drink given by parents"; and an incredulous 163 were ruined simply by "dancing school and ball rooms" (Faulkner 1894, 56; Williams 1896, 95–97).

In further support of the ruination of the young woman as a result of social dancing, Williams also cited a sermon by the Reverend S.J. Beach of Cedar Falls. The Reverend Beach, in turn, had cited the Catholic Church, who reportedly cited "strong evidence" that was compiled by the *New York Journal of Education*. Williams, therefore, presented the "strong evidence" within his book in headline fashion as follows:

NINETEEN OUT OF EVERY TWENTY WOMEN WHO
FALL CAN TRACE THE BEGINNING OF
THEIR SAD STATE TO THE
MODERN DANCE

Williams also quoted many other denominations and provided testimonials "in support" of his claim (75). Needless to say, the statistics were not substantiated.

A substantial part of Williams's 125-page publication, however, was more typical of the earlier anti-dance literature and sermons that grouped social dancing among cardplaying, alcohol, and theater. He said, "Joined to these evils, of Cards, wine, and Theater, and to some extent greater than all the others, we find the dance of modern society." In direct opposition to social dancing he provided two reasons that he summed up as follows:

- "First, the dance is unspiritual, and a positive exterminator of spiritual life."
- "Second, the dance is immoral; in fact, the hot bed of immorality and vice."

He did, though, add an explanation to this brief list asserting that "the hardest young person to reach for Christ is the young man or woman devotee of the dance" (79).

Unlike Faulkner, Williams did not condemn only the young women, he also asked, "But what of the young man?" Still, he did not necessarily condemn the "young man" directly. Actually, he leveled his admonishment directly at the young women. Williams explained,

Not a single barrier of this kind has society reared about him for protection. He is at liberty to spend his hours with you in the ball room, escort you home, and spend the balance of the night satisfying the passion which you have aroused. Society condones his offences, smiles at his brilliancy, and says, "Only sowing his wild oats; he'll come out all right one of these days, he'll marry and settle down."

Unlike Faulkner's "professional seducer," Williams called that type of man a "moral leper" (111).

For the most part, many of the prominent dance instructors did not overtly respond to any of the anti-dance crusaders. In fact, most of the dance proponents simply dismissed the writings and sermons as ludicrous and laughable. In 1875, in *The Dance of Society* for example, noted dance instructor William B. De Garmo countered the anti-dance allegations with a brief statement. He wrote,

Books, pamphlets, sermons, lectures and newspaper contributions in denunciation of dancing at times appear, and are sometimes anonymously sent to me, with such words as "please answer this" written on them. In all of them so much narrow-mindedness and bigotry are displayed, that they sufficiently condemn themselves without the assistance of a professional or amateur (13).

In 1878, in *Dancing at Home and Abroad*, C.H. Cleveland also provided a brief counterstatement. He professed,

In short, the religion of courtesy has done much more than the religion of Puritanism to elevate the mental and moral tone of societies; and it is respectfully submitted that dancing academies have had some influences in bringing about the good results (104).

At the time, one of the leading proponents of social dancing who actually seriously pondered the questions posed by the anti-dance publications was Allen Dodworth. He also administered Dodworth's Dancing Academy, which at the time was the most prominent of all the dancing schools in America.

In 1885, Allen Dodworth did not necessarily discount all social dancing as innocent. In fact, he actually was opposed to the "extravagance of expense, suppers, late hours, and other dissipations, [that] have no necessary relation to dancing." Actually, he agreed that in some cases dancing led "to many things that are sinful." The reason, however, Dodworth claimed was that the anti-dance preachers themselves had created a "dead-end" for social amusement among young people in American society. Dodworth asserted,

But these good people [the clergy] are in a measure answerable for this. They have blocked up nearly every road, except the one leading to vice. Would it not be well, now, to open a few paths through this pleasure-ground [of social dancing] which would lead to virtue?

Dodworth rationalized, "for certainly to make pleasant [dancing] motions to good music cannot be sinful." He suggested that learning social dancing within an acceptable environment was a "social virtue" that benefited all of society. He expressed his reasoning as follows:

Surely, the daily practice of these social virtues would have a softening effect, and produce a better result than sending the children into the yard or play-room for recreation which usually means to romp and practice rudeness, the strong abusing the weak, and all taking daily lessons in tyranny, imposition, and turbulence.

Dodworth continually emphasized that social dancing was always engaged in under happy circumstances and brought joy to the dancers.

Therefore, Dodworth asserted that dancing was a "social virtue." Conversely, in order to maintain the social virtue, he said that it was the responsibility of the clergy to provide an acceptable community venue for "those whose nature it is to dance." In turn, he concluded that many of the objections by the clergy would simply not exist. He asked,

What reasonable objection would there be to every "Young Men's Christian Association" [Y.M.C.A.] having weekly meetings for the enjoyment of this pleasure? Surrounded by parents, and friends, the happiness experienced by the young people would not make them less active in their Christian duties.

But Dodworth's 50 years of experience certainly taught him to be pragmatic, and he was well aware that society did not change that easily. He certainly was not overly optimistic that the opposing views or outright hostility towards social dancing would ever change. Nevertheless, he advocated that an idealistic solution to the problem was based upon a belief in the kindness of human nature. He suggested,

Not until every breath inhaled…conveys moral education, can we expect to overcome the selfishness of nature. When to make others happy is our own greatest happiness, then will come the peace that passeth all understanding.

Nevertheless, despite Dodworth's optimistic desire, hostility against social dancing still persisted (Dodworth 1900, 10–12, 23).

Apparently, not every opponent to social dancing attacked it with words. An account in *The New York Times* on February 5, 1885, indicated that some actually lashed out violently. In a brief article, under the headline "He Whipped his Wife for Dancing," newly married 17-year-old Mrs. Florence L. Foster sued for divorce from her husband, 23-year-old William H. Foster. In a Brooklyn court, she claimed that her husband routinely "beat and choke[ed] her on the slightest provocation." In fact, her accusations proved true, as the husband claimed that his wife "persisted in dancing against his commands." He admitted that upon her return from dancing, "he beat her"—actually, he brutally "whipped" her. The judge approved the divorce and "ordered a decree of separation" ("He Whipped His Wife For Dancing," 2).

Unfortunately, the constant barrage of "immoral" connotations against social dancing was not necessarily a debate that was settled in a court of law. In February 1894, an extensive three column newspaper article in *The New York Times* headlined "Parlor Dancing Denounced" recognized that the religious debate over social dancing continued. The editors openly accepted the importance of the situation as they preceded the article by stating, "*The New York Times* recognizes the gravity of the popular and clerical division thus suggested, and takes occasion to provide illustrations of it." A concise summation of the situation between the religious opponents and the religious proponents was given as follows:

> Among the clergymen the division is as marked and as profound as it is among the laity. There are clergymen of the liberal school who not merely attend balls given by their parishioners, but who applauded the waltz and the polka, and deny the responsibility of harm being inherent in either of them. On the other hand, many clergymen...make no effort to conceal their opposition to all forms and varieties of public dancing, and especially the dances so vehemently denounced at the Brooklyn revival.

Apparently, at a recent revival meeting in Brooklyn unrepressed protest was continually mounted against the "evil in the round dances." The article reported, "The evangelists, who mercilessly assailed the polka and the waltz, did not hesitate to expose the foundations of their hostility." The article surveyed many clergymen of different denominations throughout New York and Brooklyn. The results were conclusive in the sense that the debate over the social virtue of dancing was, in fact, "far more intense than one would be apt to suppose."

Actually there was a distinct division among the clergy. The Reverend Dr. E. Walpole Warren, rector of the Holy Trinity Church in Manhattan, for example, supported social dancing. He said, "There need be nothing objectionable in dancing...and I think the dance is equally harmless to most people." The Reverend Dr. David H. Greer, rector of St. Bartholomew's Church, also agreed. He pronounced, "It is a healthful recreation, and one that can well be encouraged by clergymen and church societies." On the other hand, the Reverend Dr. Arthur Brooks, rector of the Church of the Incarnation, disagreed. Brooks concluded, "I do not believe in dances being given in any connection with a church...for the Church is looked upon as a kind of fortress which should protect people from all temptations. In the ballroom we find no such fortress."

The Reverend W.C.P. Rhoades, pastor of the Marcy Avenue Baptist Church in Brooklyn, offered a different opinion. He stated, "We have no discipline condemning dancing, like the Methodists...I leave these questions to be settled by the consciences of my congregation." On the other hand, Methodist minister the Reverend James S. Chadwick affirmed, "Dancing is demoralizing, and has been the means of ruining many people." Another Methodist minister, the Reverend Dr. Van Alstyne, concurred. He added, "I thoroughly condemn the whole thing [of dancing], because it endangers the morals of society, especially those of the young people." The Reverend T. DeWitt Talmage also offered an opinion. Talmage was quite well known throughout America and even internationally; he was a personal friend of the Czar of Russia. Although he personally never witnessed the round dances, the Reverend Talmage called them "depraved" and added, "Of course, if they are wrong, I disapprove of them, as I disapprove of everything that is wrong, but, you know, I do not take such narrow views of many things as some people do." Talmage also authored two anti-dance publications, *"Dancing," Social Dynamite* (1888) and *"The Wicked Dances" Sin— A Series of Popular Discourses* (1897).

However, the debate continued and indicated that overall for as many of the clergy who routinely accepted dancing as an innocent social virtue, there was an equal number of the clergy who certainly did not. About the only thing that *The New York Times* conclusively determined was that, "It is a far cry to the fashionable dancing class from the crowded hall of the revival prayer meeting" ("Parlor Dancing Denounced," 12).

CONCLUSION

By the 1890s, although social life in general was often limited, Americans of all ethnic, economic, and social classes enjoyed some form of social dancing. But, for the most part, by the end of the nineteenth century, as it applied to the fashionable dances sponsored by the wealthy and the subsequent dance instruction and etiquette manuals, American social dancing was rather sedate. The condition was created mainly by the dancing academies and dance instructors who had "standardized" all elements of social dancing. According to dance historian Lloyd Shaw, "The academies [and] the dancing masters...had come to a sort of all-time low in dancing" (1949, 59). A major contributing factor was that Americans had basically blindly copied Europe, not only for social dancing and etiquette, but also for all aspects of culture. However, at the turn of the twentieth century, with the musical developments such as Ragtime and Jazz, America began the development of a truly unique and independent American culture.

As it applied to social dancing, those influences included the Native American Indian, Spanish, Caribbean, African, European, and other ethnic cultures that created original American social dances such as the Turkey Trot and Fox Trot. During the twentieth century, social dancing in itself offered a parallel of the social, economic, and cultural traditions of each particular time period. For example, segregation and the "Jim Crow" mentality was cemented in place all over the United States, and for most of the century dancing and dancing halls were strictly segregated. Segregation forced a mass migration from the South to northern cities and with it a transformation of the Delta Blues music into an American original—Jazz. Jazz gave birth to the Charleston Dance, as well as evolving into Swing music and the Lindy Hop. In the latter part of the twentieth century, with the technological advancement of television, shows such as "American Bandstand," "Soul Train," "Dance Fever," and eventually those watched by the MTV generation greatly influenced social dance styles and the current "new" trends in dancing such as Rock 'n' Roll, the Twist, Freestyle, Disco, Breakdancing, and Hip Hop.

Bibliography

*Publications within the bibliography preceded by an asterisk provide a good general overview for the student or scholar interested in a reference starting point on the subject of Social Dancing.

Adams, John. *Diary and Autobiography of John Adams, Volume 2, 1771–1781*. Edited by Lyman H. Butterfield. Cambridge, MA: Harvard University PRess, 1961.

*Aldrich, Elizabeth. *From the Ballroom to Hell: Grace and Folly in Nineteenth-Century Dance*. Evanston, IL: Northwestern University Press, 1991.

Ambrose, Stephen E. *Undaunted Courage: Meriwether Lewis, Thomas Jefferson, and the Opening of the American West*. New York: Simon and Schuster, 1996.

Andrews, E.D. "The Dance in Shaker Ritual." In Paul Magriel, *Chronicles of the American Dance*. New York: H. Holt, 1948, 3–5.

Arbeau, Thoinot. *Orchesographie* [1589]. Translated *Orchesography* by Mary Stewart Evans. New York: Dover Publications, 1967.

Arthur, T.S. *Advice to Young Men on their Duties and Conduct in Life*. Boston: Phillips, Sampson & Co., 1853.

Arvine, Kazlitt. *Cyclopedia of Moral and Religious Anecdotes*. New York: 1881.

The Ball-room Instructer: Containing a Complete Description of Cotillons and Other Popular Dances. New York: Huestis & Craft, 1841.

Banes, Sally, and John F. Szwed. "From 'Messin'-Around' to 'Funky Western Civilization': The Rise and Fall of Dance Instruction Songs." In *Dancing Many Drums*, edited by Thomas F. De Frantz. Madison, WI: The University of Wisconsin Press, 2002, 169–203.

Barzel, Anne. "History of Social Dancing." In *The Dance Encyclopedia*, compiled by Anatole Chuoy and P.W. Manchester. New York: Simon and Schuster, 1967.

Beadle's Dime Ball-Room Companion and Guide to Dancing. Comprising rules of etiquette, hints on private parties, toilettes for the ball-room, etc. Also, a synopsis of round and square dances, dictionary of French terms, etc. New York: Beadle and Company, 1868.

Beaumont, C.W., trans. *The Dancing-Master*. Translated from the French of Pierre Rameau. London: C.W. Beaumont, 1931.

Beecher, Catharine. *A Treatise on Domestic Economy*. New York: Harper and Brothers, 1851.

Blake, John L. *The Farmer's Every-Day Book*. Auburn, NH: Derby, Miller Company, 1850.

Blasis, Carlo. *The Code of Terpsichore. The art of dancing, comprising its theory and practice, and a history of its rise and progress, from the earliest times. Translated under the author's immediate inspection by R. Barton.* London: Printed for Edward Bull, Holles Street, 1831.

Boyer, Paul S., Clifford Clark, Jr., et al. *The Enduring Vision: A History of the American People.* New York: Houghton Mifflin, 2000.

Braden, Donna R. *Leisure and Entertainment in America.* Dearborn, MI: Henry Ford Museum and Greenfield Village.

Brathwaite, Richard. *The English Gentleman* [1630]. Norwood, NJ: W.J. Johnson, 1975.

Brathwaite, Richard. *The English Gentlewoman* [1631]. New York: Da Capo Press, 1970.

Brookes, Lawrence De Garmo. *Brookes on Modern Dancing, Containing a Full Description of all Dances, as Practised in the Ball Room and at Private Parties Together with an Essay on Etiquette.* New York: L. De G. Brookes, 1867.

Brown, Dee. *The American West.* New York: Touchstone Book, Simon and Schuster, 1995.

Bruccoli, Matthew J., Richard Layman, and Karen L. Rood, eds. *American Eras: Revolutionary Era, 1754–1783.* Detroit: Gale Research, 1998.

Bryant, William Cullen, and Sydney Howard Gay. *A Popular History of the United States.* New York: Charles Scribner's Sons, 1881.

Buckman, Peter. *Let's Dance.* New York: Paddington Press, 1978.

Burrows, Edwin G., and Mike Wallace. *Gotham: A History of New York City to 1898.* New York: Oxford University Press, 1998.

Butler, Albert and Josephine. *Encyclopedia of Social Dance.* New York: Albert Butler Ballroom Dance, 1980.

Caroso, Fabrizio. *Il ballarino.* Venice [1581]. New York: Broude Bros. 1967.

Carson, Jane. *Colonial Virginians at Play.* Charlottesville, VA: The University Press of Virginia, 1965.

Catlin, George. *Illustrations of the Manners, Customs, and Condition of the North American Indians.* 2 vols. London: Chatto and Windus, 1876.

Catlin, George. *Letters and Notes on the Manners, Customs, and Condition of the North American Indians.* Edited by Michael Mooney. New York: Clarkson N. Potter, 1975.

Catlin, George. "The Manners, Customs, and Condition of the North American Indians (1836)." In *I See America Dancing: Selected Readings 1685- 2000,* edited by Maureen Needham. Chicago: University of Illinois Press, 2002, 21–25.

Cellarius, Henri. *The Drawing-room Dances.* London: E. Churton, 1847.

The Centennial of the United States Military Academy at West Point, New York 1802–1902. Washington, D.C.: Government Printing Office, 1904.

Chalif, Louis H. *The Chalif Text Books of Dancing.* 5 vols. New York: The Chalif Normal School of Dancing, 1914–1925.

Clarke, Mary, and Clement Crisp. *The History of Dance.* New York: Crown Publishers, Inc., 1981.

Clendenen, Leslie F. *Cakewalks.* St. Louis: Author, 1900.

Cleveland, C.H. *Dancing at Home and Abroad.* Boston: O. Ditson and Co., 1878.

Collier, Robert Laird. *Every-day Subjects in Sunday Sermons.* Boston: American Unitarian Association, 1872. The 1872 edition is held in the collection "Making of American Books" at the University of Michigan Library.

Crane, Jonathan Townley. *An Essay on Dancing.* New York: Nelson and Phillips, 1849.

Cressey, Paul G. *The Taxi-Dance Hall: A Sociological Study in Commercialized Recreation and City Life.* Montclair, NJ: Patterson Smith, 1932; reprint 1969.

Csida, Joseph, and June Bundy Csida. *American Entertainment: A Unique History of Popular Show Business.* New York: Watson-Guptill Publications, 1978.

Czarnowski, Lucile K. *Dances of Early California Days.* Palo Alto, CA: Pacific Books, 1950.

Daniels, Bruce C. *Puritans at Play: Leisure and Recreation in Colonial New England.* New York: St. Martin's Press, 1995.

*Dannett, Sylvia G.L., and Frank R. Rachel. *Down Memory Lane: Arthur Murray's Picture Story of Social Dancing.* New York: Greenberg Publishing, 1954.

De Crevecoeur, John. *Sketches of Eighteenth Century America*. Edited by Bourdin, Gabriel, and Williams. New Haven: Yale University Press, 1925.

De Garmo, William B. *The Prompter: containing full descriptions of all the quadrilles, figures of the German cotillon, etc. Designed for the assistance of the pupils of Wm. B. De Garmo*. New York: Raymond and Caulon, printers, 1865.

De Garmo, William B. *The Dance of Society*. New York: W.A. Pond and Co., 1875.

*DeMille, Agnes. *America Dances*. New York: Macmillan Publishing Co., 1980.

Dick and Fitzgerald. *Dick's Quadrille Call-Book, and Ball-Room Prompter*. New York: Behrens Publishing Company, 1878.

Dodds, John W. "Living in Small-town and Rural America." In *The 1900s*. Edited by Myra H. Immell. San Diego, CA: Greenhaven Press, 2000.

Dodworth, Allen. *Assistant for A. Dodworth's Pupils*. New York: Nesbitt & Co., Printers, 1878.

*Dodworth, Allen. *Dancing and Its Relation to Education and Social Life*. New York and London: Harper and Brothers, 1900.

*Dorfman, Leon. *The Cavalcade of American Ballroom Dancing: Minuet to Hustle*. Floral Park, NY: Leon Dorfman, 1976.

*Driver, Ian. *A Century of Dance: A Hundred Years of Musical Movement, from Waltz to Hip Hop*. London: Octopus Publishing Group Limited, 2000.

Du Bois, W.E.B. *The Philadelphia Negro*. Reprinted New York: Shocken, 1967.

Durang, Charles. *The Fashionable Dancer's Casket; or, The Ball-Room Instructor. A new and splendid work on dancing, etiquette, deportment, and the toilet*. Philadelphia: Fisher and Brother, 1856.

Durang, John. Memoir excerpts "John Durang (1768–1822), First American Theatrical Dancer." In *I See America Dancing: Selected Readings 1685- 2000*. Edited by Maureen Needham. Chicago: University of Illinois Press, 2002. 140–144.

*Erenberg, Lewis A. *Steppin' Out: New York Nightlife and the Transformation of American Culture*. Westport, CT: Greenwood Press, 1981.

Escoffier, Jeffery. "Social Dancing." In *St. James Encyclopedia of Popular Culture*. Edited by Tom Pendergast and Sara Pendergast. Detroit, MI: St. James Press, 2000. Vol. 4: 450–451.

Essex, John. *For the Furthur Improvement of Dancing, A treatise of chorography or ye art of dancing country dances after a new character…translated from the French of Monsr Feuillet*. London: I. Walsh and P. Randall, 1710. London: Gregg International, 1970.

Evans, Mary Stewart. *Orchesography, translated version of Thoinot Arbeau's Orchesographie [1589]*. New York: Dover Publications, 1967.

Farrar, Mrs. John. *The Young Lady's Friend*. Boston: American Stationers Company, 1836.

Faulkner, Thomas A. *From the Ball-Room to Hell*. Chicago: R.F. Henry, 1894.

Faulkner, Thomas A. "From the Ballroom to Hell (1894)." In *I See America Dancing: Selected Readings 1685–2000*. Edited by Maureen Needham. Chicago: University of Illinois Press, 2002, 112–118.

Ferrero, Edward. *The Art of Dancing: Historically Illustrated. To which is added a few Hints on Etiquette*. New York: Dick and Fitzgerald, 1859.

Feuillet, Raoul-Auger. *Recueil de dances, composées par M. Pecour…et mise sur le papier par M. Feuillet*. Paris: Raoul-Auger Feuillet, 1709.

*Fletcher, Beale. *How to Improve Your Social Dancing with the Fletcher Count System*. Canada: The Copp Clark Company, Ltd., 1956.

Fordyce, James. *Sermons to Young Women*. Vol. I, 14th ed. London: C. Baldwin, 1814.

*Franks, A.H. *Social Dance: A Short History*. London: Routledge, Paul and Kegan, 1963.

Galbraith, R.C., Jr. *The History of the Chillicothe Presbytery from the Organization in 1799–1889*. Chillicothe: By the Presbytery, 1889.

Bibliography

Gallini, Giovanni-Andrea. *A Treatise on the Art of Dancing.* London: Printed for the author and sold by R. Dodsley, 1772.

Gardner, Ella. *Public Dance Halls: Their Regulation and Place in the Recreation of Adolescents Bureau Publication No. 189.* Washington, D.C.: United States Government Printing Office, 1929.

*Giordano, Ralph G. *Fun and Games in Twentieth Century America: A Historical Guide to Leisure.* Westport, CT: Greenwood, 2003.

Glaab, Charles N. *The American City: A Documentary History.* Homewood, IL: The Dorsey Press Inc., 1963.

Goldfield, David, Carl Abbott, et al. *The American Journey: A History of the United States.* 2nd ed. Upper Saddle River, NJ: Prentice Hall, 2001.

Grove, Lilly. *Dancing.* London: Longmans, Green, 1907.

*Harris, Jane A., Anne M. Pittmann, and Marlys S. Waller. *Social Dance: From Dance a While.* Massachusetts: Allyn and Bacon, 1998.

*Harris, Jane A., Anne M. Pittmann, Marlys S. Waller, and Cathy L. Dark. *Dance a While: Handbook for Folk, Square, Contra, and Social Dance.* 8th ed. Boston, MA: Allyn and Bacon, 2000.

*Hazzard-Gordon, Katrina. *Jookin' The Rise of Social Dance Formations in African American Culture.* Philadelphia: Temple University Press, 1990.

Heckman, George C. *Dancing as a Christian Amusement.* Philadelphia: Presbyterian Board of Publication, 1879. http://www.covenanter.org/Practical/Dancing/dancing.htm.

Hendrickson, Charles Cyril. *John Griffiths, Dancing Master, 29 Country Dances.* Sandy Hook, CT: The Hendrickson Group, 1989.

Hillgrove, Thomas. *The Scholars' Companion and Ball-room vade mecum...With hints and instructions respecting toilet, deportment, &c., &c....By Thomas Hillgrove.* New York: T.R. Turnbull and Co., printers, 1857.

Hillgrove, Thomas. *A Complete Practical Guide to the Art of Dancing. Containing descriptions of all fashionable and approved dances, full directions for calling the figures, the amount of music required; hints on etiquette, the toilet, etc.* New York: Dick and Fitzgerald, 1863.

Hillgrove, Thomas. *Hillgrove's Ballroom Guide.* New York: Thomas Hillgrove, 1868.

Holbrook, Leona. "Dancing as an Aspect of Early Mormon and Utah Culture." In *Focus on Dance: VIII Dance Heritage.* Edited by E. Carmen Imel and Gwen K. Smith. Washington, D.C.: AAHPER Publications, 1977, 4–14.

Homer. *The Iliad.* New York: Viking Press, 1990.

How to Dance. A complete ball-room and party guide. New York: Tousey and Small, 1878; Boston: A. Williams, 1858.

Ide, Jacob A.M. *The Nature and Tendency of Balls, Seriously and Candidly Considered in two Sermons, Preached in Medway, The First December 21: The Second December 28, 1818.* Dedham, MA: M. & W.H. Mann, 1818.

Jackson, Donald, and Dorothy Twohig, eds. *The Diaries of George Washington.* Vol. 5. *The Papers of George Washington.* Charlottesville: University Press of Virginia, 1979.

Jackson, Donald, and Dorothy Twohig, eds. *The Diaries of George Washington.* Vol. 6. *The Papers of George Washington.* Charlottesville: University Press of Virginia, 1979.

James, Ed. *Jig, Clog, and Breakdown Dancing Made Easy, with sketches of noted jig dancers.* New York: Ed James, 1873.

James, Henry. *Charles W. Eliot, President of Harvard University 1869–1909.* Vol. II, Boston: Houghton Miffline, 1930.

Jones, W.A. "Indian Bureau Regulations (1902)." In *I See America Dancing: Selected Readings 1685–2000.* Edited by Maureen Needham. Chicago: University of Illinois Press, 2002, 35–40.

*Kaplan, Max. *Leisure in America: A Social Inquiry*. New York: John Wiley and Sons, Inc., 1960.

*Karpeles, Maud. *Cecil Sharp: His Life and Work*. Chicago: The University of Chicago Press, 1967.

Kopp, E.H. *The American Prompter and Guide to Etiquette*. Cincinnati, New York, Chicago: The John Church Co., 1896

Leaflets of the Ball Room. Being a sketch of the polka quadrilles, the Baden, mazurka figures &c. &c. to which is appended the music of the celebrated Redowa waltz, now first published in the United States. Philadelphia and New York: Turner and Fisher, 1847.

Lyverthey, Hudson K. *Our Etiquette and Social Observances*. Grand Rapids, MI: Lyverthey, 1881.

Keller, Kate Van Winkle. *John Griffiths, Eighteenth-Century Itinerant Dancing Master*. Sandy Hook, CT: The Hendrickson Group, 1989.

Keller, Kate Van Winkle, and George A. Fogg. *Country Dances from Colonial New York, James Alexander's Notebook, 1730*. Boston: Country Dance Society–Boston Centre, 2000.

Keller, Kate Van Winkle, and George A. Fogg. *The Richmond Assemblies 1790–1797*. Annapolis, MD: The Colonial Music Institute, 2003.

*Keller, Kate Van Winkle, and Charles Cyril Hendrickson. *George Washington: A Biography in Social Dance*.Sandy Hook, CT: Hendrickson Group, 1998.

Keller, Kate Van Winkle, and Genevieve Shimer. "Playford's 'English Dancing Master' (1651) and Country Dancing in America." In *I See America Dancing: Selected Readings 1685–2000*. Edited by Maureen Needham. Chicago: University of Illinois Press, 2002, 61–65.

Keller, Kate W., and Ralph Sweet. *A Choice Selection of American Country Dances of the Revolutionary Era (1775–1795)*. New York: Country Dance and Song Society of America, 1975.

Keller, Robert M. *Dance Figures Index: American Country Dances, 1730–1810*. Sandy Hook, CT: The Hendrickson Group, 1989.

Kopp, E.H. *The American Prompter and Guide to Etiquette*. Cincinnati, New York, Chicago: The John Church Co., 1896.

Kostof, Spiro. *America by Design*. New York: Oxford University Press, 1987.

*Kraus, Richard, and Sarah Alberti Chapman. *History of the Dance: In Art and Education*. Englewood Cliffs, NJ: Prentice Hall Inc., 1981.

Latrobe, Benjamin Henry. "Sunday Afternoon Dances in Congo Square (1819)." In *I See America Dancing: Selected Readings 1685–2000*. Edited by Maureen Needham. Chicago: University of Illinois Press, 2002, 73–74.

Laussat, Pierre Clement de. *Memoirs and Correspondence of Pierre Clement de Laussat*. Translated by Henri Delville de Sinclair. Louisiana: WPA, 1940.

Lewis, Jon E. *The Mammoth Book of the West: The Making of the American West*. New York: Carroll and Graf Publishers, Inc., 1999.

Locke, John. *Some Thoughts Concerning Education*. Edited by Robert H. Quick. Boston: Cambridge University Press, 1880.

*McCarthy, Albert J. *The Dance Band Era: The dancing decades from ragtime to swing, 1910–1950*. Philadelphia: Chilton Books, 1971; reprint, 1982.

Magriel, Paul David. *A Bibliography of Dancing*. New York: Wilson, 1936.

*Magriel, Paul, ed. *Chronicles of the American Dance*. New York: Henry Holt and Company, 1948.

*Malnig, Julie. *Dancing Till Dawn: A Century of Exhibition Ballroom Dancing*. Westport, CT: Greenwood Press, 1992.

*Marks, Joseph E., III.*America Learns to Dance: A Historical Study of Dance Education in America Before 1900*. Brooklyn, NY: Dance Horizons, 1957.

Bibliography

*Marks, Joseph E., III, ed. *The Mathers on Dancing.* Brooklyn, NY: Dance Horizons, 1975.

Mather, Cotton. *A Cloud of Witness Against Balls and Dances: Darting out Light upon a Case, too Unseasonably made Seasonable to be Discoursed on.* Boston: B. Green and J. Allen, 1700. Reprinted in Joseph E. Marks III, *The Mathers on Dancing.* Brooklyn, NY: Dance Horizons, 1975, 64–75.

Mather, Increase. *An Arrow Against Profane and Promiscuous Dancing Drawn Out of the Quiver of Scriptures.* Boston: Samuel Green, 1684.

Mather, Increase. *An Arrow Against Profane and Promiscuous Dancing Drawn Out of the Quiver of Scriptures.* Reprinted in Joseph E. Marks III, *The Mathers on Dancing.* Brooklyn, NY: Dance Horizons, 1975, 29–59.

McCoy, Joseph G. *Historic Sketches of the Cattle Trade in the West and Southwest.* Kansas City, MO: Ramsey, Millett and Hudson, 1874.

McDonagh, Don. "The Evolution of Social Dancing." In *Dance: A Very Social History.* Edited by Carol Wallace et al. New York: The Metropolitan Museum of Art, and Rizzoli International Publications, Inc., 1986, 58–79.

Miller, Craig. *Social Dance in the Mormon West.* Salt Lake City: The Utah Arts Council, 2000.

Montez, Madame Lola. *The Arts of Beauty.* New York: by author, 1858.

Mooney, James. *The Ghost-dance Religion and the Sioux Outbreak of 1890.* 14th Annual Report of the Bureau of American Ethnology, 1896, Part 2.

Mooney, James A. "The Ghost Dance (1890)." In *I See America Dancing: Selected Readings 1685–2000.* Maureen Needham. Chicago: University of Illinois Press, 2002, 26–34.

*Mouvet, Maurice. *Maurice's Art of Dancing.* New York: G. Schirmer, 1915.

Nash, Gary B., et al. *The American People: Creating a Nation and a Society.* Brief 4th ed. New York: Addison-Wesley Educational Publishers Inc., 2003.

*Needham, Maureen, ed. *I See America Dancing: Selected Readings 1685–2000.* Chicago: University of Illinois Press, 2002.

Needham, Maureen. "The War of the Quadrilles: Creole vs. Americans (1804)." In *I See America Dancing: Selected Readings 1685–2000.* Edited by Maureen Needham. Chicago: University of Illinois Press, 2002, 66–72.

Negri, Cesare. *Nuove Inventioni di Balli.* Milan, Italy: G. Bordone, 1604.

*Nevell, Richard. *A Time to Dance: American Country Dancing from Hornpipe to Hot Hash.* New York: St. Martin's Press, 1977.

Nichols, Thomas L. *Forty Years of American Life.* 2 vols. London: J. Maxwell and Company, 1864.

*Page, Ralph. "A History of Square Dance in America." in *Focus On Dance: VIII Dance Heritage.* Edited by E. Carmen Imel. Washington, D.C.: AAHPER Publications, 1977, 23–32.

*Panati, Charles. *Panati's Parade of Fads, Follies, and Manias.* New York: Harper Collins, 1991.

Paxton, John A. *Paxton's Directory of 1822.* New Orleans: John A. Paxton, 1822.

Peiss, Kathy. *Cheap Amusements: Working Women and Leisure in Turn-of-the- Century New York.* Philadelphia: Temple University Press, 1986.

Pendergast, Tom, and Sara Pendergast. *St. James Encyclopedia of Popular Culture.* Vols. 1–5. Detroit, MI: St. James Press, 2000.

Playford, John. *The English Dancing-Master: or Plaine and easie Rules for the Dancing of Country Dances, with the tune to each Dance.* London: John Playford, 1651.

Playford, John. *The Dancing Master: Or, Directions for Dancing Country Dances, with the Tunes to each dance for the Treble-Violin.* 10th ed. London: Printed by J. Heprinstall for H. Playford, 1698. A machine-readable transcription. "An American Ballroom Companion: Dance Instruction Manuals Ca. 1490–1920." http://memory.loc.gov/musdi/004/0001.gif (accessed May 9, 2005).

Rameau, Pierre. *The Dancing-Master: or, The Art of Dancing Explained: In two parts. The whole containing sixty figures drawn from the life, and curiously engraved on copper plates. Done from the French of Monsieur Rameau, by J. Essex*. London: Printed and sold by him, and J. Brotherton, 1728.

Rapp, Kenneth W. *West Point: Whistler in Cadet Gray, and other Stories about the United States Military Academy*. Croton on the Hudson, New York: North River Press, 1978.

Rice, Howard C., Jr., ed. *Travels in North America in the Years 1780, 1781 and 1782 by the Marquis de Chastellux*. Vol. 1. Chapel Hill: University of North Carolina Press, 1963.

Rice, Nathan Lewis. *A Discourse on Dancing: delivered in the Central Presbyterian Church, Cincinnati*. Cincinnati: The Presbyterian Book Depository, and W.H. Moore, 1847.

Richardson, Albert D. *Beyond the Mississippi: From the Grate River to the Great Ocean, life and adventure on the prairies, mountains, and Pacific Coast, 1857–1867*. Hartford, CT: American Publishing Company, 1867.

*Richardson, Philip J.S. *The Social Dances of the Nineteenth Century in England*. London: Herbert Jenkins, 1960.

Risjord, Norman K. *Jefferson's America, 1760–1815*. 2nd ed. New York: Rowman and Littlefield Publishers, Inc., 2002.

Rivers, C.H. *A Full Description of Modern Dances*. Brooklyn, NY: C.H. Rivers, 1885.

Roberts, Kenneth, and Anna M. Roberts. *Moreau de St. Mery's American journey (1793–1798)*. New York: Doubleday and Company, 1947.

*Sachs, Curt. *World History of the Dance*. Translated by Bessie Schonberg. New York: W.W. Norton and Company, 1963.

Schouler, James. *Daily Life in Revolutionary America*. Williamstown, MA: Corner House Publishers, 1976.

Scott, Edward. *Dancing*. London: George Bell and Sons, 1905.

Sharp, Cecil. *English Country Dance, Graded Series*. 3 vols. (1911). London: Novello and Company, reprint, 1951.

Sharp, Cecil J. *An Introduction to the English Country Dance: containing the description together with the tunes of twelve dances*. London: Novello and Company Ltd., reprint, 1951.

*Shaw, Lloyd. *The Round Dance Book*. Caldwell, ID: Caxton Printers, Ltd., 1949.

Shelby, Mary Cosby. *Journal* manuscript in the Samuel Wilson Collection, University of Kentucky Library.

Sherwood, Mrs. Mary Elizabeth (Wilson). *Manners and Social Usages*. New York: Harper and Brothers, 1887.

Shurtleff, Nathaniel B., ed. *Records of the Governor and Company of Massachusetts Bay in New England*. Boston: W. White, 1853, 1854, III.

Sikes, Rev. J.R. *A Time to Dance: A Sermon on Dancing*. 2nd ed. York, PA: Office of the Teachers journal, 1879. http://www.covenanter.org/Practical/Dancing/timetodance.htm.

A Solemn Warning to Dancers. New York: Published by N. Bangs and J. Emory for the Tract Society of the Methodist Episcopal Church [between 1824 and 1832].

Spaeth, Sigmund. *A History of Popular Music in America*. New York: Random House, 1948.

*Stearns, Marshall, and Jean Stearns. *Jazz Dance: The Story of American Vernacular Dance*. New York: DaCapo Press, 1994.

Steiner, Jesse F. *Americans at Play: Recent Trends in Recreation and Leisure Time Activities*. New York: McGraw-Hill, 1933.

*Stephenson, Richard M., and Joseph Iaccarino. *The Complete Book of Ballroom Dancing*. New York: Doubleday, 1992.

St. Johnston, Thomas Reginald. *A History of Dancing*. London: Simpkin, Marshall, Hamilton, Kent, and Co., 1906.

Bibliography

Stuckey, P. Sterling. "Christian Conversion and the Challenge of Dance." In *Dancing Many Drums; Excavations in African American dance.* Edited by Thomas F. DeFrantz. Madison, WI: The University of Wisconsin Press, 2002, 39–58.

Sweet, Jill D. *Keeping the Rituals Alive* (1985). In *I See America Dancing: Selected Readings 1685–2000.* Edited by Maureen Needham. Chicago: University of Illinois Press, 2002, 40–46.

Time-Life Books. *This Fabulous Century: 1870–1900.* New York: Time-Life Books, 1970.

Time-Life Books. *This Fabulous Century: 1900–1910.* Vol. 1. New York: Time-Life Books, 1969.

Tomko, Linda J. *Dancing Class: Gender, Ethnicity, and Social Divides in American Dance, 1890–1920.* Bloomington: Indiana University Press, 1999.

Tomlinson, Kellom. *The art of dancing explained by reading and figures; whereby the manner of performing the steps is made easy by a new and familiar method: being the original work, first design'd in the year 1724, and now published by Kellom Tomlinson, dancing-master.* London: Printed for the author, 1735. (Reprinted as *The Art of Dancing.* England: Gregg International Publishers Limited, 1972.)

Trumbull, John. *The Gentlemen & Lady's Companion; Containing, The Newest Cotillions and Country Dances; To Which Is Added, Instances Of Ill Manners to be carefully avoided by Youth of both sexes.* Norwich, CT: Printed by J. Trumbull, 1798.

Trusler, John, Lord. *Principles of Politeness, and of Knowing the World, by the Late Lord Chesterfield. Methodised and digested under distinct Heads, with additions by the rev. John Trusler.* Boston: Printed by John Trusler, 1794.

Tucker, Henry. *Clog Dancing Made Easy: The Elements and Practice of that Art Arranged, Simplified, and Corrected, with Examples.* New York: Robert M. De Witt Publisher, 1874.

U.S. Census Bureau. *Statistical Abstract of the United States: 2000.* Washington D.C., 1999.

Van Buren, Anson De Puy. *Jottings of a year's sojourn in the South: or, First impressions of the country and its people; with a glimpse at school-teaching in that southern land, and reminiscences of distinguished men.* 1859. Making of America Books, University of Michigan Online collection. http://www.hti.umich.edu.

Van Cleef, Joy, and Kate Van Winkle Keller. "Selected American Country Dances and Their English Sources." In *Music in Colonial Massachusetts, 1630–1820.* Edited by Barbara Lambert. Boston: Colonial Society of Massachusetts, 1980, 2–73.

Vassar, Matthew. *Communications to the Board of Trustees of Vassar College.* New York: 1869.

*Wagner, Ann. *Adversaries of Dance: From the Puritans to the Present.* Chicago: University of Illinois Press, 1997.

Walker, Mrs. A. In *Female Beauty; as Preserved and Improved by Regimen, Cleanliness, and Dress.* New York: Scofield and Voorhies, 1840.

Walker, Caroline. *Modern Dances: Tango, Castle Walk, Hesitation Waltz, One-Step, Dream Waltz.* Chicago: Saul Brothers, 1914.

Walker, Donald. *Exercises for Ladies.* London: By Author, 1836.

*Wallace, Carol McD., Don McDonagh, Jean L. Druesedow, Laurence Libin, and Constance Old. *Dance: A Very Social History.* New York: The Metropolitan Museum of Art, and Rizzoli International Publications, Inc., 1986.

Webster, Alfred, Mrs. *Dancing, as a means of physical education; with remarks on deformities, and their prevention and cure.* London: D. Bogue, 1851.

Wharton, Anne Hollingsworth. *Through Colonial Doorways.* Philadelphia: J.B. Lippincott Company, 1893.

Wilkinson, William Cleaver. *The Dance of Modern Society.* New York: Oakley, Marson and Co., 1869.

Willcox, Asa. *Asa Willcox's Book of Figures, 1793.* [No publisher], 1793.

Williams, John R. *Philip Vickers Fithian, Journal and Letters, 1767–1774*. Vol. I. Princeton, NJ: Princeton, 1934.

Williams, M.B. *Where Satan Sows His Seed: Plain Talks on the Amusements of Modern Society*. Chicago: Fleming H. Revell Company, 1896.

Wilson, George E. *Wilson's Ball-Room Guide and Call Book*. New York: George E. Wilson, 1884.

Wilson, Marguerite. *Dancing*. Philadelphia: The Penn Publishing Company, 1899 (reprint, 1920).

Wilson, Thomas. *An Analysis of Country Dancing*. London: Printed by W. Calvert, 1808.

Wilson, Thomas. *The Complete System of English Country Dancing, containing all the figures ever used in English country dancing, with a variety of new figures, and new reels*. London: Sherwood, Neeley and Jones, 1815.

Wilson, Thomas. *A Description of the Correct Method of Waltzing*. London: Printed for the author, 1816.

Wilson, Thomas. *Analysis of the London Ballroom*. London: Thomas Wilson, 1825.

Wright, Louis B. *The Cultural Life of the American Colonies: 1607–1763*. New York: Harper and Brothers, 1957.

Wright, Mabel Osgood. *My New York*. New York: The Macmillan Company, 1926.

*Zinn, Howard. *A People's History of the United States: 1492–Present*. New York: Harper Perennial, 2003.

Unpublished Dissertation

Sarnelle, Irene Meharg. "An 1890's Ball: The Formal Ball in the Eastern United States from 1890 to 1900." Master's thesis, James Madison University, 1995.

Periodicals

"Allemande." *Microsoft Encarta Encyclopedia 2000*. © 1993–1999 Microsoft Corporation.

Allen, Zita. "From Minstrel Show to Center Stage." *Free to Dance PBS.org.*http://www.pbs.org/wnet/freetodance/behind/behind_minstrel.html (accessed November 27, 2005).

Allen, Zita. "From Slave Ships to Center Stage." *Free to Dance PBS.org.* http://www.pbs.org/wnet/freetodance/behind/behind_slaveships.html (accessed November 27, 2005).

"An American Ballroom Companion: Dance Instruction Manuals Ca. 1490–1920." Music Division, Library of Congress, Washington D.C. http://lcweb2.loc.gov/ammem/dihtml (accessed December 31, 2003).

"Arthur Murray Dictionary of Dance." Arthur Murray International Dance Schools. http://www.arthurmurray.com/htmlWS/dancdict.htm#L (accessed July 17, 2005).

Attwell, E.T. "Recreation in Colored Communities." *The Playground* 19, no. 12 (March 1926): 657.

"Band Music from the Civil War Era." *American Memory Collection*. Library of Congress. http://memory.loc.gov/ammem/cwmhtml/cwmpres06.html (accessed January 1, 2006).

Banks, Nancy. "The World's Most Beautiful Ballrooms." *Chicago History*, 206–215.

"Baroque Dance." *An American Ballroom Companion: Dance Instruction Manuals Ca. 1490–1920*. Music Division, Library of Congress, Washington D.C. http://memory.loc.gov/ammem/dihtml/diessay4.html (accessed December 31, 2003).

"Beau Nash." *Legacies UK History Local to You*. BBC Home Page. http://www.bbc.co.uk/legacies/myths_legends/england/somerset/article_1.shtml (accessed August 27, 2005).

"Boston Family History.com." http://www.bostonfamilyhistory.com/ita_1750.html (accessed August 10, 2005).

Briones, Brigida. "A Carnival Ball at Monterey in 1829." *Century Magazine*, January 1891, 460–475.

Bibliography

City of Buffalo. "Dance Halls: Ordinances Governing the Conduct of Public Dances and Dance Halls." Issued by the Common Council 1914 (Library of Congress).

"Burgundian Dance in the Late Middle Ages." *An American Ballroom Companion: Dance Instruction Manuals Ca. 1490–1920*. Music Division, Library of Congress, Washington D.C. http://memory.loc.gov/ammem/dihtml/diessay1.html (accessed December 31, 2003).

"Cakewalk Shocked Pastor." *The Brooklyn Eagle* March 22, 1902, 20. http://www.brooklynpubliclibrary.org/eagle/index.htm (accessed March 24, 2004).

Cave, Damien. "Uncle Sam Wants You. But He Needs to Adapt." *The New York Times*, May 8, 2005, WK 3.

"Clog Dance." *Microsoft Encarta Encyclopedia 2000.* © 1993–1999 Microsoft Corporation.

Cole, Arthur C. "The Puritan and Fair Terpsichore." *The Mississippi Valley Historical Review*, 29, no. 1 (June 1942): 3–34.

"Courante." *Microsoft Encarta Encyclopedia 2000.* © 1993–1999 Microsoft Corporation.

"Dance Masters Fight Jazz." *The New York Times*, August 7, 1923, 17.

"Dances for the Assembly." *Elegant Arts Society*. http://www.elegantarts.org/assembly/dances.html (accessed September 10, 2005).

Dancing as a Social Amusement by Professed Christians or their Children. American Tract Society, 1825 or 1832–33.

"The Dancing Professor, He is Sure the Glide Waltz Will Hold Its Own." *The Brooklyn Eagle*, September 8, 1889, 10. http://www.brooklynpubliclibrary.org/eagle/index.htm (accessed December 27, 2005).

De Koven Bowen, Louise. "The Public Dance Halls of Chicago." The Juvenile Protective Association of Chicago, 1917.

Duffy, George. "Old Time Dance Calls." As told to A.C. Sherbert, interview December 27, 1938. *American Life Histories: Manuscripts from the Federal Writers' Project, 1936–1940*. http://memory.loc.gov.

"Elizabeth I." *Microsoft Encarta Encyclopedia 2000.* © 1993–1999 Microsoft Corporation.

"England." *Microsoft Encarta Encyclopedia 2000.* © 1993–1999 Microsoft Corporation.

"The Enlightenment." *Microsoft Encarta Encyclopedia 2000.* © 1993–1999 Microsoft Corporation.

Erenberg Lewis A. "Entertaining Chicagoans." *The Electronic Encyclopedia of Chicago*, 2005. Chicago Historical Society. http://www.encyclopedia.chicagohistory.org/pages/428.html (accessed August 27, 2005).

Falconer, Mrs. Emma. *American Life Histories: Manuscripts from the Federal Writers' Project, 1936–1940*. Library of Congress American Memory Collection. http://memory.loc.gov/ammem/index.html.

Felson, Leonard. "Dancers Waltz Back To an Earlier Era." *The New York Times*, December 19, 1993, 12.

Fithian, Philip. "Journal." *William and Mary Quarterly* X (1953): 213.

"Galliard." *Microsoft Encarta Encyclopedia 2000.* © 1993–1999 Microsoft Corporation.

"General Nelson A. Miles on the 'Sioux Outbreak' of 1890." *New Perspectives on the West*. http://www.pbs.org/weta/thewest/resources/archives/eight/wkmiles.htm (accessed December 29, 2005).

"Girlhood Life in Portland, 1860–76." *American Life Histories: Manuscripts from the Federal Writers' Project, 1936–1940*. http://memory.loc.gov/ammem/index.html.

"Great Awakening." *Microsoft Encarta Encyclopedia 2000.* © 1993–1999 Microsoft Corporation.

Griesbeck, Christian. "Introduction to Labanotation." University of Frankfurt Uni-Frankfurt.de, 1996. http://user.uni-frankfurt.de/~griesbec/LABANE.HTML (accessed August 27, 2005).

Gushee, Lawrence. "The Nineteenth-Century Origins of Jazz." *Black Music Research Journal* 14, no. 1 (Spring 1994): 1–24. Selected Papers from the 1993 National Conference on Black Music Research.

Harris-Warwick, Rebecca. "Ballroom Dancing at the Court of Louis XIV." *Early Music Journal* 14, no. 1 (February 1986): 40–49.

Hazzard-Gordon, Katrina. "African-American Vernacular Dance: Core Culture and Meaning Operatives." *Journal of Black Studies* 15, no. 4 (June 1985): 427–445.

"He Whipped His Wife For Dancing." *The New York Times,* February 5, 1885, 2.

"Henry II (of France)." *Microsoft Encarta Encyclopedia 2000.* © 1993–1999 Microsoft Corporation.

Hightower, Annie. *American Life Histories: Manuscripts from the Federal Writers' Project, 1936-1940.* http://memory.loc.gov/cgi-bin/query/D?wpa:1:./temp/~ammem_0fdF::@@@mdb=mcc,gottscho,detr,nfor,wpa,aap,cwar,bbpix,cowellbib,calbkbib,consrvbib,bdsbib,dag,fsaall,gmd,pan,vv,presp,varstg,suffrg,nawbib,horyd,wtc,toddbib,mgw,ncr,ngp,musdibib,hlaw,papr,lhbumbib,rbp (accessed December 23, 2005).

Hinckley, David. "Eclipsing the Waltz, Polite Society Discovers Polka, 1844." *The New York Daily News,* October 15, 2004. http://www.nydailynews.com/city_life/big_town/v- bigtown_archive/story/242314p-207781c.html (accessed November 26, 2005).

"Hornpipe." *Microsoft Encarta Encyclopedia 2000.* © 1993–1999 Microsoft Corporation.

"How to Read a Dance Manual." *An American Ballroom Companion: Dance Instruction Manuals Ca. 1490–1920.* Music Division, Library of Congress, Washington D.C. http://memory.loc.gov/ammem/dihtml/dihowto.html (accessed December 31, 2003).

"Hurdy-Gurdy." *Microsoft Encarta Encyclopedia 2000.* © 1993–1999 Microsoft Corporation.

"*The Hymn of Jesus* and *The Mystery of the Cross* from *The Acts of John.*" The Gnostic Society Library. http://www.gnosis.org/library/hymnjesu.html (accessed August 9, 2005).

"Instrumental Dance Music 1780s–1920s." *The Database of Recorded American Music.* New York University. http://msdlib.home.nyu.edu/dram/Objid/26541 (accessed June 25, 2005).

"Jamestown (Virginia)." *Microsoft Encarta Encyclopedia 2000.* © 1993–1999 Microsoft Corporation.

Jewell, Andy. "Andy Jewell's Vintage Anti-Dance Bibliography." Internet http://www.geocities.com/Athens/Parthenon/9101/bib/A10.html (accessed July 4, 2004).

Kavanagh, Thomas W. "Imaging and Imagining the Ghost Dance: James Mooney's Illustrations and Photographs." The University of Indiana. http://php.indiana.edu/~tkavanag/visualb.html (accessed May 14, 2004).

Keller, Kate Van Winkle. "The Eighteenth-Century Ballroom: A Mirror of Social Change." *New England Music: The Public Sphere, 1600–1900.* The Dublin seminar for New England Folklife Annual proceedings 1996. Published by Boston University, 16–29.

Keller, Kate Van Winkle. "Early American Social Dance: A Bibliography of Sources to 1820." The Colonial Music Institute 2001. http://www.colonialmusic.org/Resource/DancBibl.htm (accessed June 18, 2005).

"Late Eighteenth-Century Social Dance." *An American Ballroom Companion: Dance Instruction Manuals Ca. 1490–1920.* Music Division, Library of Congress, Washington D.C. http://memory.loc.gov/ammem/dihtml/diessay5.html (accessed December 31, 2003).

Bibliography

"The Legacy of Cecil Sharp." *Studies in Dance History* I, no. 2 (Spring/Summer 1990): vii–xiv.

"Manning Rules Out a Puritan Sunday." *The New York Times*, February 26, 1926, 16.

"Maypole." StreetSwing.com Dance History Archives. http://www.streetswing.com/histmain/z3maypol.htm (accessed July 13, 2005).

"Mazurka." *Microsoft Encarta Encyclopedia 2000.* © 1993–1999 Microsoft Corporation.

"Muses." *Microsoft Encarta Encyclopedia 2000.* © 1993–1999 Microsoft Corporation.

Newman, Scott A. "Jazz Age Chicago: Urban Leisure from 1893 to 1934." Page authored July 1, 2000; page retrieved January 25, 2004. http://chicago.urban-history.org/sites/parks/w_city.htm (accessed January 24, 2004).

"A New Treatise on the 'Art of Dancing' first Published in the *Lady's Magazine*" (I: Volume XVI in Six Installments: February, March, April, May, June, July 1785). *Dance Research: The Journal of the Society for Dance Research* 11, no. 2 (1993): 43–59.

"Nineteenth Century Social Dance." *An American Ballroom Companion: Dance Instruction Manuals Ca. 1490-1920.* Music Division, Library of Congress, Washington D.C. http://memory.loc.gov/ammem/dihtml/diessay6.html (accessed December 31, 2003).

"Objectionable Resort Located in Flatbush." *The Brooklyn Eagle*, October 15, 1901, 20.

O'Neill, Rosetta. "The Dodworth Family and Ballroom Dancing in New York." *Dance Index* II, no. 4 (April 1943): 43–57.

"Oppose Ragtime Tunes Federation of Music Will Make Every Effort to Suppress Them." *The Brooklyn Eagle*, May 14, 1901, 1. http://www.brooklynpubliclibrary.org/eagle/index.htm (accessed March 24, 2004).

"Parlor Dancing Denounced." *The New York Times*, February 18, 1894, 12.

"Pavane." StreetSwing.com Dance History Archives. http://www.streetswing.com/histmain/z3pavane.htm (accessed July 13, 2005).

"A Plantation Cake Walk Makes Much Merriment." *The Brooklyn Eagle*, July 20, 1902, 4. http://www.brooklynpubliclibrary.org/eagle/index.htm. (accessed March 24, 2004).

"Polka." *Microsoft Encarta Encyclopedia 2000.* © 1993–1999 Microsoft Corporation.

"Polka History of Dance." CentralHome.com. *http://www.centralhome.com/ballroomcountry/polka.htm* (accessed September 17, 2004).

"Popular and Social Dancing." *Microsoft Encarta Encyclopedia 2000.* © 1993–1999 Microsoft Corporation.

"Popular Dances From the Cakewalk To the Watusi, Famous Dance Team Traces Fascinating History of American Social Dancing." *Ebony* XVI, no. 10 (August 1961): 32–38.

"Railroads in the United States." *Microsoft Encarta Encyclopedia 2000.* © 1993–1999 Microsoft Corporation.

"A Rector's Dancing Class." *The New York Times*, December 17, 1879, 5.

"Reformation." *Microsoft Encarta Encyclopedia 2000.* © 1993–1999 Microsoft Corporation.

"Renaissance Dance." *An American Ballroom Companion: Dance Instruction Manuals Ca. 1490–1920.* Music Division, Library of Congress, Washington D.C. http://memory.loc.gov/ammem/dihtml/diessay2.html (accessed December 31, 2003).

"Restoration." *Microsoft Encarta Encyclopedia 2000.* © 1993–1999 Microsoft Corporation.

Ross, Paul. "English Country Dancing in the Words of Cecil Sharp." June 7, 1999. Online Country Dance New York, Inc. http://www.cdny.org/sharp.html (accessed May 17, 2005).

"Saint Vitus." Catholic Encyclopedia. http://saintvitus.com/SaintVitus/Catholic_Encyclopedia.html (accessed August 9, 2005).

Sanders, Olcutt. "The Texas Cattle Country and Cowboy Square Dance." *Journal of the International Folk Music Council* 3 (1951): 22–26.

"Second Great Awakening." *The Reader's Companion to American History*. New York: Houghton Mifflin, 1991.

Sharp, Cecil J. "English Folk Dance: The Country Dance." *The Musical Times* 56, no. 873 (November 1, 1915): 658–661.

Shaw, Winifred Shuldham. "Cecil Sharp and Folk Dancing." *Music & Letters* 2, no. 1 (January 1921): 4–9.

A Solemn Warning to Dancers. New York: Published by N. Bangs and J. Emory for the Tract Society of the Methodist Episcopal Church [between 1824 and 1832].

"Transition From Renaissance Dance To Baroque Dance." *An American Ballroom Companion: Dance Instruction Manuals Ca. 1490–1920*. Music Division, Library of Congress, Washington D.C. http://memory.loc.gov/ammem/dihtml/diessay3.html (accessed December 31, 2003).

"United States (History)." *Microsoft Encarta Encyclopedia 2000*. © 1993–1999 Microsoft Corporation.

Van Cleef, Joy. "Rural Felicity: Social Dance in 18th Century Connecticut." *Dance Perspectives No. 65* 17 (Spring 1976): 1–45.

"Waltz." *Microsoft Encarta Encyclopedia 2000*. © 1993–1999 Microsoft Corporation.

Weaver, Charles. "Mr. Charles Weaver Square Dances or Quadrilles." As told to Frederick W. Kaul, interview January 21 and 22, 1939, South Garfield, Nebraska. *American Life Histories: Manuscripts from the Federal Writers' Project, 1936–1940*. http://memory.loc.gov.

Webster, Noah. "Importance of Female Education—and Education of Young Men in their Native Country, Addressed to every American." *American Magazine*, May 1788, 339–340.

"White House History." WhiteHouseHistory.org Web site, http://www.whitehousehistory.org/05/subs/05_e.html (accessed October 29, 2005).

Williams, Mrs. Rose. "Old Glendale." As told to William Wood on September 1, 1938. *American Life Histories: Manuscripts from the Federal Writers' Project, 1936–1940*. Library of Congress.

Wolfe, Linda. "In Step With Austen: English Country Dancing." *The New York Times*, March 7, 1997. Online Country Dance New York, Inc. http://www.cdny.org/wolfe.html (accessed May 17, 2005).

"Wovoka's Message: The Promise of the Ghost Dance." *New Perspectives on the West*. http://www.pbs.org/weta/thewest/resources/archives/eight/gdmessg.htm (accessed December 29, 2005).

VIDEO/DVD

America Dances! 1897–1948: A Collector's Edition of Social Dance in Film. Produced by Dancetime Publications Kentfield, CA, 75 mins. http://www.DancetimePublications.com.

American Indian Dance Theater: Finding the Circle. Intermediate Arts, 1987, 58 mins.

An American Ballroom Companion: Dance Instruction Manuals Ca. 1490–1920. Music Division, Library of Congress, Washington D.C. http://lcweb2.loc.gov/ammem/dihtml.

"Blind Man's Buff" (Video Clips No. 5 and 16). "Video Directory." *An American Ballroom Companion: Dance Instruction Manuals Ca. 1490–1920*. Library of Congress. http://memory.loc.gov/ammem/dihtml/divideos.html.

"Bow and Curtsy" (Video Clip No. 55). "Video Directory." *An American Ballroom Companion: Dance Instruction Manuals Ca. 1490–1920*. Library of Congress. http://memory.loc.gov/ammem/dihtml/divideos.html.

"Branle" ("Branle Simple"—Video Clip No. 40), ("Branle Double"—Video Clip No. 1), ("Mixed Branles"—Video Clip No. 43 and Video Clip No. 44), ("Haut Barrois Branle"—Video Clip No. 42), and ("Maltese Branle," "Pease Branle," and "Washerwomen's Branle"—Video Clip No. 46). "Video Directory." *An American Ballroom*

Companion: Dance Instruction Manuals Ca. 1490-1920. Library of Congress. http://memory.loc.gov/ammem/dihtml/divideos.html.

"Courante" (Video Clip No. 22). "Video Directory." *An American Ballroom Companion: Dance Instruction Manuals Ca. 1490–1920.* Library of Congress. http://memory.loc.gov/ammem/dihtml/divideos.html.

"500 Years of Social Dance: Volume I: The 15th to 19th Centuries." Dancetime DVD. Produced by Dancetime Publications Kentfield, CA, 45 mins. http://www.DancetimePublications.com.

"500 Years of Social Dance: Volume II: The 20th Century." Dancetime DVD. Produced by Dancetime Publications Kentfield, CA, 45 mins. http://www.DancetimePublications.com.

"The Fan" (Video Clip No. 4). "Video Directory." *An American Ballroom Companion: Dance Instruction Manuals Ca. 1490–1920.* Library of Congress. http://memory.loc.gov/ammem/dihtml/divideos.html.

"Galliard" ("Basic Galliard"—Video Clip No. 29), ("Five-step" variations—Video Clip No. 30), ("Eleven-step" variations—Video Clip No. 31). "Video Directory." *An American Ballroom Companion: Dance Instruction Manuals Ca. 1490–1920.* Library of Congress. http://memory.loc.gov/ammem/dihtml/divideos.html.

"The German" (Video Clips No. 16, No. 3, No. 4, and No. 5). "Video Directory." *An American Ballroom Companion: Dance Instruction Manuals Ca. 1490–1920.* Library of Congress. http://memory.loc.gov/ammem/dihtml/divideos.html.

"The Grand March" (Video Clip No. 1). "Video Directory." *An American Ballroom Companion: Dance Instruction Manuals Ca. 1490–1920.* Library of Congress. http://memory.loc.gov/ammem/dihtml/divideos.html.

"Minuet" (Video Clips No. 26 and No. 27). "Video Directory." *An American Ballroom Companion: Dance Instruction Manuals Ca. 1490–1920.* Library of Congress. http://memory.loc.gov/ammem/dihtml/divideos.html.

"*Le Pantalon*" (Video Clips No. 20 and No. 21). "Video Directory." *An American Ballroom Companion: Dance Instruction Manuals Ca. 1490–1920.* Library of Congress. http://memory.loc.gov/ammem/dihtml/divideos.html.

"Pavane" ("Basic Pavane"—Video Clips No. 36, No. 37, and No. 39) and ("Pavane Conversion"—Video Clip No. 38). "Video Directory." *An American Ballroom Companion: Dance Instruction Manuals Ca. 1490–1920.* Library of Congress. http://memory.loc.gov/ammem/dihtml/divideos.html.

"Polka" (Video Clip No. 50). "Video Directory." *An American Ballroom Companion: Dance Instruction Manuals Ca. 1490–1920.* Library of Congress. http://memory.loc.gov/ammem/dihtml/divideos.html.

"The Rope" (Video Clip No. 5). "Video Directory." *An American Ballroom Companion: Dance Instruction Manuals Ca. 1490–1920.* Library of Congress. http://memory.loc.gov/ammem/dihtml/divideos.html.

"Sarabande" (Video Clip No. 23). "Video Directory." *An American Ballroom Companion: Dance Instruction Manuals Ca. 1490–1920.* Library of Congress. http://memory.loc.gov/ammem/dihtml/divideos.html.

"Schottisch" (Video Clip No. 56). "Video Directory." *An American Ballroom Companion: Dance Instruction Manuals Ca. 1490–1920.* Library of Congress. http://memory.loc.gov/ammem/dihtml/divideos.html.

"Varsovienne" (Video Clip No. 59). "Video Directory." *An American Ballroom Companion: Dance Instruction Manuals Ca. 1490–1920.* Library of Congress. http://memory.loc.gov/ammem/dihtml/divideos.html.

"Waltz: Early Nineteenth-Century Dance" (Video Clip No. 58). "Video Directory." *An American Ballroom Companion: Dance Instruction Manuals Ca. 1490–1920*. Library of Congress. http://memory.loc.gov/ammem/dihtml/divideos.html.

"Waltz: Late Nineteenth-Century Dance" (Video Clip No. 62). "Video Directory." *An American Ballroom Companion: Dance Instruction Manuals Ca. 1490–1920*. Library of Congress. http://memory.loc.gov/ammem/dihtml/divideos.html.

"Waltz: Mid-Nineteenth-Century Dance" (Video Clip No. 58). "Video Directory." *An American Ballroom Companion: Dance Instruction Manuals Ca. 1490–1920*. Library of Congress. http://memory.loc.gov/ammem/dihtml/divideos.html.

"The Washington Post Two Step" (Video Clips No. 7 and No. 8). "Video Directory." *An American Ballroom Companion: Dance Instruction Manuals Ca. 1490–1920*. Library of Congress. http://memory.loc.gov/ammem/dihtml/divideos.html.

Web Sites

An American Ballroom Companion: Dance Instruction Manuals Ca. 1490–1920. Music Division, Library of Congress, Washington D.C. http://lcweb2.loc.gov/ammem/dihtml.

Dancing and Waltzing Academy Mr. Joseph B. Brown. "An American Time Capsule: Three Centuries of Broadsides and Other Printed Ephemera." http://memory.loc.gov/cgi-bin/query/r?ammem/rbpe:@field(DOCID+@lit(rbpe07104700)).

"Grant's Dancing academy 1860. An American Time Capsule: Three Centuries of Broadsides and Other Printed Ephemera." http://memory.loc.gov/cgi-bin/query/r?ammem/rbpe:@field(DOCID+@lit(rbpe06603600)).

"Video Directory" (75 Video Clips including: Renaissance, Baroque, 19th Century, and Ragtime dances). *An American Ballroom Companion: Dance Instruction Manuals Ca. 1490–1920*. Music Division, Library of Congress, Washington D.C. http://memory.loc.gov/ammem/dihtml/divideos.html.

A Select Bibliography of Online Dance Instruction Manuals Available from the Library of Congress

Following is a select bibliography available from *An American Ballroom Companion: Dance Instruction Manuals Ca. 1490-1920*, which is viewable online at http://lcweb2.loc.gov/ammem/dihtml. (Note: Some of the publications listed here represent a duplication from the main bibliography.) The compilation and Web site, produced and maintained by The Library of Congress in Washington D.C., can only be described as an "invaluable" reference source for any research work not only as it pertains to American social dancing up until the early twentieth century, but also for an understanding of America's social manners and habits. *American Ballroom Companion* presents a collection of over 200 social dance manuals held at the Library of Congress. Not enough can be said about the entire Library of Congress and especially the individual staff members who put together these phenomenal collections. Their credit line is listed simply as "Library of Congress, Music Division"; however, there were many individuals involved. I extend a grateful acknowledgment to those individuals as follows:

- *Music Division:* Vicky Risner
- *NDL Staff:* Martha Anderson, Marc Dudley, Lee Ellen Friedland, Amy Greenwood, Glenn Ricci, and Tracey Salley
- *ITS Staff:* Dave Woodward and Lisa Fruth
- *Conservation Office:* Mary Wootton and Alan Haley
- *Cataloguing:* Gerry Wager, Kay Guiles, and Tom Yee

- *APLO Staff:* Ardie Bausenbach
- *Rare Book Division:* Clark Evans
- *Copyright:* Melissa Levine
- *NDL/Music Team:* Morgan Cundiff, Susan Manus, David Arbury, Jeni Dahmus, Liza Vick, and Robert Sheldon
- *Special Consultant:* Elizabeth Aldrich
- *Video Performers Dancers:* The Jonquil Street Foundation, Ariane Anthony, Thomas Baird, Barbara Barr, Patricia Beaman, Christopher Caines, Charles Garth, James Martin, Maris Wolff, Cheryl Stafford, and Thomas Baird
- *Video Musicians:* Boris Gurevitch (piano), Susan Manus (violin), and members of The Library of Congress Centennial Cotillion Brass Band including Emerson Head and Robert Sheldon, Leaders (Members, Metro Washington D.C. Federation of Musicians Local 161-710, AFM).

I am sure that there were many more individuals from the Library of Congress staff who had input. If I have missed anyone—I apologize. The advantage to this particular Web site is that the manuals are viewable both in text format and also in their original published form, including the illustrations and diagrams. A companion Web site provides 75 short clip video demonstrations of the dances as described in their original form.

Chapter 1: The Minuet, Puritans, and Anti-Dance Reformation: 1607–1740

Arbeau, Thoinot. *Orchesographie.* Lengres: Imprimé par Iehan des Preyz, 1589.

Battista Dufort, Giovanni. *Trattato del Ballo Nobile,* 1728.

Caroso, Fabritio. *Nobiltà di dame del Sr. Fabritio Caroso da Sermoneta, libro, altra volta, chiamato Il ballarino.* In Venetia: Presso il Muschio, 1600.

The Dancing Master: or, Directions for dancing country dances, with the tunes to each dance, for the treble-violin. The 10th ed. corrected; with addition of several new dances and tunes never before printed. London: Printed by J. Heptinstall, for Henry Playford, 1698.

The Dancing-Master; or, Directions for dancing country dances, with the tunes to each dance, for the treble-violin. Vol. the 2d. The 4th ed., containing 360 of the choicest old and new tunes now used at court, and other publick places. The whole work rev. and done on the new-ty'd-note, and much more correct than any former editions. London: Printed by W. Pearson and sold by J. Young, 1728.

Feuillet, Raoul-Auger. *Recüeil de contredances mises en chorégraphie, d'une maniére si aisée, que toutes personnes peuvent facilement les apprendre, sans le secours d'aucun maitre et même sans avoir en aucune connoissance de la chorégraphie. Par Mr. Feuillet.* Paris: L'auteur, 1706.

Feuillet, Raoul-Auger. *For the Furthur Improvement of Dancing: A treatise of chorography, or, Ye art of dancing country dances after a new charact: in which the figures, steps & manner of performing are describ'd & ye rules demonstrated in an easie method adapted to the meanest capacity / translated from the French of Monsr. Feuillet, and improv'd with many additions, all fairly engrav'd on copperplates, and a new collection of country dances describ'd in ye same character by John Essex, dancing master.* London: Sold by I. Walsh and P. Randall and by ye author, 1710.

Isaac, Mr. *The Friendship. Mr. Isaac's new dance for the year 1715. The tune by Mr. Paisible.* London: Printed for I. Talch and I. Hare, 1715.

Isaac, Mr. *The Godolphin, Mr. Isaac's new dance made for Her Majestys birth day 1714.* London: Printed for I. Walsh and I. Hare, 1714.

Isaac, Mr. *The Pastorall, Mr. Isaac's new dance made for Her Majestys birth day 1713.* London: Printed for I. Walsh and I. Hare, 1713.

Isaac, Mr. *The Royal Ann. Mr. Isaac's new dance made for Her Majesty's birth day 1712.* London: Printed for I. Hare and I. Hare, 1712.

Kingsbury, W.H. *A Cotilion* [By] *W. H. Kingsbury.* London: S.W. Fores, 1788.

Negri, Cesare. *Nuove inventioni di balli.* Milano: G. Bordone, 1604.

Pemberton, E. *An Essay for the Further Improvement of Dancing: being a collection of figure dances, of several numbers, compos'd by the most eminent masters; describ'd in characters after the newest manner of Monsieur Feuillet. By E. Pemberton. To which is added, three single dances, viz. a chacone by Mr. Isaac, a passacaille by Mr. L'Abbe, and a jig by Mr. Pecour.* London: J. Walsh, 1711.

Playford, John. *The Dancing Master: or, Directions for dancing country dances, with the tunes to each dance, for the treble-violin. The 10th ed. corrected; with addition of several new dances and tunes never before printed.* London: Printed by J. Heptinstall, for Henry Playford, 1698.

Playford, John. *The Dancing-Master; or, Directions for dancing country dances, with the tunes to each dance, for the treble-violin. Vol. the 2d. The 4th ed., containing 360 of the choicest old and new tunes now used at court, and other publick places. The whole work rev. and done on the new-ty'd-note, and much more correct than any former editions.* London: Printed by W. Pearson and sold by J. Young, 1728.

Rameau, Pierre. *Le maître à danser. Qui enseigne la maniere de faire tous les differens pas de danse dans toute la régularité de l'art, & de conduire les bras à chaque pas...Par le Sieur Rameau.* Paris: Rollin fils, 1725.

Rameau, Pierre. *The Dancing-Master: or, The Art of Dancing Explained: In two parts. The whole containing sixty figures drawn from the life, and curiously engraved on copper plates. Done from the French of Monsieur Rameau, by J. Essex.* London: Printed and sold by him, and J. Brotherton, 1728.

Tomlinson, Kellom. *The Art of Dancing Explained by Reading and Figures: whereby the manner of performing the steps is made easy by a new and familiar method: being the original work, first design'd in the year 1724, and now published by Kellom Tomlinson, dancing-master.* London: Printed for the author, 1735.

Weaver, John. *A Collection of Ball-dances Perform'd at Court: viz. the Richmond, the roundeau, the rigadoon, the favourite, the Spanheim, and the Britannia. All compos'd by Mr. Isaac, and writ down in characters, by John Weaver, dancing- master.* London: Printed for the author, and sold by J. Vaillant, 1706.

Chapter 2: The Virginia Reel, George Washington, and the Waltz: 1740–1820

Cassidy, James P. *A treatise on the theory and practice of dancing, with an appropriate poem, in two cantos, and plates illustrative of the art.* Dublin, Ireland: Printed by W. Folds, 1810.

Dun, Barclay. *A translation of nine of the most fashionable quadrilles, consisting of fifty French country-dances, as performed in England and Scotland. With explanatory notes. To which are prefixed, a few observations on the style, &c. of the quadrille, the English country-dance, and the*

    Scotch reel. Edinburgh, England: Printed for the author and sold by W. Wilson and Co., 1818.

Fraisier, M.J. C. *The Scholars Companion: containing a choice collection of cotillons & country-dances.* Boston: Printed by D. Bowen for the author, 1796.

Gallini, Giovanni-Andrea, *A Treatise on the Art of Dancing.* London: Printed for the author and sold by R. Dodsley, 1772.

The Gentleman & Lady's Companion: containing, the newest cotillions and country-dances; to which is added, instances of ill manners, to be carefully avoided by youth of both sexes. Norwich, CT: Printed by J. Trumbull, 1798.

Gourdoux-Daux, J.H. *Elements and principles of the art of dancing, as used in the polite and fashionable circles, also rules of deportment and descriptions of manners of civility, appertaining to that art.* Philadelphia: Printed by J.F. Hurtel, 1817.

Ide, Jacob. *The nature and tendency of balls, seriously and candidly considered; in two sermons.* N.p., 1818.

Jacome Bonem, Natal. *Tratado dos Principaes Fundamentos,* 1767.

Minguet é Irol, Pablo. *Arte de Danzar a la Francesa,* 1758.

Peacock, Francis. *Sketches relative to the history and theory, but more especially to the practice of dancing. Intended as hints to the young teachers of the art of dancing.* Aberdeen: Printed by J. Chalmers and Co., 1805.

Phillips, Rev. John, *Familiar dialogues on dancing, between a minister and a dancer; taken from matter of fact with an appendix containing some extracts from the writings of pious and eminent men against the entertainments of the stage, and other vain amusements.* New York: Printed by T. Kirk, 1798.

Strathy, Alexander. *Elements of the Art of Dancing: with a Description of the Principal Figures in the Quadrille.* Edinburgh, England: Printed for the author and sold by F. Pillans, 1822.

Trumbull, John. *The Gentlemen & Lady's Companion; Containing, The Newest Cotillions and Country Dances; To Which Is Added, Instances Of Ill Manners to be carefully avoided by Youth of both sexes.* Norwich, CT: Printed by J. Trumbull, 1798.

Tucker, Henry. *Clog Dancing Made Easy: The Elements and Practice of that Art Arranged, Simplified, and Corrected, with Examples.* New York: Robert M. De Witt Publisher, 1874.

Willcox, Asa. *Asa Willcox's Book of Figures, 1793.* N.p., 1793.

Wilson, Thomas. *An Analysis of Country Dancing: wherein are displayed all the figures ever used in country dances, in a way so easy and familiar, that persons of the meanest capacity may in a short time acquire (without the aid of a master) a complete knowledge of that rational and polite amusement. To which are added, instructions for dancing some entire new reels; together with the rules, regulations, and complete etiquette of the ballroom.* London: Printed by W. Calvert, 1808.

Wilson, Thomas. *The Complete System of English Country Dancing, containing all the figures ever used in English country dancing, with a variety of new figures, and new reels.* London: Sherwood, Neeley, and Jones, 1815.

Wilson, Thomas. *The Quadrille and Cotillion Panorama, or, Treatise on quadrille dancing, in two parts: with an explanation, in French and English, of all the quadrille & cotillion figures generally adopted, as described by diagrams on the plate, by Thomas Wilson.* London: R. & E. Williamson; New York, Sold by Messrs. Geib and Co., [18–].

Wilson, Thomas. *A Description of the Correct Method of Waltzing.* London: Printed for the author, 1816.

Wilson, Thomas. *The Treasures of Terpsichore; or, a companion for the ballroom.* London: Printed for the author, and to be had of Messrs. Sherwood, Neely, and Jones, 1816.

Chapter 3: The Buffalo Dance, Cotillions, and the Polka: 1820–1865

A Solemn Warning to Dancers. New York: N. Bangs and J. Emory for the Tract Society of the Methodist Episcopal Church, [between 1824 and 1832].

The Ball-room Instructer: containing a complete description of cotillons and other popular dances. New York: Huestis and Craft, 1841.

The ball-room manual of contra dances and social cotillions, with remarks on quadrilles and Spanish dance. Boston: G.W. Cottrell, 1863.

Blasis, Carlo. *The Code of Terpsichore. The art of dancing, comprising its theory and practice, and a history of its rise and progress, from the earliest times. Translated under the author's immediate inspection by R. Barton.* London: Printed for Edward Bull, Holles Street, 1831.

Brookes, L. De G. *Brookes on Modern Dancing, Containing a Full Description of all Dances, as Practised in the Ball Room and at Private Parties Together with an Essay on Etiquette.* New York: L. De G. Brookes, 1867.

Cellarius, Henri. *The Drawing-room Dances.* London: E. Churton, 1847.

Coulon, Eugène. *Coulon's hand-book; containing all the last new and fashionable dances.* London: Jullien and Co., 1860.

Crane, Jonathan Townley. *An Essay on Dancing.* New York: Nelson and Phillips, 1849.

Durang, Charles. *The fashionable dancer's casket; or, The ball-room instructor. A new and splendid work on dancing, etiquette, deportment, and the toilet.* Philadelphia: Fisher and Brother, 1856.

Ferrero, Edward. *The Art of Dancing, historically illustrated. To which is added a few hints on etiquette; also, the figures, music, and necessary instruction for the performance of the most modern and approved dances.* New York: The author, 1859.

Hillgrove, Thomas. *The Scholars' Companion and Ball-room Vade Mecum.* New York: T.R. Turnbull & Co., printers, 1857.

Hillgrove, Thomas. *A Complete Practical Guide to the Art of Dancing. Containing descriptions of all fashionable and approved dances, full directions for calling the figures, the amount of music required; hints on etiquette, the toilet, etc.* New York: Dick and Fitzgerald, 1863.

Howe, Elias. *Howe's Complete Ball-room Hand Book, containing upwards of three hundred dances, including all the latest and most fashionable dances...with elegant illustrations, and full explanation and every variety of the latest and most approved figures, and calls for the different changes, and rules on deportment and the toilet, and the etiquette of dancing.* Boston: Ditson, 1858.

How to dance. A complete ball-room and party guide. Containing all the latest figures, together with old-fashioned and contra dances now in general use. Also, a guide to ballroom etiquette, toilets, and general useful information for dancers. Boston: A. Williams, 1858.

Jig, clog, and breakdown dancing made easy, with sketches of noted jig dancers. New York: E. James, c1873; New York: E. and J. Magnus, 1852.

The Laws of Etiquette. Philadelphia: Carey, Lea, and Blanchard, 1836.

Leaflets of the ball room. Being a sketch of the polka quadrilles. Philadelphia, New York: Turner and Fisher [c1847].

Mason, Francis. *A treatise on the use and peculiar advantages of dancing and exercises, considered as a means of refinement and physical development.* London: Sharp and Hale, 1854.

Meyen, Henry. *The ball room guide, being a compendium of the theory, practice, and etiquette of dancing, embracing the newest quadrilles, polkas...also, the Meyen quadrille, as taught by H. Meyen.* New York: E. and J. Magnus, 1852.

Palmer, B.M. *Social dancing inconsistent with a Christian profession and baptismal vows: a sermon, preached in the Presbyterian church, Columbia, S.C., June 17, 1849, by B.M. Palmer.* Columbia, SC: Printed at the office of the *South Carolinian*, 1849.

Powell, R. *Powell's Art of Dancing or, Dancing made easy By R. Powell.* Louisville, KY: Harney, Hughes, and Hughes, printers, 1848.

Rice, N.L. *A discourse on dancing, delivered in the Central Presbyterian church, Cincinnati. By N.L. Rice.* Cincinnati: The Presbyterian Book Depository, and W.H. Moore, 1847.

Théleur, E.A. *Letters on dancing, reducing this elegant and healthful exercise to easy scientific principles.* London: Author, 1832.

Thornwell, Emily. *The lady's guide to perfect gentility, in manners, dress, and conversation...also a useful instructor in letter writing.* New York: Derby and Jackson, 1857.

Webster, Mrs. Alfred, *Dancing, as a means of physical education; with remarks on deformities, and their prevention and cure.* London: D. Bogue, 1851.

Wilson, Thomas. *The danciad; or, Dancer's monitor. Being a descriptive sketch in verse, on the different styles and methods of dancing quadrilles, waltzes, country dances, &c. &c....Together with observations on the laws regarding dancing, with extracts from the acts of Parliament relating thereto.* London: The author, 1824.

Chapter 4: The Ghost Dance, the Cakewalk, and the Two-Step: 1865–1900

Ball-Room Dancing without a Master, and complete guide to the etiquette, toilet, dress and management of the ball-room; with all the principal dances in popular use. New York: Hurst and Co., 1872.

The Ball-Room Guide. London: F. Warne and Co., 1866.

Beadle's Dime Ball-Room Companion and Guide to Dancing. Comprising rules of etiquette, hints on private parties, toilettes for the ball-room, etc. Also, a synopsis of round and square dances, dictionary of French terms, etc. New York: Beadle and Company, 1868.

Brookes, James H. *May Christians dance?* St. Louis: J.W. McIntyre, 1869.

Brookes, Lawrence De Garmo. *Brookes on Modern Dancing, containing a full description of all dances, as practised in the ball room and at private parties, together with an essay on etiquette. By L. De G. Brookes.* New York: The author, 1867.

Brooks, Professor C. *The Ball-room Monitor; or, Guide to the learner; containing the most complete sets of quadrilles ever published.* Philadelphia: J.H. Johnson, 1866.

Brown, R.E. *A Treatise on the Elements of Dancing. By T. Erp. Sichore [pseud.].* San Francisco: The Bancroft Company, 1891.

Carpenter, Lucien O. *J.W. Pepper's universal dancing master, prompter's call book and violinist's guide: containing a description of all the figures and full explanation of the different steps used in dancing, together with the music of all the principal dances, arranged for violin, with the prompter's calls printed on each dance just where they occur in dancing.* Philadelphia, PA: J.W. Pepper, 1882.

Cartier, P. Valleau. *Cartier and Baron's Practical Illustrated Waltz Instructor, Ball room Guide, and Call Book. Giving ample directions for dancing every kind of square and round dances, together with cotillons—including the newest and most popular figures of "the german."* New York: C.T. De Witt, 1879.

Clendenen, Frank Leslie. *Fashionable Quadrille Call Book and Guide to Etiquette.* Chicago: C. Himmelman and Co., 1899.

Cleveland, C.H., Jr. *Dancing at Home and Abroad.* Boston: O. Ditson and Co.; New York: C.H. Ditson and Co., 1878.

Coulon, Eugène. *Coulon's Hand-book; containing all the last new and fashionable dances, and also some important remarks on dancing & deportment.* London: A. Hammond and Co., 1873.

The Dancer's Guide and Ball-Room Companion. New York: F.M. Reed, 1874.

Dancing and prompting, etiquette and deportment of society and ball room. [By] Professor Bonstein [pseud.]. Boston, Chicago [etc.]: White, Smith and Co., 1884.

Davis, Rev. George. *An Account of the Trial of Social Dance.* Rondout, NY: K. Freeman Printing House, 1899.

De Garmo, William B. *The Prompter: containing full descriptions of all the quadrilles, figures of the german cotillon, etc. Designed for the assistance of the pupils of Wm. B. De Garmo...* New York: Raymond and Caulon, printers, 1865.

De Garmo, William B. *The Dance of Society: a critical analysis of all the standard quadrilles, round dances, 102 figures of le cotillon ("the german"), &c., including dissertations upon time and its accentuation, carriage, style, and other relative matter. By Wm. B. De Garmo...Illustrations by Theodore Wùst.* New York: W.A. Pond and Co., 1875.

Dick, Harris B. *How to Lead the German.* New York: Dick and Fitzgerald, 1895.

Dick and Fitzgerald. *Dick's Quadrille Call-Book, and Ball-Room prompter...To which is added a sensible guide to etiquette and proper deportment in the ball and assembly room, besides seventy pages of dance music for the piano.* New York: Behrens Publishing Company, 1878.

Dodworth, Allen. *Dancing and its Relations to Education and Social Life, with a new method of instruction...By Allen Dodworth.* New York and London: Harper and Brothers, 1900.

Faulkner, Thomas A. *From the Ball-room to Hell.* Chicago: The Henry Publishing Co., 1892.

Gardner, William W. *Modern Dancing: in the light of Scripture and facts.* Louisville, KY: Baptist Book Concern, 1893.

Gass, Henry. *The Waltz. Respectfully dedicated to our country's centennial celebration.* Mobile, AL: 1876.

The German. How to give it. How to lead it. How to dance it. By two amateur leaders. Chicago: Jansen, McClurg and Company, 1879; New York: Dick and Fitzgerald, 1895.

Gilbert, Melvin Ballou. *Round Dancing, by M.B. Gilbert.* Portland, ME: M.B. Gilbert, 1890.

Greene, William E. *The Terpsichorean Monitor.* Providence, RI: E.A. Johnson and Co., 1889.

Harvey, J.H. *Wehman's Complete Dancing Master and Call book: containing a full and complete description of all the modern dances, together with the figures of the German.* New York: H. J. Wehman, 1889.

Heckman, George C. *Dancing as a Christian Amusement. By the Rev. George C. Heckmann.* Philadelphia: Presbyterian Board of Publication, 1879.

How To Dance: A Complete Ball-Room and Party Guide. New York: Tousey and Small, Publishers, 1878.

Howe, Elias. *The Pocket Ball-Room Prompter.* Boston: O. Ditson and Co., 1886.

Jones, John Griffing. *An Appeal to all Christians, especially the members of the Methodist Episcopal church, against the practice of social dancing. By Rev. John G. Jones.* Saint Louis: P.M. Pinckard, 1867.

Koncen, Mathias J. *Prof. M. J. Koncen's Quadrille Call Book and Ball-Room Guide.* St. Louis: Press of S.F. Brearley and Co., 1883.

Kopp, E.H. *The American Prompter and Guide to Etiquette, comp. by E.H. Kopp. Containing... full directions for calling and dancing.* Cincinnati, New York: The J. Church Company, 1896.

Link, Charles. *Unique Dancing Call Book.* Rochester, NY: Charles Link, 1893.

Penn, W.E. *There is no harm in dancing, by W.E. Penn, with an introduction by Rev. J.H. Stribling, D.D.* St. Louis, MO: L.E. Kline, 1884.

Rivers, C.H. *A Full Description of Modern Dances.* Brooklyn, NY: C.H. Rivers, 1885.

Rowe, George H. *The Prompter's Own Book; or, Rowe's calls for the ball room. Contains all the latest and best calls necessary for an all night party.* Boston: G.H. Rowe, 1878.

Sause, Judson. *The Art of Dancing, embracing a full description of the various dances of the present day.* Chicago, NY: Belford, Clarke and Company, 1889.

Segadlo, L.F. *Course of instruction in dancing and aesthetic development of the body.* Newark, NJ: 1889.

Sherwood, Mrs. Mary Elizabeth (Wilson). *Manners and Social Usages.* New York: Harper and Brothers, 1887.

Strassburg, Herman A., Jr. *Call Book of Modern Quadrilles...Arranged and explained by Herman A. Strassburg, jr.* Detroit, MI: American Music Co., c1889.

Wilkinson, William Cleaver. *The Dance of Modern Society.* New York: Oakley, Mason and Co., 1869.

Witherspoon, Mrs. Edna. *The Perfect Art of Modern Dancing.* London and New York: The Butterick Publishing Co., 1894.

Index

Index

described The Virginia Reel, 178–79; and
the Waltz, 107; described the Waltz
Position, 254–57, *256*
Dodworth Band, 250
Dodworth, Cally, 251, 252; and *The Cally
Polka* (sheet music), 172, 251, *251*
Dodworth's Dancing Academy, 250, 251–
52, 271, 272, 284; branch school in
Brooklyn operated by Frank Dodworth,
250; branch school in Brooklyn operated
by T. George Dodworth, 252, 258;
described by Mabel Osgood Wright, 252;
moved uptown, 251–52
Dodworth Family, 250
Dodworth, Frank (son), 250; and
Dodworth's Dancing Academy, 250
Dodworth, T. George (nephew), 252, 258;
and Dodworth's Dancing Academy, 252,
258
Dodworth Sr., Thomas J. (father), 250
Domesticity Role of Women, 196–97. *See
also* Double Standard for Woman and
Dancing
Dorchester, Massachusetts, and Increase
Mather, 47
Dorfman, Leon (dance historian), described
American Colonial Minuet, 73–74;
described the American Galop, 154;
described the Galop, 155
Dos-à-Dos and Virginia Reel, 82–83
Double Quadrille (dance) and Mormons,
193
Double Quadrille Set Diagram, 157–58,
*157*described by Peter Buckman, 157
Double Standard for Woman and Dancing,
299–303, 304. *See also* Domesticity Role
of Women
Downing, Andrew Jackson (architect), and
the Beechers, 196
Les Drapeaux (figure in The German), 243
The Drawing Room Polkas (1860) (sheet
music), 172, *172*
The Drawing-room Dances (1847), and the
Waltz *à Deux Temps*, 162–63
Dreiser, Theodore. *See Sister Carrie*
Drum and African Americans, 149
Duffy, George (dance hall manager), 287
Duke of Cumberland attended Almack's,
109–10
Duke of Wellington turned away at
Almack's, 109

Durang, Charles, described Redowa, 176;
described Women's Fashion of the
nineteenth century, 198–99
Durang, John (dancer), 93; describes Pigeon
wing and Buck Dancing, 93
Durang, John, and Stage Dancing, 93–94.
See also The Hornpipe
Dutch Settlements in America, 5–6

*Early American Social Dance: A Bibliography of
Sources to 1820*, 127–28
Ecclesiastes and Favorable Dance
Scriptures, 49
Edison, Thomas, 249–50. *See also* Home
Music Box; Talking Box
Education and Dancing, 128–30
Edward VI, King, 2
Edwards, Georgia, and popularity of the
Polka, 172–73
Edwards, Jonathan, 52, 110. *See also* Great
Awakening
Edwards, Timothy, and Ordination Ball,
52
El Coyote compared to Nine Pin, 241
*Elementary Treatise upon the Theory and
Practise of the Art of Dancing* (1820), 184
Eliot, Charles W. (president of Harvard),
and support of dancing as education,
129–30
Eliot, Reverend John, critic of female
education, 128
Elizabeth I, Queen, 2
English Country-dancing, 36–40, *37*, *38*,
51, 84–89, *87*, *88*, *136*; in America, 84,
85–89, *87*, *88*; etiquette for dancing, 85–
89; sets and geometric patterns, 87;
revival, 268–70, *269*; described by
Thomas Wilson, 84–86; described by
Linda Wolfe, 268, 270. *See also* Cecil
Sharp; *The English Dancing Master*; John
Playford
English Country-dancing Twentieth Cen-
tury Revival, 268–70, *269*; described by
Linda Wolfe, 268, 270. *See also* Cecil
Sharp; *The English Dancing Master*; John
Playford
English Country-dancing and "fun," 270.
See also Cecil Sharp
English Country-dancing in America,
85–89, *87*, *88*; sets and geometric pat-
terns, 87

Index

ABOUT THE AUTHOR

RALPH G. GIORDANO holds a license as a professional Registered Architect in the state of New York, a Master's Degree in Liberal Studies from the College of Staten Island–City University of New York, and a Bachelor's degree in Architecture from the New York Institute of Technology. His first book, *Fun and Games in Twentieth Century America: A Historical Guide to Leisure*, was published by Greenwood in September 2003. The book is an interdisciplinary study of how Americans spent their leisure time and the political, social, technological, and economic factors that influenced or restricted their activities.

His previous published works include three entries on the Architecture of the Gilded Age, and biographical entries on John Deere and Levi Strauss in *The Historical Encyclopedia of the Gilded Age*. He has also contributed articles to several historical journals on various topics including Rosa Parks, Thomas Jefferson, Cold War Culture, Swing music, Hip-hop, and the integrated use of popular Culture and History. Giordano is also an adjunct Professor of History and American Studies at the College of Staten Island, City University of New York.